Fishing
Florida

Kris Thoemke

FALCONGUIDES®

GUILFORD, CONNECTICUT
HELENA, MONTANA
AN IMPRINT OF THE GLOBE PEQUOT PRESS

Cover photo: Largemouth bass. Timothy O'Keefe
Back cover Photo: Permit, Walt. Jennings
All other photos by Kris Thoemke unless noted.

Cataloging-in-Publication data is on record at the Library of Congress.

ISBN 978-1-56044-231-8

First Edition/Eighth Printing

To buy books in quantity for corporate use
or incentives, call **(800) 962–0973**
or e-mail **premiums@GlobePequot.com.**

The author and The Globe Pequot Press assume no liability for accidents happening to, or injuries sustained by, readers who engage in the activities described in this book.

This book is dedicated to Albert Forte, my grandfather, who made time to take me fishing when I was young.

...And to the memory of Biff Lampton, a friend and outdoorsman extraordinaire whose love for the woods and waters was an inspiration to everyone who knew him.

ACKNOWLEDGMENTS

There is no way that I could have written this book without the help of many, many people. No single person could be an expert on fishing for the entire state of Florida. There are, however, numerous knowledgeable people in every region of the state. Scores of professional guides, bait and tackle store owners, county and city employees, and dedicated recreational anglers all contributed to this book. My sincere thanks go to them.

While I couldn't talk with every guide, store owner, and angler in the state, I did make an effort to talk with several from each region and incorporate their many years of local experience into the chapters of this book. I am deeply grateful to those mentioned by name in the text as well as many who, for whatever their reasons, wanted to remain anonymous. Others consented to having their phone numbers published; if you want more information they will be happy to answer your questions. Better yet, stop by and visit with them when you're in their area.

I would especially like to thank my friends Al Alexandre, owner of Golden Gate Bait and Tackle; Captain Mark Ward, owner of Everglades Angler; and Dan Gewant, owner of Angler's Answer. They answered many of my questions about bait and tackle. A special thank-you also goes to Jim Brown of the International Game Fish Association. Jim supplied the data on the average, big fish, and state record fish for the saltwater species.

The staff of the regional Game and Fresh Water Fish Commission (GFC) offices were a tremendous help in providing information about freshwater fishing in Florida. Tom Champeau, Dewey Weaver, Sam McKinney, Gray Bass, Stan Kirkland, and Paul Shafland are some of the most dedicated professionals that you will ever meet. Freshwater anglers owe these people and all GFC employees a great deal of credit for producing so much with so few resources. Thanks to the GFC brochures on fish management areas, the regional fishing guides and to these individuals' personal insights and expertise, the information about freshwater fishing is as up to date as is humanly possible.

A book like this is also not possible without supporters who encouraged me while I worked and sometimes struggled to complete a task which was more monumental than I ever imagined. My thanks go to my wife, Sharon, daughters Emily and Hilary, John Grassy and Randall Green at Falcon Press, and to Ernie Malone, a friend who provided invaluable support as this project began. It is gratifying to have these persons believe in my work and demonstrate their support.

CONTENTS

This sign, on Long Pier in Redington, reminds anglers about the "benefits" of fishing.

FOREWORD

Kris Thoemke continues to impress me. He is a determined, methodical, relentless researcher, a person who deals in hard facts and shuns fantasy or speculation. These talents carried Kris through all of his academic work, culminating in a Ph.D in marine biology, and they underscore the work he does today. When Kris talks about fishing in the Sunshine State, he speaks from firsthand experience or the lastest and best research. When he tells you where to fish and which methods to use, you can be sure Kris is a reliable source.

Fishing Florida looms as an instant classic, the ultimate reference for beginning and experienced anglers alike. This guide is perfect for the resident who wants to expand his collection of hotspots, and for the visitor who wants to catch Florida fish and brag about it back home. Kris's book describes over 600 specific sites based on extensive interviews with local specialists from all parts of the state. No other volume provides even a fraction of the information contained in *Fishing Florida*.

Within the pages of this book, you'll learn not only where and when to fish, but how to be successful when you get there. The introductory chapters detail angling ethics, safety factors, basic fishing tackle for all kinds of situations, and tips for hooking up with Florida's 25 most-sought-after species of gamefish.

At least two million people visit Florida each year to enjoy its fishing potential. Add to that four million anglers within the state and the problem of finding the best fishing spots is magnified. Until Kris set his keenly analytical mind and innate curiosity to this monumental task, no one had ever attempted to collect in one place the incredible angling opportunities of Florida. In this guide you'll discover piers, bridges, and fertile waters accessible only by boat. You'll also find a list of the important boat ramps, Loran and GPS numbers.

Fishing Florida is a working tool to be used repeatedly and frequently; for locating great fishing, it's just about as important as your rod and reel. All of us should commend Kris Thoemke for making many of Florida's so-called secret fishing spots common knowledge. My copy spends a lot of time out on the water with me. I know yours will, too.

Mark Sosin, Producer and Host
Mark Sosin's Salt Water Journal

PREFACE

The information presented in this book comes from many sources. The descriptions of the sites come from personal observation, printed materials supplied by the local county recreation departments and state parks, and interviews with people having specific regional knowledge.

The comments in the fishing index are based on interviews with several people and represent a consensus of their comments. For each area that is described, I relied heavily on the local knowledge of bait and tackle shop owners and managers, professional guides, trusted friends, and my personal knowledge.

The directions to each site typically begin from a major town or road intersection that can be found on the State of Florida Official Transportation Map. Distances were calculated using the odometer in my vehicle or by measurement using the Florida Atlas and Gazetteer published by DeLorme Mapping Company. If you want a good set of maps of Florida, this is the book to buy.

The businesses mentioned in this book are not necessarily the only ones near each site. They are all places that I have visited or where I have spoken with the owners/managers over the phone. My endorsement of them extends only to saying that they provided information that was determined to be accurate for their areas. There are many other equally helpful and knowledgeable businesses that are not mentioned here. Their omission is not deliberate in any way.

I claim responsibility for compiling the information and assembling it in its final form. Not everyone reading this book that has intimate knowledge of a site may totally agree with the comments. Those discrepancies are, I believe, attributable to the many and varied perspectives of anglers. If there are errors of omission or inaccuracies of fact, I'm confident that I will hear about them. Corrections will be made in future editions and the book will be updated with new information as fishing conditions and site-specific information changes, as it certainly will.

INTRODUCTION

Florida has a legacy of great fishing. I still have vivid memories of fishing the Everglades with my grandfather in the 1960s. We fished the canals along the eastern edge of the "glades," under the watchful eyes of alligators, anhingas, and great blue herons. During the summers, I spent many days from sunrise to well past sunset fishing off Anglin's Pier in Lauderdale by the Sea, trying my luck from one of the many bridges in Fort Lauderdale, or spending a morning drift fishing on the Captain Bill or Dragon party boats.

For the past thirty year's I've had the opportunity to fish in every corner of this state. Most of the hot spots I've found are described in this book along with dozens of new discoveries that I can't wait to try. In Florida you are never more than a few miles from fishable waters. The state is laced with hundreds of lakes, rivers, streams, and miles of freshwater canals which provide some of the best bass and panfish action that you will find anywhere there are fish.

Saltwater enthusiasts have thousands of miles of coastline and the blue waters of the Atlantic and Gulf of Mexico to angle for over 70 species of fish. Chum for yellow snapper in the Keys, kite fish for sailfish in the Atlantic Ocean, go grouper grabbing in the Gulf of Mexico, stalk snook among the mangroves, sight fish for redfish on the seagrass beds, test your skills on giant tarpon around Cedar Key, and fish for cobia from the Panhandle's super piers. And that's just for starters! Florida is a land where your next cast could become the fishing adventure of a lifetime.

Adding to the Florida angling fever is a new sense of optimism for fishing in the future. The evidence was clear—several species of fish were being decimated by nearshore netters. Some fish populations were close to collapse. With the state's multibillion dollar recreational fishery in danger, Florida's sport anglers took the initiative to remove entangling nets from the state's nearshore waters. As of July 1, 1995, the nets will be gone. If the Florida experience is similar to the recovery of Texas's recreational fishing after a similar net ban was enacted there, anglers should start to catch more fish in the years ahead.

No matter how much or little fishing experience you have, *Fishing Florida* offers useful, accurate advice. With hundreds of site descriptions, tips on the tackle and techniques proven to catch fish in Florida, and numerous maps and tables, all the angling information that you need to enjoy fishing in Florida is at your fingertips.

USING THIS GUIDE

This book doesn't describe every place to fish in Florida. If it did, the guide would be as thick as a big-city telephone book and still be incomplete. It does, however, give a detailed overview of the fishing conditions for every part of the state and directions to hundreds of productive places to fish.

Each of Florida's seven regions is covered in a separate chapter. Each region is further divided into sections using the region's county lines as boundaries. Entries for specific sites are numbered to correspond with the regional map accompanying each chapter.

Site entries adhere to the following format:

#. NAME OF SITE.

Fresh or salt water; types of fishing (bank, boat, etc.); Ramp (if present); $ (indicates a fee)

Description: General information about the site, a special nearby feature, and a list of amenities available at the site.

Fishing Index: Specific information about the best time to fish, the top species caught at the site, tips on how to fish here, brief interviews, and other information that will help you fish the site.

Directions: Directions relative to a city, intersection, prominent landmark, etc. Routes to many of the sites are well signed. In some instances, the signs may indicate different routes than the ones described in this book; the way you go is a matter of personal preference. State parks signs are usually brown with white lettering. Game and Fresh Water Fish Commission (GFC) boat ramp signs are small green rectangles with yellow lettering.

Access points: Some entries feature more than one access point. Additional descriptions and directions are provided as needed.

For more information: A place or person to contact for additional information such as seasonal closures, up-to-the-minute bait or lure recommendations, and current conditions. Be aware of frequently changing area codes in Florida.

A month-by-month summary at the end of each chapter highlights major fishing action for the region. Also, a species availability chart reveals at a glance

State Overview Map

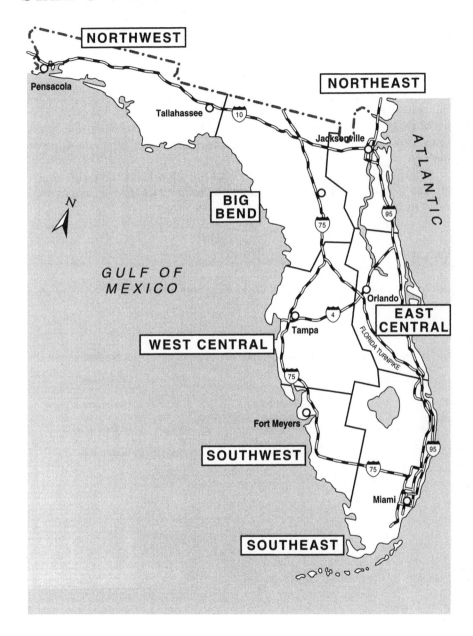

when a particular species of fish is present and whether it is a peak time of year for the species in the region. Offshore anglers will also find coordinates for some of the better known artificial reefs.

Information about the most popular species mentioned in the individual listings can be found in Chapter One, Tackle and Techniques.

The locations described in this book include piers, bridges, beaches, bank and shore spots, and even locales for those who like to wade fish. When you reach a particular site, other nearby spots may look like good places to fish. The rule to follow is: Be safe and respect private property. There are many places great places to fish, but if getting to them is dangerous or requires entering private property and you don't have permission of the land owner, don't go.

Remember, before you go fishing check with a local bait and tackle store or any Tax Collector office to determine if you need a Florida salt- and/or fresh-water fishing license.

MAP LEGEND

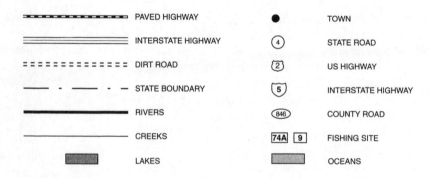

CHAPTER ONE
Tips and Techniques

Protecting Yourself from the Sun and Heat

Florida is nicknamed the Sunshine State for good reason. The daily dose of sun may be good for tourism, but overexposure to the sun's ultraviolet (UV) rays is not good for your skin. Anglers should take a few precautions to prevent sunburn and reduce their risk of skin cancer over the long haul. Remember to protect yourself from UV rays reflected off the water as well as from directly overhead—you can suffer sunburn even while standing in the shade of a boat awning or other cover. Also be aware that sunburn can occur even on cloudy days.

Use a good sunblock lotion with an SPF (Sun Protection Factor) of at least 15. If you're going to be fishing all day and there are no places to get out of the sun, or if you have very sensitive skin, use a sunblock with as high a rating as you can find. Some lotions are sweat or water-proof, an advantage in most angling situations. To obtain the maximum benefit, apply the lotion to all exposed skin about twenty minutes before going outside. Don't forget ears, nose, face, back of the neck, and—if wearing sandals or going barefoot—tops of feet. During the day, reapply as necessary especially if you've been swimming or are perspiring heavily. Overuse of sunblock is seldom a problem. Some people also use lip balm with sunscreen in it.

Consider wearing long pants and a long-sleeved shirt to minimize exposed skin. A hat (preferably with a wide brim) and sunglasses are as essential as a rod and reel. Many anglers swear by polarized sunglasses, which allow you to see beneath the surface of the water.

Hot and humid weather also places people at risk of heat exhaustion or life-threatening heat stroke. Symptoms begin with thirst, weakness, dizziness, headache, and muscle cramps. If left untreated these symptoms can quickly lead to collapse, unconsciousness, and even death.

Drinking plenty of water is the key to preventing heat-related illness. Fruit juices and sports drinks help, but avoid alcohol and caffeinated soft drinks (these tend to increase urination, hastening dehydration). Limit exposure to the sun and avoid strenuous exercise, particularly during the heat of midday.

Heat stroke—when the body's cooling mechanisms no longer work—is a medical emergency. Symptoms include red, hot, dry skin (or, conversely, pale, cool, and damp skin); lethargy; confusion or anger; dizziness; fatigue; and collapse. Move the victim to a cool, shady spot and remove or loosen tight clothing. Bathe the victim with cool water and wet cloths, especially around the head, neck, armpits, and groin. Give sips of water if the person is conscious. Heat stroke cannot be fully treated in the field; seek immediate medical help.

Potentially Problematic Plants and Animals

Florida is blessed with an abundance of plant and animals. Fortunately most of these are harmless, but a few species can turn a fun day outdoors into something less than a pleasant experience. Here's a brief rundown of some of the plants and animals to avoid.

Poison Ivy - This vine-like plant with shiny leaves in clusters of three grows along the ground and up trees and fence posts. Urushiol is the "itch" chemical in poison ivy, causing a rash, blisters, and irritation. Symptoms show up anywhere from a few minutes to several hours after contact. If you do come in contact with poison ivy, wash the oil off before it s absorbed into the skin. Use water (no soap—it removes protective skin oils) to thoroughly rinse the area. If a rash develops, apply calamine lotion. Don't worry about spreading the rash. Contrary to widespread belief, the blisters do not contain the oil from the plant and the rash is not contagious. Do see a doctor if the rash is on your face, genitals, or covers more than one-quarter of your skin surface.

Brazilian Pepper - This exotic shrub, originally brought to the country for its ornamental value, is a close relative of poison ivy. Brazilian pepper can grow almost tree-sized and is common along the banks of canals in central and south Florida.

Mosquitoes - These pesky bugs can drive anglers to distraction and they also carry diseases, including a potentially fatal form of encephalitis. But a good defense against them is as close as a can of insect repellent. Those with DEET in them seem to work best, but this harsh chemical is a skin irritant. It should not be used excessively and is not recommended for children. Citronella-based repellents are also effective. If it's not too hot, wear long pants and a long-sleeved shirt with tightly woven cloth. The clothes can be sprayed with insect repellent. Treat bites with anti-itch topical creams or ointments. Ones with hydrocortisone and an antihistamine seem to be most effective.

No-See-Ums - The no-see-um or midge is at the top of my list of annoying little critters. If you're being bitten by something but can't find anything to swat at, say hello to the no-see-um. Use insect repellents to keep them off your body. To keep them outside of a tent, cabin, or house, close the windows. Regular window screens aren't fine enough to block no-see-ums, though spraying the screen with permethrin helps.

Fire ants - Another imported pest, fire ants are now a problem for the entire southern half of the country. Fire ants build mounds that look like small piles of dirt. These are easy to avoid, but if you accidentally step on one a swarm of ants will attack in seconds. The bites are about as painful as a bee sting and some people may suffer severe allergic reactions.

If you feel one bite, expect more. The chances are good that you have more than one ant on you. Get them off as soon as possible. Be careful because many people get bites on their hands as they brush the ants off their feet and legs.

Immediate relief comes from a benzocaine saturated pad. Sawyer Products makes one of the few I've seen. It's called Sting Aid and comes in a small foil packet. Follow up with a cortisone-antihistamine cream. Puss-filled blisters usually form and may become infected.

Chiggers - Chiggers are mites, another group of mighty small creatures. They are common in wooded areas throughout Florida. The chances of seeing or feeling a chigger crawling on you is essentially zero but rises to 100 percent once they burrow under your skin. If you're going to be out in the woods, spray your shoes and ankles with a repellent specifically designed to be applied to clothing to repel chiggers and ticks. An anti-itch cream and a few days will take care of the chigger bites if you get them.

Ticks - Ticks are gaining more attention thanks to the deer tick and Lyme disease, both of which occur in Florida. We also have the more familiar and larger dog tick, which also carries unpleasant diseases.

Watch for ticks whenever you walk through tall brush or grass. They typically hitch rides on feet and legs and begin crawling upward, searching for a warm site to dig in. Flick them off before they attach. But don't try to crush them between fingertips—this can release disease-carrying body fluids. A permethrin spray on your clothing, especially from the knees to the feet, helps keep ticks off.

If a tick attaches itself, carefully remove it by gently pulling with tweezers. You may have to take a small pinch of skin with it to make sure you get all of the tick, including its mouth parts. Treat the wound to avoid infection and watch for flu-like symptoms that may signal a tick-borne disease.

Bees, hornets, yellowjackets, and wasps—Florida has them all and we probably have killer bees to look forward to. Reactions to the sting from one of these creatures range from mild to severe and life-threatening.

There is no bee and wasp repellent that you can apply to your skin or clothing. The best way to avoid being stung is to look for and avoid these insects and their hives or nests. Lessen your chances of attracting trouble by wearing white or earth-tone clothing. Avoid colognes, perfumes, and fruity or flowery shampoos. If stung, apply a paste made from water and any unseasoned meat tenderizer containing papain (a papaya enzyme). This enzyme neutralizes the protein in bee venom. Use ice packs to limit swelling and watch for signs of a serious reaction—excessive swelling, undue anxiety, shortness of breath, and itching or hives.

Scorpions - The few species of scorpions living in Florida prefer to remain hidden most of the time. Keep your hands out of dark crevasses, and shake out your shoes before putting them on. The sting of the most common scorpion in the state is on par with a good bee sting. It is not considered life threatening unless you have a special sensitivity to the venom. If a scorpion does bite someone, watch for an allergic reaction. Anti-itch lotions will help relieve some of the pain; ice reduces swelling.

Spiders - All spiders can bite but only two are considered dangerous. The black widow's venom causes abdominal pain, muscle cramps, nausea, swelling around the eyes, and possibly shock. The brown recluse's venom destroys the tissue around the bite site and results in an open wound on the skin. It is subject to infection and can take months to heal.

Spider bites are often relatively painless and may go unnoticed until secondary symptoms appear. If you suspect a black widow or brown recluse bit you, seek medical attention immediately.

Jellyfish - Jellyfish have transparent tentacles with thousands of stinging cells that can raise itching, burning welts on contact. Some stings are toxic enough to cause more severe reactions, including anaphylactic shock, which can be life-threatening. Be especially wary of the Portuguese Man-of-War; its tentacles grow to more than 10 feet long and each is armed with thousands of stinging cells. The bluish to pinkish float is a distinguishing mark for this potentially dangerous species.

Wind may blow jellyfish and Man-of-Wars into the surf zone and onto shore. Wave action may break the nearly invisible tentacles into small pieces that can still sting. Staying out of the water is the only sure way to prevent being stung (also watch where you step when walking on the lower beach). If stung, rinse the affected area with seawater (freshwater ruptures the stinging cells, making matters worse). Then rinse again with vinegar or rubbing alcohol. If the pain is severe or covers a large portion of the victim's skin, seek medical help.

Stingrays - Some species of stingrays inhabit the shallow waters where surf and wade anglers like to tread. But no one wants to step on one of these. The sting comes from a serrated barb at the base of the fish's tail. The puncture wound is painful with pronounced swelling, and often becomes infected.

Wear an old pair of shoes when walking through shallow waters. It's also a good idea to shuffle your feet to avoid stepping directly on top of these bottom dwellers. If you are stung, seek medical attention—treatment with antibiotics is usually prescribed.

Barracuda and Amberjack - What makes two fish, one with a large mouthful of razor sharp teeth and the other with a much smaller and basically toothless mouth, worthy of a listing in the dangerous plants and animals section? Rest assured it's not because the fish gobble humans whole. Actually, these fish are potentially dangerous because we might eat them. Both species, especially barracuda, can have high concentrations of ciguatera toxin, which is passed on to people who eat the meat of these fish. Actually, more than 400 species of fish can carry ciguatoxin; snapper and grouper are also high on the list of culprits.

Ciguatera toxin is produced by microscopic organisms that live around coral reefs and other hard submerged structures. The toxin accumulates in the tissues of fish feeding around the reefs.

The problem is that ciguatera has no taste or smell, you can't see it, and it isn't destroyed by cooking or freezing the meat. There's no simple way to tell if your catch of the day will make you sick. And the price for such uncertainty may be high. The toxin attacks the nervous system and intestinal tract. Symptoms include vomiting, diarrhea, and numbness or tingling around the mouth and in the arms and legs. A few people have a more severe reaction with muscle pain, dizziness, and sensations of temperature reversal. Most cases last two to three weeks, but some poor souls suffer for years. A doctor can help ease the symptoms, but there is no known cure. Consequently, those who know about ciguatera don't eat barracuda and amberjack, especially ones caught in the Florida Keys.

Health Warning

Unfortunately, the state researchers have found high enough levels of mercury in some freshwater fish around the state to issue a consumption warning. Each year they update this list and publish it in the Freshwater Sport Fishing Guide and Regulations Summary. The list includes areas that have been tested and found to be safe (unrestricted consumption), areas in which limited consumption (no more than one meal per week and one per month if you are pregnant, nursing or a child) is advised, and those areas where no consumption is advised. Largemouth bass, bowfin (mudfish) and gar are the principal species involved. **THE NO-CONSUMPTION AREAS ARE SHARK RIVER IN EVERGLADES NATIONAL PARK DRAINAGE CANALS NORTH AND WEST OF FL 27, AND WATER CONSERVATION AREAS 2A AND 3.** All are in the southeast Florida regional chapter of this book.

Fishing Regulations

The days of simply catching as many fish as you can and keeping them are a thing of the past. Regulations govern both fresh-and saltwater fishing. Before you wet a line, make sure that you know the rules. The following information comes from the Game and Fresh Water Fish Commission's (GFC) annual regulations summary booklet and from *Fishing Lines*, the Department of Environmental Protection publication covering saltwater fishing rules.

Stingrays like the same shallow water that surf anglers and swimmers enjoy. Remember to shuffle your feet when walking in the surf zone.

Freshwater licenses

Freshwater anglers must have a fishing license stamp. Both resident and non-resident licenses are available. A resident is defined as a person who has lived in Florida for six continuous months; or who has a signed domicile certificate from the local courthouse to prove an established, predominant Florida residence; or who is a military person stationed in the state or enrolled in a Florida university or college.

Annual, five-year, and lifetime licenses are available for residents. Non-residents may purchase seven-day or annual licenses. Anglers fishing in Wildlife Management Areas may need a Wildlife Management Area Stamp in addition to the fishing license stamp.

Residents 65 years of age or more can obtain a free Senior Citizen Hunting and Fishing Certificate; see your county tax collector. A similar free certificate is available to residents who are certified as being totally and permanently disabled. Children less than 16 years of age and the developmentally disabled are not required to have a fishing license stamp.

Florida also has a cane pole law that "allows a resident to fish in the county of his or her residence with live or natural bait, using poles or hand lines that are not equipped with a reel, for non-commercial purposes."

Saltwater licenses

As of January 1, 1990, Florida has had a saltwater fishing license law. The law is somewhat complicated compared to the laws regulating freshwater fishing. According to the official publication *Fishing Lines*, you don't need a Florida saltwater fishing license if:

1. You are under the age of 16.

2. You are a Florida resident fishing in saltwater from land or from a structure fixed to land.

3. You are fishing from a boat that has a valid Vessel Saltwater Fishing License.

4. You hold a valid saltwater products license, unless you are the owner, operator, or custodian of a vessel for which a saltwater fishing license is required. Only one individual may claim this exemption at any given time.

5. You are a Florida resident 65 years of age or older.

6. You are a Florida resident who is a member of the Armed Forces and not stationed in Florida while home on leave for 30 days or less, with valid orders in your possession.

7. You have been accepted by the Florida Department of Health and Rehabilitative Services for developmental services.

8. You are fishing from a pier that has been issued a Pier Saltwater Fishing License.

9. You have been assigned by a court to a Health and Rehabilitative Services authorized rehabilitation program involving training in Florida aquatic resources.

Florida has had a saltwater fishing license since 1990. Along some waterfront areas, signs remind visitors that they need a saltwater fishing license.

10. You are a Florida resident fishing for mullet in freshwater and have a valid Florida freshwater fishing license.

11. You are a Florida resident fishing for a saltwater species in freshwater from land or from a structure fixed to the land.

Florida residents certified as totally and permanently disabled can obtain a free, permanent saltwater fishing license from the county tax collector.

The bottom line is to check with an issuing agent to see if you need a license for the type of fishing that you will be doing. The county tax collector's office, most bait and tackle and sporting goods stores, and many marinas issue fishing licenses.

Seasons, Sizes, and Limits

Before you go fishing in Florida, make sure that you have a copy of the salt- and freshwater regulations. These cover the open and closed seasons, and size and bag limits. Freshwater anglers will want a copy of Fresh Water Sport Fishing Guide and Regulations Summary. Saltwater rules are summarized in *Fishing Lines*. Both are usually available where you purchase your license. Or write to the appropriate agency headquarters (see the Appendix for addresses).

Boating

While there are plenty of quality "land-based" fishing spots in Florida, fishing from a boat adds a new dimension. It allows you to search for the fish rather than waiting for the fish to find you. A boat is also the best way to see and enjoy some of the scenery and other wildlife the state has to offer.

This book lists hundreds of boat ramps that provide access to every part of the coastal and offshore waters, hundreds of freshwater lakes, dozens of rivers, and hundred of miles of canals. Read the regional chapters in this book for specific directions to all the major public ramps in each county.

Many marinas rent boats ranging from canoes and simple aluminum boats to pontoon boats and cruisers large enough for a safe, comfortable day of offshore fishing.

Whether you use your boat or rent one, safety on the water is taken seriously in Florida. In addition to the Marine Patrol and GFC Officers, many coastal communities have local marine patrol divisions. Officers frequently stop anglers to check for safety equipment, fishing licenses, and violations of fishing regulations. Before you board any boat make sure that you have the safety equipment (especially life vests) required by the Coast Guard for your size vessel, necessary fishing licenses, and a copy of the current regulations.

A special word about drinking alcoholic beverages while boating: Florida has a DUI law for boaters. If you are suspected of drinking while operating a boat, a law enforcement officer can administer a field sobriety test. If you fail, you will be arrested and your boat could be confiscated.

Fishing Guides

Fishing with a guide can make the difference between a fishing trip that is memorable rather than memory-less. Guides have the local knowledge necessary to find and catch fish. Fifty years ago just about anywhere you wet a line you could catch a fish. Fishing conditions are different now—mainly, there are fewer fish and more anglers. There are still plenty of fish to be caught, but you have to know where and when they are biting. This book is an important aid, but sometimes you'll want the extra knowledge a guide has from being on the water on a regular basis.

Finding a guide is easy. A number of them are listed in the site descriptions in this book. Virtually every large marina and many smaller ones have or know where you can hire a guide. Hotels and motels keep lists of local guides or display their brochures and business cards. Some communities have guide associations that you can contact. If all else fails, look in the local telephone directory.

How do you find the right guide? Call several guides and ask if they specialize in a particular type of fishing. If their specialty is fly fishing the flats for bonefish and you want to go grouper fishing, don't let them talk you into an outing because they have an open day when you want to go. Look for a guide that will do the kind of fishing you want to do.

Also find out if the guide is a licensed and insured captain. Be wary of those who are not. Ask how many years the person has fished the area. Remember, local experience is what you're looking for. Check to make sure the guide can supply the bait and tackle.

Finally, ask for the price. Most backwater and freshwater guides in an area charge the same price for a half or whole day of fishing. Be wary of those who charge substantially below the local going rate. For open water fishing trips

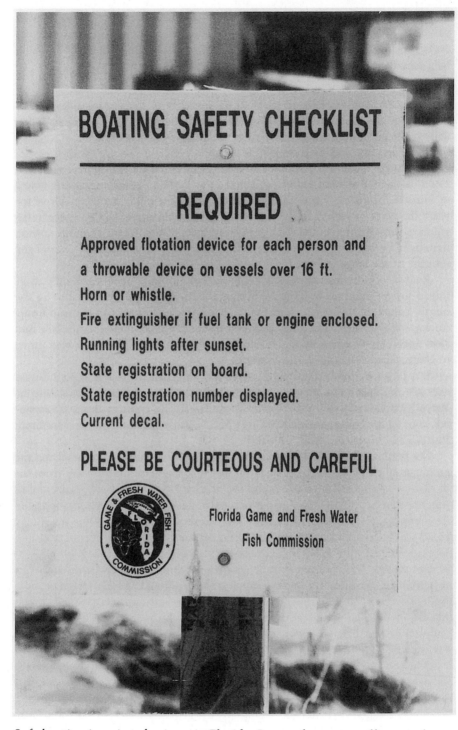

Safe boating is serious business in Florida. Law enforcement officers make frequent safety inspections and will issue citations

the price will vary depending on the size of the boat. Bigger, well-appointed yachts can cost hundreds of dollars more. The difference in cost does not necessarily reflect a difference in the quality of the trip or your chances of catching fish. It may, however, reflect your comfort level when on the water.

Special Species

Florida has its share of wildlife listed as endangered, threatened, and specially protected. Anglers, especially boaters, must be aware of the rules regarding these species. Their future is in our hands.

Manatees - The West Indian manatee is an endangered marine mammal found in coastal waters, estuaries, canals, and parts of some freshwater rivers of Florida. Migratory in nature and sensitive to the cold, manatees move toward the warmer waters in the southern part of the state or to the warm freshwater springs during winter. As coastal and river waters warm up in the spring, manatees are likely to be found anywhere along the coast, in bays, or near the mouths of the larger rivers.

Boaters are the manatee's worst enemy. Fast-moving boats can easily overtake a slower manatee and hit the mammal before it can move to safety or the boater can slow down to avoid the collision. Please obey posted speed limits on waterways where manatees may be present. Typical limits include idle and slow speed zones where manatees congregate and 20- to 30-mph speed limits in channels and areas outside channels.

It is illegal to intentionally kill, molest, annoy, or disturb a manatee. If you ever see an injured manatee or someone harassing one, call the Florida Marine Patrol's hot line at 1 800 DIAL FMP. To get more information about the manatee, contact the Save the Manatee Club, 500 North Maitland Avenue, Maitland, Florida 32751 or call (407) 539-0990.

Sea turtles - Florida's waters are home to the threatened loggerhead and the endangered green sea turtle. The main threat to these animals comes from the trash we thoughtlessly toss in the water. Plastic bags and other plastic items are the biggest concern. Turtles mistake them for food and the plastic lodges in the digestive tract, blocking the flow of food and often killing the animal. All boaters should carry a trash bag and put everything, especially plastic items, in the bag. Deposit it in a dumpster back on shore.

Dolphins - The Atlantic bottlenose dolphin (not to be confused with the dolphin fish) is a common sight in the state's coastal waters. This air-breathing mammal is protected by the marine mammal act. Sadly, an increasing number of well-intentioned people lure these animals to their boats for a closer look by offering the dolphins food. Healthy wild animals don't need us to give them a free meal. The bottom line is don't feed dolphins or any other wild animal.

Pelicans - One species that can use our help under certain circumstances is the brown pelican. This bird likes to hang around fishing piers and bridges looking for an easy meal. But pelicans sometimes fly into fishing lines and become entangled. If you accidentally hook a pelican, never cut your line and let the bird fly away. It is a death sentence for the bird.

Instead, try to reel the pelican in and remove the line. To calm the bird down, gently but firmly grab the bill, fold the wings down, and hold the bird so it can't move. With two people, one can hold the pelican while the other looks for line and cuts it off. If a hook is through the flesh, cut off the barbed end and back it out. If the barb is embedded, cut the line off and leave the hook. Saltwater will quickly corrode the hook and the bird should recover without further treatment. Once all the line is off the bird, let it go.

Angling Ethics

The ethics of fishing are rather simple: don't litter, tread lightly on land and water, obey the regulations, and respect your fellow anglers and other recreationists. Two other actions go the next step toward sustaining the future of fishing.

Catch-and-release fishing - More and more anglers are releasing the fish they catch. For some species, or during specific seasons, this may be mandatory. But catch-and-release makes sense in nearly all situations, and it may be the single most important factor in preserving Florida's fisheries.

To reduce injury to the fish, use a barbless hook. Some stores sell these, but you can make your own by pinching the barb down on a standard hook or filing it off.

Fish that swallow the hook are more difficult to successfully release. To help prevent swallowed hooks, set the hook quickly when the fish bites. If the hook was swallowed, it will be easier to remove if it is barbless. Carry a de-hooking device in your tackle box.

As a last resort, if the hook is hopelessly stuck cut the line and leave the hook in the fish. This may not save the fish, but it gives it a fighting chance. Get the hook out if you can.

Play a caught fish quickly—don't let it fight to exhaustion. Once you get the fish to the boat or the shore, leave it in the water. If you must handle the fish, use a gloved hand or a wet towel to grab the fish. Avoid a landing net if possible. Keep your fingers off the fish's gills and eyes. Remove the hook and get the fish back in the water as quick as possible. If you want a picture, have the camera ready ahead of time.

To release the fish place it carefully in the water. Don't toss it back in with a splash. Hold the fish from underneath and gently by the tail. Wait for the fish to swim away from you. If the fish can't swim normally wait for it to recover. If the fish is weak or lethargic, gently resuscitate it by slowly moving it back and forth in the water to force water through its gills. Some anglers that I know have spent a half an hour or more helping a big snook or tarpon recover. Every one of them says that it was time well spent.

Offshore anglers that bring fish up from deep water may have to contend with distended air bladders. Fish have these organs to control their buoyancy under water. When an angler brings a fish to the surface too fast the bladder distends and bloats the fish. Before releasing a fish with an expanded air bladder, use a pin, sharp hook, or for very large fish an ice pick, and puncture the air bladder. If you don't do this the fish will be unable to return to the deep water it came from and it will most likely die.

Mounting a trophy - When anglers catch a big fish or one of an unfamiliar species, many want to have the fish mounted. In the old days, that meant sacrificing the fish to get the skin and scales for the mount. Taxidermists can still do this, but it's no longer necessary to kill the fish you want to mount.

Most taxidermists use molds to create a fiberglass replica of your catch. Simply give them a measure of the fish's length and girth. Taking a picture will also help illustrate any distinctive marks or color patters. Doing this allows you to release the fish and let it survive.

WHICH ROD AND REEL?

A multitude of fishing conditions faces anglers in Florida. No single rod and reel combination is best for a specific set of fishing conditions, but there are general guidelines.

Fresh Water

When chasing any of Florida's freshwater fish (except the 30-pound-plus catfish in the big rivers) use either a spinning rod and reel or a bait-casting rod and reel. Spinning combinations are the most popular choice because they are easier to use. A 6-foot rod with a spinning reel rated for 6- to 12-pound test line is as close to a standard freshwater rig as you will find. Those who like to use bait-casters prefer a 6-foot rod with a compatible reel that is free spooling, level winding, and has a star drag.

When the cover is heavy, largemouth bass anglers use a technique called flipping. For this type of fishing try a 7-foot, stiff-action rod with bait-casting reel and 20-pound test or higher line. The heavy cover limits casting so you must swing the bait to the target. Heavy-duty line gives you a reasonable chance to land the fish.

Fly fishing for largemouth bass and panfish is growing in popularity. Depending on your skill level, a 7.5- to 8.5-foot rod and reel rated for 5- to 8-weight line is a good overall choice.

For pure simplicity, try a cane pole. It is especially effective for panfish or when fishing with a young child who isn't ready for a spinning rod and reel.

Salt Water

Bays and Backwaters

The traditional tackle for most species in the backwaters is a fast-action, 6- to 7-foot rod with a spinning reel that accommodates a minimum of 150 yards of 8- to 17-pound test line. Using this rig you can fish with jigs, lures, or live bait to catch most of the fish you're likely to encounter. To go after large tarpon try a stiffer rod with a reel that can hold 150 to 300 yards of 15- to 20-pound test line.

Saltwater fly fishing is all the rage now in Florida's bays and backwaters. A 7- to 9-weight rod and reel will suffice for all but the big tarpon. Big tarpon require an 11- or 12-weight combination. If you plan to buy only one saltwater fly rod, go with the 9 weight. Weight-forward floating or slow sinking line generally gives the best results.

Piers and Bridges

"Keep the fish's head up." That's the key to fishing off the piers and bridges according to Dan Gewant, owner of Angler's Answer Bait and Tackle store in Naples. To do this you need a stout 6- to 8-foot rod rated to handle 30- to 40-pound test line even though you can fish using 20-pound test. The lighter tackle used to fish the bays and backwaters can be used from small piers and bridges but not off the numerous high coastal piers and big bridges. When used from these structures a light-weight rod and reel doesn't have the stiffness and drag ability to keep the fish from heading to the pilings and cutting off your line.

A stout rod and reel that can get the fish up is also a necessity when fishing from a crowded bridge or pier. If you hook a sizable fish and can't get it up to the surface before it swims up and down the length of the pier and entangles a half dozen or more of your neighbors, the other anglers may use you for bait.

Boat tackle, used for offshore fishing and described later in this section, will work from piers and bridges if you plan to fish straight down from the structure. If you want to cast away from the pier or bridge, a heavy spinning rod and reel like ones used by surf anglers, is necessary. An 8- to 12-foot rod with a reel holding 200 yards of 15- to 20-pound test line is what the veteran bridge and pier anglers use.

Surf

Surf fishing is popular along both coasts. But there are significant differences in the type of gear that you need to fish one side versus the other.

Gulf Coast - Florida's west coast features a gently sloping bottom and fairly

small waves. Thus, anglers do not need the large surf rods used on the Atlantic side. A 6.5- to 7-foot fast-action rod capable of handling 10- to 17-pound test line is sufficient for most surf fishing. If you're after the big tarpon that occasionally cruise the shoreline, a beefier rod and reel would be appropriate.

Along much of the west coast, a shallow trough runs a few feet to a few yards from the water's edge. Although it is usually less than 2 feet deeper than the surrounding bottom, snook, redfish, pompano, and flounder seem to prefer these areas. Thanks to the generally small waves along the Gulf coasts, anglers can wade out waist deep on the seaward side of the trough and cast back into the trough on a diagonal. This tends to produce a more realistic presentation of the bait.

Atlantic Coast - To fish along the state's east coast, you need a stiff 9- to 12-foot rod with a reel capable of handling 15- to 30-pound test line. Anglers usually use a 2- to 5-ounce sinker to heave their bottom rigs far enough offshore to reach the fish.

Offshore

Anglers after permit, amberjack, small dolphin, and other non-bottom dwellers can use tackle similar to that used in the bays and backwaters or saltwater fly rods and reels used for the big nearshore tarpon. I've caught permit up to 30 pounds using a 7-foot fast-action rod and a 6- to 12-pound test rated spinning reel. I wouldn't recommend this however unless you are using top quality products, especially a reel with an excellent drag system. Remember, quality pays and this is never more evident than when you have a big fish on the line.

Most offshore fishing involves heavy-duty boat tackle. It is designed to be used for bottom fishing and trolling. Typically anglers use a 5.5- to 6.5-foot stiff rod and a free-spooling reel with a star drag. The size of this rig depends of the line rating of the rod and reel. Dedicated offshore anglers will have several different sizes of rods and reels. Which one they use depends on the size and strength of the fish they're after. In any case, the reel must have at least 200 yards of line on it and you may want twice that amount for some of the strong, long running fish. An increasing number of anglers are using the new generation of "braided" lines. The lack of stretch with these lines gives you more of a chance to get the fish off the bottom.

Fishing for the big saltwater game fish requires special gear that most anglers don't have. The easiest way to fish for these species is to charter a boat and captain that provide the bait and tackle.

Terminal Tackle: The end of the line

Terminal tackle is the stuff at the end of the fishing line—leaders, sinkers, floats, hooks, and swivels. The hook size, sinker weight, need for a leader, and type of leader material varies depending on fishing conditions. The key to success is combining the correct leader, if you're using one, with the properly sized hook to get your bait to where the fish are while making the entire rig as inconspicuous as possible.

Fresh Water

Freshwater anglers can tie their hooks or lures directly to the end of the line. This works when angling for panfish and small largemouth bass. You can use a snap or a snap swivel at the end of the line if fishing with an artificial lure. This allows you to change lures quickly, but fish may notice it and refuse the bait.

Anglers after bass usually use a 2- to 4-foot length of 10- to 30-pound test monofilament leader. The poundage you choose depends on the rod and reel involved. A 10- to 12-pound test leader will be sufficient for ultra-light rigs, but a 20- to 30-pound test leader would be appropriate for a rig with 6- to 12-pound test line. It can be tied directly to the fishing line or connected to the swivel. The leader reduces the chance that the bass can abrade or nick the line with its small teeth or gill covers, or by dragging the line through heavy weeds and submerged branches or rocks.

Hook choice depends on the bait you use and the species you're fishing for. In freshwater, anglers using live shiners for bass bait, employ an offset hook. The fish's mouth size and the size of the bait you're using determines the range of hook sizes that will work.

The Carolina or Texas rig is common when using a soft bait like a worm or lizard. It makes the bait weedless, a great benefit when fishing in most of Florida's freshwater.

Salt Water

The terminal tackle for saltwater anglers generally includes a leader. There are a few instances, such as when bonefishing the flats in southeast Florida, when a leader is not necessary.

A 4- to 6-foot length of monofilament line is the most popular leader. The poundage of the leader material depends on the size rod and reel being used and the species you're after. When fishing for snook, redfish, spotted seatrout, and the other common coastal species, 6 feet of 30- to 40-pound leader is sufficient. Bigger fish, like tarpon, require stronger leader material. There is no standard and I've seen anglers use anywhere from 40- to 100-pound test line.

Wire leaders are also used when fishing for species with sharp teeth such as king mackerel and barracuda and big game species like marlin. To get the maximum strength and suppleness, use a multi-strand wire. The length varies depending on the type of fishing you're doing.

Saltwater hooks are coated with a rust-resistant plating of nickel or gold. Offset hooks make good live bait hooks but you can use straight hooks (ones that lay flat on a flat surface). Never use offset hooks on artificial lures or when trolling. Their shape interferes with the bait's motion.

For backwater and coastal fishing with a spinning or bait-casting rod, there are five basic types of terminal tackle rigs to use. The simplest is a straight monofilament leader tied to the fishing line and a hook or jig head. With just a hook and a piece of live or dead bait on, you have the typical free-line rig. It is used when you want the bait to have a natural, unattached action. When using this rig, leave the bail open or the line in free-spool setting and let the fish take

Barracuda have an impressive set of teeth. Use a steel leader if you're fishing for these efficient predators.

the bait and swim off with it. When a jig head is tied on, cast the jig and then retrieve it. A short jerk followed by a pause and then a wind or two of the handle is one of the basic retrieval methods.

Add an egg sinker to the line above the leader and you have the standard bottom fishing rig called the sliding sinker rig. The "sliding" part refers to the fact that the sinker is not tied into position and is free to slide up and down the line. A swivel is usually used to connect the line to the leader. This rig is castable and is used when fishing the backcountry, off piers and bridges, and when fishing hard bottoms, wrecks, and reefs.

Surf, bridge, and pier anglers use a modified bottom rig called a pyramid rig. The line is tied to one part of a three-way swivel. A separate length of leader material is tied to a second part, and a pyramid-shaped sinker is attached to the other end. Off the third part is a second piece of leader material with the hook. This rig holds its place better in a current.

The last two rigs involve floats. The fixed float rig uses a free-line rig with a float (bobber) clipped at a fixed height above the hook. This sets the depth for the bait at the level that you choose. The rig is very useful in keeping bait off the bottom where saltwater catfish reign.

The other rig using a float is a popping cork. It also suspends the bait at a fixed depth but it has an added feature to attract fish. The cork makes a popping sound when you twitch your rod tip, and this draws fish. This is a popular rig to use when fishing for spotted seatrout.

A Dozen Tackle Tips

1. Learn how to correctly tie knots. At a minimum learn the improved clinch and palomar knots to hold terminal tackle (hooks, swivels, snaps) to your line and the surgeon's knot to tie line to line or line to leader. Another useful knot for saltwater anglers is the Bimini Twist.

2. Monofilament line stretches up to 20 percent. This is an advantage because it reduces the sudden stress a big fish puts on a line when pulling against the drag. Its disadvantage is that this gives fish a chance to head towards cover before you can turn its head toward the boat. If you want to reduce the line stretch problem, consider switching to one of the high-tech braided fishing lines. They have virtually no stretch so all the shock of the fish is transferred to the rod and drag on the reel. A cheap reel won't survive.

3. Re-spool your reels with new line on a regular basis. How often this needs to be done depends on how often you fish. Charter captains replace lines every few days if they are catching a lot of fish. Recreational anglers who fish once a month or so may only have to put new line on once or twice a year. Monofilament line gets stretched out after catching fish. You cannot see when this happens nor tell how bad the problem is until your catches break the line. Fishing line is inexpensive so change your line sooner rather than later.

4. Frequently examine the working end of your line for cuts, nicks, and abrasions. Some anglers do this after every fish they catch. If the leader or end of the line looks or feels rough, replace it. Monofilament line's strength is greatly diminished when cut or abraded. Re-rigging whenever you notice the damaged line might take a few extra minutes but you will loose far fewer fish this way.

5. Don't leave monofilament line exposed to the sun. The ultraviolet rays destroy it. The problem is serious if the line looks or feels chalky. Line in this condition should be replaced.

6. Don't discard pieces of fishing line in the water. For that matter, never throw any trash in the water. Fishing line is especially bad. It does not break down over time and it can become fouled in birds and fish and lead to their death (see the section on pelicans in the Safe and Responsible Angling chapter). Fishing line can be recycled at many bait and tackle stores.

7. Saltwater angling requires using a leader. Monofilament line in the 20- to 60-pound test range is the most commonly used material. Some anglers prefer to use steel cable when fishing for sharks and larger open water fish.

8. As a general rule use a swivel to connect the leader to the line if you're using a sinker in the terminal rig. If no sinker is used, or if using small split shot on your line, tie the leader and line directly together using a strong knot such as a surgeons knot.

9. When fishing with lures that don't come with a split ring, use a loop knot. This will allow full action of the lure. Split rings function like loops so you can use an improved clinch knot or other tight knot.

10. Saltwater corrodes metal. Always rinse off your rods and reels with freshwater after a day of saltwater fishing. Follow the manufacturer's directions for doing this and keep your reels properly lubricated. Rinsing lures in freshwater and letting them dry before storing them in your tackle box will help delay the rusting of hooks.

11. Use a hook sharpener. Most anglers don't do this and they loose fish as a result.

12. Buying quality tackle pays off. Yes, you can go to the mass merchandisers and purchase a rod and reel combination for under $30. But, don't count on catching a saltwater fish of any size. The drags on these low-end reels are very weak and the guides of the rods tend to rust quickly. Your best bet is to buy quality products. You can always get professional help from the independent tackle shops. They can help you select a combo that fits your budget and will work for the type of fish you want to catch.

Baits: What turns a fish on

There is general consensus about baits for certain types of fishing. Live shrimp is the best overall saltwater bait, a trolled ballyhoo is a great all-around bluewater bait, live shiners are the best live bait for trophy largemouth bass, and live Missouri minnows are the best bait for crappie. The debate rages on over other lives baits and artificial lures.

Fresh Water

Live bait - For largemouth bass, live shiners are a good choice, especially for inexperienced anglers. Native shiners are preferable to aquacultured ones, but to get the native baits anglers must catch their own or be willing to pay over a dollar apiece for the big ones trophy anglers relish. As an alternative to wild shiners, it is legal in Florida to use a live bluegill or other panfish as bait for largemouth bass. Other live baits used for bass fishing around the state include crayfish, frogs, and worms (big night crawlers are preferred).

For what the GFC calls panfish, small minnows (especially Missouri minnows), crickets, grasshoppers, freshwater shrimp, insect larvae, and redworms are the most popular live baits. Panfish include crappie, bluegills, shellcrackers, stumpknockers, warmouth, and redfin pickerel.

Artificial lures - There are far too many lures to discuss the merits of each one individually, so let's look at the major groups. The most widely used artificial bait is the "plastic worm" and its relatives. It is commonly used for largemouth bass. These soft baits come in a wide range of colors, shapes, sizes, and lengths. Many of them contain scented fish attractant.

These versatile lures can be fished on or below the surface. Their natural tendency is to float so to get them deep, anglers use split shot or a bullet weight.

Darker colors are most productive—black, grape, and dark blue. Some anglers swear that worms with glitter in the plastic are even more effective.

Most of Florida's lakes and rivers have problems with excessive growth of one or more exotic aquatic plants. While these water weeds provide great cover for fish, it is essential that you use a weedless worm when fishing these areas. The traditional method is to use a weedless hook, but in Florida the Texas rig is most commonly used. In this rig, the point of the hook is embedded in the plastic bait and the lure can easily be cast and retrieved through the thickest weeds.

Spinner baits are very popular for largemouth bass and panfish. Larger weedless styles make good choices, especially on windy days. The smaller ones are deadly on panfish and can bring a strike on almost every cast in some areas.

Surface plugs are a good choice on cooler days and early in the morning or late in the day during the hot summer months. Spoons and shallow- and deep-diving crank baits can be used along the edges of submerged vegetation and in the open areas of reservoirs and lakes. Accurate casting is required when fishing these lures around the weeds. Their treble hooks readily snag on plants. Because of this they are not used as much in Florida as they are in other parts of the country.

Freshwater jig fishing is underused in Florida. It seems that only the most experienced bass anglers will use a jig and they only do that when their other traditional favorites aren't producing.

Flies - Most of the freshwater fly fishing in Florida is for panfish and bass. There is no reason why you couldn't fly fish for any other freshwater species. Experiment with which type of fly works best, something fly fishing enthusiasts like to do anyway.

Finding out which flies are best for each region may take some extra field research. Although the number of bait and tackle store owners that carry flies and fly tying material is on the upswing, fly fishing information is hard to come by outside of the larger cities.

Popping bugs are one of the favorite styles for bass and panfish. These small floating flies entice a fish to bite by the popping sound they make when the angler twitches the rod tip as he or she strips the line. Wet flies, including streamers, are also used. Experimentation is the key and anglers who can fish the same lake or river on several occasions and can tie their own flies can learn which patterns work best.

Saltwater

Live bait - Because of their widespread distribution and reasonably abundant supply, live shrimp are a natural target for fish living in the bays, backwaters, and nearshore waters. They are almost always a safe and productive choice for bait.

Shrimp work best when they are alive. Many boats have live bait wells with aerators and recirculating pumps. Anglers with more basic boats can make a live well with a cooler and a submersible pump, or simply use a flow-through-style bait bucket.

One common problem when using live shrimp is the bait's rapid demise on the hook. The trick is to pass the hook through the shrimp's head in front of the dark spot, which is the heart. Avoid the heart and the shrimp will stay alive much longer.

Most saltwater fish won't pass up a shrimp, but some fish truly relish other bait. Permit and tarpon love small crabs. Pompano show a strong preference for an odd looking crab called a sand flea. It lives in the surf zone along the beach and is easily harvested with a sand flea rake or by hand. Sheepshead find another crab, the fiddler, irresistible.

Live fish are also a popular bait. Any size fish works as long as it's smaller than the one you're trying to catch. Several species of small baitfish roam the nearshore waters in huge schools. Catch them with a cast net or small gold hooks. A cast net opens wide when thrown and can catch over a hundred fish in one cast. To make the net open correctly and catch fish by surprise, however, takes skill acquired only by practice. Cast nets can be used from land, low bridges, and boats.

Anglers fishing from boats, piers, and high bridges can also catch their own bait by using a series of very small gold hooks tied sequentially on a light line and jigged up and down. The glistening hooks look like small crustaceans and baitfish will strike at them without any bait on the hooks.

Catch larger fish in the 6- to 12-inch range, such as grunts, pinfish, and squirrelfish, to use as bait on offshore grouper and snapper excursions. Use light tackle to catch the bait, then keep them in the live well until you're ready to grab the heavy tackle.

Cut bait - Dead shrimp, squid, and fish make excellent bait for saltwater

Throwing a cast net takes some practice. This youngster made a good cast and was rewarded with a couple of dozen "whitebaits" for his effort.

anglers on some fish. It is the easiest bait to use and you don't have to worry about killing the bait when hooking it. Cut bait works well because oils and other chemicals ooze from it, attracting nearby fish.

Pieces of shrimp are used alone or are tipped on a jig. The latter makes a particularly effective combination for the most popular backwater species like snook, redfish, and spotted seatrout.

Pieces of squid and fish are good bait for bottom fish. Fresh dead bait is preferable, but frozen bait also works and is available at most every bait shop. Or get some of the by-catch (fish pulled up in the net) from a shrimp boat; use some for cut bait and the remainder for chum.

Artificial lures - The choices facing saltwater anglers are staggering. Artificial lures come in hard and soft varieties. The hard lures are plastic, wood, or metal. They include floaters, shallow, medium- and deep-diving lures, jigs, and spoons. Soft baits are injection-molded plastic. They are shaped to imitate earthworms, shrimp, different types of baitfish, eels, crabs, and marine worms. These molded baits look remarkably like the real thing and if properly presented by the angler they will entice a fish to bite. Like their freshwater cousins, most are made with a flavor enhancer cooked into them.

Which ones work best is highly subjective and dependent on fishing conditions, casting and retrieving expertise, and an angler's local knowledge. Jigs tipped with a piece of shrimp are widely used. While the speed of the retrieval varies depending on what you're fishing for, the general pattern of cast (pause) jig-the-lure (pause) crank-the-line-in-a-few-feet is the most effective and is relatively easy to master. And it never hurts to stop by one of the local bait and tackle stores and find out what lure is currently hot.

Flies - Saltwater fly fishing is the fastest growing segment of the fishing industry. Thousands of anglers are taking up the sport and specialty shops are opening throughout the state. In many of these stores anglers can learn how to cast, tie flies, and choose effective flies for particular species. Look in the phone book for fly fishing shops.

Streamers are the most widely used flies. They tend to be large and are made of animal hair, feathers, and flashy materials like mylar. They are designed to look like a small baitfish, crab, or shrimp.

Chum - Saltwater anglers use chum to stir up the action and get fish in the mood to bite. Chum has an infinite variety of forms. Just about any leftover fish or part of fish can be cut or ground into chum. There are dozens of recipes for chum and all work. Strange ingredients go into some recipes. I've heard of people using vegetables, dog food, cat food, and sand. The only rules for making chum is to make it smell.

Fresh chum can be tossed overboard by the scoop. Doing this every few minutes creates a chum slick—a plume of ground or cut bait streaming out behind the boat. Fish gather in the slick and that's when you throw them your bait.

You can also buy blocks of frozen chum which can be put in a mesh bag and suspended from the stern of a boat or off a dock or pier. As the chum thaws a slick will develop. That same block of frozen chum can also be dropped to the bottom in a weighted bag and used to attract a crowd of bottom feeders.

Tides

For success, saltwater anglers must know the stages of the tides, especially the amount of time between a high and low tide. Fish are most active when the water is ebbing or flowing. The longer the time between tides, the longer the period of best fishing. Anglers may debate over whether the incoming or outgoing tide is better for fishing, but the important point is that fishing is better during the ebb and flow than during the slack times at high and low tide.

Experienced anglers also know that there are certain times each day when fishing activity reaches a peak. These times correspond to the times the moon is directly over or under the earth. For approximately one hour on either side of the moon over or moon under time, fishing should be the best for that part of the tidal cycle.

Every bait and tackle store that deals with saltwater anglers will have a tide chart for their area. Several companies publish yearly tide chart books, and charts are usually included in the saltwater fishing magazines. *Florida Sportsman* magazine provides detailed tide times for the entire state in each month's issue.

Much of the Florida coast experiences two highs and two low tides per day. Remember that the times and actual levels of tides may vary due to winds and storms.

Fish Hangouts

Finding fish is easier if you understand their habits. The most important point to remember, except with open water fish, is that fish like to be around reefs, pilings, mangroves, wrecks, artificial reefs, or other structures. (Ocean-going fish like mackerel, wahoo, and marlin are less dependent on structures—they focus more on following the schools of baitfish.) These structures provide food and shelter, the fish's basic requirements for staying alive.

To take advantage of this knowledge, anglers must know how to find submerged structures. Some, such as shoreline, are obvious. If the water is deep enough, any spot along a shoreline can hold fish. Especially good spots are overhanging or downed branches, undercut banks, and points along the shoreline. Channel markers, towers, floating debris, and even crab pot markers are also easy to find and provide enough structure to attract fish.

One of the best ways to find submerged structures is to visit the area during low tide. Oyster bars, reefs, rocks, and even wrecks may be exposed then, or at least are close enough to the surface to be seen. Note locations on a nautical chart.

Depth finders reveal deeper structures. The sonar displays a running track of the bottom beneath your boat. On a smooth, flat bottom such as is found along much of the Gulf of Mexico coast, the smallest amount of relief will have fish around it. With LORAN and GPS technology, anglers can accurately locate submerged structures found with the depth finder, store the coordinates in the LORAN or GPS unit, and then use the instruments to return to the spot at any time.

Ten Tips on Techniques

1. When bottom fishing use just enough weight to get your bait to the bottom. Too much weight makes it difficult to feel a bite and not enough allows the current to sweep your bait off the bottom and suspend it in the water where the fish can't find it.

2. When bottom fishing let the line free spool until the bait reaches the bottom. Close the bail or lock the spool and reel in the slack until you can see and feel tension on the line. Keep light tension on the line at all times so you can see and feel the bite.

3. When fishing over hard bottom, artificial reefs, wrecks, coral reefs, or any other submerged structure for bottom fish, turn the fish's head up toward the surface as soon as possible. In a matter of seconds, the fish can and will head for cover and if it gets there before you respond, the fish wins. When you feel a bite, set the hook and start reeling.

4. Casting requires accuracy, whether it's dropping your line past a wall of hydrilla or plunking it close to a weed-choked bank. Too far and you're tangled, too short and the fish never see the bait. Practice, practice, practice.

5. The retrieval or trolling speed to use depends on water temperature and the species you're fishing for. In general, the colder the water the slower your retrieve or trolling speed should be. Fish slow down when the water cools off and they just aren't as interested in moving as fast as they would on a warmer day. The retrieval speed is relevant only when comparing the same species. Some fish, such as Spanish and king mackerel, are fast swimmers and are fished at a faster retrieval speed than spotted seatrout or redfish for example.

6. When surf fishing, learn how to read the water along the beach. Fish will be in the troughs that parallel shore. Perpendicular to the troughs are washouts. They allow water in the troughs to move back out to sea. Washouts constantly shift position but they're easy to see and are good places to fish.

7. Along the Gulf coast surf anglers should try wading offshore to the first sand bar parallel to the beach, usually less than 100 feet out. Cast back toward shore. This gives the bait the natural appearance of coming from shore into deeper water.

8. Buy and learn how to use a cast net. Live baitfish are one of the best baits, but most shops don't sell live saltwater baitfish. The only way to get them is to catch them yourself. A cast net is the most efficient method.

9. When fishing from bridges and piers fish straight down or under the bridge or pier unless you know that the fish are away from the bridge. Fish love to be around the pilings. Remember to use stout tackle so you can get a hooked fish away from the pilings before it breaks the line.

10. Boaters angling for fish that make long line-peeling runs should use a quick-release anchor system. When a fish is on the line and you need to drift with the fish, take your anchor line off the cleat and throw it in the water. A float attached to the line allows you to recover your anchor after the battle.

CHAPTER TWO

Florida's Top Twenty-five Game Fish

Some anglers, it seems, always catch more fish than others. They usually know more about the fish they're after and have experimented with a wider range of lures, baits, and techniques. Good anglers keep notes on when, where, and how they catch fish, and try to learn as much as they can about the behavior of each species. To give you a start, here is some basic information and tips on how to catch 25 of the most sought-after species in Florida.

SALTWATER SPECIES

Barracuda

Sphyraena barracuda
GREAT BARRACUDA

Distribution - Widely distributed. Usually caught offshore and on the flats in the Florida Keys. Resides year-round in southern waters; moves north during warmer months. Look for barracuda around any submerged structure.

Tackle and techniques - Use spinning or bait-casting gear with a minimum 15-pound test line and a heavy monofilament or wire leader. The fish may also be caught when trolling for bluewater species. Barracuda on the flats can be taken by fly rod. Use at least a rod and reel rated for an 8-weight line. Barracuda are most dangerous when hooked and being brought into the boat; beware the 'cuda's razor sharp teeth.

Bait - Use any small fish or fishlike lure. The tube lure is best. Barracuda is said to be tasty but few people eat the meat because of the risk of ciguatera poisoning (see page 4).

Bluefish

Distribution - The largest concentrations and the biggest fish are caught on the Atlantic side. Bluefish are most numerous in Florida during winter, and stay close to shore, providing good action for surf and pier anglers.

Tackle and techniques - Surf fishing is the most popular method of catching

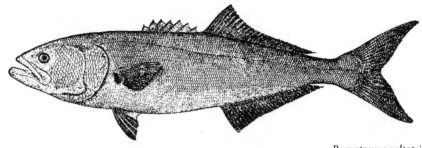

Pomatomus saltatrix
BLUEFISH

bluefish. When the surf is rough and the fish are farther offshore, use a big surf rod and reel. From the piers and on calm days from the surf you can use a 6-foot rod and standard spinning or bait-casting reel with 12-pound test line. Use a heavy monofilament or light wire leader to withstand the bluefish's sharp teeth.

State regulations apply to this fish. Check the latest edition of the rules and regulations for size and bag limits and open and closed seasons.

Bait - Live baitfish, taken by cast net from the schools the bluefish are feeding on, is a sure way to catch one of these fish. Other small fish, when tossed into a feeding frenzy, will also work. Gold and silver spoons are very effective in schools of bluefish, or try a jig tipped with a piece of shrimp. Pieces of cut bait and large spoons work when trolling from a boat. Bluefish meat is good to eat but does not freeze well.

Bonefish

Distribution - Limited to Biscayne Bay in south Florida and the Florida Keys. Bonefish move onto the flats to feed when the water temperature is between 74 and 86 degrees.

Tackle and techniques - A 6- to 7-foot spinning rod and reel with 150 yards of 6- to 12-pound test line is the standard tackle. Go without a leader if the sea bottom isn't rough. Bonefish have good eyesight and can see line. When fly fishing for bonefish use an 8- or 9-weight rig with at least 200 yards of backing. Hire a guide if unfamiliar with the area or this species.

State regulations apply to this fish. Check the latest edition of the rules and regulations for size and bag limits and open and closed seasons.

Bait - Live shrimp is best but a jig tipped with fresh shrimp also works well. Fly fishing with specially designed bonefish flies is your best bet. Strictly a game fish to catch and release. Very seldom eaten.

Cobia

Distribution - Widely distributed offshore and in large bays such as Tampa Bay and Charlotte Harbor. Cobia migrate north in spring and south in fall (often accompanying large rays) but reside year-round in south Florida. Cobia like structure. Most are caught from boats but some are taken from ocean piers, particularly along the Panhandle's Gulf coast. Cobia can grow to 2 feet in two years.

Tackle and techniques - Medium- to heavy-duty spinning tackle with 15- to 30-pound test line works best on these strong fighting fish. Use a heavy monofilament leader. When the water is warm the fish may be close enough to the surface to sight fish for them. Keep a hooked fish away from pilings or other cover. A reel with lots of line and a good drag system is essential.

State regulations apply to this fish. Check the latest edition of the rules and regulations for size and bag limits and open and closed seasons.

Bait - Cobia readily take a small live fish or crab. If the cobia are near the surface, free-line the bait. If they are closer to the bottom, use enough lead to get your bait down but still allow it some freedom to move. The most successful artificial lure is a big jig tipped with a piece of squid or other cut bait. Cast ahead of the fish and bring it toward them.

Dolphin

Distribution - Dolphin travel in schools in open water. Year-round residents in southeast Florida and the Keys, these fish move north in summer and can be found all along the Atlantic coast, sporadically along the lower and mid-Gulf coast, and in good numbers offshore from the Panhandle.

Young fish grow rapidly, reaching 3 feet long in their first year. Dolphin less than 3 pounds are called chickens. Three- to 8-pound fish are known as "schoolies." "Gaffers" are the ones you need to gaff in order to get in the boat; big fish weighing more than 30 pounds are known as "slammers." Large males, known as "bull" dolphin, have a distinctive vertical forehead.

Tackle and techniques - Look for schools of dolphin around anything floating offshore. This includes lines or patches of seaweed and any type of floating debris. Boat tackle with 20-pound test line or higher works when trolling. If casting to floating debris or weedlines, use a medium-duty spinning reel with 15-pound test line for small and medium-sized fish.

State regulations apply to this fish. Check the latest edition of the rules and regulations for size and bag limits and open and closed seasons.

Bait - Trolling baits include a rigged ballyhoo, a piece of cut bait, or an offshore lure designed for dolphin and other big game species. When casting use cut bait or a ballyhoo. When a school is nearby and they're in a feeding frenzy, anything light colored and flashy will get a strike. When you catch the first fish, leave it in the water. Chances are good that other dolphin will show up to keep the hooked fish company. Highly regarded food fish. Called mahi mahi in restaurants.

Flounder

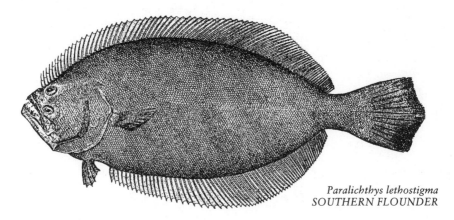

Paralichthys lethostigma
SOUTHERN FLOUNDER

Distribution - Flounder are caught statewide but the bigger fish are fouind from central Florida northward. Some flounder reach almost 20 pounds, but few fish that size are caught in Florida waters. Fall is generally the best time. The fish like passes, inlets, nearshore waters, and sheltered areas. Most are caught near the bottom though they feed at all depths.

Tackle and techniques - A medium-duty spinning or bait-casting combination is sufficient. Use 6- to 20-pound test line and a monofilament leader. Light-duty boat tackle also works when fishing from a boat, bridge, or pier. Flounder bite lightly, nothing more than a soft tap. Wait—up to 30 seconds—before setting the hook. Then do it hard.

State regulations apply to this fish. Check the latest edition of the rules and regulations for size and bag limits and open and closed seasons.

Bait - Small live fish are the bait of choice. Along the Atlantic coast anglers prefer finger mullet; along the upper Gulf coast, bull minnows are the top pick. Lures are seldom used to fish for flounder although they will occasionally hit a shrimp-tipped jig bounced along the bottom.

Grouper

Distribution - The gag and red groupers and the jewfish are the most widely distributed species. The adults are offshore bottom dwellers. Younger fish are often caught in seagrass beds, around mangroves and in the deeper holes of backwater tidal creeks. The other species—Nassau, red hind, rock hind, black, yellowfin, and scamp—are caught around the coral reefs of extreme south Florida.

Tackle a d techniques - Most grouper fishing is on the bottom and done from a boat. In some places slow trolling over hard bottom also produces fish. In either case, boat tackle with 20- to 40-pound test line is necessary to get these strong fish to the surface. Also use a 40- to 80-pound test leader.

When a grouper bites it is seldom more than a few feet from a place of refuge. Reel in as much line as you can as quickly as possible. The goal is to turn the fish's head up to keep it from going under a rock or into a hole.

State regulations apply to this fish. Check the latest edition of the rules and regulations for size and bag limits and open and closed seasons.

Bait - Small live fish and dead whole or cut bait are the baits of choice. Grouper will eat anything that comes their way. Jigs can be used when at anchor or drifting, and deep diving saltwater plugs work when trolling. One of the most popular and best-tasting food fish.

King mackerel

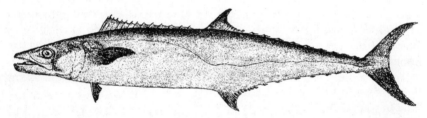

Scomberomorus cavalla
KING MACKEREL

Distribution - Along the Atlantic coast, king mackerel are caught year-round south of Jupiter Inlet; only during warmer months do they venture farther north. In the Gulf the fish migrate along the west coast in spring and fall, summering off the Florida Panhandle. The Atlantic and Gulf populations appear to be separate. Most fish are taken offshore, but some larger fish move into nearshore waters and can be caught from ocean piers and in the surf.

Tackle and techniques - From a boat anglers can use standard boat tackle with 20-pound test line or higher to troll or drift. Use either a heavy monofilament or wire leader. Get your bait down below the surface. From the surf or a pier, you will need a medium to heavy rod and reel with at least 20-pound test line on it to handle the big fish that come close to shore. Jigging may also work once you've found a school. The big king, called smokers, are excellent smoked.

State regulations apply to this fish. Check the latest edition of the rules and regulations for size and bag limits and open and closed seasons.

Bait - Small live fish are the preferred bait. A piece of whole or cut bait with a plastic skirt is often used when trolling, or try large fish-shaped plugs.

Marlin

Distribution - White and blue marlin spend their entire lives at sea. Both are warm water species. In Florida, white and blue marlin are caught along the Atlantic coast from St. Augustine to the Florida Keys. The fish are also taken during the summer months offshore from the Panhandle. The best marlin fishing is from Palm Beach south to the Keys. The blue marlin is larger of the two species, averaging about 300 pounds compared to a 60-pound average for white marlin. In both species, females are larger than males.

Tackle and techniques - Marlin are caught by trolling. Use 50- to 130-pound test line and tackle to match it (which tends to be expensive). Landing one of these fish also requires a special fighting chair. Anglers are strapped in so they aren't pulled out of the boat. The boat's captain is an integral part of the battle. He or she must maneuver the boat to keep the fish from breaking off. Unless you have the boat and equipment to do it right, charter a boat and captain.

State regulations apply to this fish. Check the latest edition of the rules and regulations for size and bag limits and open and closed seasons.

Bait - Trolling a live bait such as a bonita works, but you must troll at a relatively slow speed to keep the bait alive. Trolling with an artificial bait is a popular method of fishing. Specially designed bluewater trolling lures for big game saltwater fish like marlin and sailfish can be towed at a much faster speed. This allows anglers to cover more territory, increasing the chances of a hookup. A typical lure has a hard plastic "fish" head with a soft plastic skirt attached. Rigged to this lure are the hooks. There are many ways to rig the lures with one or more hooks, typically 10/0 to 14/0 in size. If you don't know how to rig trolling lures you can buy them in a ready-to-fish form.

Permit

Distribution - Permit are most prevalent on the flats of Biscayne Bay and the Florida Keys. They are also commonly caught offshore in southwest Florida around wrecks.

Tackle and techniques - Sight fish for permit on the flats using light spinning tackle or a fly rod. A 7-foot spinning rod with a reel of 6- to 12-pound test line on it is ideal. Fly fishers generally use a rod and reel rated for 7- to 9-weight line with at least 150 yards of backing. The same gear will work offshore in the Gulf. Permit usually swim close to the surface; cast in their direction once you see them. This fish has a tough mouth; when you feel a bite, set the hook hard and do it a couple of times.

State regulations apply to this fish. Check the latest edition of the rules and regulations for size and bag limits and open and closed seasons.

Bait - Permit love small live crabs. They will also hit live shrimp and cut bait, but crabs are much higher on their list of thing to eat. When fishing for them

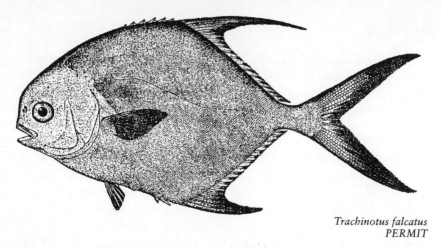

Trachinotus falcatus
PERMIT

off the southwest Florida coast, take along a long-handle dip net. Once you are 10 miles or more offshore, look for floating clumps of seaweed. Clinging to them are 3- to 5-inch crabs. Dip them with a net and use them for bait. The chances of a permit passing one by are very slim. Soft plastic artificial baits in a crab shape also work, as well as jigs tipped with shrimp. A crab imitation fly is a top choice for fly rodders.

Pompano

Distribution - Pompano are common along both Florida coasts, usually close to shore. Surf and ocean pier anglers catch most of the fish. North Florida anglers won't see pompano except during the warmer months.

Tackle and techniques - Light spinning or bait casting tackle is all you need to catch this fish. The fish are great fighters on ultra-light gear with 4- to 6-pound test line. A leader is recommended. Fly rodders can fish for pompano with a rod and reel rated for 7-weight line.

State regulations apply to this fish. Check the latest edition of the rules and regulations for size and bag limits and open and closed seasons.

Bait - Live sand fleas are the favorite bait for pompano. Some tackle store sell them but you can easily collect your own. They live beneath the surface of the beach in the surf zone. On a receding tide look for ripples or bubbles coming from the sand and dig out the sand fleas. Pompano have small mouths so use a small hook, a #1 or 1/0. Around Melbourne and Cocoa Beach on the Atlantic coast, surf anglers like to use clams for bait. Live shrimp also works well.

Small jigs with a piece of fresh dead shrimp are the most effective artificial lures. Retrieve with a slow bounce across the bottom. The bouncing stirs up the sand and that attracts the attention of pompano.

Redfish

Distribution - Since the end of commercial harvesting in 1989, the redfish is thriving and is now common throughout Florida's coastal and nearshore waters. Red drum and red bass are other common names for redfish. Redfish grow quickly, reaching 12 inches in their first year.

Tackle and techniques - You can catch redfish using a variety of tackle. How light you go, in terms of line strength, depends on how brave you want to be. If you're fishing the flats where there is not much chance of the fish heading for cover and cutting you off, an ultralight rod and 2-pound test line will give you the ultimate challenge. If you fish deeper waters, around the passes, a heavier line is in order, perhaps a 12- to 15-pound test line with a 40-pound test leader. Fly fishers will find plenty of challenge using an 8- or 9-weight rig and varying the tippets from 2- to 12-pound test.

Finding redfish is easy once you understand their preferences. Look on the flats when the water temperature is above 70 degrees. The best time is when the water is coming onto or falling off of the flats. Getting to the fish then requires a shallow draft boat and a trolling motor or a good pole. Redfish are sensitive to noise and are easily scared off, so some anglers prefer to get out of the boat and wade. Protect your feet with an old pair of running shoes or other footwear.

When the water is less than 18 inches deep, the fish's tail will break the surface as it noses in the mud to feed—this is what anglers call *tailing* redfish. When a redfish is tailing, wait for the fish to finish feeding and start moving to a new location. That's when you cast. Toss your bait ahead of the fish to intersect its path. If you run the bait by when the fish is feeding, it could go unnoticed.

When fishing an incoming tide, eventually the water gets too high and signs of tailing activity diminish, but you can still locate fish by looking for humps of water created by schools of moving redfish. Cast ahead of them and bring the lure across their path.

Also look for redfish around stingray muds. Stingrays, when they feed, stir

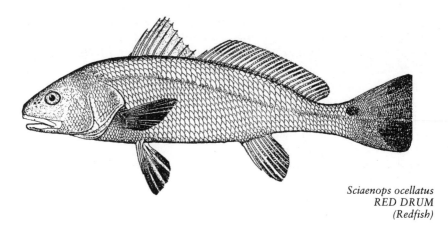

Sciaenops ocellatus
RED DRUM
(Redfish)

up the bottom and create what anglers call a "mud." Redfish often follow close behind, looking for a meal of their own.

When the water cools below 70 degrees, redfish head for deeper water. Look for them in channels near the flats and in the passes. This pattern becomes even more apparent as colder weather approaches. When the fish head for deeper water you won't be able to sight fish for them. Try soaking a live bait or blind casting until you find fish. Many anglers use lures to cover a lot of territory until they find the fish, then switch to live bait.

Redfish tend to remain in the same area for extended periods. If you find fish on a flat or in a channel one day, there is a good chance that the fish will be there tomorrow.

State regulations apply to this fish. Check the latest edition of the rules and regulations for size and bag limits and open and closed seasons.

Bait - With an underslung mouth, redfish prefer to feed on the bottom for small crabs and shrimp. A live shrimp under a popping cork is one of the most widely used baits.

Experienced redfish anglers also know that this fish will eat just about anything presented to them if they are hungry, and they always seem to be hungry. Redfish go for small baitfish, jigs, spoons, and topwater plugs. The latter is an interesting bait to use when fishing the flats because the fish must come to the surface and partially rollover to get the bait. It makes for some exciting action.

Sailfish ——————————————

Distribution - Sailfish roam widely. They are found off the Atlantic coast during summer and early fall. In the Keys, these year-round residents are most abundant in winter. In the Gulf, sailfish are found off the Panhandle during summer. Most fish are taken from boats but they are also routinely caught from the Lake Worth Pier near Palm Beach and occasionally caught from ocean piers in the Panhandle.

Tackle and techniques - Sailfish tire easily compared to their marlin cousins. That doesn't mean they aren't fun to catch. Their aerobatic maneuvers are hard to beat. It does mean that you can use lighter duty boat tackle with line in the 20- to 50-pound range and a 6- to 8-foot length of 40- to 80-pound test leader. You can even use medium-weight spinning tackle for a real challenging fight. Make sure you have at least 200 yards of line on the spool or this technique probably won't work. Fly rodders using big 12-weight rigs can also tackle sailfish anywhere they can see one to cast to. Trolling in the bluewater and at the blue-green water line marking the edge of the Gulf Stream are where many anglers look for sailfish. Anglers must also know the depth of the day for the sailfish. It can change daily and listening to your marine radio may give you a clue as to where other boats are finding the fish.

Slow trolling or drift fishing a live or dead bait is a popular technique. Bluewater trolling lures also work well. They can be trolled faster and therefore can cover more ground.

Take a charter boat trip to learn bill-fishing techniques and strategies from an experienced captain. Remember that handling the fish once it's brought alongside the boat is dangerous and requires an experienced hand.

State regulations apply to this fish. Check the latest edition of the rules and regulations for size and bag limits and open and closed seasons.

Bait - Sailfish have a wide-ranging appetite. Live pinfish, blue runners, mullet, goggle eyes, and ballyhoo will attract a sailfish's attention. A rigged dead fish or large piece of cut bait also works.

Shark

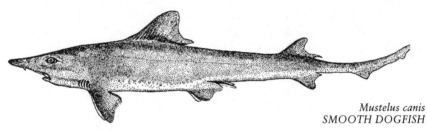

Mustelus canis
SMOOTH DOGFISH

Distribution - The future of shark populations is of increasing concern. Many species give birth to live young only one or two at a time. As angling pressure on sharks increases, such a low reproductive rate may mean severe declines for some species unless further regulations are enacted.

Collectively, sharks are widely distributed throughout the state. Anglers can catch sharks in the nearshore and offshore waters, in bays, and even on the flats. Some of the more commonly sought after and caught species are the blacktip, lemon, hammerhead, spinner, sandbar, and bull sharks.

Tackle and techniques - The tackle used depends on the size shark you're fishing for and where that species lives. Light spinning tackle and fly rods are adequate for small blacktip sharks caught on the flats and in the backwaters. The big sharks of the coastal and open waters require much stouter gear. Wire leaders and rod and reels capable of handling from 20- to 100-pound test line are the order of the day. Shark fishermen have their own subculture. New members are always welcome but be prepared to dedicate yourself to the sport because that's the way shark anglers are.

Go with an experienced shark angler before trying it on your own. Bringing a 5-foot or larger shark alongside or into a boat is dangerous if you've never done it before (and sometimes even if you have).

State regulations apply to this fish. Check the latest edition of the rules and regulations for size and bag limits and open and closed seasons.

Bait - The bait of choice, with few exceptions, is a live fish or a freshly killed one. The bloodier species such as bonita make the best dead baits. What most anglers would consider a good-sized fish to catch makes a great bait for a shark.

Sheepshead

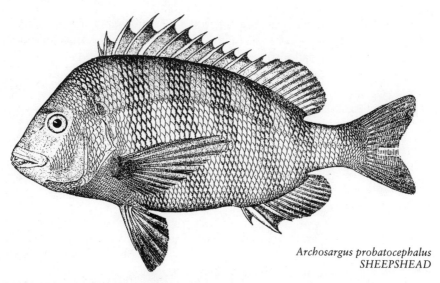

Archosargus probatocephalus
SHEEPSHEAD

Distribution - Sheepshead are year-round residents throughout the state. They are most commonly found around bridge and dock pilings, oyster bars, and nearshore reefs and wrecks. They also visit the flats in some areas.

Tackle and techniques - Light to medium spinning and bait-casting tackle with 6- to 12-pound test line is sufficient. When fishing for bigger, stronger sheepshead on the offshore reef and wrecks, use boat rods and reels.

Use a small, sharp hook and set it quickly when you feel the fish start to move off with the bait. You will feel a few light taps as the fish takes the bait into its mouth. Ignore those and wait a moment or two for a heavy feeling. That's when to set the hook. Use as little weight as necessary to get the bait to the bottom. The more weight you use, the less sensitivity you have in feeling the fish bite.

State regulations apply to this fish. Check the latest edition of the rules and regulations for size and bag limits and open and closed seasons.

Bait - Among the most popular baits are live fiddler crabs, live or dead shrimp, and sand fleas. Sheepshead are great bait stealers. Their small mouth and ability to nip bait off a hook before you can set it makes them a challenge to catch. When fishing around a bridge some anglers scrape barnacles off the pilings with a flat blade shovel. This serves as a chum and attracts fish.

Snapper

Distribution - Fifteen species of snapper live in Florida's waters. The top five are the mangrove (also known as gray), lane, red, yellowtail, and mutton. Mangrove snapper are found throughout the coastal waters from the mangroves and nearshore sea grass beds to the hard bottoms, wrecks, and coral reefs offshore. Lane snapper are also widely distributed but are more abundant in the warmer offshore waters of south Florida. Lanes are the smallest of the top five, maturing when they reach 6 inches long.

Red snapper are most common in the deeper, northern offshore waters. They are slow growers; a 20-year-old red snapper weighs about 35 pounds.

Yellowtail snapper are found in most of the state's coastal waters but in significant numbers only in southeast Florida, especially the Keys. Mutton snapper are found around the state in moderate numbers but the best fishing is in the Keys.

Tackle and techniques - When fishing inside waters for mangrove snapper and offshore for lane and yellowtail snapper, use light spinning or bait-casting tackle with 6- to 12-pound test line. For the larger specimens—the reds, big offshore mangroves and muttons—boat tackle with 20- to 30-pound test and a heavy monofilament leader is necessary.

There is no magic to the technique of catching snapper. You drop down a bait, they bite, you set the hook and reel them in. Any fish over a few pounds gives a good fight. Just don't be too anxious to set the hook at the first nibble.

Mutton snapper are the only species that routinely visit the flats in the Keys. Anglers fishing for permit on the flats will have the right tackle for mutton that come their way. Use a 7-foot spinning rod with a reel of 6- to 12-pound test line or a rod and reel rated for 7- to 9-weight line. Reels should have at least 150 yards of backing.

State regulations apply to this fish. Check the latest edition of the rules and regulations for size and bag limits and open and closed seasons.

Bait - Small live fish such as pinfish, squirrel fish, and ballyhoo are excellent snapper or grouper bait. Cut bait is also very effective and is all that you need

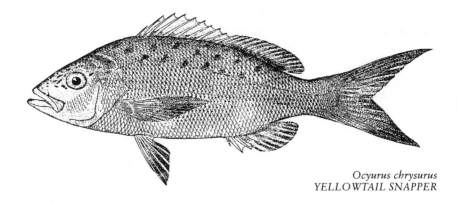

Ocyurus chrysurus
YELLOWTAIL SNAPPER

if you're chumming, which is a popular snapper strategy. It is standard procedure when fishing for yellowtail in the Keys and for any night fishing offshore (snapper are active feeders after dark).

When mutton fishing on the flats use a small crab or a live shrimp. For artificial lures try a soft plastic crab lure, a fly designed to imitate a crab or shrimp, or a streamer in a small fish pattern.

Snook

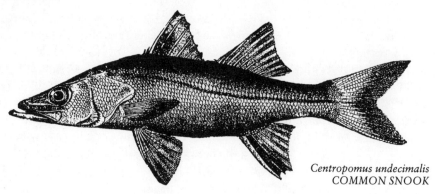

Centropomus undecimalis
COMMON SNOOK

Distribution - The Snook may be the perfect saltwater gamefish—it is a great fighter and makes delicious eating. Four species are lumped under the snook moniker, but three of them never get larger than 18 inches. These must be released if caught because of the 24-inch minimum size limit on snook. The fourth species, common snook, is the big one, growing in excess of 40 pounds.

Snook are primarily inshore fish that don't migrate far from where they spawn. From April to October, adults move from the estuaries to spawn offshore. Juveniles and adults tolerate freshwater and often move into coastal canals and tidal creeks. Snook are common from Tampa Bay south on the west coast and from Cape Canaveral south on the east coast. The fish is very cold sensitive. When the water temperatures drop below about 60 degrees, snook head for warmer waters. Fish kills from cold are often noticed at the northern limits of their range. Look for snook around overhanging mangroves, dock pilings, and other submerged structures.

Tackle and techniques - A medium-weight spinning or bait-casting rod and reel with 8- to 20-pound test line is necessary for this strong fighting fish. Use heavier tackle when fishing around good cover such as bridges. Snook are adept at running into the cover and breaking lines. A heavy monofilament line helps to reduce break-offs caused from abrasion and the fish's razor sharp gill covers.

Snook like moving water for the food it brings. The fish wait in eddies for small fish or crabs carried on the current. For this reason, snook fishing is usually good when the tide is moving in or out of passes.

Night fishing is fun and highly productive. The fish love to hang around lighted areas close to the water. Look for docks with lights or take a lantern and hang it just above the water's surface. Snook will dart in and out of the light eating small fish. On cold days snook move far up small tidal creeks, into freshwater regions on the coldest days. Fish the deep spots.

State regulations apply to this fish. Check the latest edition of the rules and regulations for size and bag limits and open and closed seasons.

Bait - Snook will eat anything that looks good and is easy to catch. Although they will eat small crabs and shrimp, their favorite food is small fish. Cast net your own bait, particularly if you can catch what the snook are feeding on locally. Free lining the baitfish and letting it go with the current is the most popular technique. In areas where the current is especially strong, a small weight may be necessary.

Casting artificial lures is also popular. Any of the fish-shaped lures, jigs tipped with shrimp, and gold or silver spoons are traditional favorites. MirrOlures and Zara Spooks are two brand names that are reportedly productive snook lures. Cast the lure as close to a structure as you can. Snook may not move from their spot unless the lure is dragged right across the fish's nose.

Spanish mackerel

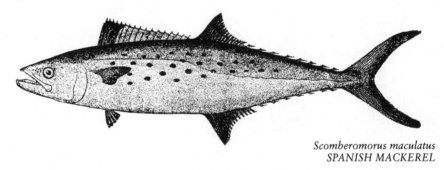

Scomberomorus maculatus
SPANISH MACKEREL

Distribution - This species is commonly found along both coasts of Florida. They travel in large schools and are highly migratory— they may be around in great numbers one day and virtually gone the next. The general trend is northward in spring and south in late fall to wintering grounds off the south Florida coast. Spanish mackerel can be caught from the surf, off ocean piers, and in boats within 1 or 2 miles of shore along the Atlantic coast and up to 5 miles offshore along the Gulf coast.

Tackle and techniques - Medium duty spinning or bait-casting tackle with 6- to 12-pound test line is suitable. Use a heavy monofilament leader or a small diameter wire leader. This fish has a mouthful of small sharp teeth.

To find the schools of fish, look to the sky. Spanish mackerel like to feed on baitfish and so do pelicans, terns, and frigate birds. If you see a large patch of disrupted water and a number of birds diving into the area, you've located a school of bait. If mackerel are nearby, they are likely to be under the baitfish actively feeding. Get within casting distance of the school and you will catch fish.

If there are no signs of surface activity, troll with a spoon or jig. When you hook the first fish, throw a milk jug marker buoy overboard. Return to the site and begin casting. Where there's one Spanish mackerel there's bound to be a school.

All the fish in a school will be close to the same size and age. If you are looking for bigger fish, try around the edges of the school you're fishing or look elsewhere for another school. If you are working a school and there isn't much action try smaller bait or lures.

State regulations apply to this fish. Check the latest edition of the rules and regulations for size and bag limits and open and closed seasons.

Bait - When fishing a school of Spanish mackerel you can use a live baitfish or free lined shrimp but a spoon or jig works just as well and is easier to use. If the school is in a feeding frenzy, this fish will strike at any shiny object, including a bare hook.

Spotted seatrout ───────────────────

Distribution - This is a common species in the estuarine and coastal waters of Florida except from south of Lake Worth to Miami and the lower Florida Keys. Seatrout prefer estuaries, spawning there and growing up among the sea grass beds. The fish won't move far from the area in which they grew up. Females tend to live longer than males and eventually grow to a larger size.

The ban on commercial netting should help this species to rebound within five years, regaining its as one of the most popular and abundant sport fish.

Tackle and techniques - Light spinning or bait-casting tackle is sufficient. Some anglers fly fish with a rod and reel rated for 7-weight line. Use a free-lined bait with or without a popping cork, troll or cast with spoons, slowly bounce a jig on or near the bottom, or cast a variety of hard and soft lures.

Fish of similar size tend to school together. When you catch one fish, mark the site with a buoy and return to it for a casting session.

State regulations apply to this fish. Check the latest edition of the rules and regulations for size and bag limits and open and closed seasons.

Bait - This species is an active predator with a wide ranging appetite. A live shrimp is the most widely used bait. Dead shrimp, when used with a popping cork or tipped on a jig is also effective. A variety of baitfish, including finger mullet, pinfish, and pigfish (small grunts), also work well. Deceivers, Bend Backs, and Dahlberg Divers are some of the fly rodders' choices.

Tarpon

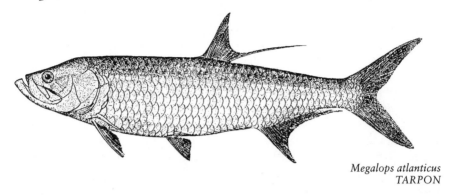

Megalops atlanticus
TARPON

Distribution - Tarpon begin to spawn in mid May and reach a peak in June and July. Within 30 to 45 days the fish grow to about an inch long and move into the estuaries during the height of the rainy season. High water levels allow them to move far inland and some become land-locked in small ponds and ditches as summer rains subside and mangrove forests dry out.

Tarpon take 10 to 13 years to mature. Males weigh about 40 pounds and females are close to 60 pounds. Once sexually mature a tarpon can reproduce for up to 45 years.

Tarpon can also breath air. The swim bladder connects to the fish's throat. Inside the bladder is a mass of lung-like tissue which can remove oxygen from air. One of the ways to scout for the presence of the "silver king" is to look and listen for tarpon to "roll" on the surface. That's when they gulp air and pass it into the swim bladder.

The best tarpon fishing is along the coast in the southern half of the state. But tarpon are caught anywhere along the coast during summer when the water is warm.

Virtually no one keeps a tarpon for eating. They are exclusively a sport fish. This helps prevent over fishing. So does the $50 special tag required for keeping a tarpon. This special permit, instituted in 1989, lowered the number of tarpon kept by sport anglers from 300 a year to about 80 in 1993.

Tackle and techniques - A 7- to 8-foot stout rod rated at a minimum of 20-pound test with a reel capable of holding 150 to 300 yards of at least 12-pound test line is the type of spinning or bait-casting tackle to use. Most tarpon rigs use 15- to 30-pound test line. A good bass flipping stick will work in lieu of buying a special tarpon rod. Fly rodders will want to use a rod and reel rated for 11- or 12-weight line. A 7- to 9-weight combination works for tarpon up to 30 pounds. Use 30-pound test backing and have at least 200 yards on the spool in addition to the fly line.

Whether using a conventional or fly rod, use 20-to 40-pound leader tied to the end of the line. Attach a 1-foot piece of 100-pound test line to the end of the leader and tie the hook to that. The heavy line is necessary to prevent the fish from fraying or chewing through the line. Many anglers tie a Bimini Twist on the end of their spinning or plug rods and then tie the leader to that. This knot doubles the end of the line and makes a stronger connection with the leader. Use hooks ranging from 3/0 to 7/0 depending on the size of the bait. Tarpon have very hard, bony mouths. Sharpen hooks before you use them, even ones fresh out of the package. When you feel a fish on the line, let it run with the bait for a few seconds then set the hook hard.

Tarpon spook very easily when there is noise in the water. Try to turn the motor off when close to your site and use a trolling motor or push pole to get within casting distance.

Let big tarpon have control the first few minutes. This is when they do the most jumping and all you can really do is hold on anyway. Dip your rod when the fish jumps. This gives the line some slack and you are less likely to have the fish spit out the lure or break the line.

State regulations apply to this fish. Check the latest edition of the rules and regulations for size and bag limits and open and closed seasons.

Bait - Mullet or crabs are the preferred live baits. They are one of the tarpon's favorite natural foods and anyone with a cast net can catch some 5- to 10-inch mullet. Tarpon will also take other live baits such as large shrimp, ladyfish, catfish, and pinfish. Don't rule out fishing with cut bait. When tarpon are feeding on a school of baitfish, they will stun some fish as they attack the school. A piece of cut bait apparently resembles a stunned fish close enough for a tarpon to go after it.

Spinning and casting anglers can use lures that resemble mullet and other baitfish. Some of the more popular lures used by tarpon anglers are the Zara Spook, Creek Chub Darter, Chartreuse Bomber Long A, 52m MirrOlure, Bagley Finger Mullet, Ratlin' Flash, and Ratl' Trap. Experienced anglers usually replace the hooks that come on the lures with 3X strength hooks because of the tremendous biting force of the fish.

Streamers are considered one of the best tarpon flies. Orange and red are popular colors. The cockroach is another widely used fly.

When using artificial lures or flies, make your retrieve slow and straight. Don't retrieve the lure so that it is coming at the fish as this usually scares them off. Make a presentation that brings the lure across or at a quartering diagonal away from the direction in which the fish is swimming.

Fresh water Species

Black crappie

Distribution - This member of the panfish clan forms schools and is most active during the colder months of the year when it is spawning. Specs, as some people call crappie, are found in most lakes and rivers in Florida. They prefer cooler water and are more abundant in northern Florida with one notable exception. Lake Okeechobee is famous for crappie.

Tackle and techniques - Crappie average 1 to 2 pounds, so anglers can use any type of freshwater tackle including cane poles, ultra-light spinning tackle, and fly rods. Crappies are an easy fish to catch once you locate a school of them, a baited hook and a bobber are all the terminal tackle needed. The best time of year to fish for crappie is during spawning, which lasts from December to early or mid March.

State regulations apply to this fish. Check the latest edition of the rules and regulations for size and bag limits and open and closed seasons.

Bait - Missouri minnows are the most popular bait. Other small shiners will work as well. Experienced anglers looking for more of a challenge will use small jigs or spinner baits. The Hal Fly jig is one of the most widely used lures for crappie.

Largemouth bass

Distribution - Largemouth bass are found in most every freshwater body in the state. Typically, they are in the shallows during the nesting season and then disperse throughout the area. During summer, the fish tend to stay in deeper, cooler water during the day. They move into shallower water to feed early in the morning or late in the day.

Tackle and techniques - A variety of spinning and bait-casting rods and reels are used. A typical combination is a 6-foot rod with either a spinning reel rated to hold 4- to 20-pound test line or a bait caster rated for 6- to 20-pound test line. The wide range of line strengths relates to the type of cover where you are fishing and the skills and preferences of the angler. Use heavier tackle in heavy cover to avoid break-offs.

The basic techniques are to cast, flip, or pitch a bait to the fish. Bass anglers have dozens of variations from these techniques and each angler seems to have one or two methods that he or she likes best.

State regulations apply to this fish. Check the latest edition of the rules and regulations for size and bag limits and open and closed seasons.

Bait - To catch a trophy fish, one over 10 pounds, your best chances for success come from using live wild shiners. Inexperienced anglers also should use live shiners. Large live worms are popular with kids.

Veterans like to use artificial lures. Soft plastic worms, rigged to run weedless, are the most popular lures. Hard lures, including surface plugs, jigs, and diving bait, also work but each has limitations depending on which aquatic weed is choking your favorite fishing ground.

Panfish

Distribution - Included in this group are bluegills, shellcrackers (redear sunfish), stumpknockers (spotted sunfish), warmouth, and redfin pickerel. The state also includes crappie in this group for bag limit purposes. The Oscar, an escapee from tropical fish farms on the east coast, is also considered a panfish but there are no bag limits.

Native panfish are abundant in nearly all the state's fresh waters. Oscars, because they are tropical, are limited to south of Lake Okeechobee.

Tackle and techniques - Light and ultra-light conventional tackle, or a fly rod and reel rated for 5-weight line, or a cane pole are ideal for taking these small fish. The spring and summer spawning season provides the best action for native panfish, often reaching a monthly peak a few days on either side of the full moon.

State regulations apply to this fish. Check the latest edition of the rules and regulations for size and bag limits and open and closed seasons.

Bait - These fish will take live grass shrimp, earthworms, and crickets. Small lures such as spinner baits, popping bugs, and jigs are the most effective artificial baits. Oscars will bite year-round. For Oscars, one of the easiest and most effective baits is a small piece of dead shrimp.

Striped bass

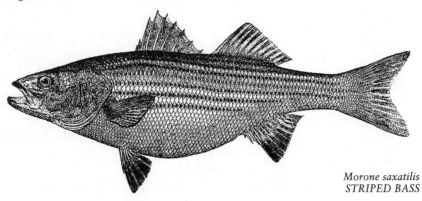

Morone saxatilis
STRIPED BASS

Distribution - Most of Florida's stripers are hatchery raised and are stocked only in north Florida rivers and reservoirs. The majority of the fish go into the St. Johns, Nassau, and St. Marys rivers in northeast Florida, and the Apalachicola and Ochlockonee rivers in the Panhandle. They are also stocked in Lakes Seminole and Talquin. A few are occassionally stocked in the other rivers of the Panhandle. Because of its preference for cold water, this fish seldom is found farther south than Lake George on the St. Johns River. They also rarely venture into saltwater.

By their second spring, stripers form schools and feed on shad as they migrate upriver as if they were going to spawn. By June the water is starting to warm up and the fish seek out cold water sites at which to spend the summer. When cooler fall weather arrives the fish start to move downriver for winter.

Tackle and techniques - Use stout tackle when fishing for hybrids and stripers.

A stiff rod and a reel with 15- to 25-pound test line and a good drag will handle any big fish that decides to bite. One of the best times of year to fish for stripers is from February through April. During this time, stripers congregate at the tailraces (the area immediately downriver from the dam) of the dams on Lakes Seminole and Talquin.

During warmer weather the fish head for cooler water and deeper holes. They will stay here from about June to October if the water remains warm. During summer, getting these fish to bite is tough. Your best bet is to fish for them at night or very early in the morning or late in the day. Even then the fishing is nowhere near the quality it is in February and March.

State regulations apply to this fish. Check the latest edition of the rules and regulations for size and bag limits and open and closed seasons.

Bait - Live bait, especially live shad, is one of the most popular baits to use for trophy fish. For everyday angling, GFC experts recommend yellow- or white-headed jigs. The weight used depends on how deep the fish are. Spoons also produce good results when deep jigging. The Redfin lure is effective if the fish are on the surface feeding on shad.

Sunshine (hybrid) bass ─────────────

Distribution - Sunshine are a cross between striped bass and the smaller white bass. These fish don't grow as large as the stripers, averaging 3 to 4 pounds in north Florida and 1 to 2 pounds at the southern end of their range. Sunshine can tolerate warmer temperatures than stripers. As a result, hybrids can be stocked in lakes as far south as Lake Manatee near Bradenton and Lake Osborne in West Palm Beach. The fishery is strictly a put-and-take effort; sunshine bass are sterile and cannot reproduce.

Tackle and techniques - Medium-weight spinning or bait-casting tackle with 12- to 20-pound test line is suggested for north Florida fishing especially in the rivers. Because these fish coexist with stripers in north Florida, a big striper is as likely to grab your bait. Much lighter gear is appropriate when fishing in central and south Florida where the fish seldom weigh more than 2 pounds.

State regulations apply to this fish. Check the latest edition of the rules and regulations for size and bag limits and open and closed seasons.

Bait - Like striped bass, sunshine love live shad, white and yellow jigs, spoons, and some surface lures.

IS IT A RECORD?

So you caught a big fish. One for the record books? The Game and Fresh Water Commission (GFC) maintains the official state record list for freshwater fish. If you've hooked one for the list, contact the closest regional GFC office. To be recognized as a record, the fish must be caught by a legal sport-fishing method, must be identified by a GFC biologist, and must be weighed on a certified scale. The phone numbers for the regional offices are in the Appendix. You should have little trouble getting a local bait and tackle shop to help you track down a certified scale and a biologist.

If your fish doesn't break the record but is a big fish, it may qualify for the GFC's "Big Catch" program. Anglers who catch a fish that exceeds the qualifying weight established by the GFC are eligible to receive a full color "Big Catch" citation. Special recognition is also noted on the citation if you release the fish after catching it. To be eligible for a citation, the angler must have a valid freshwater fishing license or be legally exempt from having one. The fish must be weighed at a public scale with a witness present. The angler then fills out an application and sends it to the GFC for approval.

A complete list of the record fish and qualifying weights for the "Big Catch" program is in the annual regulations summary published by the GFC.

The state record program for saltwater fish is administered by the International Game Fish Association (IGFA). This organization also maintains world records for the most popular fresh- and saltwater gamefish. The state keeps records for more than 70 species of saltwater fish in two categories: conventional and fly fishing. To register a state record fish, contact the Office of Fisheries Management at the Department of Environmental Protection or the IGFA to request an application.

The state uses the IGFA rules to determine if you have a record fish. Only fish caught in state waters, within 3 nautical miles of the shoreline of the Atlantic Ocean or 9 nautical miles of the shoreline of the Gulf of Mexico are eligible for a state record. The fish must be weighed on an accurate scale, and the application completed and mailed to the IGFA for verification.

CHAPTER THREE
Northwest Florida

COUNTIES: ▪ Escambia ▪ Santa Rosa ▪ Okaloosa ▪ Walton ▪ Holmes ▪ Washington ▪ Bay Jackson ▪ Calhoun ▪ Gulf ▪ Liberty Gadsden ▪ Franklin Leon ▪ Wakulla

Convenient, great fishing is the best way to summarize angling in northwest Florida. It's convenient because you can switch from fresh- to saltwater fishing in less than an hour's drive and, in many instances, with only a few minutes' boat ride. It's great because of the diversity of fish caught in this part of the state. From small but strong fighting bluegills to giant blue marlin far off shore in the Gulf's blue waters, there is something to please all anglers.

The western half of this region features miles of white "sugar sand" beaches and resort communities like Pensacola Beach, Fort Walton Beach, and Panama City. Between these cities are miles of undeveloped beach, much of it accessible to the public. East of Panama City is St. Joseph Bay and some of the best scalloping beds in the state. A little farther to the east is Apalachicola Bay, home of one of the most productive oystering communities in the country.

Northwest Florida is the Old South: spring blooms of magnolia trees and azaleas, sprawling moss-covered oaks, plantation style homes, sweet iced tea, and grits. There are four distinct seasons, miles of rolling hills, and plenty of southern hospitality.

As this book goes to press, residents of the Panhandle are beginning the arduous process of cleaning up from Hurricane Opal. If you plan to visit this area check ahead to see if the sites described for the western part of this chapter are open and whether any changes resulted from the storm.

SALTWATER FISHING

The bays here, including Pensacola, Choctawhatchee, St. Andrews, St. Joseph, Apalachicola, Apalachee and others, are rich in seagrass beds and oyster bars. Numerous artificial and natural reefs fringe the deep, blue offshore waters of the Gulf of Mexico. For land-bound anglers, miles of public beach, including Gulf Islands National Seashore, afford great surf fishing, and many of the region's bridges are open to anglers. Boaters will find enough boat ramps to ensure easy and quick access to all of the region's bays and coastal waters. Plus, charter boats operate from Destin (perhaps the best), Pensacola, Gulf Breeze, Panama City and several other communities. Fishing is so good that some charter boat captains go so far as to guarantee that if you don't catch fish you don't pay. I haven't heard of too many people getting a refund.

The region supports year-round fishing, but most of the activity occurs from May to October. This is when the Gulf water heats up and fish that spend their winters farther south move north (see the fish availability chart and month-by-month summary).

The key to understanding the region's saltwater fishing, then, is to follow

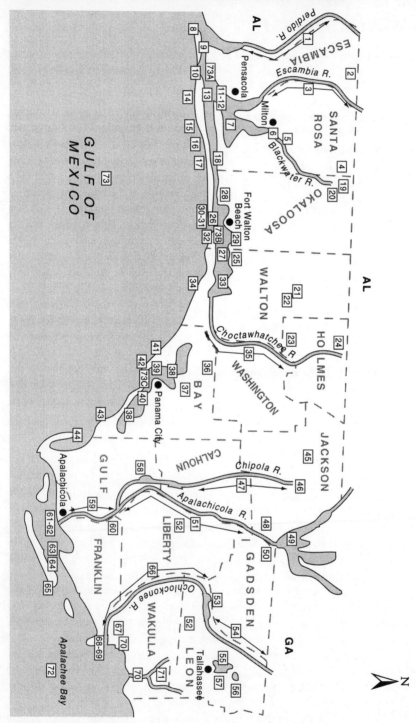

the Gulf of Mexico water temperature. Fishing activity really takes off in March when the Gulf water temperature surpasses the 65-degree mark. Fish begin arriving from their wintering grounds to the south and stay in the northern reaches of the Gulf through summer. Then in the fall, usually around October, the water temperature drops below the fishes' comfort level and there is a reverse migration to the south.

FRESHWATER FISHING

Some of the most scenic freshwater fishing, which also happens to be the most productive in the state, is in northwest Florida. No other part of the state has as many rivers, such as the Perdido, Escambia, Blackwater, Choctawhatchee, Apalachicola, and Ochlockonee, and they are well known for largemouth, sunshine (hybrid), and striped bass, and several species of panfish, regionally called bream.

Fishing activity is related to the rivers' water levels. Each year the rivers cycle through periods of high and low water. When the water level is low, parts of some of the rivers become too shallow for most boats. While fishing may be good during these times, getting to the fish can be a problem. When the water levels are high and the bottomlands along the rivers flood, the fish move in among the flooded forests and it is harder to find them. Always check with one of the local bait and tackle stores near the river you are planning to fish. Timing is important.

This part of the state also has numerous natural and man-made lakes open to the public. Many of them have free boat ramps constructed by the GFC. Some of the lakes are designated fish management areas. Angler success is enhanced in these lakes thanks to periodic stocking, aquatic weed management, placement of fish attractors and feeders, and the construction of fishing fingers and piers.

Lakes Seminole, Talquin, and Jackson are three of the most popular freshwater fishing sites in northwest Florida. Lakes Talquin and Jackson, within miles of downtown Tallahassee, are renowned for big bass.

ESCAMBIA AND SANTA ROSA COUNTIES

1. PERDIDO RIVER ————————————————————

Fresh; Boat; Ramp.

Description: One of the state's "blackwater rivers," named because of the dark, tannin-stained waters. One of the less fished rivers in Florida.

Fishing Index: Largemouth bass fishing is better on the lower part of the river. Boats can safely navigate below the US 90 bridge and for about 3 to 4 miles north of the bridge. Fish anytime of the year. Because it is not one of the more popular rivers, it has the reputation of being hard to fish. One of the few Florida rivers with spotted bass.

Directions: Forms the Panhandle's western boundary with Alabama.

Access Points:
1A. FL184 RAMP—*Fresh; Boat; Ramp*
Description: A GFC ramp near Muscogee.
Directions: From the intersection with US 29 north of Pensacola, take FL 184 west about 5.5 miles to the ramp.

1B. US 90 BRIDGE—*Fresh; Bank*
Directions: From the Alt. US 90 exit off I-10, take Alt. 90 west 4.5 miles to the junction with US 90. Continue west on US 90 an additional 2.2 miles to the bridge.
For more information: Call the GFC regional office at (850) 265-3677.

2. LAKE STONE

Fresh; Boat; Bank and Ramp.

Description: A 130-acre GFC Fish Management Area. The lake is a flooded timber area managed to enhance fishing. There is camping, a fishing pier, and several fishing fingers, which make this lake very good for land-bound anglers. No gas motors allowed. Supplies available in Century.

Fishing Index: Lake Stone holds natural populations of largemouth bass, bluegill, and shellcracker and a stocked population of channel catfish. Bass bite best on live threadfin shad which are also stocked in the lake.

Directions: In northeastern Escambia County, about 30 miles north of Pensacola. From the intersection with US 29 in Century drive 1.4 miles west on FL 4 to the lake.

For more information: Call the GFC regional office at (850) 265-3677.

3. ESCAMBIA RIVER

Fresh; Boat; Bank and Ramp.

Description: A river with plenty of oxbows and a good fishing reputation.

Fishing Index: The marshy area where the river empties into Escambia Bay is a good place to fish for bass and bream. The river is stocked with sunshine bass (hybrids). Spotted bass are in the upper part of the river.

Directions: Forms the boundary between Escambia and Santa Rosa counties.

Access Points:
3A. MC DAVID RAMP—*Fresh; Boat; Ramp*
Directions: From the US 29 exit off of I-10, take US 29 north approximately 25.5 miles. Look for the GFC boat ramp sign on the highway. Turn right and follow the road 0.5 mile to the ramp.

3B. MOLINO RAMP—*Fresh; Boat; Ramp*
Directions: From the US 29 exit off of I-10, take US 29 north approximately 15.5 miles to the intersection with FL 182. Turn right and go 2.3 miles east to the ramp.

ESCAMBIA AND SANTA ROSA COUNTIES

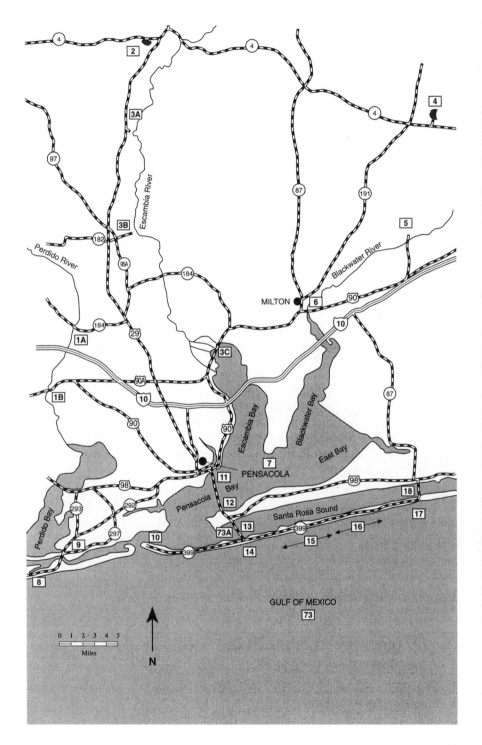

3C. The US 90 Causeway—*Fresh and Salt; Boat; Bank and Ramp*

Description: Two fish camps, Jim's and Bob's are just off the US 90 Causeway near the Pensacola side.

Directions: From the US 29 exit off of I-10 in Pensacola, take US 90 east approximately 3.9 miles to the fish camps.

For more information: Call the GFC regional office at (850) 265-3676.

4. Bear Lake

Fresh; Boat; Bank, Pier and Ramp.

Description: A 107-acre fish management area in the Blackwater River State Forest. The Division of Forestry maintains the campground. There is a barrier-free fishing pier and large area for bank fishing. Supplies available in Munson and Crestview. No gas motors allowed.

Fishing Index: Sunshine bass, channel catfish, and threadfin shad are stocked by the GFC. There are natural populations of largemouth bass, bluegill, and shellcrackers. Part of the lake is flooded timberland that provides excellent cover for the fish.

Directions: From Crestview drive 4 miles west on US 90. Turn right on FL 4 and drive 15.6 miles west to the entrance to Bear Lake. Or from Munson drive 2 miles east on FL 4 to the entrance. Follow the dirt road 0.5 mile to lake.

For more information: Call the GFC regional office at (850) 265-3676.

5. Blackwater River State Park

Fresh; Boat; Bank, and Ramp, $.

Description: The Blackwater is popular with canoers. Small boats may have difficulty navigating parts of the river during dry months. Camping and hiking opportunities also exist.

Fishing Index: The best bream and largemouth bass fishing is in the lower part of the river. According to Gray Bass, a fisheries biologist with the GFC, wade fishing for spotted bass is good upriver from the park.

Directions: From Milton drive about 10 miles east on US 90. Look for the state park signs and follow the entrance road about 2.9 miles north to the park.

For more information: Call the park office at (850) 983-5363.

6. Carpenter's Union Park

Fresh; Bank and Boat; Ramp.

Description: A community park with a nice boat ramp that provides access to the lower Blackwater River.

Fishing Index: Boats going upriver from here may encounter unnavigable conditions due to low water. Downriver, fish for bass, bluegills, and shellcrackers. In the fall look for a few redfish and speckled trout to move into the freshwater parts of the river and for largemouth bass to mix with these species in the slightly brackish waters.

Directions: In Milton. From US 90, drive north 0.8 mile on FL 87 to FL 191. Take FL 191 north for 0.3 mile. Park is on right.

7. PENSACOLA, EAST, ESCAMBIA, AND BLACKWATER BAYS
Salt; Boat

Description: These bays make up the estuarine system near the city of Pensacola.

Fishing Index: In winter, when the water is saltier, legal-size grouper may move into the lower part of the bay, creating some exciting fishing. To find these spots you will need LORAN numbers directing you to submerged structures. Fish with live bait. Beginning in fall and on into winter, speckled trout and redfish may move up the rivers to escape the shallow, cold bay waters, while largemouth and sunshine bass may move downriver to feed on schools of shrimp that are often abundant during the latter part of the year. Sheepshead love to hang around pilings and rocky bottoms. In summer, Spanish mackerel, bluefish, and cobia venture into the lower part of the bay. Flounder are always around.

Directions: Refer to the site descriptions for the **US 90 Causeway** between Milton and Pensacola (site 3C), **Carpenters Union Park** (site 6), and **Big Lagoon State Recreation Area** (site 9). There are also numerous marinas in the area.

8. PERDIDO KEY STATE RECREATION AREA
Salt; Surf; $.

Description: Surf fish anywhere along the park's 1.4 miles of beach.

Fishing Index: Surf fish for speckled trout, sheepshead, flounder, bluefish, and redfish.

Directions: From Pensacola take FL 292 west, cross over the Intracoastal Waterway, and go about 4 miles. The park is on the Gulf of Mexico.

For more information: Call the Park office at (850) 492-1595.

9. BIG LAGOON STATE RECREATION AREA ————————
Salt; Bank; Ramp; $.

Description: The boat ramp provides access to Big Lagoon and the Gulf of Mexico. Camping and nature trails help make this a popular site.

Fishing Index: Grand Lagoon is a popular place for crabbing and castnetting mullet. Fish for speckled trout, sheepshead, flounder, bluefish, and redfish. Long Pond, a freshwater pond, has bass and bream.

Directions: From Pensacola take FL 292 (Gulf Beach Highway) to FL 297. Turn left and go 5.2 miles to the park.

For More Information: Call the park office at (850) 492-1595.

10. FORT PICKENS
(GULF ISLANDS NATIONAL SEASHORE) ————————
Salt; Surf and Pier; $.

Description: The fort is one of several Civil War era forts on the upper Gulf coast. The park offers camping, swimming, SCUBA diving, miles of white sand beaches, and nature trails. A good family place.

Fishing Index: Fish from the pier on the bay side near Fort Pickens or anywhere along the beach so long as there are no swimmers nearby. A good place for sheepshead, redfish, flounder, speckled trout, and Spanish mackerel.

Directions: From the traffic light by the Pensacola Beach water tower, bear west 4 miles on FL 399 (Fort Pickens Road) to the park entrance. Continue 6.3 miles to Fort Pickens at road's end.

For more information: Call (850) 934-2600 for information or (850) 932-5302 for the Superintendent's Office.

11. PENSACOLA BAY PIER ————————————
Salt; Pier.

Description: The pier is part of the old-automobile-bridge-turned-fishing-pier over Pensacola Bay.

Fishing Index: Fish for Spanish mackerel, pompano, and speckled trout in summer. When the water gets colder there may be some big sheepshead around the pilings.

Directions: Adjacent to the Pensacola Bay Bridge (US 98) on the Pensacola side of the bay.

For more information: Call the City of Pensacola at (850) 432-7199.

12. GULF BREEZE PIER

Salt; Pier; $.

Description: The pier is the other part of the old bridge over Pensacola Bay on the Gulf Breeze side of the bay. Cars (no RVs) are allowed on this pier, making fishing very convenient. Maximum water depth is 30 feet.

Fishing Index: You will catch sheepshead, bluefish, whiting, and Spanish mackerel during their seasons. In winter look for some grouper and snapper to move into the deeper areas along the pier.

Directions: Adjacent to the Pensacola Bay Bridge (US 98) on the south side of the bay.

13. BOB SIKES BRIDGE

Salt; Bridge.

Description: The pier is part of the old bridge over the Intracoastal Waterway in Santa Rosa Sound. No fee. Parking can be a problem in this area. Ask permission before parking on private property.

Fishing Index: Spanish mackerel, bluefish, speckled trout, and sheepshead are likely catches.

Directions: This is the FL 399 bridge over the Intracoastal Waterway from Gulf Breeze to Pensacola Beach.

14. PENSACOLA BEACH PIER

Salt; Pier; $.

Note: Pier destroyed in hurricane since original printing.

Description: The westernmost Gulf of Mexico fishing pier in Florida. A popular and productive fishing location. The pier attracts fish because baitfish con-

The waters around the Pensacola Beach Pier are almost always gin clear. From the pier you can often see schools of fish approaching the pier.

gregate around the submerged rocks around the pier. The pier has rod and reel rentals and a snack bar (with good, fresh fried mullet sandwiches).

Fishing Index: In spring look for pompano, cobia, Spanish mackerel, and flounder. In summer add some king mackerel, bonita, and crevalle jacks. "Most of the time the water is so clear, you can see the fish coming and cast to them," according to Bob Payne, who works at the pier. Feathered jigs and heavy rods are necessary to go for the big fish like cobia.

Directions: Just off FL 399 as you enter Pensacola Beach from Pensacola. The pier parking lot is at the base of the water tower.

For more information: Call the pier office at (904) 932-0444.

15. SANTA ROSA ISLAND
Salt; Surf.

Description: Along FL 399, the island's Gulf-front road, there are numerous places to pull safely off the pavement, park and walk over the dunes to the beach. On the beach you can surf fish and enjoy a relatively undeveloped and unpopulated part of the coast. To protect the fragile dune vegetation use the wooden boardwalks to reach the beach whenever you can.

Fishing Index: Bluefish, redfish, flounder, speckled trout and pompano are common catches from the surf.

Directions: Places to pull off FL 399 begin at the outskirts of Pensacola Beach and continue to the Gulf Islands National Seashore boundary about 7 miles east of Pensacola Beach on FL 399.

16. GULF ISLANDS NATIONAL SEASHORE, SANTA ROSA AREA
Salt; Surf.

Description: Surf fish both in the Gulf of Mexico and Santa Rosa Sound at this day-use area. Fishing is allowed anywhere except in swimming areas where lifeguards are on duty. Bait and tackle are available at the concession store. To protect fragile dune plants use the boardwalk to reach the beach.

Fishing Index: On the bay side try wading in the flats for redfish and speckled trout during summer. Bluefish, redfish, flounder, speckled trout, and pompano are common catches from the surf.

Directions: On FL 399 7 miles east of Pensacola Beach or 4 miles west of Navarre.

For more information: Call (850) 934-2600 for information and (850) 932-5302 for the Superintendent's Office.

17. NAVARRE BEACH FISHING PIER

Salt; Pier.

Description: This 880-foot pier is a popular place in summer. There is no charge.

Fishing Index: The pier is noted for king mackerel, which give anglers a thrill when they arrive around April, and as a hot spot for big cobia in late spring and summer. Spanish mackerel, tarpon, flounder, and pompano also are caught during summer. In late summer blackfin tuna occasionally visit here.

Directions: On FL 399 in Navarre Beach. The pier is across the street from the water tower.

18. NAVARRE BEACH BRIDGE

Salt; Bridge and Bank.

Description: Fish along the wide road shoulders of the causeway leading to the bridge or from the walkway on the bridge.

Fishing Index: Look for speckled trout, redfish, sheepshead, and flounder.

Directions: This is the FL 399 bridge connecting the mainland to the east end of Santa Rosa Island.

OKALOOSA, WALTON, AND HOLMES COUNTIES

19. HURRICANE LAKE

Fresh; Boat and Bank; Ramp.

Description: A 318-acre GFC Fish Management Area in the Blackwater River State Forest. There are two paved ramps (locations described below), two un-improved ramps, and a beautiful, campground. No gas motors allowed.

Fishing Index: Much of the lake is flooded timberland. Submerged logs provide excellent cover for largemouth bass, bluegills, and shellcrackers. Several fishing fingers make this a good lake for bank fishing. Note the daily bag limit of 6 channel catfish.

Directions: From the intersection of US 90 and FL 85 in Crestview, take US 90 west for 4 miles to the intersection with FL 4. Turn right and go west on FL 4 for 11 miles. Turn north on Beaver Creek Road and go 2.5 miles. The road makes a bend to the right and continues another 3.3 miles. The first access point is Forest Road 24 (Kennedy Bridge Road). Turn right and go 2.4 miles to the campground entrance road. To reach the second access point go about 2.6 miles past Kennedy Bridge Road on Beaver Creek Road. Turn right on Forest Road 41 and go about 1.8 miles to the ramp and campground.

For more information: Call the GFC regional office at (850) 265-3676.

Fishing fingers like this one at Hurricane Lake (see previous page) provide anglers with plenty of shoreline to fish from.

20. KARICK LAKE

Fresh; Boat and Bank; Ramp.

Description: A 58-acre GFC Fish Management Area in the Blackwater River State Forest. There are two paved ramps and campgrounds on the lake. Fish fingers provide ample opportunity for bank fishing. Daily limit for channel catfish is ten. No gas motors allowed No bait and tackle nearby. Stock up in Crestview or Baker.

Fishing Index: The GFC stocks this lake with channel catfish and sunshine bass to supplement the natural bass and bream populations. The lake has several marked fish attractors.

Directions: In the northeast corner of Blackwater River State Forest. From the US 90 and FL 85 intersection in Crestview, take US 90 west for 4 miles. Turn right on FL 4 and go 3.6 miles. Turn north on FL 189, drive 7.25 miles, and look for the sign to the ramp and a dirt road on the right. Follow the dirt road to the ramp and campground. A second access point is 0.75 mile farther north on FL 189. Look for the sign and follow the dirt road to the ramp and campground.

For more information: Call the GFC regional office at (850) 265-3676.

OKALOOSA, WALTON, HOLMES COUNTIES

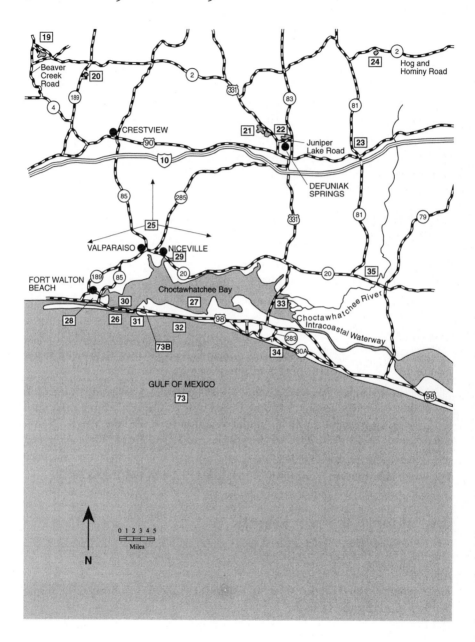

21. Kings and Holley Lakes

Fresh; Boat; Ramp.

Description: The two lakes, formerly connected, are now separated by a small dam. The only access is via ramps at private campgrounds.

Fishing Index: The lakes are known as very good bass lakes, particularly in February and March. Sometimes, if the weather is warm enough in January, the pre-spawning bass will be biting.

Directions: From De Funiak Springs, drive 2 miles west on US 90. Turn north on US 331 and drive about 4.2 miles to the lakes.

For more information: Call Kings Lake Campground at (850) 892-7229 or Lake Holley/Kings Lake Resort at (850) 892-5914.

22. Juniper Lake

Fresh; Boat and Bank; Ramp.

Description: This 665-acre lake is managed to enhance fishing. The Juniper Lake Campground (904) 892-3445), open only in the summer, is 0.2 mile east of the ramp. Camping, bait and tackle, groceries, and licenses are available at the campground.

Fishing Index: Like other lakes in the Panhandle, this is a good place for bass, bream, and catfish. Average depth is 6 feet. The lake is mostly flooded timber and marked trails provide access to remote areas.

Directions: From US 90 in De Funiak Springs, drive 2.4 miles north on FL 83 to Juniper Lake Road. Turn left and go 0.8 mile to the GFC ramp and county park. To reach a second ramp along the north shore of the lake, drive 3.9 miles north on FL 83 from US 90 and turn onto Catt Island Road. Follow the road 1.2 miles to the ramp at road's end.

For more information: Call the GFC regional office at (850) 265-3676.

23. Ponce De Leon Springs State Recreation Area

Fresh; Bank; $.

Description: Fishing is allowed in areas not set aside for swimming. Swimming is allowed in the spring boil.

Fishing Index: A place to take the kids fishing for bream and small bass.

Directions: From the Ponce De Leon springs exit on I-10 (11 miles east of De Funiak Springs), drive 1.1 miles north on FL 81 to US 90. Turn right and go 0.6 mile to FL 181A. Turn right and follow signs to the site.

For more information: Call the park office at (850) 265-3676.

24. LAKE VICTOR

Fresh; Boat and Bank; Ramp.

Description: This 130-acre lake is intensively managed for fishing. The center of the lake is flooded timber. Average depth is 8 feet. Fishing fingers provide ample opportunity for bank fishing. No gas motors allowed.

Fishing Index: In addition to naturally occurring bass, bluegill, shellcrackers, and crappies, the lake is stocked with channel catfish. Ten-fish limit on channel catfish.

Directions: Exit I-10 at Ponce De Leon Springs and drive 13.5 miles north on FL 81 to FL 2 (Hog and Hominy Road). Turn right and head 4.6 miles east to a dirt road on the right that goes to the paved boat ramp and a picnic area.

For more information: Call Riddle Bait and Tackle (850) 956-2444.

25. EGLIN AIR FORCE BASE

Fresh; Bank and Boat.

Description: The public is welcome to fish inside the base but there are some special regulations to follow. Most important is to obtain an Eglin AFB Fishing Permit from the Eglin Natural Resources Branch Office at 107 FL 85 North, Niceville, FL 32578. You may also call the office at (904) 882-4164 and request a permit and copy of the regulations book. All Florida fishing laws apply on Eglin. Except for a few lakes where motors up to 10 hp are allowed, no gas motors can be used.

Fishing Index: Fish for bream and bass. It's a good idea to check at one of the local bait and tackle shops to see if they have any current information on which of the ponds are producing the best action and to get directions.

Directions: The base includes most of the land surrounding Valpariso and Niceville. There are numerous small ponds and lakes to fish within the reservation.

For more information: Call the Eglin Air Force Base Natural Resources Branch at (850) 882-4164.

26. OKALOOSA ISLAND PIER

Salt; Pier; $.

Description: This 1,228-foot pier in Fort Walton Beach draws people from around the south. It's open 24 hours during summer. Bait and tackle are available, and rod and reels can be rented. No saltwater license needed. Pier owner Rhett Cadenhead said that, "people from out of state come here every year and some stay and fish for a month."

Fishing Index: Summer is the time to fish from the pier. Schools of cobia swim by and many are caught on the jigs that pier employees make during the slower winter season. Spanish and king mackerel, flounder, bluefish, redfish, sheepshead, black drum, and whiting are common catches reported at the pier. Occasionally a sailfish is hooked by an angler fishing off the end of the pier.

Directions: In Fort Walton Beach drive 1.2 miles east on US 90 from the intersection with FL 85. Look for the pier parking lot just past the bridge over the Intracoastal Waterway.

For more information: Call the pier office at (850) 244-1023.

27. CHOCTAWHATCHEE BAY ———————————————
Salt; Boat.

Description: The river with the same name is the major freshwater source for this bay. The bay has good seagrass flats along much of the shoreline. It opens to the Gulf of Mexico through East Pass near Destin, and the Intracoastal Waterway passes through the bay. At the east end, a dredged portion of the waterway connects to West Bay and the Panama City area.

Fishing Index: Fish the flats for speckled trout and redfish during warmer months. When the water cools down look for these fish to move into the deeper holes in the bay and to go up the river and tidal creeks, sometimes venturing into freshwater. It's possible to catch redfish, speckled trout, and largemouth bass in the same area. Flounder are always in the bay and sometimes up the rivers in freshwater. White trout fishing can be very good in January and February. Another place to try is the "old ship," a partially submerged wreck off Basin Bayou along the bay's north shore. You may find some tarpon hanging around in summer.

Directions: Refer to the site descriptions for Jackson Park, Rocky Bayou State Recreation Area, Gulf Islands National Seashore, East Pass, and US 331 Bridge. There are also many marinas in the area.

28. JACKSON PARK ———————————————
Salt; Boat and Pier; Ramp.

Description: The ramp at this Fort Walton Beach city park provides access to eastern Santa Rosa Sound and Choctawhatchee Bay. There is a small fishing pier in the park.

Fishing Index: This is a good place to launch a boat to fish "The Narrows," that part of Santa Rosa Sound between Fort Walton Beach and Navarre. The seagrass flats along this stretch of the Intracoastal Waterway are a top spot for speckled trout.

Directions: In Fort Walton Beach. From the intersection with FL 85 drive 1.6 miles west on US 98.

29. ROCKY BAYOU STATE RECREATION AREA

Salt, Boat and Bank; Ramp; $.

Description: Rocky Bayou is part of the Choctawhatchee Bay system. The park has a campground, hiking trails, swimming, and picnicking.

Fishing Index: Fish for redfish, speckled trout, and flounder. Flounder fishing can be very good on the flats in fall.

Directions: From the intersection with FL 285 in Niceville, drive about 2.5 miles east on FL 20 to the park.

For more information: Call the park office at (850) 897-3222.

30. GULF ISLANDS NATIONAL SEASHORE, OKALOOSA AREA

Salt; Surf; Ramp.

Description: This part of the national seashore has a boat ramp that accesses the western part of Choctawhatchee Bay, Santa Rosa Sound, and the Gulf of Mexico via East Pass.

Fishing Index: Try wading the flats east of the boat ramp for speckled trout and redfish. Boaters are only a few miles from East Pass. Fish around the US 98 bridge for Spanish mackerel, flounder, bluefish, and sheepshead.

Directions: 1.1 miles east of the Okaloosa Pier on US 98.

For more information: Call (850) 934-2600 for information and (850) 932-5302 for the Superintendent's Office.

31. EAST PASS

Salt; Boat and Bank.

Description: This is the only entrance to Choctawhatchee Bay from the Gulf of Mexico. Fish from the shore along the west side of East Pass or from a boat.

Fishing Index: Fish for Spanish mackerel, redfish, flounder, bluefish, and sheeps–head. Some days the pass is too rough for boaters to anchor and fish. Use caution.

Directions: Drive about 7 miles east of Fort Walton Beach on US 98.

For more information: Call Half Hitch Tackle and Marine Supply at (850) 837-3121

32. HENDERSON BEACH STATE RECREATION AREA ———

Salt; Surf; $.

Description: A beachfront park.

Fishing Index: Surf fish where people are not swimming. Fish for whiting, reds, and bluefish.

Directions: From the intersection with Gulf Shores Drive in Destin, drive 2.1 miles east on US 98 to the park.

For more information: Call the park office at (850) 837-7550.

33. US HIGHWAY 331 BRIDGE ———————————

Salt; Pier and Bank.

Description: The pier is part of the old bridge over the bay. Fish off it or along the causeway south of the bridge.

Fishing Index: Sheepshead and speckled trout like the pier's pilings and the rocky shoreline of the causeway.

Directions: The highway spans the eastern end of Choctawhatchee Bay. From Destin take US 98 east about 20 miles. Turn north on US 331 and go 0.25 mile to the bridge. From I-10 take the De Funiak Springs exit and drive about 20 miles south on US 331.

34. GRAYTON BEACH STATE RECREATION AREA ———

Salt; Surf;Boat and Ramp; $.

Description: There are nature trails, picnicking, and a campground at this beachfront park.

Fishing Index: From the ramp in the park you can access Western Lake, a brackish water lake along the coast. The lake holds speckled trout and few small bass. Surf fish for whiting, reds, and bluefish.

Directions: From the intersection with US 331 drive 1.5 miles east on US 98. Turn onto FL 283 and go 1.7 miles to FL 30A. Turn left and go 0.6 mile to the entrance.

For more information: Call the park office at (850) 231-4210.

35. CHOCTAWHATCHEE RIVER ———————————

Fresh; Boat and Bank; Ramp.

Description: The river flows from southern Alabama to the eastern end of Choctawhatchee Bay.

Fishing Index: For something unusual try fishing for alligator gar. Fish that weigh more than 70 pounds are eligible for the GFC's Big Catch Program. The most popular way to catch these fish is by bowfishing for them. The river is a good place to fish for channel catfish. Stan Kirkland of the GFC says that a piece of shrimp fished on the bottom is the best bait on this river.

Directions: There is a GFC ramp on FL 20, 1.4 miles west of the intersection with FL 79.

Washington, Bay, and Gulf (Southwestern portion) Counties

36. Sandhill Lakes

Fresh; Boat and Bank.

Description: These small, natural lakes are generally deep and filled with clear water. The lakes are best fished with a small boat. Most of the ramps are primitive. Local knowledge is very helpful in finding the ramps because many are poorly marked.

Fishing Index: The lakes are known for their bass fishing and, to a lesser extent, for bream. Tom Putnam, one of the owners of Half Hitch Tackle and Marine Supply, says that your best bet may be to hire a guide. Check at the local bait and tackle shops for more information.

Directions: The primary access road is FL 77 beginning about 14 miles north of Panama City and 16 miles south of Chipley.

For more information: Try Half Hitch Tackle and Marine Supply in Panama City Beach at (850) 234-2621.

37. Deer Point Lake

Fresh; Boat; Ramp.

Description: A popular lake used by anglers and swimmers. The lake is an impounded marsh at the south end that grades into flooded timberland at the north end.

Fishing Index: Stan Kirkland of the GFC's regional office in Panama City say that this lake is "one of the best places to fly fish at night for bream." This is also a good lake for crappie in winter.

Access Points:
37A. Ira Hutchinson Park—*Fresh; Boat; Ramp.*
Description: The county park has a ramp that accesses the south end of Deer Point Lake. In summer, sunbathers and swimmers use the area and many locals avoid using the ramp from May through August.
Directions: From Panama City, drive north about 6.3 miles on US 231 to CR 2321. Turn left and drive 5.2 miles to the park.

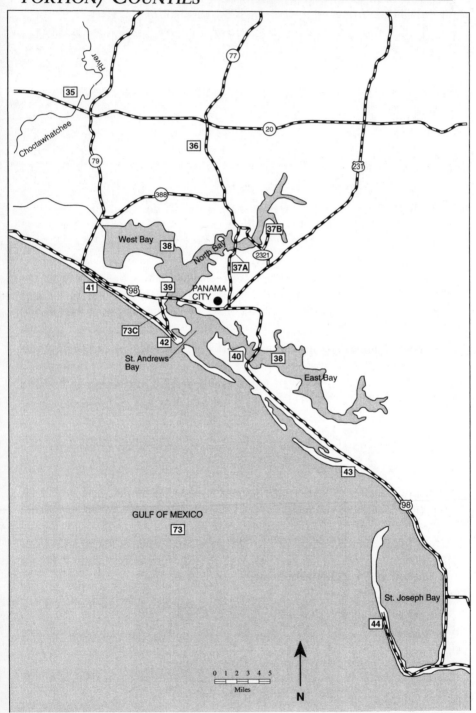

37B. High Point Landing—*Fresh; Boat; Ramp.*

Description: This ramp is used year-round to access Deer Point Lake.

Directions: From the intersection with US 98 in Panama City, drive north for 6.3 miles on US 231 to CR 2321. Turn left and go north about 1.4 miles to CR 2311. Take CR 2311 north 4.7 miles to the ramp.

38. WEST, NORTH, EAST AND ST. ANDREWS BAYS ———
Salt; Boat; Bank and Pier; Ramp.

Description: These bays in and around Panama City all have good seagrass flats except for North bay, which is influenced by freshwater runoff from Deer Point Lake. East Bay may be the best bay because the combination of grassflats and oyster bars provides good habitat for speckled trout and redfish.

Fishing Index: Tom Putnam, a long-time resident and knowledgeable angler from Panama City Beach recommends fishing for speckled trout and redfish in the bayous and deeper waters during winter. The fish move onto the flats in spring and remain there until early fall. When the fish are on the flats, Jim Wilson, host and producer of *Jim Wilson Outdoors*, suggests wade fishing for speckled trout. "Use as light a line as possible and freeline a shrimp." Spanish mackerel move into St. Andrews Bay and the lower parts of West and East bays in spring. Redfish are in the pass from St. Andrews Bay to the Gulf of Mexico almost all year Putnam says, but "90 percent are over the current maximum size limit."

Directions: Refer to the site descriptions for the Hathaway and Dupont bridges and St. Andrews State Recreation Area. There are many marinas in the area.

39. HATHAWAY BRIDGE ——————————
Salt; Bank; Ramp.

Description: Fish around the bridge embankments on either side of the bridge. The ramp is on the west side.

Fishing Index: Fish for sheepshead and redfish.

Directions: This is the US 98 bridge entering Panama City from the west.

40. DUPONT BRIDGE ——————————
Salt; Pier.

Description: This is one of many old road bridges that was left for anglers to use when the replacement bridge was built. Half Hitch Tackle and Marine Supply store owner Tom Putnam thinks this is an "underutilized" spot that more people should try.

Fishing Index: A very good place for redfish, speckled trout, and sheepshead. Putnam suggests using live shrimp and pinfish for bait.

Spanish mackerel provide a flurry of action for anglers whenever a school move through. In northwest Florida the fish is a summertime favorite.

Directions: This is the US 98 bridge crossing East Bay when approaching Panama City from the east. Fish on the east (Tyndall) side of the bridge.

41. DAN RUSSELL CITY PIER

Salt; Pier; $.

Description: The Panama City Beach pier stretches 1,642 feet, making it the longest pier in the Gulf of Mexico. Bait and tackle, rod rentals, and snack bar are on site. Park across the street from the pier.

Fishing Index: The best fishing is from March to October when migratory species including cobia, Spanish and king mackerel, pompano, blackfin tuna, and sailfish will be around.

Directions: From the center of Panama City Beach drive about 5 miles west on Alternate US 98.

For more information: Call the pier office at (904) 233-5080.

42. ST. ANDREWS STATE RECREATION AREA

Salt; Boat, Pier and Surf; Ramp; $.

Description: The boat ramp accesses St. Andrew Bay and the Gulf of Mexico. Camping, nature trail, and picnicking make this a popular park for tourists.

Fishing Index: Fish from either of the two piers or the jetties. Bluefish are caught all year, redfish in summer and fall, Spanish mackerel in spring, and king mackerel in summer. A few cobia are taken in summer.

Directions: At the east end of Panama City Beach. From the US 98, Alt. US 98 and Thomas Drive intersection, take Thomas Drive 3.4 miles to the beach. The park is on the left.

For more information: Call the park office at (904) 233-5140.

43. MEXICO BEACH

Salt; Pier and Boat.

Description: Two types of fishing are popular in this small community about 20 miles east of Panama City. The free fishing pier is rather short (385 feet) compared to other piers in the Panhandle but still popular in summer. There are no facilities. Inshore fishing is the other activity. A private boat ramp (across the highway from the pier) allows access to the Gulf of Mexico and St. Joseph Bay. Also, a few charter boats operate from town.

Fishing Index: From the pier, anglers catch whiting, flounder, and a few Spanish mackerel. Captain Dave Mullis fishes in the Gulf of Mexico for his favorite fish, cobia, from May to October. He also catches Spanish and king mackerel, wahoo, and amberjack. When dolphin arrive in late spring he suggests fishing the buoy line that runs out from Port St. Joe. In late fall he recommends flounder fishing in the Gulf. "This area has a lot to offer," Mullis says, "and if you're nice you can get all the help you want—just ask." Stop by any of the local marinas and ask for the free fishing map local marine dealers made up; it includes useful LORAN numbers for some popular inshore sites. You can call Mullis at (904) 647-8783.

Directions: The pier is one block off US 98 on 37th St. in Mexico Beach. The charter boats are in the waterway on the north side of US 98.

44. St. Joseph Peninsula State Park ─────────
Salt; Boat and Surf; Ramp; $.

Description: On the tip of the St. Joseph peninsula, this is a popular park in the summer. There is a boat ramp and plenty of beach for surf fishing. Amenities include a large campground, cabins, a camp store with bait and tackle, and a wilderness hiking area. This is also a great place for bird watchers to catch the fall hawk migration.

Fishing Index: The extensive seagrass flats in St. Joseph Bay are a productive place to fish for speckled trout beginning in April and lasting into fall. Surf fishing is very good along the St. Joseph peninsula because migrating species, such as Spanish and king mackerel, cobia, and pompano, come close to shore. Look for troughs between the beach and the sand bars just offshore. Fish the troughs and wear polarized glasses. They will make it easy to see the fish, and once you do, cast ahead of the fish and bring your lure or bait toward the fish. Don't sneak it up from behind, that's not normal behavior for prey. The grassflats also draw a huge crowd every summer when the recreational scallop season opens. The bay has one of the last remaining sizable population of succulent bay scallops. Check for season dates and daily bag limits.

Directions: From Port St. Joe take US 98 east to FL 30A. Turn south and go about 6.6 miles. Where the road bends left (east), turn right instead on FL 30E and drive 7.9 miles to the park entrance.

For more information: Call the park office at (850) 227-1327.

Calhoun, Jackson, Gadsden, Liberty (northern portion), and Leon Counties

45. Florida Caverns State Park ─────────
Fresh; Bank and Boat; Ramp; $.

Description: The Chipola River is a cold-water, spring-fed river. The park features a series of limestone caves. Take time for the tour. Camping, canoeing, swimming, and a nature trail are also available.

Fishing Index: The best bet along this part of the river is redbreast and blue-gills in the spring.

Directions: The park entrance is 3 miles north of Marianna on FL 166.

For more information: Call the park office at (850) 482-9598.

46. MERRITT'S MILL POND

Fresh; Boat and Bank; Ramp.

Description: Anglers come from around the country to fish this 200-acre, spring-fed pond. A small dam at the south end created the pond.

Fishing Index: Merritt's is famous for its spring shellcracker fishing. The best action comes around the time of full moon. The water is crystal clear so the fish can see you as well as you can see them. Days when there are ripples on the water usually produce more action.

Directions: The pond is 2.6 miles east of Marianna on US 90. Easiest access is the ramp at Arrowhead Campground (call (904) 482-5583) on US 90. To reach the GFC ramp, take FL 71 north from US 90 in Marianna about 1.2 miles. Turn onto CR 164 and go about 1.5 miles; watch for Hunter Fish Camp Road on the right. Look for the boat ramp sign. Turn onto the road and follow it about 0.9 mile to the ramp. The road ends just beyond the ramp.

For more information: Call The Bait Shop across the highway from Arrowhead Campground at (850) 482-8425.

The crystal clear water of Merritts Mill Pond is a top spot for shellcracker fishing.

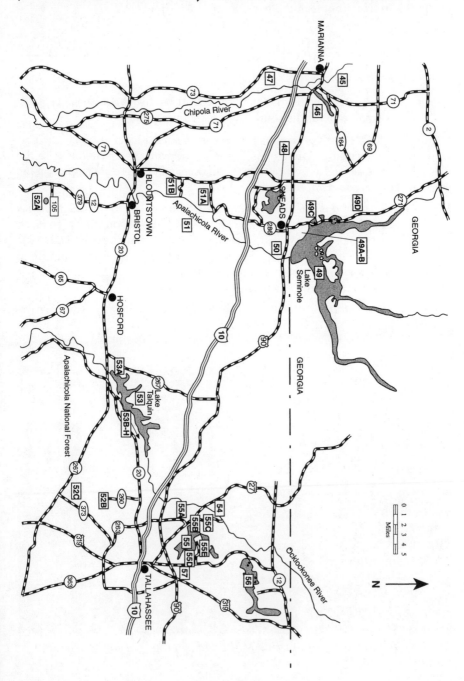

47. CHIPOLA RIVER

Fresh; Boat; Ramp.

Description: This spring-fed river has its origins along the Florida-Alabama border. It empties into the Apalachicola River.

Fishing Index: This is the only river in Florida that has shoal bass. The best place to fish for them according to Gray Bass, a fisheries biologist with the GFC, is the reach of river south of the I-10 bridge and north of the CR 278 bridge. Fish for this species around the numerous rock shoals.

Directions: There is a ramp just south of I-10. Exit onto FL 71 south and go 0.5 mile. Look for the GFC ramp sign and turn right. Follow the road to the ramp.

48. OCHEESEE POND

Fresh; Boat; Ramp.

Description: This is an impounded and flooded cypress swamp. It's easy to get lost among the standing flooded timber. Ocheesee is popular among local residents but not well known to many others. If the water is too rough on nearby Lake Seminole, make the short trip southwest of Sneads to the pond.

Fishing Index: A good lake for bass and large bream. Bring along a long-handled, small mesh net and catch your own grass shrimp. They are excellent bream bait.

Directions: From Sneads take FL 286 (Gloster Avenue) south 3.2 miles to FL 280. From the I-10 exit take FL 286 north 2 miles to FL 280. Turn onto FL 280, go west for 2.3 miles, and look for the GFC ramp on the north side of the road.

49. LAKE SEMINOLE (JIM WOODRUFF RESERVOIR)

Fresh; Boat and Bank; Ramp.

Description: The lake, formed by Jim Woodruff Dam, partially impounds the Flint and Chatahoochee rivers. Anglers with a Florida license can fish the Florida waters of this lake and a part of the reservoir in Georgia. Before you fish this lake consult with a local fish camp or bait and tackle shop and make sure you know and respect the boundaries.

Fishing Index: The lake is well known for its largemouth, sunshine, and striped bass fishing. Largemouth bass fishing is best in winter in the deeper waters and in the shallows when the water temperature is warmer. Striped bass also school during late winter; the trick is finding the schools. Sunshine bass fishing is very good in fall and winter. This is also a good place for crappie in winter. Live Missouri minnows are the preferred bait. Special size and bag limits may be in effect. Check with a local bait and tackle shop for specific information.

Directions: On the Florida-Georgia border, 8,000 acres of this 37,500 reservoir are in Florida. Access in Florida is primarily off FL 271 north of Sneads. There are also numerous access points in Georgia.

Access Points:

49A. Sneads Landing—*Fresh; Bank and Boat; Ramp.*

Description: Operated by the US Army Corps of Engineers. There is a free boat ramp and plenty of bank fishing along the lake. Lake Seminole Lodge is 0.1 mile down the road from the recreation area.

Directions: From US 90 on the east side of Sneads turn north onto Legion Road. Go 1.6 miles to Sneads Landing recreation area.

For more information: Call the US Army Corps of Engineers office at (850) 662-2001.

49B. Three Rivers State Recreation Area—*Fresh; Boat, Bank and Pier; Ramp; $.*

Description: The park has a 100-foot fishing pier, several places for bank fishing, a campground, and two nature trails.

Directions: The entrance is 2 miles north of US 90 in Sneads on FL 271.

For more information: Call the park office at (850) 482-9006.

49C. Jackson County Ramp—*Fresh; Boat and Bank; Ramp*

Description: Bank fish in the area around the boat ramp. Across the highway from the ramp is Chestney's Fish Camp (call (850) 593-6935). Camping, bait and tackle, and groceries are available.

Directions: On FL 271 about 2.8 miles north of US 90. Ramp is on the west side of the road.

49D. Apalachee Wildlife Management Area—*Fresh; Boat and Bank; Ramp.*

Description: There are boat ramps accessing Lake Seminole via the Chatahoochee River located about 3.5 miles (Arnold's Landing), 12 miles (Buena Vista Landing), and 17 miles (Neal's Landing) from the Jackson County ramp. Bank fish wherever you can safely pull off the road.

Directions: From the Jackson County ramp on FL 271 you can fish at numerous places along the road in the Wildlife Management Area. The ramps are along FL 271.

50. Jim Woodruff Dam Fishing Deck ──────
Fresh; Bank.

Description: The waters immediately below a dam are called the tailrace. This fishing and observation deck is a very popular and productive place to fish. To reach the site you must drive across the Florida-Georgia border, then loop back into Florida at the parking lot.

Fishing Index: In February and March white bass spawn on the sand bars below the dam. Fish for them and sunshine and striped bass, which have followed the shad upriver. This is a place to catch your limit and have a shot at some big sunshines and stripers. The sunshine bass make a second strong showing in fall.

Directions: From Chatahoochee, drive west on US 90; turn onto the signed access road to the US Army Corps of Engineers office at the dam.

51. APALACHICOLA RIVER (WOODRUFF DAM TO CHIPOLA CUTOFF CANAL) ——————————
Fresh; Boat and Bank; Ramp.

Description: This river is an important waterway for barges headed to ports in Georgia above Jim Woodruff Dam. The upper part of the river, from the dam to the intersection of the Gulf, Calhoun, and Liberty county lines, has steep bluffs along much of its length.

Fishing Index: This river has something to offer any type of freshwater angler. Sunshine, striped, and white bass migrate upriver in spring and create excellent fishing, especially close to Woodruff Dam. The entire length of the river has good to very good largemouth bass fishing in spring and summer. After the annual spawn is over the bass move into the river to spend late spring and summer.

Access Points:
51A. OCHEESEE LANDING—*Boat; Ramp.*
Description: A GFC ramp.
Directions: Exit I-10 onto CR 286 (the Sneads exit) and drive south about 3.8 miles. Look for a dirt road and the GFC boat ramp sign. Turn east on the dirt road and go about 1.2 miles to the ramp at the end of the road. Or exit I-10 onto FL 69 and go south about 5.8 miles to CR 274. Take CR 274 east about 3.5 miles to the ramp.

51B. REDD'S LANDING—*Boat; Ramp.*
Description: A GFC ramp.
Directions: Exit I-10 onto FL 69 and drive south for 9.7 miles; look for the boat ramp sign. To reach the ramp turn east on a dirt road and go about 2 miles to the river and the ramp. If the sign is missing on the highway, the dirt road is 0.7 mile south of the small bridge over Graves Creek on FL 69.

52. APALACHICOLA NATIONAL FOREST ————————
Fresh; Boat and Bank; Ramp.

Description: Fishing within the national forest is on several small lakes and the Ochlockonee and Apalachicola rivers. The non-river sites described here have campgrounds and boat ramps (except Trout Pond) and bank fishing. Unless specifically indicated there are no fees to use these sites.

Fishing Index: Fishing in the lakes is for bass and bream.

Directions: The national forest covers much of the land south and west of Tallahassee in Leon, Wakulla, and Liberty counties.

Lakes:

52A. CAMEL LAKE CAMPGROUND—*Fresh; Bank; Ramp.*
Description: A small lake with a 10 horsepower limit on motors. Camping, picnicking.
Directions: From Bristol, take CR 12 south about 10.3 miles. Turn and go 2 miles east on Forest Road 105.

52B. SILVER LAKE—*Fresh; Boat and Bank; $.*
Description: A 23-acre lake only 5 miles from Tallahassee. Unpaved ramp. No gasoline motors allowed on lake. Campground, picnicking, swimming beach, nature trail. Barrier-free bathhouse.
Directions: From the intersection of FL 20 and FL 263 (Capital Circle) in Tallahassee, take FL 20 west 3.4 miles to CR 260. Drive south on CR 260 about 3.2 miles and look for the sign to the site. Turn left and follow the paved road.

52C. TROUT POND—*Fresh; Bank and Pier.*
Description: A day-use area with a barrier-free fishing pier. Open April 1 to October 31.
Directions: From the intersection of FL 263 (Capital Circle) and CR 373 (Springhill Road) in Tallahassee, take CR 373 south 3.6 miles to FR 375. Turn west (right) and go 0.5 mile to the site.

53. LAKE TALQUIN
Fresh; Boat, Bank, and Pier; Ramp.

Description: At 8,850 acres this lake is more than twice the size of nearby Lake Jackson. The lake, an impounded portion of the Ochlockonee River, was formed in 1927 when Jackson Bluffs Dam was built. Much of the lake is flooded timberland, so exercise care when on the water. In addition to the public access sites described below, there are a number of privately operated fish camps on the lake.

Fishing Index: This is one of Florida's famous fishing lakes, boasting great year-round fishing. The GFC stocks this lake with striped bass. They begin to school in January. Native white bass also form schools at this time. February and March are traditionally the best months for trophy largemouth bass. Bluegill and shellcracker fishing is very good in spring, and crappie action is excellent in winter. Special size and bag limits may be in effect. Check with a local bait and tackle shop for specific information.

Directions: This reservoir begins about 10 miles west of Tallahassee and continues another 10 miles to the west. Access to the ramps and fish camps is off FL 20 in Leon County and FL 267 in Gadsden County.

Access Points:
53A. PAT THOMAS PARK (HOPKIN'S LANDING)—*Fresh; Boat, Bank and Pier; Ramp; $.*
Description: This is a Gadsden County park with a campground, hot showers, electric hookups, and a dump station. There is a fee for camping and using the ramp. A park ranger is on-site.

Directions: Go 9.2 miles south of I-10 or 3.3 miles north of FL 20 on FL 267. Turn onto Hopkin's Landing Road and go 1 mile to the park.
For more information: Call the park ranger at (850) 875-4544.

53B. BLOUNT'S LANDING—*Fresh; Boat and Bank; Ramp.*
Directions: From the intersection with Capital Circle (FL 263), go 17.9 miles west on FL 20. Turn onto Blount's Landing Road and go 1 mile to the lake.

53C. WAINRIGHT LANDING—*Fresh; Boat and Bank; Ramp.*
Directions: From the intersection with Capital Circle (FL 263), go 17.2 miles west on FL 20. Turn onto Wainright Landing Road and go 0.5 mile to the lake.

53D STOUTAMIRE LANDING—*Fresh; Boat; Bank; Ramp.*
Directions: From the intersection with Capital Circle (FL 263), go 16.9 miles west on FL 20. Turn onto Stoutamire Road and go 0.7 mile to the lake.

53E. HALL'S LANDING—*Fresh; Boat, Bank, and Pier; Ramp.*
Description: This is a county operated park with free camping. Bank fish around the boat ramp or fish off the piers near the campground.
Directions: From the intersection with Capital Circle (FL 263), go 14 miles west on FL 20. Turn onto Hall's Landing Road and go 1.4 miles to the lake.

53F. RIVER BLUFF STATE PICNIC SITE—*Fresh; Pier.*
Directions: From the intersection with Capital Circle (FL 263), go 11 miles west on FL 20. Turn onto Vause Road and go 0.6 mile to the entrance.

53G. WILLIAM'S LANDING—*Fresh; Boat, Bank and Pier; Ramp.*
Description: This is a county operated park with free camping. Bank fish around the boat ramp or fish off the piers near the campground.
Directions: From the intersection with Capital Circle (FL 263), go 10.4 miles west on FL 20. Turn onto William's Landing Road and go 0.8 mile to the lake.

53H. COE'S LANDING—*Fresh; Boat, Bank, and Pier; Ramp.*
Description: This is a county operated park with free camping. Bank fish around the boat ramp or fish off the piers near the campground. A private marina with bait and tackle is across the street from the campground.
Directions: From the intersection with Capital Circle (FL 263), go 7.6 miles west on FL 20. Turn onto Coe's Landing Road and go 1.2 miles to the lake.

54. OCHLOCKONEE RIVER
(HEADWATERS TO LAKE TALQUIN)
Fresh; Boat and Bank; Ramp.

Description: The upper part of the river begins in Georgia. From the Florida - Georgia line south, the river is fishable with a small boat.

Fishing Index: The upper part of the river, above Lake Talquin, has fair to good bass and bream fishing. It is also the only place in Florida besides the Suwannee River where anglers can catch the Suwannee bass.

Directions: To reach the GFC's boat ramp, take US 27 north from Tallahassee.

At the north end of Lake Jackson turn north onto CR 157 and go about 3.5 miles to the river and the ramp.

55. LAKE JACKSON

Fresh; Boat and Bank; Ramp.

Description: This 4,000-acre lake is just north of Tallahassee.

Fishing Index: Lake Jackson is regarded as one of the best bass fishing lakes in Florida. January to March, when the bass are bedding, is the best time, but it's also fun to try night fishing in summer. Red's daughter Martha of Red and Sam's Fish Camp says the shellcrackers bite good during the full moon in March and April. Crappie action is very good during the winter months using Missouri minnows for bait. Special size and bag limits may be in effect. Check with a local bait and tackle shop for specific information.

Directions: The lake is about 7 miles north of the state capitol building. The main access road is US 27.

Access Points:
55A. US 27 NORTH—*Bank; Ramp.*
Directions: Exit I-10 onto US 27 and drive 3.9 miles north.

55B. RED AND SAM'S FISH CAMP—*Boat and Bank; Ramp.*
Directions: Exit I-10 onto US 27 and drive 4.5 miles north.
For more information: Call Red and Sam's at (850) 562-3083.

55C. SUNSET ROAD—*Boat; Ramp.*
Directions: From the intersection of US 27 and FL 157 in Havanna drive 1.1 miles northeast on FL 157. Turn right at Sunset Road and go 1 mile to the ramp at road's end.

55D. RHODEN COVE ROAD—*Boat; Ramp.*
Directions: From the intersection of Thomasville and Meridian roads in Tallahassee, take Meridian 3.7 miles north to Rhoden Cove Road. Turn left and drive about 1.3 miles to the ramp.

55E. MILLER'S Landing—*Boat; Ramp.*
Directions: Take Meridian Road 5.1 miles north from Thomasville Road. Turn left on Miller's Landing Road and follow it for 2.1 miles to the ramp.

56. LAKE IAMONIA

Fresh; Boat; Ramp.

Description: This heavily-vegetated lake is north of Lake Jackson but is still only a short drive from Tallahassee.

Fishing Index: The lake has a reputation for very good bluegill and shellcracker fishing.

Directions: Exit I-10 onto US 319 and drive north about 12.5 miles to FL 12.

Turn left and go 2.3 miles to Lake Iamonia Road. The public ramp is next to Reeve's Fish Camp.

For more information: Call Charlie Harrell's Fish Camp at (850) 893-0361.

57. MACLAY STATE GARDENS

Fresh; Boat and Bank; Ramp; $.

Description: Fish in Lake Hall and enjoy the beautiful ornamental gardens. The peak blooming season is mid to late March.

Fishing Index: Fish for largemouth bass and bream throughout the year.

Directions: Exit I-10 onto US 319 and drive 0.5 mile north.

For more information: Call the park office at (850) 487-4556.

GULF (EASTERN PORTION), LIBERTY (SOUITHERN PORTION), FRANKLIN AND WAKULLA COUNTIES

58. DEAD LAKES STATE RECREATION AREA

Fresh; Boat and Bank; Ramp; $.

Description: Dead Lakes is an impoundment on the Chipola River. The park has areas for bank fishing, a ramp that provides access to the lake, a campground, and nature trails. There are several privately operated fish camps just north of the park on the lake.

Fishing Index: Shellcrackers, bluegills, and bass are the three popular species caught on the lake. Like many parts of northwest Florida, spring is the best time to fish.

Directions: From the intersection with FL 22 in Wewahitchka, drive 2 miles north on FL 71 to the park entrance.

For more information: Call the park office at (850) 639-2702.

59. APALACHICOLA RIVER (CHIPOLA CUTOFF CANAL TO APALACHICOLA BAY)

Fresh; Boat and Bank; Ramp.

Description: The lower part of the river passes by the western edge of the Apalachicola National Forest. Most of the river is bounded by tupelo and cypress swamps that make up the river's extensive flood plain.

Fishing Index: The Apalachicola River has an excellent reputation for catfish, specifically channel and flathead catfish. To catch the channel cats, locals use a bait called the catalpa worm. Actually this is a larvae from a moth that lays its eggs on the catalpa tree. The 2-inch black and yellow worm-like larvae are

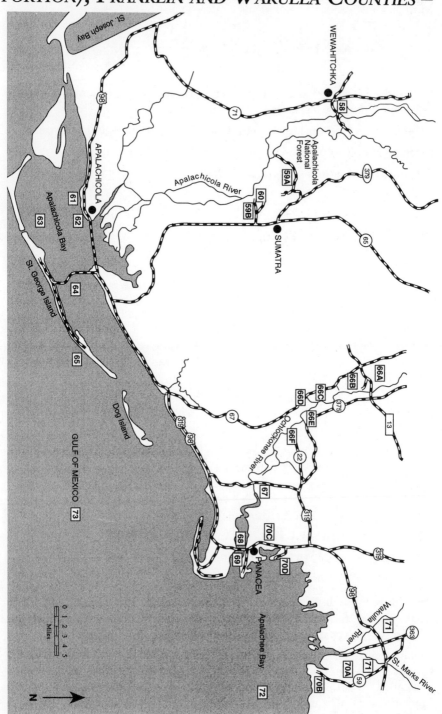

great bait according to regular catfish anglers. To get some "worms" ask at a local bait and tackle shop if there are any trees around where you can literally pick up some bait. If you can't find them, wigglers (earthworms) are also an excellent bait. Anglers in search of flathead catfish, an introduced fisheating species, will find a healthy population of them in the river, with some fish exceeding 30 pounds. According to Stan Kirkland from the regional GFC office, the key to catching flatheads is to use heavy tackle, a small bream for bait, and to fish in the deeper holes from February through April.

Access Points:

59A. COTTON LANDING—*Boat and Bank; Ramp.*
Description: An Apalachicola National Forest recreation area. Access to the Apalachicola River is via Kennedy Creek. A small, primitive campground is open all year. No drinking water on site. No fees.
Directions: From FL 65 in Sumatra, take CR 379 north 3.2 miles. Turn west (left) on FR 123 and go 2.8 miles to FR 123B. Turn west (left) and go 0.7 mile to the site.

59B. HICKORY LANDING—*Boat and Bank; Ramp.*
Description: An Apalachicola National Forest recreation area. Access to the Apalachicola River is via Owl Creek. A small, primitive campground is open all year. No fees.
Directions: From Sumatra, take FL 65 south 2 miles. Turn west on FR 101 and go 1.5 miles to FR 101B. Turn south (left) and go 1 mile to the site.

For more information: For information about fishing on the river, call the GFC regional office at (850) 265-3676. For information about recreational opportunities, contact the Apalachicola National Forest, Apalachicola District, at (904) 643-2282. Ask for the brochure, National Forests in Florida Recreation Area Directory.

60. WRIGHT LAKE

Fresh; Bank and Canoe.

Description: This site is within the Apalachicola National Forest. A small lake with bank fishing. No boat ramp but canoes could be launched from the shoreline. Camping, picnicking, nature trails. Barrier-free bathhouse.

Fishing Index: Fish for bass and bream.

Directions: From Sumatra, drive 2 miles south on FL 65. Turn west on FR 101 and go about 2 miles. Turn north (right) at the sign and go 0.25 mile to the site.

61. LAFAYETTE PARK PIER

Salt; Pier.

Description: A 100-foot city-owned pier into Apalachicola Bay. While in town, visit the John Gorrie State Museum. Gorrie invented a machine that changed the ways of commercial fishermen. It's worth the stop.

Fishing Index: The best action is speckled trout in fall.

Directions: At the intersection of 13th, 14th, or 15th Streets and US 98 in Apalachicola, turn towards the water (southeast) and go three blocks to the park.

For more information: Call the Apalachicola Bay Chamber of Commerce at (850) 653-9419.

62. BATTERY PARK PIER

Salt; Pier; Ramp.

Description: A 500-foot pier in Apalachicola Bay; a six-lane boat ramp is nearby. The headquarters for the Apalachicola National Estuarine Research Reserve is in town. To learn more about the area stop by the visitor center.

Fishing Index: Speckled trout, flounder, and a few redfish are caught from the pier; fall is the best season. In winter when a front passes through, speckled trout and redfish move upriver and the activity at the pier may increase.

Directions: The park is on the south side of US 98 in downtown Apalachicola. If east bound on US 98, turn right off of US 98 just before leaving town and crossing the Gorrie Bridge over East Bay. If west bound on US 98, turn left just after crossing the Gorrie Bridge and entering town.

For more information: Call the Apalachicola Bay Chamber of Commerce at (850) 653-9419.

63. APALACHICOLA BAY

Salt; Boat.

Description: The fertile waters of this bay are home to one of the largest oyster fisheries in the country. The shallow bay has extensive grassflats along the inside of St. George Island, and numerous oyster bars are regularly enhanced by the state to keep oyster production up. The bay's rich environment results from freshwater from the Apalachicola River mixing with saltwater from the Gulf of Mexico.

Fishing Index: Speckled trout and redfish are the most sought-after fish in the bay. They are present year-round but spring and fall are the best times to fish. In summer, some tarpon, Spanish mackerel, and tripletail show up. Bob Sikes Cut, a man-made channel through St. George Island, and East Pass, at the eastern end of St. George Island, are popular places to catch Spanish mackerel, big speckled trout, redfish, and pompano in summer. Winter fishing is best a few days after a front passes through the area. Redfish, speckled trout, and flounder move north of US 98 into the waterways forming the Apalachicola River delta. Largemouth bass also reside year-round in this area.

Directions: The bay is about a two-hour drive from Tallahassee. Take US 319 south to US 98 and stay on US 98 to Apalachicola. The public boat ramp at Battery Park is a good place to launch. There are several other private ramps in the area. A small fleet of charter boats operates out of Bay City Lodge in Apalachicola (call (850) 653-9294). The Gibson Inn is a beautifully restored turn-of-the-century Victorian inn (call (850) 653-8282).

64. ST. GEORGE ISLAND CAUSEWAY. ————————

Salt; Bridge and Bank.

Description: This toll road is the only route to St. George Island. The causeway and bridge span Apalachicola Bay.

Fishing Index: Fish along the causeway for redfish, Spanish mackerel, and flounder. Boaters can fish around the bridge pilings for sheepshead.

Directions: From Apalachicola, take US 98 east across East Bay to Eastpoint. Turn at the sign for St. George Island.

65. ST. GEORGE ISLAND STATE PARK ————————

Salt; Surf; Ramp; $.

Description: This barrier island park offers miles of beach for surf fishing and swimming. There are ramps at two locations within the park that access Apalachicola Bay. Camping, nature trails, and picnicking are available.

Surf fishing enthusiasts will love the miles of uninhabited beaches along the Florida Panhandle.

Fishing Index: An excellent place to surf fish for redfish, speckled trout, flounder, Spanish mackerel, bluefish, and an occasional cobia.

Directions: At the east end of the island. Cross the causeway onto the island (see site 64) and turn left on FL 300. The entrance to the park is about 3 miles east.

For more information: Call the park office at (850) 927-2111.

66. OCHLOCKONEE RIVER (LAKE TALQUIN TO OCHLOCKONEE BAY)

Fresh; Boat and Bank.

Description: The lower part of the river, below Lake Talquin, is fished from just below Jackson Bluff Dam to Ochlockonee Bay. Parts of the river are not navigable when water levels are low.

Fishing Index: There is very good fishing for striped bass in the tailrace below the Lake Talquin dam. further downriver is a popular place for largemouth bass angling.

Access Points (in the Apalachicola National Forest):
66A. PORTER LAKE—*Boat and Bank.*
Description: River access is via a small tributary. No developed ramp. Primitive campground and hiking on the Florida National Scenic Trail.
Directions: Off CR 67 about 18 miles south of Hosford or 24 miles north of Carabelle. From CR 67, take FR 13 east 2.6 miles to the site.

66B. WHITEHEAD LAKE—*Ramp; Boat and Bank.*
Description: A good place to enter the river. Primitive camping.
Directions: Off CR 67 about 18 miles south of Hosford or 24 miles north of Carabelle. From CR 67, take FR 13 east 1.5 miles to FR 186. Go south on FR 186 1.5 miles to the site.

66C. REVELL LANDING—*Ramp; Boat and Bank.*
Description: Primitive camping with no other facilities. No fees.
Directions: Off CR 67 about 22 miles south of Hosford or 20 miles north of Carabelle. From CR 67, take FR 152 about 1 mile to the site.

66D. HITCHCOCK LAKE—*Ramp; Boat and Bank.*
Description: A small primitive campground open all year. No drinking water.
Directions: Off CR 67 about 25 miles south of Hosford or 17 miles north of Carabelle. From CR 67, take FR 184 east (left) 1.5 miles to the site.

66E. MACK LANDING—*Ramp; Boat and Bank.*
Description: Access to the river is via a small creek. Primitive camping, open all year.
Directions: From Sopchoppy, drive west about 7.5 miles on FL 375 to FR 336. Go west (left) about 1 mile to the site.

66F.   WOOD LAKE—*Ramp; Boat and Bank.*

Description: Access to the river is via a small creek. Primitive camping, open all year. No fees.

Directions: From Sopchoppy drive 0.5 mile northwest on FL 375 to FL 22. Go west (left) 1 mile and turn left onto CR 399. Go south 1.7 miles to FR 338. Turn west (right) and go about 1.8 miles to the site.

For more information: For information about fishing on the river call the GFC regional office at (904) 265-5991. For information about recreational opportunities contact the Apalachicola National Forest, Wakulla District, at (850) 926-3561.

67.   OCHLOCKONEE RIVER STATE PARK

Fresh and Salt; Bank and Boat; Ramp; $.

Description: The park has a riverfront campground.

Fishing Index: Going upriver the bass and bream fishing is good. Striped bass live in the river and fishing can be good if you catch the fish feeding on the shad as they migrate upriver. Head south to the river mouth at Ochlockonee Bay to fish for speckled trout and redfish in the bay's deeper holes in winter. In July a few tarpon will show up in the bay.

Directions: From Sopchoppy, drive south about 3.7 miles on US 319 to the park entrance.

For more information: Call the park office at (850) 962-2771.

68.   OCHLOCKONEE BAY

Salt; Boat and Bank.

Description: The road on the north side of the bay, FL 372, ends at a small county park where you can fish at the confluence of the river and Apalachee Bay. On the south side FL 372 ends near Bald Point. Park at the end of the road and walk to the point.

Fishing Index: A good place to wade and fish for speckled trout, flounder, redfish, and whiting. Some tarpon are in the bay in summer. Sheepshead are around the bridge pilings.

Directions: For northside access, take FL 372 east from US 98 about 2.3 miles to the end of the road. For south side access take FL 370 from US 98. Follow 370 about 5.7 miles to a fork in the road. Bear to the left and follow the road to the end. Park and walk to Bald Point. Boats can launch at one of the private ramps in the area or at the state park about 5 miles upriver.

69. OCHLOCKONEE BAY BRIDGE

Salt; Bank; Ramp.

Description: Fish along the shoreline on the south side of the bridge. The town of Panacea is on the north side of the bridge. Campgrounds, bait and tackle, food, and restaurants are in the area.

Fishing Index: Fish for speckled trout, redfish, and flounder.

Directions: Go to the south end of the US 98 bridge over Ochlockonee Bay.

70. ST. MARKS NATIONAL WILDLIFE REFUGE

Salt and Fresh; Bank and Boat; Ramp; $.

Description: Freshwater fishing opportunities exist in the lakes and ponds in the Panacea and Wakulla units. Some access areas are free and others charge an entrance fee. There is no camping allowed in the refuge.

Fishing Index: Fish the freshwater ponds for bass and bream. Bank fishing is permitted all year. Boats are allowed on the ponds from March 15 to October 15, the period when the migratory ducks are not present. The ponds are mostly shallow and surface lures work well. Also try fly fishing with small poppers. Spring is usually the best time. Saltwater anglers launch from the refuge to get easy access to the grassflats in Apalachee Bay.

Directions: The refuge is south of Tallahassee near the coast in Wakulla County. The Refuge Headquarters is on FL 59.

Access Points:

70A. WAKULLA UNIT, REFUGE IMPOUNDMENTS—*Fresh and Salt; Bank and Boat; Ramp.*
Description: Some of the impoundments are freshwater and some are brackish. The most popular freshwater one is East River Pool. The most popular brackish one is Stoney Bayou Pool #1. There is a 10 horsepower motor limit. The ramp is open from March 15 to October 15. Try bank fishing year-round on any of the impoundments. The brackish pools are popular crabbing sites. Watch for alligators.
Directions: Access to the impoundments is from FL 59 inside the fee area about 5.8 miles south of the intersection with US 98. There is a ramp on FL 59 accessing Stoney Bayou #1 and East River pools.

70B. ST. MARKS SALT WATER RAMP—*Salt; Boat; Ramp.*
Description: Access to the Gulf of Mexico. Open daylight hours. Night-time operation may vary. Consult refuge office for more information. Although there is no charge to use the ramp, it is located within the refuge fee area.
Directions: At the end of FL 59, about 9.8 miles south of US 98.

70C. PANACEA UNIT, OTTER LAKE—*Fresh; Boat and Bank; Ramp.*
Description: There is a boat ramp and bank fishing. The ramp is open from March 15 to October 15; try bank fishing year-round.

Directions: From the US 98 and US 319 intersection north of Panacea, take US 98 south 3.6 miles to CR 372A. Turn west at the sign for Otter Lake and go 1.5 miles to the site.

70D. BOTTOMS ROAD RAMP—*Salt; Bank and Boat; Ramp.*
Description: Direct access to the Gulf of Mexico. The refuge is considering discontinuing this ramp. Check with the refuge office before using.
Directions: From US 98, turn onto FL 372A just north of Panacea. Go about 4 miles east to the ramp at road's end.

For more information: Call the refuge office at (850) 925-6121.

71. ST. MARKS AND WAKULLA RIVERS
Fresh; Boat.

Description: The Wakulla joins the St. Marks, which then empties into Apalachee Bay. Both rivers are scenic and good canoeing sites.

Fishing Index: Both rivers are spring fed and offer very good summer fishing for bass and bream.

Directions: There are private ramps just off US 98 where it crosses each river. There is a canoe rental facility on the Wakulla at the US 98 crossing. Access is also easy from the boat ramp in St. Marks National Wildlife Refuge (see site 70B).

72. APALACHEE BAY
Salt; Boat.

Description: This bay is formed by the coastline's curve to the south. The bay is shallow with extensive seagrass flats.

Fishing Index: Speckled trout and redfish are on the flats from spring to late fall. In winter and early spring, the fish take to the deeper holes or move up the St. Marks River. Along the outer edges of the grassflats, migratory species—including Spanish and king mackerel, dolphin, and cobia—will bite in spring and to a lesser extent in fall.

Directions: Any ramp, public or private, from Panacea to Steinhatchee provides access to the bay.

73. GULF OF MEXICO
Salt; Boat.

Description: Two types of offshore fishing are popular along this part of the coast: nearshore fishing, which is heavily oriented toward bottom fishing; and bluewater fishing in which free-swimming species are the target.

Fishing Index: Snapper, primarily red snapper, and gag grouper are two year-

This group of hopeful anglers is ready to depart for a half day fishing trip. Party boats are a good way to experience offshore fishing without spending a lot of money.

round targets for bottom anglers fishing the nearshore waters off Pensacola Beach. In spring and summer many of these anglers will also fish for king mackerel, cobia, dolphin, and sometimes sailfish. Bluewater fishing is a summertime activity that takes boats 20 to 25 miles offshore and beyond in search of blue and white marlin, sailfish, and yellowfin tuna. It requires special tackle and a good boat. Captain Skip Mason operates a charter boat out of Pensacola Beach. "Most captains specialize in bottom fishing," he says. "We fish from 4 to 5 miles offshore all the way out to the edge at about 180 feet. In April and May, when the cobia run begins, we will sight fish for them on the surface. After the run is over we continue to fish for them but now they're on the bottom." If you plan to use your own boat Mason recommends stopping at one of the area's dive shops and getting GPS numbers for some of the popular offshore wrecks. "Use cut squid or a cigar minnow for bait," Mason says, "Get the fish up off the bottom as fast as you can and hope it doesn't have the endurance to get back to the wreck. If the fish gets in there chances are you'll loose it."

The charter boats leaving from Destin fish for grouper, snapper, king mackerel, cobia, amberjack, and dolphin close to shore in spring and summer. Some captains specialize in making the 25-mile trek offshore to try for billfish, yellowfin tuna, and wahoo in summer. If you happen to be in the area during the off season (November through February) and the weather is nice, try a day of bottom fishing for grouper and snapper.

The focus for offshore anglers leaving from Panama City is on bottom fishing for grouper, snapper, amberjack, and king mackerel. Billfishing is possible but it is 10 miles farther offshore to the 100-fathom line and the fish than from the Destin area.

Fleet Locations:
73A. PENSACOLA BEACH
Directions: There is a modest sportfishing fleet operating from Pensacola Beach and another one in Pensacola.
For more information: contact the local Chambers of Commerce or try Skip Mason at (850) 477-4033.

73B. DESTIN
Description: Destin is home to a major charter fishing fleet. Most of the 50 to 60 boats operate out of Destin Harbor. There is no central charter boat association number so you must rely on advertisements, the local Chamber of Commerce, or walking the docks and finding the boat that you like. Prices are competitive. Both small charter (6 anglers) and party boats operate in this area.

Tom Moody, a prominent charter boat operator in Destin, suggests that you pick a good captain before making a commitment. To determine which one to choose, ask around the docks. Find out who's catching fish. One way to do this is to show up as the boats are returning. See what they bring in and talk to some of the people who were fishing on the boat that day. If you want Tom's opinion, give him a call at (850) 837-1293.

Directions: Destin is on US 98 about 7 miles east of Fort Walton Beach.
For more information: Call the Chamber of Commerce at (850) 837-6241.

73C. PANAMA CITY

Description: The offshore fishing fleet in Panama City Beach is centered at Captain Davis' and Anderson's Dock and Treasure Island Dock. Party boats and sportfishing charters are available.
Directions: The docks are along Thomas Drive in Panama City Beach.

MONTH BY MONTH IN NORTHWEST FLORIDA

Note: Offshore is defined as greater than 5 miles from the coast. Coastal waters include open waters inside of five miles including surf fishing, and all brackish water area such as bays, the saltwater regions of rivers, and lagoons. Freshwater includes, lakes, ponds, reservoirs, rivers and phosphate pits.

JANUARY

Offshore: Can be a tough month for Gulf fishing; the weather is the problem. Best bet is red snapper and gag grouper in the deeper water.

Coastal: Redfish and trout will be in the deeper holes of the bays unless the water has been warm for several days. On windy days, try the small creeks where it's warmer for the fish and you; this time of year the speckled trout and redfish may move into the freshwater sections of the rivers; if fishing with lures work them slowly, go slowly if trolling—fish move slower when it's cold just like you. Look for bluefish around the jetties; plenty of sheepshead around any type of piling. Peak season for white trout.

Freshwater: Bass are active in the deeper parts of the region's lakes. A top month for crappie fishing with Missouri minnows being a favorite bait. Striped, sunshine, and white bass may be schooling in the lakes and rivers.

FEBRUARY

Offshore: Grouper and red and black (mangrove) snapper are out there in the deep water but weather still a factor. GPS numbers are essential to find fish.

Coastal: Sheepshead around structures is best bet; black drum and white trout fishing usually very good. Cold water means look in the holes for speckled trout and redfish; bluefish scattered around the region.

Freshwater: Prime time for largemouth bass; the females are bedding this month. Shad migrating up the rivers with sunshine and striped bass following in schools. White bass spawning; action is great; Crappie fishing continues to be good.

MARCH

Offshore: Some Spanish and king mackerel and dolphin may arrive. Cobia activity picks up; sight fish for them. Top month for grouper.

Coastal: Flounder fishing can be very good. Trout move onto the flats when the water rises above 60 to 65 degrees. Pompano can be caught in the surf and around the jetties;fish with sand fleas if you can get them. Top month for tripletail in Apalachicola Bay.

Freshwater: Last month for top bass action. Shellcrackers are bedding and fishing is great. Sunshine and striped bass activity gradually declining from peak activity; fishing will be very good.

APRIL

Offshore: Great time for red snapper, gag grouper; fish starting to move closer to shore. King and Spanish mackerel increasing in numbers and moving closer to shore.

Coastal: A good month for trout, redfish, pompano, flounder, croaker, crevalle jack, bluefish, and Spanish mackerel. A few tarpon toward the eastern end of the region.

Freshwater: Shellcrackers and bluegills are bedding; fishing will be excellent. Bass spawn over and the fish are dispersing.

MAY

Offshore: As the water warms, cobia, Spanish and king mackerel, grouper, and snapper move closer to shore and action gets hot. Don't overlook the numerous public reefs. Billfish start to trickle in; those who can't wait may find them plus some wahoo and blackfin tuna.

Coastal: Nice time to surf fish for pompano, bluefish, trout, and redfish.

Freshwater: Bluegill fishing is prime, especially on the full moon. Best bass fishing will be in shallow water of lakes and rivers.

JUNE

Offshore: King and Spanish mackerel action into prime time. Consistent grouper and snapper fishing. Wahoo, billfish, and dolphin good.

Coastal: Trout on the grassflats, redfish around oyster bars; Spanish mackerel in the bays; tarpon spreading through the region; have fun with a big jack.

Freshwater: Bream activity is still the best. Bass have settled into their summer pattern of hanging around the deeper waters; stripers and sunshine bass are there but don't bite well in summer when the water is too warm.

JULY

Offshore: Anything swimming offshore is biting—grouper, snapper, both mackerels, cobia, billfish, tuna, dolphin, and wahoo. Except for marlin, most are found close to shore.

Coastal: If you are looking for a tarpon this is one of the best months; fish for them on the flats and in the tidal rivers. Don't overlook the really good Spanish mackerel and some decent speckled trout, flounder, and bluefish action. Scallop time in St. Joe Bay but check on regulations on the exact time and bag limit.

Freshwater: Use the summer pattern for largemouth bass—fish early in the morning and late in the day to avoid the heat. Many locals also fish at night this time of year; the results can be surprisingly good.

AUGUST

Offshore: Prime time for billfish and yellowfin tuna but it's a long ride out to the fish. Lots of amberjack around. Grouper and snapper are good but watch for barracuda stealing your catch as it comes off the bottom.

Coastal: Prelude to the best redfish time; you might get in on the action early. Good supply of trout, flounder, bluefish, Spanish mackerel, and jacks in the bays, passes, and surf.

Freshwater: Typical summer pattern: bass early and late in the day, bream action is still better than anything else.

SEPTEMBER

Offshore: Billfish action still hot. Fall migration of king and Spanish mackerel, cobia, and pompano begins.

Coastal: One of the best months for redfish, speckled trout, and flounder; don't miss the action.

Freshwater: Bass may be in the brackish water feeding on the abundant shrimp. Possible to catch a largemouth, redfish, and trout within casting distance of where you anchor the boat. In some areas sunshine bass are schooling and the fish will bite.

OCTOBER

Offshore: Traditionally the peak month for the king mackerels' southward migration. Dolphin, cobia, wahoo numbers are declining; angler's choices becoming limited. Think offshore grouper; great offshore flounder time.

Coastal: Top redfish month; look around oyster bars. If it cools off early, the trout and redfish will head for the warmer and deeper holes.

Freshwater: Bass will be deeper in the shallower lakes; may still be near the shallows on the bigger lakes. Crappie action awakening from the summer doldrums.

NOVEMBER

Offshore: Migrant species mostly gone; a few resident cobia stay behind. Offshore flounder fishing is good; snapper and grouper are probably the best bet. Keep an eye on the weather.

Coastal: Redfish moving to deeper areas and up some of the rivers. Flounder fishing is very good; bluefish in the passes. Attention turns toward sheepshead around pilings and rocky bottoms.

Freshwater: Bass still in the brackish waters; action can be good. Stripers and sunshine bass will be more inclined to bite now that the water is cooler. Crappie action noticeably better than in October.

DECEMBER

Offshore: Not one of the best fishing months but determined anglers can try for snapper and grouper. Fish may be close to shore; ask locally what is biting and how far offshore.

Coastal: Best bet will be sheepshead. This is big fish time; redfish and trout are there but the action is not fast and furious unless it is unseasonably warm. Ever-present bluefish and flounder will be biting.

Freshwater: Top crappie month. Largemouth bass are hanging around the deeper and warmer water.

NORTHWEST FLORIDA FISH AVAILABILITY

NOTE: Information in this chart represents the seasonal patterns observed over the past three years. For saltwater species, the arrival of the migrant species and the peak times for each species is heavily dependent on water temperature. Unusually warm or cold periods will effect the patterns described above. Bream is the local name for bluegills and shellcrackers. Speckled trout is the local name for spotted seatrout. Speckled trout is the local name for spotted seatrout. Health Advisory (see intro for details).

■ signifies a reasonable chance of catching this species in that month.

□ signifies the optimal months for catching the species. Refer to the month by month table for additional information.

SPECIES	JAN	FEB	MAR	APR	MAY	JUN	JUL	AUG	SEP	OCT	NOV	DEC
Redfish	■	■	■	■	■	■	■	■	□	□	■	■
Speckled trout	■	■	■	■	□	■	■	■	□	□	■	■
Sheepshead	□	□	□	□	■	■	■	■	■	□	□	□
Mangrove Snapper	■	■	■	■	■	■	■	■	■	■	■	■
Red Snapper	■	■	■	□	□	■	■	■	■	■	■	■
Red Grouper	■	■	■	■	■	■	■	■	■	■	■	■
Gag Grouper	■	■	□	□	□	■	■	■	■	■	■	■
Cobia	■	■	□	□	□	■	■	■	■	■	■	■
Amberjack	■	■	□	■	■	■	■	■	■	■	■	■
Bluefish	■	■	■	■	■	■	■	■	■	■	■	■
Flounder	■	■	■	■	■	■	■	■	□	□	□	□
Black Drum	□	□	■	■	■	■	■	■	■	■	■	□
White (Silver) Trout	□	□	■									■

Species	Jan	Feb	Mar	Apr	May	Jun	Jul	Aug	Sep	Oct	Nov	Dec
Whiting	■	■	■							■	■	■
Pompano			■	■	■	■	■	■	■			
Spanish Mackerel			■	■	□	□	□	■	■	■	■	
King Mackerel			■	■	□	□	□	■	■	□	■	
Wahoo			■	■	■	■	■	■	■	■		
Tripletail			□	□	□	■	■	■	■			
Crevalle Jack				■	■	■	■	■	■	■		
Tarpon				■	■	■	■	■	■	■		
Shark (all species)				■	■	■	■	■	■	■		
Dolphin				■	■	■	■	■	■			
Blackfin Tuna						■	■	■	■	■		
Sailfish						■	■	■	□	■		
White Marlin						■	■	■	□	□	■	
Blue Marlin						■	■	■	□	□	■	
Yellowfin Tuna							■	□	■	■		
Largemouth Bass	■	□	□	■	■	■	■	■	■	■	■	■
Catfish	■	■	■	■	■	■	■	■	■	■	■	■
Shellcracker	■	■	□	□	□	□	■	■	■	■	■	■
Spotted Bass	■	■	□	□	■	■	■	■	□	□	□	■
Sunshine Bass	■	□	□	■				■	□	□	■	
Striped Bass	■	□	□	■				■	■	□	■	
White Bass	■	□	□	■								
Crappie	□	■	■							■	■	□
Bluegill			■	□	□	□	■	■	■	■	■	

CHAPTER FOUR: BIG BEND

COUNTIES: ▪ Jefferson ▪ Madison ▪ Hamilton ▪ Taylor ▪ Lafayette ▪ Suwannee ▪ Columbia ▪ Dixie ▪ Gilchrist ▪ Alachua ▪ Levy

The Big Bend region, where the Florida peninsula curves west to the Panhandle, is the place to fish if you want a spot that the hordes of tourists haven't discovered. This is the original Florida, no big cities or shopping malls, and no condominiums along the coast. What's there is what nature created, miles of attractive river bends and fishy looking marshes, sea grass beds, and tidal creeks.

Anglers visiting the area will find enough boat ramps, both public and private, in the region to make it a short run to most of the good fishing locations. Land-bound anglers will be limited to bank fishing along the rivers. Fishing from the land along the coast is challenging. There is no coastal highway in the Big Bend. Most of the roads run perpendicular to the coast and dead end once they reach the Gulf, leaving a limited number of undeveloped areas to fish. Unlike other regions of Florida, there are no big piers and very few bridges in the Big Bend.

SALTWATER FISHING

The coastline here is a squiggle of irregular indentations—small bays separated by tiny capes and points—created by numerous tidal creeks. From an angler's point of view, such a coastline is a sure sign of some great fishing opportunities.

The Big Bend coastline won't disappoint. Along the shore are extensive salt marshes with a broad, shallow flats area seaward of the vegetation. These shallow, clear waters harbor extensive seagrass beds. The shallows extend well offshore. Five miles offshore the water is usually less than 10 feet deep.

This part of the coast is ideal habitat for two of Florida's top saltwater species, spotted seatrout and redfish. Both are year-round residents.

Cedar Key and Steinhatchee are the major towns along the coast, small communities that caters to anglers heading for coastal waters or further out in the Gulf of Mexico. The hamlets of Horseshoe Beach and Suwannee are becoming increasingly popular and are usually crowded on the weekends.

FRESHWATER FISHING

Freshwater anglers have miles of shoreline to fish along the Suwannee, Santa Fe, Aucilla, Econfina, and Steinhatchee rivers, some of the best bass and bream rivers in the state. There is little development along these rivers and plenty of access points. Fishing during the week, when most people are at work, almost guarantees a place of your own.

The Suwannee River is the dominant river in this region. Beginning in Georgia, this river flows unimpeded by dams more than 280 miles to the Gulf of Mexico. The Suwannee is fed millions of gallons of water each day by dozens of springs along its course.

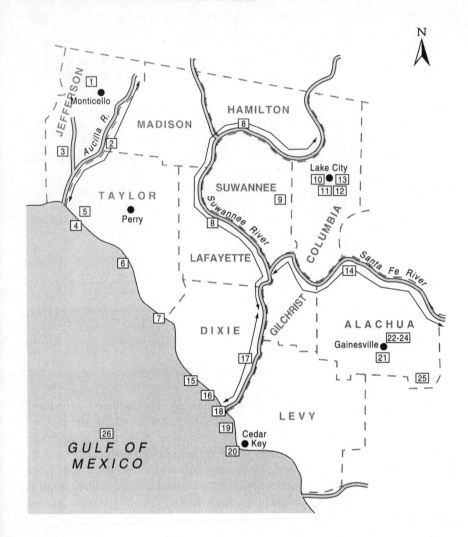

N

JEFFERSON

1 ● Monticello

MADISON

HAMILTON

8

Lake City
10 ● 13
11 12

Aucilla R.

3

2

TAYLOR

5

4 ● Perry

SUWANNEE

9

Suwannee River

8

COLUMBIA

Santa Fe River

6

LAFAYETTE

14

DIXIE

GILCHRIST

7

17

ALACHUA

22-24
Gainesville ●
21

15

16

18

25

19 ● Cedar Key

26

20

LEVY

GULF OF
MEXICO

According to Dewey Weaver of the Game and Fresh Water Fish Commission (GFC), the best fishing is from Suwannee River State Park to the mouth of the river. From the park to Old Town, a distance of about 100 miles, the river is narrow and rocky. The top species along this part of the river is redbreast (also known as stumpknocker). Below Old Town the river widens and slows down. There are a lot of lily pads and this is an excellent part of the river for largemouth bass, Weaver says.

Because it is still a wild river, water levels can fluctuate dramatically and this affects fishing success. Although the river can rise or fall at any time of the year, it is often at or near flood stage from December to February and fishing is not as good as at other times of the year. The best fishing, Weaver believes, occurs when the river is just dropping back into its banks after a high water period.

The Suwannee bass occurs only in this river system and the upper part of the Ochlockonee River near Tallahassee. In the Suwannee system, the best place to catch this small bass is in the last few miles of the Santa Fe River before it joins the Suwannee.

Lake lovers have a number of large lakes to choose from around Lake City and Gainesville. The most popular are the lakes around Gainesville, including Orange and Lochloosa Lakes, Newnans Lake, and Lake Santa Fe.

The key to lake fishing in this region is to know the water levels. A drought in the early 1990s dropped lakes to their lowest recorded levels. Ramps were hundreds of feet from the water's edge. The lakes that remained accessible saw fishing patterns change. The situation seems to be returning to normal: lake levels are rising, and fishing predictions for these lakes are the brightest they've been in years. If possible, call ahead to some of the fish camps or bait and tackle stores to ask about the lake you want to fish.

JEFFERSON, MADISON AND TAYLOR COUNTIES

1. LAKE MICCOSUKEE

Fresh; Boat; Ramp.

Description: A 6,226-acre weed-filled lake between Tallahassee and Monticello.

Fishing Index: Follow easy-to-see "trails" through this weed-choked lake. Try fishing the edges of the weedlines for bass and bluegill. Local knowledge of where the fish are biting is helpful.

Directions: From Monticello, drive west 6.8 miles on US 90 to the lake and boat ramp. From I-10 near Tallahassee, take US 90 east 11.2 miles to the ramp.

For more information: Call Stewart's Bait and Tackle in Monticello (850) 997-2143.

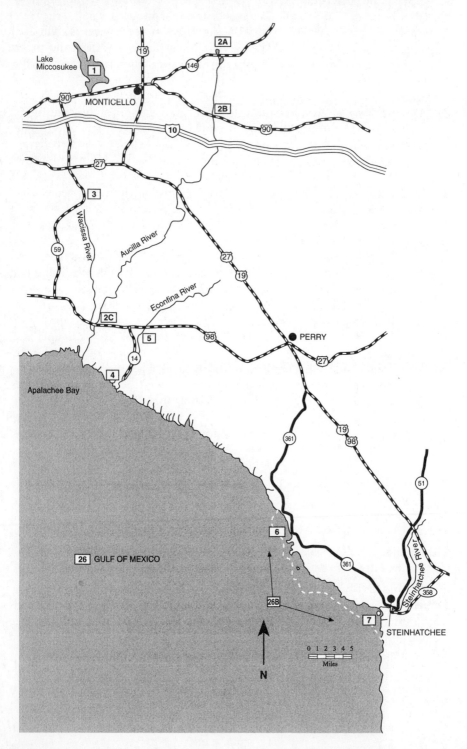

Lake
Miccosukee

1

MONTICELLO

2A

2B

3

Wacissa River

Aucilla River

Econfina River

2C

5

14

4

Apalachee Bay

PERRY

26 GULF OF MEXICO

6

26B

7

STEINHATCHEE

Steinhatchee River

0 1 2 3 4 5
Miles

N

2. AUCILLA RIVER

Fresh; Boat and Bank; Ramp.

Description: This very scenic river has little development along its shoreline. There are no major cities along the river. The Wacissa River is the major tributary. South of US 27 the river disappears underground several times before reappearing near the confluence with the Wacissa. The Aucilla is a good canoeing river.

Fishing Index: Historically known for its bream fishing; anglers can also catch some bass and catfish. Fish for redfish and spotted seatrout closer to the Gulf.

Directions: Forms the border between Jefferson County and Taylor and Madison counties.

Access Points:
2A. FLORIDA HIGHWAY 146—*Fresh; Boat.*
Description: A good place to fish with a car-top boat or canoe. No ramp, but you can launch a small boat from the banks around the bridge. Limited bank fishing. Good spot for bass and bream
Directions: From Monticello, drive 9.2 miles east on FL 146. The highway crosses Sneads Smokehouse Lake on the upper part of the river.

2B. US HIGHWAY 90—*Fresh; Boat and Bank.*
Description: Access is possible with a boat that can be launched from the banks around the bridge. Limited bank fishing in this area.
Directions: From Monticello, drive 9.3 miles east on US 90 to the river.

2C. US HIGHWAY 98—*Fresh; Boat and Bank; Ramp.*
Description: There is a ramp and limited bank fishing opportunities on the east side of the river and at the end of the dirt road about 0.5 mile east of the river. Look for the boat ramp sign on the highway.
Directions: The US 98 bridge over the Aucilla river is about 24.1 miles west of Perry or 13.2 miles east of Newport.

3. WACISSA RIVER

Fresh; Boat; Ramp.

Description: This is a remote, scenic river that is popular with canoeists. It is a tributary of the Aucilla River

Fishing Index: Try float fishing for bass in the spring. Bream and catfish are present year-round. The river is wider south of the ramp.

Directions: From the intersection of US 27/19 with FL 59, go south about 4.6 miles on FL 59 to the end of the road at the river.

4. ELITE RESORT ON THE ECOFINA

Salt and Fresh; Boat and Bank; Ramp.

Description: Privately operated fish camp and campground. One of the few good access points to the eastern side of Apalachee Bay and the freshwater region of the Econfina River.

Fishing Index: Fish for spotted seatrout (also called speckled trout) and redfish around the river's mouth. In winter these species migrate toward freshwater to look for deeper, warmer water. The grassflats accessible from here are remote and not fished as heavily as those on the bay's west side. A great place to get away from civilization.

Directions: From Perry, drive 19.5 miles west on US 98. Turn left on FL 14 (Econfina Road) and go 5.8 miles to the fish camp.

For more information: Call the campground office at Elite Resort (850) 584-2135.

5. ECONFINA RIVER, US 98

Fresh; Boat; Ramp.

Description: A narrow winding river in a sparsely developed part of the state. Much of the land around the river is owned by paper companies and is off limits to the public.

Fishing Index: Bass and bream bite best in the spring.

Directions: From Perry drive 17.5 miles west on US 98. Just before crossing the bridge look for the GFC ramp.

6. Keaton Beach. Salt; Boat; Ramp.

Description: This small, out-of-the-way coastal community is one of the few access points to the miles of flats and crystal clear water that characterize the Big Bend region. Keaton Beach Marina is the only local marina. It has motel rooms, cottages, a restaurant, boat lift, and ramp. Guides are available.

Fishing Index: Travis Beach, owner of the marina, says this area has some of the best spotted seatrout fishing in the state. Redfish and trout fishing is good year-round, but Beach says the best times for these species are April through May and September to November. In July and August the scalloping season brings people to Keaton Beach in search of the tasty mollusks. From here it is only 9.2 miles to Steinhatchee Reef and some good sheepshead fishing.

Directions: From Perry, drive 17 miles south on FL 361 to Keaton Beach. Yates Creek has a county boat ramp, but during some low tides the ramp becomes unusable. To reach the ramp from US 19/98 drive 11.5 miles south on FL 361 and turn onto Yates Creek Road.

Follow the road to a "Y", bear left, and go to the ramp.

For more information: Call Keaton Beach Marina at (850) 578-2897.

6   KEATON BEACH

Salt; Boat; Ramp.

Description: This small, out-of-the-way coastal community is one of the few access points to the miles of flats with crystal clear water that characterize the Big Bend region. Keaton Beach Marina is the only marina in the area. It has motel rooms, cottages, a restaurant, a boat lift and ramp. Guides are available.

Fishing Index: Travis Beach, owner of Keaton Beach Marina, says this is area has some of the best spotted seatrout fishing in the state. Redfish and trout fishing is year-round but Beach says the best times for these species are April and May and September to November. Like other coastal sites north of the Suwannee river, the scalloping season of July and August brings people to Keaton Beach in search of the tasty mollusks. From here it is only 9.2 miles to Steinhatchee Reef and some good sheepshead fishing.

Directions: From Perry, take FL 361 for 17 miles south to Keaton Beach. There is a Taylor County boat ramp at Yates Creek but caution is advised in using it. During some low tides, the ramp becomes unusable. To reach the ramp, turn onto Yates Creek Road off of FL 361, 11.5 miles from the FL 361-US 19 and 98 intersection south of Perry. Follow the road to a "Y", bear left and go to the ramp.

For more information: Call Keaton Beach Marina, (850) 578-2897.

7.   STEINHATCHEE

Salt; Boat; Ramp.

Description: This town has several marinas, restaurants, and places to stay. Steinhatchee Landing is the largest and newest facility. There is a public boat ramp on the Steinhatchee River at the end of Jena Highway (CR 358). Numerous local charter guides specialize in fishing the flats; a few offshore charter boats are also based here.

Fishing Index: Extensive grassflats here extend offshore 2 to 3 miles. Fish year-round for Spanish mackerel, speckled trout, and redfish. When the water is colder, sheepshead, flounder, and black drum fishing can be good too. The mouth of the Steinhatchee River supports a productive scallop bed. Offshore anglers looking for king mackerel and grouper will find some good fishing about 20 to 25 miles offshore. Gil Parker, manager of River Haven Marina recommends fishing the flats and using a Florida Flats Equalizer, a type of rattling, popping cork. "Use a live shrimp, or a jig and grub tail with the popper, and work it along the bottom. Floating and sinking MirrOlures work good too."

Directions: From Cross City, drive about 11.2 miles north on US 98 to the intersection with CR 358 in Jonesboro. Take CR 358 west about 6.8 miles to the town of Steinhatchee. If traveling south on US 19/98, turn south on FL 51, which is the main intersection in Tennile. Take FL 51 about 8 miles to town.

Steinhatchee, a small community along the Big Bend coast, is a former commercial fishing community that is making the change to catering to recreational anglers.

For more information: Call River Haven Marina at (352) 498-0709 or Steinhatchee Landing at (352) 498-3513.

HAMILTON, LAFAYETTE, SUWANNEE, AND COLUMBIA COUNTIES

8.   SUWANNEE RIVER (WHITE SPRINGS TO BRANFORD)——
Fresh; Bank and Boat; Ramp.

Description: The Suwannee River is one of the state's least polluted rivers. It is classified as an Outstanding Florida Water and has very little development along its banks. The river begins in southeast Georgia's Okefenokee Swamp and runs south and west about 210 miles through Florida before emptying into the Gulf of Mexico. The Suwannee River is considered the dividing line between northwest Florida and the peninsular portion of the state. The Withlacoochee and Santa Fe rivers are the two major tributaries of the Suwannee.

The river's level fluctuates in winter and spring as cold fronts bring rain to the watershed. The substantial rises and lack of flood control structures on the river help to limit development along the Suwannee. High water can also make it difficult to use some of the river access points described below.

Fishing Index: Fifty-eight native fish species inhabit the river including the Suwannee bass, a species that occurs only here and in the Ochlockonee River to the northwest. When the river is low, the most commonly caught species is

100

redbreast sunfish. When the water levels rise above normal, catfish catches usually show a dramatic increase. The river also has a good largemouth bass population and fair numbers of other panfish such as stumpknockers, bluegills, and shellcrackers.

Access Points:

8A. BIG SHOALS WILDLIFE MANAGEMENT AREA.—*Fresh; Canoe and Bank; Canoe Launch.*
Description: Fish along the banks of the river or from a canoe. The Suwannee is very narrow here but is quite scenic. There are two nature trails and picnic facilities.
Directions: From White Springs drive 3.8 miles north on FL 135 to Old Godwin Bridge Road. Turn right and go about 1.7 miles to the canoe launch area.

8B. WHITE SPRINGS—*Fresh; Boat and Bank; Ramp.*
Directions: On US 41 about 1 mile south of the junction of US 41 and FL 136 in White Springs.

8C. HAMILTON COUNTY PARK—*Fresh; Boat and Bank; Ramp.*
Description: The park includes a campground.
Directions: From the intersection of FL 249 and US 90 in Live Oak, drive about 11.5 miles north on FL 249 to the county park.

Many of the ramps to the state's freshwater are on side roads. Look for these signs along the major roads to help direct you.

8D. SUWANNEE RIVER STATE PARK—*Fresh; Boat and Bank; Ramp; $.*
Description: The park sits at the confluence of the Withlacoochee and Suwannee rivers. Camping, picnicking, hiking, and canoeing are popular activities. The park is seldom crowded and is a good place to enjoy the river.
Directions: The park entrance is on US 90 about 12 miles west of Live Oak and 16 miles east of Madison. Exit I-10 at the Live Oak (US 90) exit and go 5.7 miles west.
For more information: Call the park office at (904) 362-2746.

8E. FLORIDA 51 RAMP—*Fresh; Boat and Bank; Ramp.*
Description: A roadside park on the river's southeast bank.
Directions: From US 27 in Mayo, drive 2.9 miles north on FL 51.

8F. OWEN'S SPRING—*Fresh; Boat and Bank; Ramp.*
Description: One of many natural springs that occur along the river.
Directions: From Mayo drive 8.1 miles south on US 27 to FL 251. Drive north about 2.3 miles on FL 251 to the spring.

8G. BRANFORD—*Fresh; Bank and Boat; Ramp.*
Description: This riverside community marks the dividing line between the upper and lower parts of the river.
Directions: From Gainesville drive 43 miles north on US 27.

For more information about all Suwannee River sites: Call the Suwannee River Water Management District at (904) 363-1001 or (800) 226-1066 (Florida only). The district is continually purchasing more land and opening new access points.

9. SUWANNEE LAKE

Fresh; Bank, Boat and Pier; Ramp.

Description: This 63-acre lake was built as a fish management area by the GFC in 1967. It has several fishing fingers and two piers for land bound anglers.

Fishing Index: The lake is managed to enhance fishing for largemouth bass, sunshine bass, and bream.

Directions: From Live Oak, drive 2.6 miles east on Suwannee Lake road. Turn onto an access road to the lake. From US 90 in Houston, turn north on CR 417 and go 2.9 miles to Suwannee Lake road. Turn left (west) and go about 1 mile to the lake access road. Look for signs.

For more information: Call the GFC office at (904) 758-0525.

10. LAKE JEFFREY

Fresh; Boat; Ramp.

Description: Access to this lake is via a private ramp at Alma John's Landing. The scenic lake boasts crystal clear water and cypress trees. Outboards are allowed.

Hamilton, Lafayette, Suwannee, and Columbia Counties

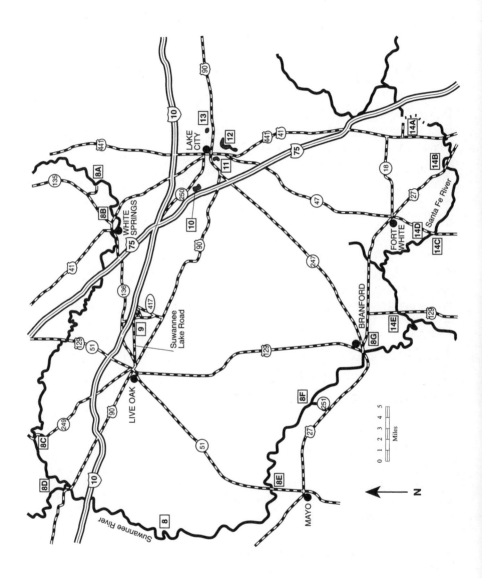

Fishing Index: A good lake for small bass, crappie, and, according to Dewey Weaver of the GFC, an excellent place to catch bluegill, especially in August.

Directions: From the intersection of FL 250 (Lake Jeffrey Road) and US 41 in Lake City, take FL 250 west for approximately 4 miles to the intersection with Scenic Lake Drive. Turn left onto Scenic Lake Dr. and continue to the boat ramp.

11. MONTGOMERY LAKE

Fresh; Boat; Ramp.

Description: A 36-acre GFC Fish Management Area (also known as Lake Hamburg or Hamburger Lake) that can be plagued with aquatic vegetation. The fishing pier is barrier free. Electric motors only.

Fishing Index: The lake supports largemouth and sunshine bass, bream, catfish, and crappie. Threadfin shad are established as a food source for the sunshine bass. The lake, because it is intensely managed, produces bass in excess of 10 pounds.

Directions: The lake is located off Baya Avenue, a road that runs diagonally between US 90 and US 41 in Lake City. From the US 41-US 90 intersection, take US 41 approximately 0.3 mile to Baya Avenue. Turn right; the lake is 0.35 mile down the road.

For more information: Call the GFC at (904) 758-0525.

12. ALLIGATOR LAKE

Fresh; Boat, Bank and Pier; Ramp.

Description: This 338-acre lake is very shallow and has an abundance of aquatic vegetation. It is managed by the GFC to enhance fishing conditions. An active sinkhole causes extreme water level fluctuations. This lake may not be fishable so don't plan a trip just to fish here; have an alternate lake in mind.

Fishing Index: Alligator Lake is a popular place for bass enthusiasts. Bluegill fishing is also good. Sunshine bass are stocked, aquatic weeds are controlled, and several quarter-acre brush piles placed by the GFC serve as fish attractors, including one within casting distance of the fishing pier at the lake's south site.

Directions: In Lake City. There are two access points. From the intersection of US 441 and US 90, take US 441 south for 1.9 miles to Oleander Road. Turn left and continue 0.25 mile to the ramp. NOTE: Low water levels often make this ramp unuseable. A second access point is 3.4 miles south of the US 411 - US 90 intersection on US 441. Look for a ramp sign on US 441 and turn left onto an unmarked road by the Columbia High School football field.

For more information: Call the GFC at (904) 758-0525.

13. WATERTOWN LAKE

Fresh; Pier and Boat; Ramp.

Description: A 46-acre GFC Fish Management Area that has a maidencane- and stump-lined shoreline that provides good habitat for fish. The fishing dock is barrier free.

Fishing Index: The lake has good largemouth bass and crappie fishing. It is periodically stocked with sunshine bass and channel catfish. In places the lake is 25 to 30 feet deep; try fishing deep for largemouth bass.

Directions: In Lake City. Drive east from downtown on US 90 and turn left onto CR 100A at the western outskirts of town. Drive north about 0.5 mile to CR 278B. Turn right and follow this road to the lake.

For more information: Call the GFC at (904) 758-0525.

14. SANTA FE RIVER

Fresh; Bank and Boat; Ramp.

Description: This major tributary of the Suwannee River forms the southern boundary of Columbia County and flows into the Suwannee south of Branford. It disappears below the surface and flows underground for several miles near O'Leno State Park.

Fishing Index: The last 5 miles of the river before it joins the Suwannee River is the best place to fish for Suwannee bass. Dewey Weaver of the GFC says that this section of the Santa Fe has a lot of rock ledges and bedrock bottom, the preferred habitat for this fish. "The best bait," he added, "is a Snagless Sally with a piece of pork rind on it."

Access Points:
14A. O'LENO STATE PARK—*Fresh; Canoe and Bank; Canoe Launch.*
Description: The river disappears at the park and flows underground for almost 3 miles before reappearing. The park has several campgrounds and a nature trail around the river sink.
Directions: The park entrance is on US 441 about 6.3 miles north of High Springs.
For more information: Call the park office at (352) 454-1853.

14B. US 27 RAMP—*Fresh; Boat; Ramp.*
Directions: From High Springs, take US 27 north for 2.4 miles to the bridge. The ramp is on the west side.

14C. FL 47 COUNTY RAMP—*Fresh; Boat; Ramp.*
Directions: The ramp is on the south side of the river on FL 47. Turn south on FL 47 off of US 27 in Fort White and go 4 miles to the turnoff for the ramp.

14D. FL 47 GFC RAMP—*Fresh; Boat; Ramp.*
Directions: On the north side of the river, turn west onto Hollinsworth Road. The ramp is a short distance down the road.

14E. US 129 RAMP—*Fresh; Boat; Ramp.*
Directions: From the junction of US 129 and US 27, 4 miles south of Branford, take US 129 south for 2.8 miles to the ramp.

DIXIE, GILCHRIST, ALACHUA, AND LEVY (SUWANNEE RIVER TO CEDAR KEYS) COUNTIES

15. HORSESHOE BEACH ——————————————
Salt; Boat; Ramp.

Description: This small community is a good access point for fishing the coastal and offshore waters of the Big Bend. There is a county park with a camping facilities and two marinas, Dockside and Horseshoe.

Fishing Index: Trout and redfish are the year-round favorites for the nearshore waters with mid-March to mid-June and September to mid-December being the best times of the year according to Horseshoe Marina owner Dick Powell. January and February, the coldest months, are slow because the trout and redfish like to move into the rivers then and Horseshoe Beach isn't at the mouth of a river. Preferred baits are MirrOlures, gold spoons, and live shrimp. In the heat of the summer, when scallop season opens, scallopers head north from Horseshoe Beach to Pepperfish Keys and try their luck. Offshore anglers like to fish the artificial reefs for grouper, sheepshead, and amberjack.

Directions: The park and commercial facilities are located at the end of CR 351. From US 19/98 in Cross City, drive about 18 miles south on CR 351. The county park and boat ramp are on the right.

For more information: Call Horseshoe Beach Marina at (352) 498-5687 or Dockside Marina at (352) 498-5768.

16. SHIRED CREEK COUNTY PARK ——————————
Salt; Boat; Ramp.

Description: This remote county park has a campground for anglers looking to spend a few days close to the water. There are few facilities at this site.

Fishing Index: Boaters have access to the extensive salt marshes and seagrass flats along the coast. Fish for redfish and spotted seatrout. Spanish mackerel come close enough to shore for anglers to occasionally hook up with one of these toothy predators. Some flounder are caught here, especially around the numerous oyster bars.

Directions: From Cross City drive 7.5 miles south on CR 351. Turn south on CR 357 and drive 10.3 miles to the park and ramp.

DIXIE, GILCHRIST, ALACHUA, AND LEVY (SUWANNEE RIVER TO CEDAR KEYS)

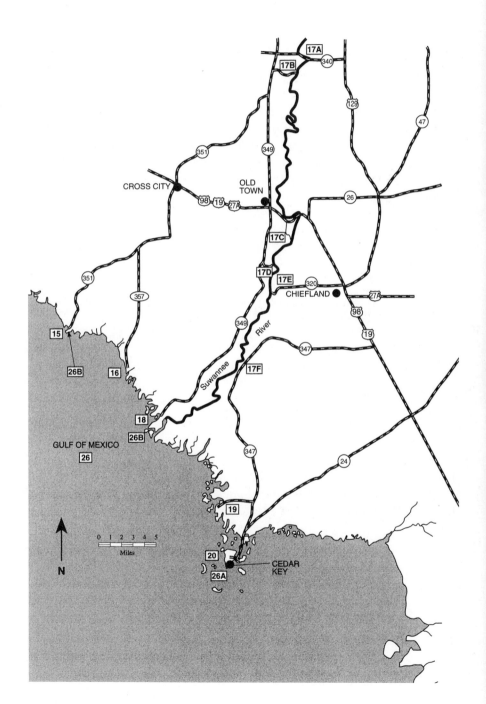

17. SUWANNEE RIVER (BRANFORD TO GULF OF MEXICO)

Fresh and Salt; Boat and Bank; Ramp.

Description: Numerous springs boil to the surface and discharge their clear, cool water into the Suwannee River along this part of the river. Just north of Rock Springs Bluff, the Santa Fe River joins the Suwannee and the river begins to widen. The effects of the tides, minus the saltwater, are seen as far up the Suwannee as Fowler's Bluff. Saltwater usually doesn't penetrate very far up the river because of the tremendous flow of freshwater. The water is often fresh enough for bass and bream to survive at the river mouth.

Fishing Index: This lower section of the river is good for largemouth bass. Fishing is usually good to very good year-round. Spotted seatrout and redfish make their way up the river during colder months in search of deeper and slightly warmer water. They rarely move past Fowler's Bluff.

Access Points:

17A. ROCK BLUFF SPRINGS—*Fresh; Boat and Bank; Ramp.*
Directions: From the intersection of US 129 and US 27 near Branford, drive south on US 129 approximately 10.4 miles to FL 340. Turn right (west) and continue 3.2 miles to river. The ramp and small roadside park are located on the north side of the road.

17B. GUARANTO SPRING COUNTY PARK—*Fresh; Boat and Bank; Ramp.*
Description: A Dixie County park. Camping allowed.
Directions: From US 27 near Branford, drive 11.5 miles south on FL 349. Look for the park sign about 1.5 miles past the junction with FL 340. Turn right onto a gravel road and follow it to the park.

17C. HINTON LANDING COUNTY PARK—*Fresh; Boat; Ramp.*
Description: A Dixie County park. Camping allowed.
Directions: The park is at the end of CR 317 approximately 2.1 miles south of Old Town.

17D. NEW PINE LANDING COUNTY PARK—*Fresh; Boat; Ramp.*
Description: A Dixie County park. Camping allowed.
Directions: The park is off FL 349 about 4.7 miles south of Old Town. Look for the park signs along FL 349 for the turnoff.

17E. MANATEE SPRINGS STATE PARK—*Fresh; Boat; Ramp; $.*
Description: A popular place for swimming and diving. There is a campground, picnic area, and hiking and biking trail.
Directions: From Chiefland, drive 1.7 miles north on US 19/98. Turn west on FL 320 (Manatee Springs Road) and go approximately 5 miles to the park.
For more information: Call the park office at (904) 493-6072.

17F. FOWLER'S BLUFF—*Fresh and Salt; Boat; Ramp.*
Description: The bass fishing is usually better upstream of this point. From here it is about 13 miles to the Gulf of Mexico.

The Suwannee River is one of the state's most scenic rivers. Fishing success depends, in part, on the river level. With no control structures, the level goes up and down depending on the amount of rain. Check on fishing conditions before you go.

Directions: From the junction of US 19/98, US 129, and Alternate US 27 in Chiefland, drive 5.1 miles south on US 19/98. Turn west on FL 347 and drive 13.2 miles to Fowler's Bluff.

For more information: Call Treasure Camp (adjacent to the ramp) at (352) 493-2950

18. SUWANNEE

Salt and Fresh; Boat; Ramp.

Description: This small fishing village at the mouth of the Suwannee River has a public ramp plus several private ramps at the fish camps. Jimmy Greene, owner of Suwannee Shore Marina, says, "Anglers like to fish the flats, which in this area can extend out as far as 5 miles. Anywhere inside of that there are lots of patches of sand and sea grasses." His best advice for first-timers to the area is a friendly warning. "You can't just go fishing blind around here. You must know something about the area or you're likely to run aground on an oyster bar or mud flat." This holds true for the entire Big Bend coastal area.

Fishing Index: Most of the anglers fishing out of Suwannee are looking for spotted seatrout and redfish along the coast. Trout fishing also brings the chance to catch a Spanish mackerel or two from spring through fall. In winter redfish move up the Suwannee into freshwater more readily than the trout do according to Greene. "The trout will go upriver when the water is cold, but they don't like to do it unless the river water is clear. Normally the river water is tannic and the trout don't seem to like it." Anglers fishing 28 to 32 miles offshore will find some good grouper actions in all but the coldest months.

Directions: From US 27 in Old Town, drive about 21 miles south on FL 349 to Suwannee. A public ramp is maintained by the county but it has little public parking. The commercial facilities all have ramps or hoists and will put your boat in the water for a reasonable fee. A couple of the marinas don't charge for the use of their ramps, but they do hope you will at least buy your bait from them. All of the facilities are in Suwannee on FL 349.

For more information: Call Suwannee Shores Marina at (352) 542-7482.

19. SHELL MOUND

Salt; Boat; Ramp.

Description: This is a Dixie County park. There is a small campground next to the ramp. The ramp allows boaters access to the waters north of Cedar Key.

Fishing Index: Like most of the other sites in this area, the top species for nearshore anglers are spotted seatrout and redfish.

Directions: From US 19/98 in Otter Creek, drive toward Cedar Key on FL 24. Go about 18 miles to FL 347. Go 2.2 miles north on FL 347 and turn west onto CR 326. Follow CR 326 for 3.2 miles to the county ramp.

20. CEDAR KEY

Salt; Boat, Bridge, and Pier; Ramp.

Description: Cedar Key is the best known community in the Big Bend region. The town sits on several islands linked together by short bridges. The area has reputation as a great place to fish and is developing some renown as an artist's haven.

Fishing Index: Seahorse Reef, a 5-mile bar laced with patches of seagrass beds, is one of the most popular places to fish. Spanish mackerel, cobia, sheepshead, and king mackerel hang around this reef. Spotted seatrout, redfish, and sheeps–head are caught by anglers fishing from the bridges around town. Captain Jim Dupre (call (352) 371-6153) specializes in fly fishing the flats. He says, "Fishing for redfish is always good around Cedar Key. If there was anytime that it's a little slow, I'd say that was in June." Land-bound anglers can fish from the area's bridges and from the county finger pier and dock adjacent to the boat ramp and city marina.

Directions: From US 19/98 at Otter Creek, drive about 24 miles southwest on FL 24 to Cedar Key. When the road ends, turn left at the stop sign onto 2nd Street. Go one block and turn right onto C Street. Go one block and turn left onto 1st Street. The city marina and boat ramps, one accessing the Gulf of Mexico and the other the backwaters between the islands and the mainland, are on the right. The county operated dock and finger pier are adjacent to the boat ramps and city marina.

The city dock at Cedar Key attracts plenty of anglers on the weekends. This out-of-the way coastal community provides good access to the extensive salt marshes of the Big Bend.

For more information: Call Cedar Key City Hall at (352) 543-5132 or the county pier and dock at (352) 543-5461.

ALACHUA COUNTY

21. PAYNES PRAIRIE STATE PRESERVE
Fresh; Boat and Bank; Ramp; $.

Description: The park has a campground, hiking and horseback trails, and good opportunities for bird watching. Only electric motors are allowed on the lake. Fish from the boardwalk along the lake or anywhere along the shore within the park.

Fishing Index: Lake Wauberg is fished year-round for largemouth bass, crappie, and bream.

Directions: The entrance road to the site is 7 miles south of Gainesville on US 441.

22. NEWNANS LAKE
Fresh; Boat and Bank; Ramp.

Description: This 7,500-acre lake, fringed with cypress trees, is a very scenic place to fish. This lake had problems in the past due to a dam that affected the water quality. That dam was removed in 1991 and the fishing made a strong recovery. In addition to the public ramps, there are several fish camps on the lake.

Fishing Index: This relatively shallow lake has some good bass fishing. The fishing is best when the water level is low enough so that the cypress forest surrounding the shoreline isn't flooded. When that happens the bass move into the trees and fishing drops off. This lake also has a good reputation for producing nice stringers of crappie.

Directions: The lake is a few miles east of Gainesville off FL 20.

Access Points:
22A. EARL POWERS PARK—*Fresh; Boat; Ramp.*
Directions: From University Avenue (FL 26) turn onto Hawthorne Road (FL 20) and go east about 4.0 miles.

22B. COUNTY ROAD 234 RAMP—*Fresh; Boat; Ramp.*
Directions: From University Avenue (FL 26) Turn onto Hawthorne Road (FL 20) and go east about 6.5 miles to the intersection with CR 234. Turn left on CR 234 and go 2.6 miles to the access road to the ramp.

For more information: Call McGilvary's Fish Camp at (352) 376-3452.

23. LAKE ALTHO
Fresh; Boat; Ramp.

Description: This 540-acre natural lake is not heavily fished. The lake is low in nutrients. Anglers who frequently fish here have the best success.

Fishing Index: The lake produces a moderate supply of small bass and panfish.

Directions: From Waldo, take US 310 south to the intersection with CR 325. Drive 1.4 miles north on CR 325 to the turnoff for the lake and the ramp.

24. SANTA FE LAKE
Fresh; Boat; Ramp.

Description: A 5,850-acre lake fringed with cypress trees 15 miles east of Gainesville. Years ago, a number of fish camps operated around the lake. They are all "dead and buried and the lake has become a pretty expensive piece of property," according to one local resident.

Fishing Index: This lake is considered one of the better fishing lakes in the region. Bass fishing is good year-round and several deep holes hold crappie, especially in the winter. The GFC stocked threadfin shad in the lake to create a food supply for largemouth and sunshine bass.

Access Points:

24A. LITTLE SANTA FE LAKE—*Fresh; Boat; Ramp.*
Directions: From FL 26 in Melrose, turn north on FL 21 and go 3.5 miles to
FL 21B. Drive 3.1 miles west on FL 12B.

24B. MELROSE—*Fresh; Boat; Ramp.*
Directions: From FL 26 in Melrose, turn onto Trout Street and go 0.3 mile to
the ramp.

24C. COUNTY PARK—*Fresh; Boat; Ramp.*
Directions: From Melrose drive 1.2 miles west on FL 26. Look for the sign and turn right at the paved road leading to the park.

25. ORANGE AND LOCHLOOSA LAKES —————

Fresh; Boat and Bank; Ramp.

Description: These lakes, located between Gainesville and Ocala, are connected by Cross Creek, a small waterway made famous by author Marjorie Kinnan Rawlings. Her home, between the lakes on FL 325, is a state historic site and is open for tours.

Fishing Index: The water level in these lakes fluctuates over time creating some good and not-so-good fishing conditions. Bass fishing is usually good year-round with the best times being March and April and October and November according to Ann Thomas, owner of Twin Lakes Camp. Beginning in mid-March the bream, shellcracker (redear sunfish), and warmouth fishing turns on and provides good action throughout the summer months. "We use grass shrimp on these lakes for these fish," according to Thomas, who has owned the camp for 21 years. You can fish from the bank of Cross Creek in the county park.

Access Points

25A. LOCHLOOSA RAMP—*Fresh; Boat; Ramp.*
Description: The ramp accesses Lochloosa Lake.
Direction: From the intersection of US 301 and FL 20 in Hawthorne, drive south on US 301 for about 6.2 miles to the community of Lochloosa.

25A. MAJORIE RAWLINGS COUNTY PARK—*Fresh; Boat and Bank; Ramp.*
Description: The park is adjacent to the state historic site.
Directions: Drive north on FL 325 for 4.3 mile from the US 301 intersection or 8.1 miles south on FL 325 from FL 20. Additional access to Orange Lake is from the numerous fish camps on the lake.

For more information: Call the Game and Fresh Water Fish Commission regional office at (904) 758-0525; Twin Lakes Fish Camp at (352) 466-3194; or South Shores Fish Camp at (352) 595-4241.

26. GULF OF MEXICO

Salt; Boat.

Description: Anglers with small, shallow-draft boats fishing within 2 or 3 miles of the coast have a multitude of seagrass flats, oyster bars, and tidal creeks to explore. With numerous oyster and sand bars in this area, running aground is easy to do. Larger vessels can venture farther offshore to fish the artificial reefs and rocky bottom areas of the Gulf.

Fishing Index: The primary target species for nearshore anglers are redfish and spotted seatrout. Around the reefs are sheepshead, Spanish and king mackerel, cobia, and some grouper and mangrove snapper. The rocky bottoms farther offshore produce the best grouper and sea bass action. Red and gag grouper are the two most common species. While there is a relatively consistent supply of fish, the catching slows down in the winter because bad weather keeps the anglers off the water more during this time of year. The general pattern for grouper is the same one seen along the state's west coast. The red grouper tend to move into deeper water while the gags move into shallower water during colder months. The movement reverses itself when the water warms up.

Fleet locations:

26A. CEDAR KEY.
Description: The largest number of boats operate from Cedar Key. There is one party boat and numerous six-pack boats based in town. Six packs are charter boats that take six or fewer persons and are the boats that families or groups of friends usually hire for a day's fishing.
For more information: Call the Gondola Party Boat at (352) 543-6148; Captain Jim Dupre at (352) 371-6153; Captain Bill Roberts at (352) 543-5690; or Norwood Marina at (352) 543-6148.

26B. SUWANNEE, HORSESHOE BEACH, STEINHATCHEE, AND KEATON BEACH.
Description: A few boats operate from each of these small fishing villages.
For more information: In Suwannee call Suwannee Shores Marina at (352) 542-7482; in Horseshoe Beach call Horseshoe Beach Marina at (352) 498-5687 or Dockside Marina at (352) 498-5768; in Steinhatchee call River Haven Marina at (352) 498-0709 or Steinhatchee Landing at (352) 498-3513; and in Keaton Beach call Keaton Beach Marina at (352) 578-2897.

Month by Month in the Big Bend

Note: Offshore is defined as greater than 5 miles from the coast. Coastal waters include open waters inside of five miles including surf fishing, and all brackish water area such as bays, the saltwater regions of rivers, and lagoons. Freshwater includes, lakes, ponds, reservoirs, rivers and phosphate pits.

January

Offshore: A tough month because of the weather. When the northwesters aren't blowing through get out for some great sheepshead fishing and decent grouper and sea bass action.

Coastal: Look for spotted seatrout and redfish in the deeper water of the region's rivers and tidal creeks; sand trout action is red hot at the river mouths once you find them you'll have non-stop action.

Freshwater: A top month for largemouth bass; Crappie action is good on some of the lakes; ask around because some are better than others and the situation changes from year to year.

February

Offshore: Pretty much a repeat of January. Sheepshead is the best bet.

Coastal: The redfish and spotted seatrout are still in the deep holes of the lower parts of the rivers. If the weather warms up for a few days, they will move onto the flats during the warmest part of the day; sand trout action is still hot.

Freshwater: Crappie action is very good, largemouth bass are bedding and trophy fish will be taken on large live shiners.

March

Offshore: The water temperature starts its upward swing and the first Spanish mackerel of the year will probably arrive. Don't give up on the sheepshead action, it will still be good.

Coastal: The spotted seatrout and redfish will start to move onto the flats.

Freshwater: Largemouth bass will finish spawning this month; bream, shellcracker and warmouth, the three top panfish in the region, will start to turn on.

April

Offshore: King mackerel are what everyone is looking for this month, once they arrive expect some great fishing for about six weeks or so; the cobia will also arrive; Spanish mackerel action will be at its peak; Cedar Key anglers will be flocking to Seahorse reef.

Coastal: Spotted seatrout and redfish are on the flats. The fishing will be great.

Freshwater: Largemouth bass activity goes from great to very good; bream, shellcracker and warmouth action goes from good to great.

MAY

Offshore: Spanish and king mackerel should continue to be the best bets; cobia, bluefish, tripletail and crevalle jacks will make the fishing interesting.

Coastal: Redfish and spotted seatrout are abundant throughout the region, that's what the area is famous for.

Freshwater: Bluegills, a.k.a. bream, shellcrackers, a.k.a. redear sunfish, and warmouths are plentiful this month; as the waters warm the better bass fishing tends to be in the rivers, the fish seem to bite better when the water is flowing.

JUNE

Offshore: The king mackerel are gone and won't be back until the fall; their smaller cousins, the Spanish, stay in the area throughout the summer but not in the numbers seen in the spring; the summer months provide good fishing for cobia, tripletail, amberjack, grouper, and jacks.

Coastal: Nothing new to report, redfish and spotted seatrout are the staples of the coastal anglers.

Freshwater: If you want a largemouth and like to fish on the lakes, try the early morning hours and late afternoons; panfish action is still strong in most areas.

JULY

Offshore: Triggerfish, which are around much of the year, can be plentiful on some reefs and rocky bottoms; if you want to catch a dolphin and this is the only place in Florida that you will fish, now is the time to try, the fish aren't plentiful but there are some out there; some spotted seatrout will be caught on the deeper seagrass beds, they're there to escape the summer heat of the shallow waters.

Coastal: This is thunderstorm season so keep an eye out for the big storms especially in the afternoon; tarpon will join the coastal regulars; fish the cooler times of the day for redfish and spotted seatrout.

Freshwater: Bream and friends are your best bet; try largemouth bassfishing on the lakes at night, it can produce very good results; river largemouth bass fishing is very good.

AUGUST

Offshore: The heat of the summer makes for a hot day on the water when there's no wind; with Spanish mackerel, grouper, triggerfish, cobia, dolphin, barracudas and amberjacks around the action is good and you never know what's on the end of your line until you get the fish to the boat.

Coastal: Look for the spotted seatrout to be in slightly deeper water than the redfish this month, they seem to be less tolerant of the heat.

Freshwater: The water is warm and the fish are sluggish, early and late in the day are the keys to success for largemouths and panfish; maybe it's time to try for a mess of catfish, with some grits, hushpuppies and a fresh sliced tomato you've got a great meal.

SEPTEMBER

Offshore: Thunderstorm season isn't over yet, watch the sky late in the day; Spanish mackerel, grouper, cobia, amberjacks and a few others are the typical mixed bag during the heat of the year.

Coastal: Only the heat of the day will keep anglers off the water and not catching the abundant redfish of the Big Bend; the spotted seatrout will be over the deeper grass flats.

Freshwater: Fish early and late in the day for largemouth bass and panfish.

OCTOBER

Offshore: This is the month the king mackerel usually return; the summer species will also be around unless the temperatures take an early nose-dive

Coastal: The redfish will start to move out of the shallow water as the weather cools off but the action is likely to be some of the best of the year; ditto for spotted seatrout.

Freshwater: Largemouth bass fishing is much improved on the lakes now that the summer heat is gone.

NOVEMBER

Offshore: If you like grouper, this is one of the best month for the tasty fish; chances are also very good that the king mackerel will be around, at least for the first part of the month.

Coastal: The spotted seatrout and redfish will be working their way towards deeper water, especially as the month wanes and the water really begins to cool.

Freshwater: Crappie action starts to pick up; largemouth bass fishing can be very good on the lakes and in the rivers.

DECEMBER

Offshore: Another top month for grouper, weather permitting; sheepshead action goes from good to great; mackerel and summer residents have moved way south to warmer waters.

Coastal: The spotted seatrout and redfish are moving to the river mouths and looking for the deeper and warmer water, some will move up the rivers and mingle with the largemouth bass.

Freshwater: Crappie action is the best bet for those lakes with a good fishery.

Big Bend Fish Availability Chart

NOTE: The information contained in this chart represents the seasonal patterns observed over the past two or three years. For saltwater species, the arrival of the migrant species and the peak times for each species are heavily dependent on water temperature. Unusually warm or cold periods will effect the patterns described above. Bream is the local name for bluegills and shellcrackers. Speckled trout is the local name for spotted seatrout.

Species	Jan	Feb	Mar	Apr	May	Jun	Jul	Aug	Sep	Oct	Nov	Dec
Redfish	■	■	■	□	□	■	■	■	□	□	■	■
Speckled trout	■	■	■	□	□	■	■	■	□	□	■	■
Sheepshead	□	□	□	■	■	■	■	■	■	■	□	□
Mangrove Snapper	■	■	■	■	■	■	■	■	■	■	■	■
Red Grouper	■	■	■	■	■	■	■	■	■	■	■	■
Gag Grouper	■	■	■	■	■	■	■	■	■	■	■	■
Amberjack	■	■	■	■	■	■	■	■	■	■	■	■
Flounder	■	■	■	■	■	■	■	■	■	■	■	■
Black Sea Bass	■	■	■	■	■	■	■	■	■	■	■	■
Sand Trout	□	□	□	□	■	■	■	■	■	■	■	■
Black Drum	■	■	■	■						■	■	■
Spanish Mackerel				■	□	□	□	■	■	■	□	□
King Mackerel				■	□	□			■	□	□	
Cobia				■	□	□	□	□	□	□	■	■
Tripletail				■	■	■	■	■	■			
Crevalle Jack				■	■	■	■	■	■			
Tarpon				■	■	■	■	■	■			
Shark (all species)				■	■	■	■	■	■	■		
Bluefish				■	■	■	■					
Dolphin						■	■	■	■			
Largemouth Bass	□	□	□	■	■	■	■	■	■	■	■	■
Catfish	■	■	■	■	■	■	■	■	■	■	■	■
Shellcracker	■	■	□	□	□	□	■	■	■	■	■	■
Sunshine Bass	■	■	■	■	■	■	■	■	■	■	■	■
Crappie	□	■	■	■	■	■	■	■	■	■	■	□
Bluegill	■	■	□	□	□	□	■	■	■	■	■	■
Warmouth	■	■	□	□	□	□	■	■	■	■	■	■

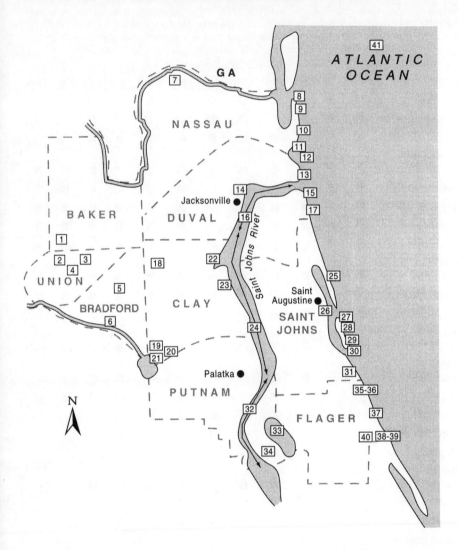

CHAPTER FIVE
Northeast Florida

Counties: ▪ Baker ▪ Union ▪ Bradford ▪ Nassau ▪ Duval ▪ Clay ▪ St. Johns ▪ Putnam ▪ Flagler

"The First Coast" is how people along the Atlantic Ocean coast refer to this part of the state. Visiting anglers, in a rush to head south to the Florida seen on the postcards, pass by the fertile fishing grounds along the coast and in the St. Johns River. Florida's longest river, the northward-flowing St. Johns cuts through downtown Jacksonville. From just north of the tall office buildings to the coast, there are miles of marshy shoreline and tidal creeks to fish for saltwater species. South of the downtown area, largemouth bass and panfish anglers have more places to fish than they could handle in a lifetime. Adding variety to the angling in northeast Florida is the annual upriver run of shrimp, an event that brings hungry recreational shrimpers to the shores of the river hoping to catch their limit of the tasty crustaceans.

SALTWATER FISHING

Local residents love to fish the miles of coastal marshes where rivers like the St. Marys, St. Johns, and Nassau meet the Atlantic. And they know about the outstanding opportunities to catch redfish, spotted seatrout, and flounder. Similar conditions exist along the Intracoastal Waterway, the boater's highway along the state's east coast. The inlets are also a popular gathering spot for fish and anglers. Most are accessible from land via the rock jetties protecting the openings or from a boat.

Northeast Florida also has miles of beach and there are many perfect places for surf fishing. Access is as easy as parking your car and walking over the dune to the beach. Surf anglers have excellent luck catching whiting, redfish, and bluefish. In the summer, some pompano are around to add excitement. Surf fishing in this region is perhaps one of the most overlooked types of angling in the entire state. The best sites are where a trough of water runs between the beach and an offshore sand bar. Look for places where the waves first break just off the beach and cast your bait into the trough between you and the sand bar.

Fort Clinch State Park, at the very northern tip of the state, is a scenic place to camp and there is some very good fishing from the jetty and along the shore of the inlet. At the other end of this region, Flagler Beach Pier always draws a crowd.

Offshore anglers will find plenty of action to keep them happy. Close to shore, the cobia, Spanish and king mackerel, grouper, snapper, and tarpon keep anglers busy in all but the coldest and windiest months. Nearshore anglers get excited in the spring when the northward moving mackerel pass through the region. The cobia also show up then and sometimes move so close to shore they can be caught by anglers on the piers or in the surf.

Far out to sea—beyond 35 miles—the big bluewater boats fish the edge of the Gulfstream for wahoo, dolphin, tuna, and billfish. May is the top month so plan ahead and book a charter. This is the way to go because bluewater fishing requires a seaworthy, well-appointed boat and expensive tackle and lures. Saltwater anglers looking for an offshore adventure will find plenty of charter boats to choose from in St. Augustine.

FRESHWATER FISHING

The St. Johns River provides anglers with a nearly unlimited supply of places to fish. Largemouth bass bite year-round and that's supplemented by some outstanding winter and spring crappie action. Numerous access points make this an easy place to get on the water.

The big river isn't the only one with good fishing. The St. Marys River forms the border between Nassau County in Florida and the state of Georgia. This river, many anglers claim, supports a native population of striped bass, a fish at its southern limit in north Florida. Winter angling can produce some big fish as they move up the river to spawn.

The lakes are interesting places to fish. Some are much better than others. The amount of nutrients in a lake are what make the difference. The ones with low levels are sometimes referred to as sterile. That doesn't mean they are devoid of life. No lake in Florida is that bad off. What it does mean is that the water is usually very clear and the fishing is seldom better than good. The better lakes are ones with enough nutrients in them to sustain a fair amount of aquatic vegetation.

Besides being affected by nutrient levels, fishing in the lakes of this region is also influenced by local rainfall. During the early 1990s water levels dropped in some lakes so much that ramps were hundreds of feet from the water and docks were useless. The trend in the mid 1990s shows the levels rising but how long that pattern will continue cannot be determined. If you plan to fish this part of the state, call ahead and make sure the lake you want to fish is fishable.

BAKER, UNION, AND BRADFORD COUNTIES

Freshwater lake fishing is the only type of angling in this area. All of the lakes have largemouth bass, bream, and crappie, but fishing conditions vary from lake to lake. It seems like the most scenic lakes are the ones with the lowest nutrients and the most limited fishing. Still, this doesn't mean you should pass these lakes up. If you're in the area or passing through, give any of them a try. The biggest bass will be taken from January through March in the shallow areas along the shore. Crappie fishing is pretty good on most of these lakes.

1. OCEAN POND ——————————————

Fresh; Boat, Bank and Pier; Ramp; $.

Description: A 1,760-acre natural lake fringed with cypress, located within Osceola National Forest.

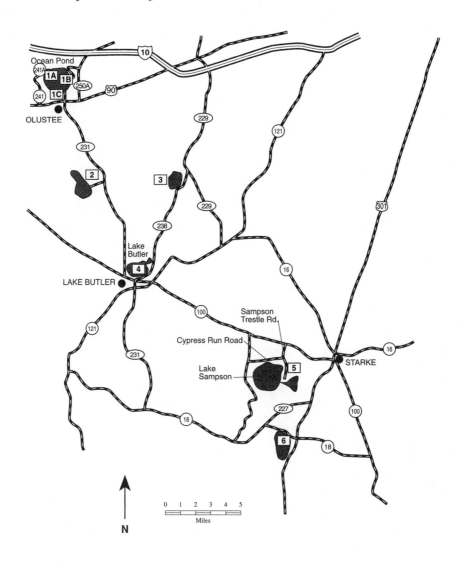

Fishing Index: The GFC classifies this as an infertile lake. For anglers this implies that it is only fair to good for largemouth and sunshine bass and panfish. Bank fishing is possible at each site and there is a fishing pier at Olustee Beach. Best bet is to fish for sunshine bass and crappie during the colder months. February and March, during the largemouth bass spawn, is the best time for this species.

Directions: In Osceola National Forest near Olustee, about 12 miles east of Lake City and 7.5 miles west of the US 90/I-10 interchange. Access to the three recreation areas is off US 90.

Access points:

1A. Hog Pen Landing—*Ramp; Boat and Bank.*
Description: An Osceola National Forest recreation area. Primitive camping.
Directions: From Olustee, drive about 2 miles west on US 90 and turn north onto FR 241. Go 3 miles to FR 241A, turn right, and enter the site.

1B. Ocean Pond—*Boat and Bank; Ramp; $.*
Description: An Osceola National Forest recreation area. Site has a developed campground, swimming beach, and warm showers.
Directions: From Olustee, drive about 1.1 miles east on US 90 and turn north onto CR 250A. Go about 4 miles to the entrance.

1C. Olustee Beach—*Boat, Bank and Pier; Ramp; $.*
Description: An Osceola National Forest recreation area. Barrier-free fishing pier, swimming beach, and picnic tables.
Directions: From US 90 in Olustee, take CR 231 north about 1 mile.

For more information: Call the Osceola National Forest office at (904) 752-2577.

2. PALESTINE LAKE

Fresh; Boat; Ramp.

Description: A remote 972-acre lake surrounded by cypress forested lowlands.

Fishing Index: Best fishing is for crappie and sunshine bass. Largemouth bass fishing is fair.

Directions: From Olustee, take CR 231 south 5.75 miles. Turn right onto Palestine Lake Road and go 1 mile to the boat ramp.

3. DOWLING LAKE (SWIFT CREEK POND)

Fresh; Boat; Ramp.

Description: Part of the Creek Swamp region, this rural lake is very scenic thanks to its undeveloped shoreline. The ramp is unimproved.

Fishing Index: Crappie are the best bet in this lake. The colder months are the best. Compared to other lakes in the region, this is not considered a top producing lake.

Directions: About 20 miles east of Lake City. From Lake Buler take CR 238 about 7.5 miles north.

4. LAKE BUTLER

Fresh; Boat; Ramp.

Description: In addition to the ramp, there is a swimming beach and picnic facilities.

Fishing Index: A fair to good lake for largemouth and sunshine bass.

Directions: On the north side of the city of Lake Butler. The city is about 20 miles southeast of Lake City on FL 100.

5. SAMPSON AND ROWELL LAKES
Fresh; Boat; Ramp.

Description: The lakes are connected by a navigable canal.

Fishing Index: Sampson Lake is less fertile than Rowell Lake but both offer good fishing opportunities for bass and panfish. Fish along the outer edge of the emergent vegetation and along the part of the lakes where cypress lines the shoreline. The lakes also have good bream and crappie fishing. Both are stocked with sunshine bass.

Directions: From US 301 in Starke, drive 4 miles west on FL 100 to Sampson Trestle Road. Turn south, drive 0.9 mile, and turn right on Cypress Run Road. Go about 0.9 mile to the ramp and day-use park on Lake Sampson.

6. LAKE HAMPTON
Fresh; Boat; Ramp.

Description: An 823-acre lake managed by the GFC. The lake has a natural shoreline of maidencane, water lilies, and cypress trees. The GFC has transplanted bulrush and placed several quarter-acre brush piles to serve as fish-attractors.

Fishing Index: The lake has a threadfin shad population that serves as a food source for largemouth and sunshine bass. The biggest fish are caught in spring during the spawning period. The lake has a very good reputation for crappie, especially in the winter months.

Directions: From Starke drive about 3 miles south on US 301. Turn west on FL 18 and go 0.4 mile to the ramp.

NASSAU AND DUVAL COUNTIES

7. ST. MARYS RIVER
Fresh; Bank; Ramp.

Description: The St. Marys originates in Okefenokee Swamp and winds 130 miles before emptying into the Atlantic Ocean.

Fishing Index: The freshwater part of the river has excellent striped bass fishing (the best of local rivers) in February and March. These are native Atlantic stock fish. They come into the river to spawn. Good places to try are around the pilings of the US 1, US 17, and I-95 bridges. Bass and bream fishing is good to excellent.

Directions: The St. Marys forms part of the northern border with Georgia.

Access Points:

7A. US 1/301 BRIDGE—*Boat; Ramp.*
Description: A GFC-maintained ramp.
Directions: The ramp is on the south side of the river just off the highway.

7B. KING'S FERRY—*Boat and Bank;Ramp.*
Description: A GFC-maintained ramp.
Directions: Turn off of US 1/301 in Boulonge onto King's Ferry Road (CR 108). Take CR 108 east about 8 miles.

8.   FORT CLINCH STATE PARK ──────────────
Salt; Surf and Pier; $.

Description: The fort dates from the Civil War and was occupied by Confederate troops. There are two campgrounds, a swimming beach, and a nature trail.

Fishing Index: Fish from the shoreline along St. Marys Inlet, from the park's fishing pier, or in the surf south of the pier and the fishing area on the jetties along the south side of Fernandina Inlet. Fish for spotted seatrout, sheepshead, redfish, and flounder from the pier and shore. The pier is not always the best place to fish. The waters around it are shallow and cut off from the inlet flow by a rock jetty closer to the inlet.

Directions: From I-95, take the A1A exit and drive east about 15.4 miles.The park is at the north end of Amelia Island. The entrance is on Atlantic Boulevard (A1A) in Fernandina Beach just before the road turns and heads south along the beach.

For more information: Call the park office at (904) 277-7274.

9.   FERNANDINA BEACH ──────────────────
Salt; Boat; Ramp.

Description: This coastal community at the north end of Amelia Island is the gateway to the brackish waters of the St. Marys River and adjacent tidal creeks.

Fishing Index: The numerous tidal creeks around the mouth of the St. Marys River and the river inlet are great places to fish for redfish, spotted seatrout, sheepshead, and flounder. Try fishing the rocky shoreline around town for trout in spring and fall. Use a free-lined live shrimp. Tarpon arrive in the summer and can be especially abundant in the inlet. You can also surf fish along most of the beach. Don't forget to stay clear of swimmers.

Directions: To reach the public ramp in Fernandina Beach, turn onto Centre Street from A1A (8th St.). Take Centre Street until it ends along the riverfront.

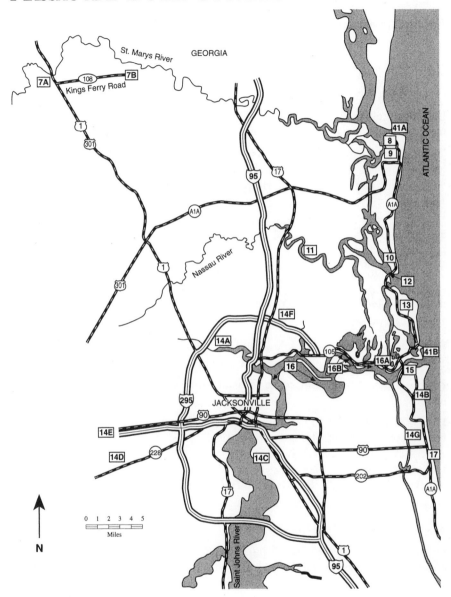

10. Amelia Island State Recreation Area ————

Salt; Surf; $.

Description: This coastal park features a stable that rents horses for guided rides along the Atlantic beach.

Fishing Index: The undeveloped beaches here are a good place to fish for bluefish, whiting, and redfish.

Directions: The park entrance is on A1A at the south end of Amelia Island, about 12 miles south of Fernandina Beach.

For more information: Call the park office at (904) 251-2320.

11. NASSAU RIVER
Salt; Boat.

Description: The river forms the boundary between Nassau and Duval counties. As with other tidal rivers in this region, numerous creeks flow into it.

Fishing Index: Not as renowned as the St. Marys River for striped bass, it is a locally popular place for some anglers. Try fishing around the US 17 and I-95 bridges. Fish the lower part of the river for flounder, redfish, sheepshead, and spotted seatrout.

Directions: The best ramps to launch from are the public ramps in Fernandina Beach and Mayport (see sites 9 and 15). Follow the Intracoastal Waterway to the river and head upstream.

12. NASSAU SOUND BRIDGE
Salt; Bridge.

Description: This is the A1A highway bridge over mouth of the Nassau River. There is an extensive series of constantly shifting sand bars in the sound.

Fishing Index: A very good place to fish for black drum, flounder, and sheepshead.

Directions: Take A1A south from Fernandina Beach about 12.5 miles or north from Mayport about 9 miles to the bridge.

13. BIG TALBOT ISLAND AND LITTLE TALBOT ISLAND STATE PARKS
Salt; Boat and Surf; Ramp; $.

Description: These two coastal parks have swimming beaches, hiking trails, and outstanding canoeing through the tidal marsh creeks between the Nassau and St. Johns rivers. A campground in Little Talbot Island State Park also rents canoes.

Fishing Index: Fish the surf for bluefish and whiting. Fish the A1A bridge over Fort George Creek and the tidal creeks on the west side of the islands from a canoe or small boat for redfish, spotted seatrout, flounder, and sheepshead.

Directions: Both parks are on A1A between Mayport and Amelia Island. The entrance to the campground at Little Talbot Island State Park is about 4.6 miles north of the Mayport ferry docks. There is a small boat ramp in the campground area. Canoe access is possible at the campground and along A1A between Big Talbot and Little Talbot Islands.

For more information: Call the parks office at (904) 251-2320.

14. JACKSONVILLE URBAN PONDS
Fresh; Bank and Boat; Ramp.

Description: These seven Fish Management Areas in the Jacksonville area offer anglers easy access to intensively managed freshwater fishing ponds. Each site has boat ramps, but gasoline motors are prohibited. There is heavy emphasis on providing year-round bank fishing. Consider these sites as places to take the kids fishing or as a quick get-away for anglers caught in the city with an hour or two to spare.

Fishing Index: The ponds are stocked by the GFC with largemouth and sunshine bass, bluegills, shellcrackers, crappie, and catfish. Numerous fish feeders and brush attractors enhance the fishing.

Directions: All seven sites are within the City of Jacksonville. But because the city limits and the county boundaries are the same as Duval County, the sites are spread over a large area. Three of the best sites are ponds within city parks.

Access:
14A. BETHESDA FISH MANAGEMENT AREA—*Boat and Bank; Ramp.*
Directions: Exit I-295 at Dunn Road and go 1.2 miles east to the entrance.

14B. HANNA PARK FISH MANAGEMENT AREA—*Boat and Bank; Ramp.*
Directions: Near Mayport. Turn off A1A onto Wonderwood Road. The entrance is 0.2 mile down this road.

14C. ST. AUGUSTINE ROAD FISH MANAGEMENT AREA—*Boat and Bank; Ramp.*
Directions: Near the Lakewood section of Jacksonville, on the east side of the St. Johns River. The entrance is a few blocks south of St. Augustine Road on Stetson Road.

Other sites in the Urban Pond Project are:
14D. LEE ADAMS FISH MANAGEMENT AREA—*Boat and Bank; Ramp.*
Description: The oval-shaped pond has a road around it providing access to the entire pond.
Directions: Exit I-295 at Normandy Boulevard (FL 228) and drive 5.7 miles southeast.

14E. POPE DUVAL FISH MANAGEMENT AREA—*Boat and Bank; Ramp.*
Description: The area is barrier-free.
Directions: Drive 4.5 miles east on US 90 from the US 90-US 301 intersection or 7.5 miles west on US 90 - I-295 exit.

14F. OCEANWAY FISH MANAGEMENT AREA—*Boat and Bank; Ramp.*
Description: Adjacent to the Oceanway Sports Complex.
Directions: Take US 17 north from Jacksonville. Turn onto New Berlin Road,

*Automatic fish feeders are found in most of the fish management areas
maintained by the Florida Game and Fresh Water Fish Commission.*

which is just north of the US 17 intersection with I-295. Turn right onto Palm
Avenue and follow it to the pond.

14G. Huguenot Fish Management Area—*Boat and Bank; Ramp.*
Directions: In Jacksonville Beach. The park is 1.2 miles north of the A1A-FL
202 (J. Turner Butler Highway). Turn off of A1A onto 16th Street and go 2
blocks east to the park.

15. Mayport

Salt; Boat and Bank; Ramp.

Description: This town is at the mouth of the St. Johns River. From here you
can fish in the Atlantic or the tidal waters of the St. Johns, or explore some of
the numerous small creeks that branch off the river and the Intracoastal Waterway.

Fishing Index: Spotted seatrout, redfish, sheepshead, flounder, and black drum
are the mainstays for anglers in this area. There is good bank fishing around
the Mayport Ferry docks and the public boat ramp. Some locals say there is
very good flounder fishing near the ferry docks on the north side of the river.
The jetties in the inlet are popular places to fish if you have a boat. Local guide
John Dryssen ((904) 223-4181) says, "we have a lot of water around here and
90 percent of it is desert when it comes to fish. The other 10 percent has most
of the fish. This makes blind fishing tough. I suggest that anyone new to the
area stop by one of the local bait and tackle shops to get some information and
tips on where to go." As far as bait to use, Dryssen believes "live shrimp is the

way to go. Everything eats it." He recommends using a slip bobber to keep the bait at the same depth as the fish, usually just above the bottom.

Directions: To reach Mayport from Jacksonville take Atlantic or Beach Boulevards east to A1A. Head north until you reach Mayport. If approaching from the north side of the Saint John River, take FL 105 (Heckscher Drive) to the Mayport Ferry docks. The boat ramp is in Mayport just past the ferry dock.

For more information: Two local bait and tackle shops to try are A1A Discount Bait and Tackle at (904) 247-4424 and B&M Bait and Tackle at (904) 249-3933.

16. St. Johns River (River Mouth to Buckman /I-295 Bridge)
Salt; Boat and Bridge; Ramp.

Description: Most of the fishing is in the river and the numerous tidal creeks along the north side of the river from Reddie Point to the mouth.

Fishing Index: The new Dames Point Bridge over the St. Johns is a hot spot for spotted seatrout and black drum. Anglers also have good luck with trout in Trout River. Redfish, which some locals call red bass, are making a strong return to the tidal creeks that flow into the St. Johns River. Summer flounder fishing is very good in this area. See the Mayport listing for more information about fishing near the inlet.

Directions: There are numerous fish camps and marinas along the river. Many have private ramps. You can also use the Mayport boat ramp described in site 15.

Access Points:
16A. County Boat Ramp—*Salt; Boat; Ramp.*
Directions: The ramp is on FL 105 1.1 miles east of the FL 105 bridge over the Intracoastal Waterway (about 4.5 river miles from the mouth).

16B. FL 105 Bridges—*Salt; Bridge.*
Directions: You can fish from the FL 105 (Heckscher Drive) bridges over Dunn Creek, Browns Creek, and Clapboard Creek.
For more information: Call White Shell Fish Camp at (904) 251-3388.

17. Jacksonville Beach Pier
Salt; Pier; $.

Description: This 1,000-foot pier is a popular place for land-bound anglers. Bait and tackle and rod rentals are available. No saltwater fishing license is needed.

Fishing Index: Flounder activity is very good from May to July. King mackerel fishing, using live bait, is popular from May through September. Some big crevalle jacks will also take your bait this time of year. Tarpon cruise the beaches in summer and a number of big fish are caught from the pier. There are runs of spotted seatrout and bluefish in the fall, some pretty good whiting fishing in the winter, and some good days for redfish in April and May and September and October.

Directions: The pier is on 6th Avenue South. From the intersection with US 90, take A1A south 0.4 mile to 6th Avenue South. Turn left and go two blocks to the pier.

For more information: Call the pier office at (904) 246-6001.

CLAY AND ST. JOHNS COUNTIES

18. KINGSLEY LAKE

Fresh; Boat; Ramp.

Description: This partly developed lake is only accessible via a private ramp. It is a very popular lake for swimming.

Fishing Index: Kingsley is a deep lake with fair to good largemouth and good sunshine bass fishing according to Dewey Weaver of the GFC. Most of the bass are caught in 30 to 40 feet of water. It is also a good place for bluegills and shellcrackers.

Directions: The private ramp is at Strickland's Landing. Strickland's is 7 miles east of Starke on FL 16, along the north side of the lake.

For more information: Call Strickland's Landing at (904) 533-2321.

19. MAGNOLIA AND LOWERY LAKES

Fresh; Bank and Boat; Ramp.

Description: These two lakes in southwest Clay County are GFC fish Management Areas. Lowery Lake, referred to as Sand Hill Lake on some maps, is a deep lake with a white-sand bottom. Magnolia Lake is highly regarded by some anglers.

Fishing Index: Largemouth bass, bream, and crappie are the targeted species. The GFC stocks some hybrid (sunshine) bass in the lakes. Both lakes have fish attractors and brush piles to enhance fishing activity. Best times to fish are in spring and fall for bass and winter for crappie. For the largemouths use a live bait or troll with a deep diving plug. The intense summer heat drives most anglers away, but you may have good results fishing at night.

Directions: From Keystone Heights drive 1.7 miles north on FL 21. Turn left onto Treat Road and drive about 1.5 miles to the Magnolia Lake ramp. Continue 1.9 miles to the access road to the Lowery Lake ramp.

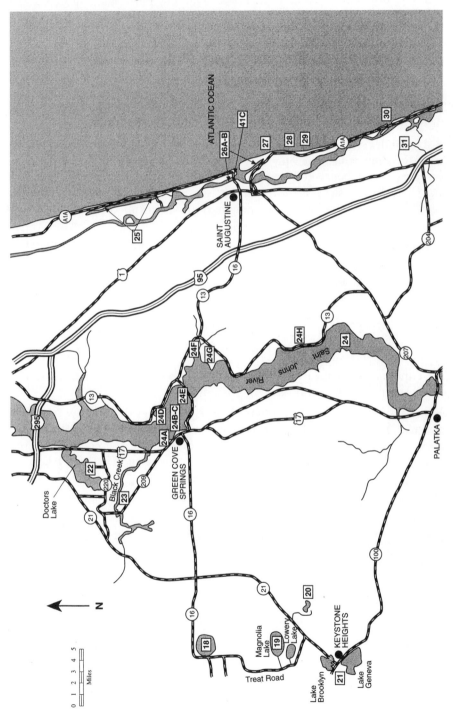

For more information: Call the GFC office at (904) 758-0525. Local lake condition information is available at Perrets Hunting and Fishing Shop at (904) 473-3801.

20. GOLD HEAD BRANCH STATE PARK

Fresh; Bank and Boat; Ramp; $.

Description: This 1,500-acre park is in the sandy hills of Florida's central ridge. The park has a campground, nature trails, and canoes for rent.

Fishing Index: As of early 1995 the water level in Lake Johnson was so low the ramp was unusable. The only way to fish the lake is from the banks or by carrying a small boat or canoe from the ramp to the water. Once the lake level rises, bass fishing should recover and be very good for a few years. Under low water conditions, anglers are catching bass and panfish, especially during the cooler months.

Directions: From Keystone Heights drive about 5.7 miles north on FL 21 to the park entrance.

For more information: Call the park office at (352) 473-4701.

21. LAKE GENEVA AND BROOKLYN LAKE

Fresh; Bank and Boat; Ramp.

Description: Two of the numerous clear-water, white-sand bottomed lakes typical of this region. Geneva is heavily used by water skiers.

Fishing Index: The best largemouth bass fishing is in the shallow waters in spring. Other times of the year, fish the deep waters of these lakes for this species. Use a deep diving crankbait or live shiners. The best crappie action is during the colder months. Shellcracker fishing is also good on both lakes.

Directions: The lakes are in Keystone Heights. Lake Geneva is on the south side of this small community. Brooklyn Lake is to the north. Public ramps to both lakes are on FL 100 in Keystone Heights.

For more information: Call Perret's Hunting and Fishing Shop in Keystone Heights at (904) 473-3801.

22. DOCTORS LAKE

Salt and Fresh; Bank and Boat; Ramps.

Description: This lake has a direct attachment to the St. Johns River. Although the water is brackish and tidal, fresh and saltwater fish are caught in the lake year-round.

Fishing Index: Billy Hamm, owner of Whitey's Camp on the south shore of Doctors Lake, says that most anglers target largemouth bass from late winter through spring. In summer, bass fishing continues, but at least half the anglers turn their attention to redfish and spotted seatrout. A run of shrimp in summer brings cast netters to work the waters at Doctors Inlet, the opening of the lake into the St. Johns River. You can also catch bream through much of the year and a few striped bass in winter.

Directions: The lake is immediately south of the city of Orange Park. There is a public ramp on the south side of the lake. From the intersection with US 17 drive about 1 mile east on Doctors Inlet Road (FL 220). Turn north onto Lakeshore Drive and follow the road about 1.5 miles to the ramp. There are private ramps at Doctors Lake Marina near the US 17 bridge over Doctors Inlet and Whitey's Camp. You can also rent a boat, hire a guide, or fish from the docks at Whitey's.

For more information: Call Whitey's Camp at (904) 269-4198.

23. BLACK CREEK
Salt and Fresh; Boat; Ramp.

Description: This unusual creek has some 30- to 40-foot-deep sections and is a "hard place to fish," according to John Stone, manager of nearby Whitey's Camp. The creek is a small tributary of the St. Johns River.

Fishing Index: Fish the shallower waters along the shoreline for largemouth bass, bream, and spotted seatrout. In fall some striped bass move into the creek and are caught with live shiners around the upper part of the creek near Middleburg.

Directions: Drive about 3 miles east from Blanding Boulevard (FL 21) or 6.3 miles west from US 17 on Doctors Inlet road (FL 220). Turn south onto Russell Road and go about 1.7 miles to the turnoff for the ramp.

For more information: Call Whitey's Camp at (904) 269-4198.

24. ST. JOHNS RIVER (BUCKMAN BRIDGE TO PALATKA)——
Fresh; Boat, Bank and Pier; Ramp.

Description: This segment of the river, from the Buckman Bridge (I-295) to a few miles north of Palatka, is primarily a freshwater fishery with the exception of the north section of the river. Although the river is still tidal at this point, the amplitude is small and the wind plays just as important a role as the tides in determining water levels in the river. Numerous small creeks flow into the St. Johns and should not be overlooked when fishing in this area.

Fishing Index: Fish year-round for largemouth bass, crappie, bream, and catfish. A few striped bass are caught around the Shands Bridge (FL 16). The river is still more than a mile wide and most of the fishing is done close to shore in shallow water. The area also has a good blue crab fishery and a shrimp run in July and August.

C.C. Corey, a veteran guide who specializes in fishing the St. Johns River, says fishing for largemouth bass isn't that complicated. "It has basic needs and reacts accordingly." Based on that he follows a definite pattern when looking for this famous gamefish. "In February and March, when the fish are spawning, fish the shallow coves along the river. Look for eelgrass beds because that's the fish's favorite spawning bed. When the fronts come through, move out to slightly deeper water. In the May and June post-spawn period, the fish may not bite as much. Try the deeper eelgrass beds. In the hot summer months the largemouths move into deeper water. This time of year it's important to fish where there's current. The best places to try are the deep creeks, bridge pilings, and shell beds. Beginning in October, the fish will move back into the shallow water. Look for them in the coves around the floating cover like hydrilla weeds. And in December and January, when it's cold, fish the deeper waters or try some of the warm spring runs."

Pinkham Pacetti's family has operated Pacetti's Marina on the St. Johns River since 1929. An avid angler, he had this tip for bream fishing in the spring. "In March and April we use live crickets for bream. For the best results they need to be alive when in the water. The way to do this to hook them through the collar behind the neck. This also makes the cricket float in the natural face-down position."

Access Points:

24A. GOVERNORS CREEK—*Fresh; Boat and Pier; Ramp.*
Description: A small pier next to the ramp allows anglers to fish in the cove near the creek's confluence with the St. Johns River. The water around the pier is shallow but anglers still report good catches of bass, panfish, and mullet.
Directions: On US 17 about 1 mile north of Green Cove Springs.

24B. SPRING PARK—*Pier.*
Description: A good place to take a kid fishing and have a fun family outing. During the shrimp run, this is a popular place to net the tasty crustaceans.
Directions: In Green Cove Springs, turn on Walnut Street and go two blocks to the park.

24C. SHANDS PIER—*Pier; Ramp.*
Description: The recently reworked pier is part of the old road bridge over the St. Johns River. Besides being a popular place to fish, it is an excellent place to cast net shrimp during the summer run. Shrimp are attracted to the lights on the pier. Shrimpers use chum to bring the shrimp close enough to cast net.
Directions: Just south of Green cove Springs. From the west side of FL 16 (Shands Bridge), turn onto Shands Pier Road and follow it to the free pier and boat ramp.

24D. ORANGEDALE PIER—*Pier.*
Description: This is the St. Johns County side of the old Shands Bridge.
Directions: The pier is on FL 13 about 1 mile north of FL 16.

24E. SHANDS BRIDGE—*Bridge and Bank.*
Description: There is a narrow walkway on this bridge for anglers to use. You

can also fish from the embankments around the east and west sides of the bridge.

Directions: This is the FL 13 bridge over the St. Johns River. Green Cove Springs is on the west side of the river.

24F. TROUT CREEK PARK—*Boat and Bank; Ramp.*
Description: A county park.
Directions: The park is 2.3 miles south of the Shands Bridge off FL 13. Turn onto Collier Road and follow it a short distance to the park.
For more information: Pacetti's Marina is also on Trout Creek and is near the park. They have bait and tackle, boat rentals, and a ramp. Call them at (904) 284-5356.

24G. PALMO—*Ramp; Boat.*
Description: This is a GFC-maintained ramp.
Directions: From the junction with FL 16, drive about 5.1 miles south on FL 13. Turn onto Palmo Fish Camp Road and go 1.9 miles to the ramp.

24H. RIVERDALE PARK—*Ramp; Boat and Bank.*
Description: A small county park where you can fish from shore and launch a small boat.
Directions: The park is on FL 13 about 1.5 miles south of CR 214.

25. GUANA RIVER STATE PARK
Salt; Boat, Bank and Surf; Ramp; $.

Description: This unique coastal park features large sand dunes and an unspoiled beach for surf fishing in the Atlantic Ocean. On the west side of A1A is Guana Lake, a brackish-water lake created by a small dam at the south end of the lake. The lake is a wildlife management area and boats using it are limited to ten horsepower. This is a day-use facility and services are limited. Bring all the bait and tackle you'll need for the day.

Fishing Index: Surf fish for whiting and pompano. The lake has good fishing for spotted seatrout and flounder. This is also a popular place to catch blue crabs.

Directions: Six Mile Ramp is maintained by the GFC. It is near the park's south beach use area, about 10 miles south of Jacksonville Beach and 10 miles north of St. Augustine on A1A. Take the access road to the ramp. Land-based anglers can fish around the dam at the south end of Guana Lake. There is a primitive ramp for small boats at the dam that allows access to the Guana River, which flows south to St. Augustine. To reach the dam drive 8 miles north on A1A from the bridge over the Tolomato River near St. Augustine. Turn off of A1A onto a dirt road and look for the park signs.

For more information: Call the park office at (904) 825-5071.

26. St. Augustine

Salt; Boat; Bridge, and Pier; Ramp.

Description: The nation's oldest city, St. Augustine is a major stop for many Florida tourists. Visitors with some free time can surf fish from the area's beaches, dangle a hook off some of the local bridges, or charter a boat for a day of backwater or Atlantic Ocean fishing.

Fishing Index: Along the Intracoastal Waterway and the tidal creeks associated with it, anglers will find redfish, spotted seatrout, flounder, and sheepshead. At the inlet, you can catch any of these species plus bluefish, tarpon, and Spanish mackerel. Along the beach, you might find all of the above plus pompano and, in the heat of summer, some king mackerel. See the Atlantic Ocean listing for information on offshore angling.

Access:

26A. Vilano Road Bridge—*Salt; Bridge; Ramp.*
Description: One of the best places to fish from land is this bridge which spans the Tolomato River on the north side of Saint Augustine.
Directions: Drive 1 mile west on A1A (first called May Street and then Vilano Road). The ramp is on the west side of the bridge.

26B. Lighthouse Park—*Salt; Pier; Ramp.*
Description: The park is on Salt Run, a dead end spur south of Saint Augustine Inlet.
Directions: Turn off of US 1 onto A1A in Saint Augustine and drive south about 1.8 miles to Old Beach Road. Turn left and go to the park.

The art of throwing a cast net takes some practice, but once mastered, virtually guarantees you'll have fresh, live bait whenever it's around.

27. ANASTASIA STATE RECREATION AREA

Salt; Bank and Surf; $.

Description: The park has a campground, picnic area, nature trail, and swimming beach. It is also a good place for watching shorebirds.

Fishing Index: Surf fish in the Atlantic Ocean for whiting and pompano. Fish from the shore of Salt Run Lagoon for redfish, spotted seatrout, and flounder.

Directions: The park entrance road is 1.4 miles south of the A1A bridge over the Intracoastal Waterway in St. Augustine.

For more information: Call the park office at (904) 461-2033.

28. OCEAN PIER

Salt; Pier; $.

Description: This is a 600-foot pier. No saltwater fishing license is needed. Bait and tackle and rod rentals are available at the pier.

Fishing Index: In spring, anglers do well on black drum, sheepshead, Spanish mackerel, and cobia. Flounder soon join the crowd and are a summer favorite. Whiting and bluefish are year-round residents along the beach, thus anglers will always have something to fish for from the pier.

Directions: The pier is about 5.3 miles south of St. Augustine on A1A in St. Augustine Beach.

For more information: Call the pier office at (904) 461-0119.

29. FRANK BUTLER PARK

Salt; Surf, Bank and Boat; Ramp.

Description: This is a county park. You can fish the Matanzas River from the shoreline and surf fish on the Atlantic side.

Fishing Index: According to Gene Hurley, manager of nearby Devil's Elbow Fishing Camp, the river is a good year-round place to fish for redfish, sheepshead, and blue crabs. Tarpon and mangrove snapper are in the river from May to September and there is good spotted seatrout fishing from November to March.

Directions: The ramp is 2.4 miles south of the A1A-FL 3 intersection on A1A. Turn onto Palmetto Road and go a short distance to the ramp. The access road to the Matanzas River is 0.2 mile south of Palmetto Road, and the beach access is an additional 0.2 mile south on A1A.

For more information: Call Devil's Elbow Fishing Camp at (904) 471-0398.

30. MATANZAS PASS

Salt; Bridge, Surf, and Bank.

Description: This is an uncharted pass subject to constant change. Boaters without local knowledge and experience should not attempt to use this inlet. Fort Matanzas is just north of the pass on A1A. The stone tower, built in 1742, was a watching post to help the Spanish protect St. Augustine from the British.

Fishing Index: Fish around the inlet for redfish, spotted seatrout, tarpon, sheeps–head, and flounder. In the surf are whiting and pompano. Look for sandbars and submerged rocks; the fish love to congregate in these areas. The river has year-round redfish and fall and winter runs of spotted seatrout and a few snook during the warmer months.

Directions: The pass is 15 miles south of St. Augustine on A1A. Try fishing off the A1A bridge over the inlet, a smaller bridge 0.9 mile to the south, in the surf south of the pass down to the county line, and along the river beginning 1.5 miles south of the bridge.

31. FAVER-DYKES STATE PARK

Salt and Fresh; Bank and Boat; Ramp; $.

Description: This secluded park has campsites and picnic facilities. You can also rent canoes and paddle Pellicer Creek. The ramp allows small boats to access the brackish waters of Pellicer Creek, which runs into the Matanzas River. You can also go upstream and do some freshwater fishing. Land-bound anglers can fish from the dock by the ramp or from the shoreline in the picnic area.

Fishing Index: Fish this area for the same species found in the Matanzas River; spotted seatrout, redfish, flounder, and tarpon. In the freshwater part of the creek there are largemouth bass and panfish.

Directions: The entrance road to the park is just north of I-95 on US 1.

For more information: Call the park office at (904) 794-0997.

PUTNAM AND FLAGLER COUNTIES

32. ST. JOHNS RIVER (PALATKA TO LITTLE LAKE GEORGE)

Fresh; Boat; Ramp.

Description: The St. Johns is your source for freshwater fishing. The river narrows as you go south and upriver. If you head up Dunns Creek, a tributary of the big river, you'll end up in Crescent Lake (see site 33), not a bad place to be if you like to fish for crappie.

Moving upriver from Palatka, the river narrows considerably until you get to Little Lake George where it begins to widen again. The largemouth bass pat-

PUTNAM AND FLAGLER COUNTIES

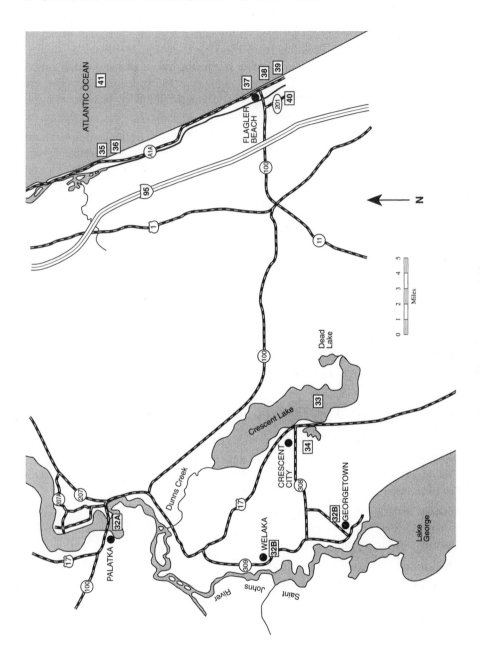

tern is very similar to the pattern described by C.C. Corey in the Palatka-to-I-295 segment of the river (see site 24).

Fishing Index: Striped bass fishing is popular along this part of the river. One of the best known spots for stripers in the summer is the "Croaker Hole," a freshwater spring that boils up from the river bottom. In July and August, when the shrimp migrate up the river, try using live shrimp to catch largemouth bass. Use a slip float to get your bait near the bottom in areas where there is current. Anchor upstream and drift back to where the bass are congregating.

Directions: The "Croaker Hole" is along the west shore of the St. Johns about 2 miles south of where the Ocklawaha River flows into the St. Johns.

Access Points:
32A. PALATKA—*Boat; Ramp.*
Description: There is one public ramp in downtown Palatka and two across the river in East Palatka. To reach the city ramp turn off of US 17 onto 2nd Street. Go 2 blocks and turn onto River Street. One of the East Palatka ramps is off US 17. About 0.8 mile from the US 17-FL 207 intersection turn onto Boat Ramp Road and follow it to the ramp. The other is a GFC ramp 4.3 miles north of the US 17-FL 207 intersection on FL 207. Turn right at CR 207 A and follow the road to the ramp.

32B. WELAKA TO GEORGETOWN—*Boat; Ramp.*
Description: There are public ramps at Welaka and Georgetown. Both are a short distance off FL 309. Also, there are numerous private fish camps along FL 309. Most have ramps, bait and tackle, and other amenities.

33. CRESCENT AND DEAD LAKES ——————————

Fresh; Boat; Ramp.

Description: Crescent Lake, a 16,000-acre natural lake, and the much smaller Dead Lake connect to the St. Johns River via Dunns Creek. The lakes harbor a lot of natural cover including lily pads, stumps, and grasses.

Fishing Index: Joe Howell, owner of Lake Crescent Resort, says the crappie fishing is very good on the lake. "Trolling with a crappie jig, like a Halfly, usually produces good results."

Directions: The lakes are southeast of Palatka. Access to the western shore is via a ramp on US 17 in Crescent City. Parking is limited. Access to the eastern shore is via the ramp on FL 100. From the intersection with US 17, drive about 9.2 miles east on FL 100 to the turnoff for the ramp. Or from US 1, drive about 14 miles west on FL 100 to the ramp.

For more information: Call Lake Crescent Resort at (904) 689-2485.

Black crappie, also called specs or speckled perch, are a favorite fish of freshwater anglers.

34. LAKE STELLA ──────────────

Fresh; Boat; Ramp.

Description: This small lake is across the highway from Crescent Lake in Crescent City. Joe Howell of Lake Crescent Resort suggests fishing Lake Stella on windy days instead of the much larger and rougher Crescent Lake.

Fishing Index: The lake has good bass and bream fishing.

Directions: There is a public boat ramp in Crescent City. From US 17, turn onto FL 308 and go east about 0.6 mile to the ramp.

For more information: Call Lake Crescent Resort at (904) 689-2485.

35. WASHINGTON OAKS STATE GARDENS ──────────

Salt; Surf and Bank; $.

Description: The site was originally part of the Bella Vista Plantation and dated back to the mid 1800s. A formal garden was added to the native coastal hammock by Owen Young, former chairman of the board of General Electric. The property was donated to the state in 1964. Anglers can fish the Matanzas River from the seawall near the interpretive center or surf fish around the exposed rock along this part of the beach.

Fishing Index: Fish in the river for spotted seatrout, redfish, flounder, and some snook. Surf casters will find bluefish, whiting, and pompano. Limestone outcrops provide cover for fish just off the beach; fishing around them is usually excellent.

Directions: The park is on A1A about 19 miles south of St. Augustine and 30 miles north of Daytona Beach.

For more information: Call the park office at (904) 446-6780.

36. BING LANDING COUNTY PARK ──────────────

Salt; Boat and Pier; Ramp.

Description: This small park provides anglers with another access point to the Matanzas River.

Fishing Index: Fish in the river for redfish, spotted seatrout, and flounder.

Directions: The park is 0.8 mile south of Washington Oaks State Gardens on A1A.

37. VARN BEACH

Salt; Surf.

Description: A county beach access area for swimmers and surf fishing. In addition, there is a 2.5-mile stretch of beach 1.5 miles south of Varn Beach where you can park and fish in the surf.

Fishing Index: The typical surf fare—whiting, pompano, and maybe a redfish or two—are what anglers can expect along this part of the beach.

Directions: Varn Park is 5.2 miles north of Flagler Beach on A1A.

38. FLAGLER PIER

Salt; Pier; $.

Description: A 1,500-foot city-owned pier. Bait, tackle, and rod rentals are available.

Fishing Index: The pier is a popular place to catch whiting and bluefish year-round. Spanish mackerel and pompano are caught in spring and summer.

Directions: The pier is 0.1 mile south of FL 100 on A1A in Flagler Beach.

For more information: Call the pier office at (904) 439-4169.

39. GAMBLE ROGERS MEMORIAL STATE RECREATION AREA

Salt; Surf, Bank and Boat; Ramp.

Description: This coastal facility has a plush beachfront campground, picnic area, and nature trail. Bank fishing and the ramp are on the Intracoastal Waterway.

Fishing Index: Flounder, spotted seatrout, and redfish are the target species along the Intracoastal Waterway. In the surf anglers catch pompano, whiting, and bluefish.

Directions: The park is on A1A in Flagler Beach 3.1 miles south of FL 100.

For more information: Call the park office at (904) 517-2086.

40. BULOW PLANTATION RUINS STATE HISTORIC SITE

Salt; Boat; Ramp.

Description: This site of an old plantation dates back to the Second Seminole Indian War. Bulow Creek can be fished from a small boat, but a low bridge prevents access to the Intracoastal Waterway. This is a good place to canoe.

Fishing Index: The winding creek is a good place to fish for redfish, flounder, spotted seatrout, and an occasional small snook or tarpon.

Directions: The park is west of Flagler Beach. Take FL 100 west 1.2 miles to CR 201 (Anderson Highway). Take CR 201 south for 2.2 miles to the park entrance.

For more information: Call the park office at (904) 517-2084.

41. ATLANTIC OCEAN

Salt; Boat.

Description: The Atlantic is home to big, bluewater fish: migrating schools of cobia and king mackerel and bottom-dwelling groupers and snappers. There's good offshore angling from a few miles offshore to more than 50 miles out in the Gulf Stream. Several charter fleets operate in this part of the state with the biggest centered in St. Augustine.

Fishing Index: King mackerel, tarpon, and some cobia are the common targets of the close-in offshore anglers. Cobia are the first of the big migrating fish to show up near the coast. May is the top month around St. Augustine. Anglers look for this fish by watching for the big manta rays as they move north for the summer. The rays, with wingspans in excess of 5 feet, are easy to spot and there always seem to be some cobia around them. The kings reach their peak from June to August. The fish move close to shore throughout the entire region, sometimes getting close enough for pier and surf anglers to catch them. Tarpon also move into the area in the summer. They are also close to shore, usually within 3 miles.

Bottom fishing for grouper, snapper, and seabass is popular from the artificial reefs and wrecks close to shore to the deeper rocky bottoms and step slopes of the continental shelf farther out. Visitors to the area who want to try this type of fishing should consider one of the head boats. Generally they have half- and full-day trips and always return to port with some fish.

Bill Kerr of Commanche Cove Sport Fishing Charters in St. Augustine says, "there is excellent bluewater fishing off the coast of St. Augustine and perhaps the best wahoo fishing in the state." April to mid-June are the best times to make the long trip offshore to the edge of the Gulf Stream. Anglers have a very good chance of catching sailfish, blue marlin, wahoo, dolphin, and blackfin and yellowfin tuna. Robert Johnson, one of the captains operating out of the St. Augustine area, summed up offshore fishing this part of the Atlantic coast by saying, "You will find something that's fun to catch and good to eat year-round. No day is a total loss because we have such a big variety of fish to catch."

Fleet Locations:

41A. FERNANDINA BEACH.

Description: About 20 boats operate out of the area. Not too many of the boats fish the Gulfstream because it is so far offshore from here compared to other locations along the coast.

For more information: Call the Amelia Charter Boat Association at (904) 261-2870. If he's available, talk to Captain Terry Lacoss.

41B. Mayport.

Description: Only a few head boats operate out of this small port. They dock near the Mayport Ferry.

For more information: Consult the local telephone directory.

41C. St. Augustine.

Description: The northeast's largest fleet, about 40 boats, operate from this popular tourist city.

For more information: Several boats dock at Commanche Cove; call (904) 825-1971. A few boats use Matanzas Pass 13 miles south of St. Augustine. Alan Zamba is one of them at (904) 471-1841.

Month by Month in Northeast Florida

Note: Offshore is defined as greater than 5 miles from the coast. Coastal waters include open waters inside of 5 miles including surf fishing, and all brackish water area such as bays, the saltwater regions of rivers, and lagoons. Freshwater includes, lakes, ponds, reservoirs, rivers, and phosphate pits.

January

Offshore: Weather is a major factor in the ability to get offshore. Best times are a few days after the most recent front has passed. Best bets are seabass and gag grouper.

Coastal: An excellent time to surf fish for whiting; redfish can be plentiful on parts of the St. Johns and in the numerous tidal creeks along the ICW north and south of the St. Johns River, the key to success is to fish the deeper holes especially when the weather is cold.

Freshwater: Striped and sunshine bass fishing is very good in the St. Marys, Nassau, and St. Johns rivers; fish around structures such as pilings and docks. A top month for crappie in the lakes and rivers.

February

Offshore: Another month where you must keep an eye on the weather; the best bets continue to be grouper and seabass.

Coastal: Very good whiting action on the Jacksonville Beach Pier and surf fishing. Fish around the inlets with jetties for a mixed bag of sheepshead, bluefish, redfish, black drum, and flounder; the best days will be the warmer ones.

Freshwater: This month marks the beginning of the best big largemouth bass months. The females start to bed especially in the shallow lakes where the water warms up faster than in the deeper lakes and rivers. Crappie and striped bass fishing continues to be excellent throughout the region.

March

Offshore: The pelagic, migratory fish begin to move through the region on their way north. Wahoo fishing along the edge of the Gulfstream begins to really turn on along with some dolphin and blackfin tuna. Closer to shore the gag grouper and seabass fishing is good; cobia action begins to pick up around the reefs and wrecks.

Coastal: Start looking for migrating manta rays close to shore, the cobia will be close by. Traditionally a good time for whiting, sheepshead, and giant black drum. The big spotted seatrout show up around St. Augustine; crevalle jacks make their annual appearance and remain through summer and early fall.

Freshwater: Largemouth bass and crappie are the top freshwater fish; live shiners for the largemouths and Missouri minnows for the crappie are favorite baits. Don't overlook angling for catfish—it's always good and the small ones are easy to catch. Stripers are still good especially on the St. Marys River; hybrids are in the waning days of their peak time.

APRIL

Offshore: A top month for cobia. To increase your chances try using some chum to stir up the action. At the edge of the continental shelf near the Gulf Stream waters the wahoo will be very good. This is the beginning of the prime time for dolphin, blackfin and yellowfin tuna, sailfish, and blue marlin off St. Augustine; overall a good offshore month exceeded only by May.

Coastal: This is a very good month for coastal species. Top month for close-in cobia, many fish are caught by anglers fishing from the surf. Peak time for giant black drum; fish for them around structures. Also one of the best months for big "gator" spotted seatrout. Spanish mackerel fishing will be very good around the inlet and in the St. Johns River up to Mill Cove. Flounder fishing is at its springtime peak.

Freshwater: Last month for trophy bass in cooler water locations; try the eel-grass-covered coves along the St. Johns River. Bream fishing, which is for shellcrackers and bluegills, enters prime time; live crickets are a great bait.

MAY

Offshore: Traditionally the best "bluewater" month. Along the edge of the Gulf Stream there will be best-of-the-year action for dolphin, wahoo, tuna, sailfish, and marlin. King mackerel activity is on the upswing 10-15 miles out; lots of cobia out there too.

Coastal: A strong month for big spotted seatrout and flounder. Spanish mackerel move from the inlets to the nearshore waters. Redfish activity improves. Maybe a few tarpon showing up at the south end of the region. Continued great surf and nearshore fishing for cobia. Look for pompano in the surf.

Freshwater: Shellcracker and bluegill action gets into high gear as largemouth bass and crappie action slows down.

JUNE

Offshore: A very good month for wahoo, marlin, dolphin, and blackfin tuna. Sailfish may be as close as 80-foot contour. Prime time to chum up some king mackerel in the 10-15 mile range. Can be very productive month for amber-jacks in less than 100 feet of water.

Coastal: Some of the best redfish action is going on especially around the inlets with jetties. Try fishing at night for spotted seatrout. Tarpon move into the nearshore area and up the St. Johns River. Some big "smoker" king mackerel will be near the inlets and along the beach; cobia will mix with the kings close to shore.

Freshwater: Shellcracker and bluegill action is at peak. Start fishing for large-mouth bass in the deeper waters.

JULY

Offshore: King mackerel top the action this month. Mangrove snapper enter their prime time. Sailfish action has been good in recent years. Amberjack and cobia are good bets over the reefs.

Coastal: Prime time for tarpon; look for the fish a couple of miles offshore and in the inlets. Big king mackerel are close to shore; some are caught from the beach. Redfish action is very good around the inlets. Try night fishing from the bridges for small tarpon, seatrout, ladyfish, and jacks, plus it's a lot cooler than midday.

Freshwater: Summer pattern in place; fish early in the morning and late in the day on the lakes. On the St. Johns, fish for largemouth bass in the deep sections of the creeks emptying into the river; fish where there is current. If the shrimp run is on in the St. Johns River, use live shrimp for bait. Don't overlook catfish; they're always biting.

AUGUST

Offshore: Last of the best months for king mackerel. Top month for mangrove snapper. Sailfish action is good. Amberjack, barracuda, and sharks on the reefs and wrecks.

Coastal: Last month for hot tarpon, king mackerel, and cobia action. Redfish activity is usually strong. Continue to fish at night for good action and comfort. Usually the last good month for pompano.

Freshwater: It's the heat of summer; fish deep and stay out of the midday heat. For something different, fish for largemouths with live shrimp on the St. Johns River; the action should be very, very good.

SEPTEMBER

Offshore: The familiar favorites—wahoo, dolphin, tuna, sailfish, and marlin—are around but none is at peak time.

Coastal: A prime month for flounder and spotted seatrout in the south part of the region. Above average redfish action along the ICW. Last good month to get a tarpon; the fish are migrating south to keep warm.

Freshwater: Not much change in activity or strategy since June.

OCTOBER

Offshore: Average fishing for the Gulf Stream species (wahoo, dolphin, tuna, marlin). Average fishing for amberjack, barracuda, king mackerel, and cobia. Gag grouper action may be slightly better than average.

Coastal: Lots of spotted seatrout and flounder available especially around Mayport. Redfish action is good around the inlets; try the surf too.

Freshwater: Largemouth bass start to move to shallower waters. Crappie action will improve.

NOVEMBER

Offshore: Yellowfin tuna can be abundant and may be the best bet. Fair action on the Gulf Stream species. Gag grouper action is good. Weather becomes a factor in making long trips offshore.

Coastal: Flounder fishing is outstanding. First real good month of the winter whiting season; fish for them from the surf. Lots of spotted seatrout around and plenty of redfish unless the cold weather arrives early.

Freshwater: A mixed bag. Largemouth bass fishing can be pretty good if its warm. If it's cold striped bass and crappie action will pick up.

DECEMBER

Offshore: Gag grouper and red snapper fishing is a good bet as long as the weather is good. The Gulf Stream species are out there but not in the numbers seen in May and June; keep in touch with local contacts on the advisability of heading offshore.

Coastal: No outstanding species this time of year. Sheepshead, which are consistent all year, might look pretty good because not much else is biting. Some areas on the inside will have good periods of redfish activity.

Freshwater: Crappie action begins its best time. Largemouth bass will be in deeper water especially if it's cold. Striped bass action can be very good in the St. Marys River; ask locally before taking to the water.

NORTHEAST FLORIDA FISH AVAILABILITY CHART

NOTE: Refer to the month-by-month table for additional information. Information in this chart represents the seasonal patterns observed over the past three years. For salt water species, the arrival of the migrant species and the peak times for each species is heavily dependent on water temperature. Unusually warm or cold periods will effect the patterns described above.

■ signifies a reasonable chance of catching this species in that month.

❏ signifies the optimal months for catching the species.

SPECIES	JAN	FEB	MAR	APR	MAY	JUN	JUL	AUG	SEP	OCT	NOV	DEC
Redfish	❏	■	■	■	■	❏	❏	■	❏	❏	❏	❏
Spotted Seatrout	■	■	■	❏	❏	■	■	■	■	❏	❏	■

Species	Jan	Feb	Mar	Apr	May	Jun	Jul	Aug	Sep	Oct	Nov	Dec
Sheepshead	■	■	■	■	■	■	■	■	■	■	■	□
Mangrove Snapper	■	■	■	■	■	■	□	□	□	■	■	■
Seabass	■	■	■	■	■	■	■	■	■	■	■	■
Red Snapper	■	■	■	■	■	■	■	■	■	■	■	■
Gag Grouper	■	■	■	■	■	■	■	■	■	■	■	■
Bluefish	■	■	■	□	■	■	■	■	■	■	■	■
Flounder	■	■	■	□	□	■	■	■	□	□	□	■
Black Drum	■	■	□	□	■	■	■	■	■	■	■	■
Dolphin	■	■	■	■	□	□	■	■	■	■	■	■
Blackfin Tuna	■	■	■	■	□	□	■	■	■	■	■	■
Blue Marlin	■	■	■	■	□	□	■	■	■	■	■	■
Wahoo	■	■	□	□	■	■		■	■	■	■	■
Whiting	□	□	□	■	■	■			■	■	□	□
Amberjack	■	■				■	■	■	■	■	■	
Sailfish		■	■	■	■	■	□	□	■	■	■	
Little Tunny			■	■	■	■	■	■	■	■		
Cobia				■	□	□	■	■	■	■	■	
Spanish Mackerel			■	□	■	■	■		■	■	■	
Yellowfin Tuna			■	■	■					■	■	■
King Mackerel				■	■	■	□	■	■	■		■
Crevalle Jack				■	■	■	■	■	■	■	■	
Shrimp					■	■	■	■	■			
Shark (all species)					■	■	■	■	■	■		
Tarpon						■	■	□	□	■		
Largemouth Bass	■	□	□	□	■	■	■	■	■	■	■	■
Bluegill	■	■	■	□	□	□	■	■	■	■	■	■
Catfish	■	■	■	■	■	■	■	■	■	■	■	■
Shellcracker	■	■	■	□	□	□	■	■	■	■	■	■
Sunshine Bass	□	□	■	■				■	■	■	■	■
Striped Bass	□	□	■	■				■	■	■	■	■
Crappie	□	□	□	■	■			■	■	■	■	□

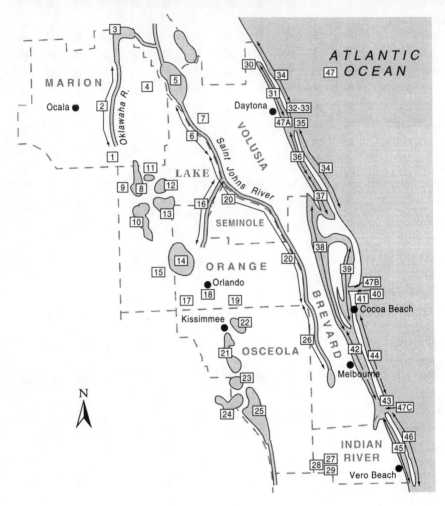

CHAPTER SIX
East Central Florida

COUNTIES: ▪ Marion (eastern) ▪ Putnam (southeastern)▪ Lake ▪ Volusia ▪ Seminole ▪ Orange ▪ Osceola ▪ Brevard ▪ Indian River

SALTWATER FISHING

Indian River Lagoon—1 mile wide and 3 feet deep for much of its expanse—is the major coastal feature along much of east-central Florida. Along with the Halifax River, another coastal lagoon, the two systems stretch the entire length of the coast. The shallow, seagrass-rich environment is prime fishing grounds for redfish and spotted seatrout. The Indian River system is home to 700 salt- and freshwater fish species and harbors one-third of the state's population of manatees. Nearly all the clams harvested in Florida come from the lagoon. Nationally, this adds up to 15 percent of the total harvest. One part of the Indian River system, Mosquito Lagoon, reportedly has the best redfishing in the state, and the nearby Banana River is high on the list.

After decades of urban growth, pollution, and subsequent clean-up programs, Indian River is again healthy but it still needs help. Several programs are already in place, including the Indian River Lagoon National Estuary Program, the St. Johns Water Management District, and the Surface Water Improvement and Management program. For more information about the important programs and activities coordinated by the National Estuary Program staff, call 1 800 226-3747 in Florida or (407) 984-4950 from out of state.

The lagoons are linked to the Atlantic Ocean by a series of inlets that are magnets for fish and anglers. Snook, Florida's ultimate saltwater game fish, is one of the most sought-after inlet inhabitants from spring to fall. In winter, doormat-sized flounder show up, while snook seek out warmer waters in the creeks emptying into the lagoon.

Offshore, dolphin and sailfish give meat and sport anglers something to fish for. This part of the coast benefits from the spring and fall run of the pelagic species: Spanish and king mackerel, cobia, dolphin, and blackfin tuna. Of course grouper and snapper feed on the bottom all year. From the beach to more than 50 miles offshore, the chances are really good that you will catch some fish. It's almost guaranteed if you take a charter boat and rely on the captain's expertise.

FRESHWATER FISHING

The clear-water lakes in Ocala National Forest, even the small ones, are good places to fish for big largemouth bass and specs, the regional name for crappie. Local experts say it's necessary to use light line (in both pound test and color) and small baits when fishing these lakes. The clear water makes it easy for the bass to see the line attached to your bait. That, combined with the fact that these fish have seen every type of lure ever made, gives the advantage to the fish. That doesn't mean they're uncatchable. Eventually the bass get hungry and patient anglers will reap the rewards.

Billy Snell, owner of Big Bass Guide Service in Astor, has some good advice. "If you see a spot and think it's good, don't give up. Stick with it. Usually most people are fishing the good spots but don't use the right technique for that spot at that time. Don't be disheartened if you have one bad day. All baits work and if the one you're using today wasn't successful try it tomorrow because it may be the one that works. Patience is real important."

The waters of Ocala National Forest are only the beginning of places to wet a line. The St. Johns and Ocklawaha rivers offer a number of well-known fishing holes. Lake Oklawaha, a reservoir on the Oklawaha River, and lakes George and Woodruff along the St. Johns River have long-standing reputations as great bass waters.

The large Harris chain of lakes and the smaller Clermont chain provide angling opportunities in scenic surroundings. The action on one or two lakes in each chain always seems to be really hot. Hydrilla, an introduced aquatic plant, plagues both lake chains. Fishing conditions among these lakes vary widely from month to month. "The lakes take turns," is how Diane Henning of Al Jana Fish Camp explains the panfish angling. Stop at local bait and tackle shops to check on the latest conditions.

Farther south, the Kissimmee chain, Stick Marsh, and Garcia Reservoir are some of the most famous bass fishing waters in Florida. Although these areas aren't as great as they once were, the fishing is still above average. The Kissimmee River begins in the swamps and lakes south of the Kissimmee-St. Cloud area. The lakes are linked by canals. Some are open to boaters and others have water control structures that prevent access.

MARION (EASTERN PORTION), PUTNAM (SOUTHEASTERN PORTION), LAKE (NORTHERN PORTION), AND VOLUSIA (NORTHWESTERN PORTION) COUNTIES

1. LAKE WEIR

Fresh; Boat; Ramp.

Description: A popular recreational lake that is heavily used on the weekends. Fishing tends to be more relaxed during weekdays.

Fishing Index: Fish for largemouth bass, which is best in early spring. In summer, fish for bluegills.

Directions: From Ocala, take US 441, 301, and 27 south to Belleview. Turn onto CR 25 and go about 8.7 miles to Hampton Beach. Look for the boat ramp sign and turn right onto the access road.

MARION (EASTERN PORTION), PUTNAM (SOUTHEASTERN PORTION), LAKE (NORTHERN PORTION), AND VOLUSIA (NORTHWESTERN PORTION) COUNTIES

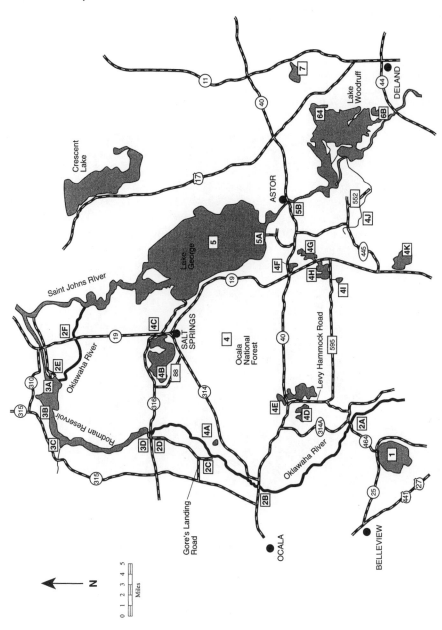

2.   OKLAWAHA RIVER ————————————————

Fresh; Boat and Bank; Ramp.

Description: The Oklawaha River has its origins in the Harris chain of lakes near Leesburg. The river flows north and eventually empties into the St. Johns River near Welaka. A series of dams along its course regulate water levels on the river. According to Eddie White of the US Army Corps of Engineers, the river has numerous obstructions and boaters must always watch out for them. "Most obstructions happen overnight when a tree falls down and blocks part or all of the river. If boaters see a hazard they should contact our office and we will remove it." To check on the status of the river or to report an obstacle call (904) 328-1002.

Fishing Index: Most of the fishing is from Eureka Dam upriver to Moss Bluff.

A bucketful of bream is the common outcome of a few hours of fishing in any of the freshwater lakes in east central Florida.

This stretch is popular for bluegills, shellcrackers, and catfish. Jeanne Knepper, owner of Forest Tackle and Archery, has fished the river all her life. She says largemouth bass fishing is good but you must know how to fish for them in the river's swift waters. The secret to success is to use a one-ounce egg sinker and a five-foot leader. The weight gets the bait to the bottom and keeps it there while the leader gives the bait, preferably a live shiner, some freedom to swim around. Most Florida anglers aren't used to fishing this way so they don't catch as many fish as they could. Another method she recommends is to anchor in the protected and slower waters of one of the numerous river bends and shiner fish using a bobber to keep the bait a few feet off the bottom..

Directions: The river is in Marion and Lake counties.

Access Points:
2A. Moss Bluff—*Bank, Pier, and Boat; Ramp.*
Description: There are two ramps, one above the Moss Bluff Lock and Dam and the other below it. There is bank fishing and a fishing pier on the upriver (south) side of the lock and dam.
Directions: From FL 25, along the north shore of Lake Weir, turn north onto FL 464 and drive about 4 miles to the lock and dam. Or from FL 40 in Ocala National Forest turn south on CR 314A and go 7 miles to the junction with FL 464. Turn right and go 0.3 mile to the lock and dam.

2B. Marion County Boat Basin—*Bank and Boat; Ramp.*
Description: This easy to reach facility has a very scenic location on the river.
Directions: The ramp is on FL 40, on the west side of the river, about 9.5 miles east of the US 27 and FL 40 intersection in Ocala.

2C. Gore's Landing—*Boat; Ramp.*
Description: The ramp is midway along the river between FL 40 and Eureka Dam.
Directions: From Silver Springs, drive 2 miles east on FL 40 and turn north on FL 315. Drive about 6.3 miles to Gore's Landing Road. Turn right and drive 3.5 miles to the ramp at road's end. About halfway, the road makes a turn to the right.

2D. Eureka Dam—*Boat and Bank; Ramp.*
Directions: From the intersection of FL 315 and FL 316 in Fort McCoy, take FL 316 east about 4 miles. The ramp is on the east side of the river, just below the dam.

2E. Oklawaha Recreation Area—*Bank, Pier, and Boat; Ramp.*
Description: This facility, formerly operated by the US Army Corps of Engineers, is now operated by the state's Office of Greenways Management. The site provides anglers with access to the segment of the Oklawaha River between the Rodman Dam and the Saint Johns River. The pier is barrier-free. Camping is at the nearby Rodman Recreation Area on the lake.
Directions: From the intersection of FL 19 and Rodman Dam Road, take Rodman Dam Road 2.6 miles to the recreation area.

2F. FL 19 Ramp—*Boat; Ramp.*
Directions: The ramp is about 9.2 miles north of the FL 19-Fl 314 intersection in Salt Springs. It is on the southwest side of the FL 19 bridge over the river.

3. Rodman Reservoir (Lake Oklawaha)

Fresh; Boat and Bank; Ramp.

Description: The Rodman Dam, about 6.5 miles upriver from the Ocklawaha's junction with the Saint Johns, forms the Rodman Reservoir (also known as Lake Oklawaha). The reservoir extends almost 13 miles upriver to the Eureka Dam which controls the flow from the river into the reservoir. A remnant of the Cross Florida Barge Canal connects the reservoir to the Saint Johns River. The lake is flooded timberland and there are many stumps along the edge of the lake that provide good cover for fish and dangerous boating conditions. Be careful.

State government officials want to remove the Rodman Dam and restore the natural flow of Oklawaha River. If done, it would lower levels on the lake up to 14 feet, effectively eliminating the lake and returning the water to the old river channel. Anglers who mostly oppose the idea, say it would destroy a significant trophy bass fishery. If the dam is removed, access via these sites will be affected.

Fishing Index: The well-known lake has a reputation as a trophy fish lake. There is very good largemouth bass fishing throughout the year. The fishing is notably good during the warmer months of the year, a departure from the normal pattern for largemouth bass. Look for the fish in places where they can get under some type of cover. Striped bass migrating up the Saint Johns River move into Rodman Reservoir in the winter and spring.

Directions: The reservoir is on the Putnam-Marion County line.

Access Points:
3A. Rodman Recreation Area—*Bank, Pier, and Boat; Ramp.*
Description: This facility, formerly operated by the US Army Corps of Engineers, is now operated by the state's Office of Greenways Management. There is a campground and picnic facilities.
Directions: From the intersection of FL 19 and Rodman Dam Road, take Rodman Dam Road 2.3 miles to the entrance to the recreation area.

3B. Kenwood Recreation Area—*Bank and Boat; Ramp.*
Description: This facility, formerly operated by the US Army Corps of Engineers, is now operated by the state's Office of Greenways Management. Primitive camping is permitted.
Directions: From the intersection of FL 19 and FL 310, take FL 310 west about
8 miles until the road ends at FL 315. Turn left and go 1.1 miles to the small settlement of Kenwood. FL 315 bends to the right. Look for the recreational area entrance sign and follow the access road to the ramp.

3C. ORANGE SPRINGS RECREATION AREA—*Boat; Ramp.*
Description: This facility, formerly operated by the US Army Corps of Engineers, is now operated by the state's Office of Greenways Management. There are no other facilities than the ramp.
Directions: From the turn-off to the Kenwood Recreation Area, continue on FL 315 an additional 4.5 miles to the community of Orange Springs. Look for the sign and turn onto the access road. If you are approaching from the west, take FL 315 north about 20 miles from its intersection with FL 40 near Silver Springs.

3D. EUREKA DAM—*Boat; Ramp.*
Description: The ramp provides access to the headwaters of the Rodman Reservoir. Another nearby ramp provides access to the river.
Directions: From the intersection of FL 315 and FL 316 in Fort McCoy, take FL 316 east about 4 miles. The access road to the ramp is on the west side of the river, just above the dam.

4. OCALA NATIONAL FOREST

Fresh; Bank, Pier, Boat and Canoe; Ramp.

Description: This 382,000-acre national forest has 23 spring-fed streams and nearly 600 lakes. While most can be fished, many are accessible only on foot or with a 4x4 vehicle. The lakes have some vegetation around them but are acidic and usually low in nutrients. Nonetheless many of them have produced bass in excess of 10 pounds. The springs and lakes listed here are easily accessible by any type of vehicle.

Fishing Index: Fish the lakes for largemouth bass, bluegills, shellcrackers, and crappie, locally referred to as "specs." Jeanne Knepper, owner of Forest Tackle and Archery, says, "You need patience to catch largemouth bass fishing on the lakes. The fish are very finicky and they have seen just about every bait manufactured. Although it's tougher now to catch a 10-pounder than it used to be, you can still catch these fish but you must wait them out." Fish the clear water lakes with small lines and baits. Some of the local guides use a camouflage line. It changes colors every foot so the line will look broken.

The creeks emanating from the springs hold largemouth bass, bluegills, specs, and, in the springs feeding Lake George, striped bass.

Directions: Ocala National Forest begins about 10 miles east of Ocala.

For more information: For up-to-the-minute information call Forest Tackle and Archery at (352) 625-5545. Talk to Jeanne Knepper. The Ocala National Forest Interpretive Association publishes a booklet entitled "Fishing Opportunities in the Ocala National Forest." It is available at the visitors centers on FL 19 and FL 40.

Access Points:
4A. FORE LAKE—*Pier; Boat.*
Description: No gasoline engines are allowed on this lake. Boats are allowed but they have to be small enough to be hand-carried to the launching site.

Fishing is best around the vegetated shoreline. There is a campground next to the lake.

Directions: From the FL 40-FL 314 intersection, a few miles west of Salt Springs take FL 314 towards Salt Springs for about 5.4 miles to the lake entrance.

4B. LAKE KERR—*Boat; Ramp.*

Description: This semistained-water lake is shallow and has considerable vegetation. Most of the property around the lake is privately owned and the lake receives heavy use by water-skiers and personal watercraft.

Directions: From the intersection of FR 88 and FL 314 a few miles west of Salt Springs take FR 88 3.4 miles to the entrance road. Drive 0.3 mile to the public boat ramp.

4C. SALT SPRINGS RUN—*Boat; Ramp.*

Description: A popular place for anglers. The run empties into Lake George and is wide enough to accommodate large boats. Swimming in the spring and camping are also popular. Look for striped bass—drifters from Lake George—in the run. Rental boats are available in Salt Springs.

Directions: The ramp is just off of FL 19 in Salt Springs.

4D. LAKE BRYANT—*Boat; Ramp.*

Description: Access is via Lake Bryant Camp.

Directions: From the intersection of FL 40 and FL 19 take FL 40 about 12 miles west and look for Levy Hammock Road (SE 183 Avenue). Turn south and go 2.4 miles Lake Bryant Camp.

For more information: Call Lake Bryant Camp at (352) 625-2376.

4E. MILL DAM LAKE—*Boat; Ramp.*

Description: A popular and convenient place to fish. The ramp may be unusable during low water.

Directions: From the intersection of FL 40 and FL 19 take FL 40 west about 11.5 miles. Turn north onto FR 79, go 0.3 mile to FR 59, turn right, and follow the road 0.3 mile to the lake.

4F. WILDCAT LAKE—*Boat; Ramp.*

Description: A clear water lake with vegetation that extends into the deeper water. Billy Snell, owner of Big Bass Guide Service, suggests using lightweight line and pitching a small shiner into the heavy vegetation. It's a good place to find a big bass but you may experience more break-offs than usual.

Directions: From the intersection of FL 40 and FL 19 take FL 40 east 0.9 mile to the entrance road to the lake.

4G. GRASSHOPPER LAKE—*Pier; Boat; Ramp.*

Description: A 147-acre clear water lake with dense vegetation along the shoreline.

Directions: From the intersection of FL 40 and FL 19 take FL 19 south 2.6 miles to the entrance road to the lake.

4H. BEAKMAN AND SELLERS LAKES—*Boat; Ramp.*

Description: These two lakes are linked by a waterway that is navigable except during low water. Both are clear water lakes that reportedly have some of the biggest bass in the region. These are difficult lakes to fish, requiring good angling skills and patience.

Directions: The ramp to Lake Beakman is just off FL 19, 3 miles south of the FL 19-FL 40 intersection. Access Sellers Lake via the channel connecting the lakes.

4I. BUCK LAKE—*Boat; Ramp.*

Description: A 52-acre lake that supports trophy-sized bass. The lake has several brush attractors. Crappie are stocked here. There is a 20-horsepower limit on outboard motors.

Directions: From the FL 19-FL 40 intersection, go south 4.5 miles on FL 19 to FR 595. Turn right and go about 1 mile west to the entrance road.

4J. ALEXANDER SPRINGS CREEK—*Canoe; Ramp.*

Description: This is one of the most popular sites in the national forest. It is a great place to launch a canoe or jonboat and fish the swift moving creek. At the head of the creek is Alexander Springs, which features swimming and camping.

Directions: From FL 19 about 12.5 miles north of Eustis, go east on CR 445 about 5 miles to the bridge over Alexander Springs Creek. The put-in spots for canoes and jonboats are on either side of the bridge. The take-out is at the end of FR 552. To reach it from CR 445, drive 0.3 mile past the Alexander Springs Creek Bridge to FR 552. Follow FR 445 about 4.5 miles to the ramp.

4K. LAKE DORR—*Boat; Ramp.*

Description: The lake, despite a convenient location and nice campground, is not heavily fished. Try it in spring for largemouth bass and in fall for crappie.

Directions: There are two good ramps both off FL 19. One is 11 miles south and the other is 11.3 miles south of the FL 40-FL 19 intersection.

5. LAKE GEORGE

Fresh; Boat; Ramp.

Description: Technically, this 46,000-acre lake is a wide spot in the St. Johns River. It is a very popular place to fish. The depth seldom exceeds 10 feet and a shelf only 1 to 4 feet deep runs around the entire lake. These flats harbor eelgrass beds and are an excellent place to fish. There is an active military bombing range in the middle of the lake. Anglers can fish around the clusters of pilings placed by the military. From time to time the military jets "buzz" anglers as a friendly way of asking them to leave the area before they start their bombing runs.

The lake can become rough if the wind begins to blow; keep an eye on the weather. If it turns bad, return to home port or head up the spring runs along the lake's western shore. Salt Springs is one of the most popular destinations.

Fishing Index: The lake is well known for its largemouth and striped bass fishing. Largemouth bass spawn in the shallow waters around the edge of the lake in spring. At other times of the year, anglers fish around the deeper water structures. The lake has several brush attractors, small deep holes, and some jetties at the south end which are good places to try for both bass species. Crappie fishing is excellent in winter with Missouri minnows the preferred bait.

Several saltwater species make their way into the Lake George area. The summer shrimp run often brings the crustaceans into the lower part of the lake. Redfish and blue crabs appear to be established in Lake George. Catching a redfish is not unusual and there are enough blue crabs to support a small commercial fishery. Anglers also occasionally catch mangrove snapper, flounder, and tarpon. On this lake, you might be in for a surprise when the fish gets to the boat.

Access Points:
There are numerous commercial marinas and fish camps in Georgetown at the north end of the lake and in Astor about 1 mile upriver from the south end of the lake. The most popular public access points are:

5A. BLUE CREEK—*Boat; Ramp.*
Directions: From the FL 40 bridge over the St. Johns River in Astor, drive 4.6 miles west on FL 40 to Blue Creek Road (FR 9983). Turn right and go 2.4 miles to Lake George Road (FR 9984). Turn left and follow Lake George Road 1 mile to the ramp.

5B. ASTOR RAMP—*Boat; Ramp.*
Description: Head downriver to reach Lake George. Upriver leads to lakes Dexter and Woodruff.
Directions: Turn off of FL 40 on the west side of the St. Johns River onto Front Street. Go one block to Pearle Street and turn left.

For more information: At the north end of the lake, call Camp Henry Resort and Marina at (904) 467-2282. At the south end of the lake, call Big Bass Guide Service at (352) 759-2795 or Astor Tackle and Marine at (352) 759-2278, both in Astor.

6. ST. JOHNS RIVER (ASTOR TO FL 44 BRIDGE INCLUDING LAKE WOODRUFF) ─────────────

Fresh; Bank and Boat; Ramp.

Description: Heading upriver from Astor, it's a little more than 4 miles to reach Lake Dexter and the marshes of Lake Woodruff National Wildlife Refuge. Both lakes are totally undeveloped. Boaters just passing through can simply follow the channel markers. But to explore the wilderness, take along a good map. Most of the local marinas and tackle stores carry them. Access to this stretch of the river is from Astor to the north, DeLeon Springs to the east, and off FL 44 to the south. Remember, the St. Johns River flows northward.

Fishing Index: From Astor upriver to Lake Dexter, anglers fish for largemouth bass. Lake Dexter is the destination for crappie enthusiasts in fall and winter. The lake is considered a top spot for the tasty panfish. In summer, lakes Dexter and Woodruff produce good stringers of big bluegills. The best times are roughly four days on either side of the full moon. Lake Woodruff is also noted for its bass fishing. Try for them around the many lily pads.

Access Points:
The Astor Ramp, described in the Lake George site (see previous site, page 161), is used by anglers approaching these lakes from the north.

6A. DeLeon Springs State Recreation Area—*Bank, Boat; Ramp; $.*
Description: The park features swimming in the spring boil, the remains of an old sugar mill, and picnicking. Anglers can fish from the banks in Spring Garden Lake. Access to lakes Woodruff and Dexter is via Spring Garden Creek, a winding waterway that connects to Lake Woodruff.
Directions: From the intersection with US 92 in Deland take US 17 north 7.2 miles to Ponce DeLeon Boulevard. Turn left and go 0.8 mile to the park.
For more information: Call the park office at (904) 985-4212.

6B. Ed Stone Park—*Bank and Boat; Ramp.*
Description: A county facility adjacent to the St. Johns River Bridge on FL 44. Anglers can fish in the river off of the seawall. Several commercial marinas are nearby.
Directions: From US 17 and US 92 in Deland, take FL 44 west 5 miles to the park.

7.   Lake Dias
Fresh; Bank and Boat; Ramp.

Description: This 711-acre lake is a GFC Fish Management Area. The land around the lake is relatively undeveloped.

Fishing Index: Fish congregate around four fish attractors in the lake and anglers fishing near them generally have good luck. The lake is noted for its crappie fishing and has fair largemouth bass fishing; spring is the best time of year.

Directions: From the intersection of FL 44, US 17, and 92 in Deland, drive about 2.9 miles north on US 17. Where the highway bends left, go straight on FL 11 about 6.9 miles. The lake is on the right.

For more information: Call the Central Region office of the GFC at (352) 732-1225.

Lake (southern portion), Orange, Seminole and Volusia (southwestern portion) Counties

8. Lake Griffin

Fresh; Boat and Bank; Ramp.

Description: Water in the Harris chain flows north into Lake Griffin and exits at the north end of the lake as the Oklawaha River. Most of the land along the shoreline is undeveloped or minimally so. Cypress trees line the shoreline and shallows around the lake support extensive eelgrass beds.

Fishing Index: This is the favorite lake of veteran guides Larry Fetter and Jerry Sloan. Both guides claim Griffin produces more trophy-sized bass than others in the chain. "March to May, when the bass are entering their post spawn, is a good time to fish this lake," according to Larry Fetter of Pine Island Fish Camp. "The fish are hungry when they come off the beds and are very aggressive."

Access Points:

8A. Hurlong Park—*Bank and Boat; Ramp.*
Directions: The park is just off US 441 in Leesburg. Turn off of US 441 at the Minute Maid orange processing plant.
For more information: Call Al Jana Fish Camp and talk to the owners, Diane and Harry Henning at (352) 787-2429.

8B. Pine Island Fish Camp—*Boat; Ramp.*
Description: This commercial facility provides access to the north end of the lake.
Directions: From the intersection of FL 44 and US 27 in Leesburg, take US 27 north about 8.1 miles to the community of Lady Lake. Turn right onto Lake Griffin Road and go 4.5 miles to the camp.
For more information: Call Larry Fetter, owner of the camp, at (352) 753-2972.

9. Lake Griffin State Recreation Area

Fresh; Boat and Bank; Ramp; $.

Description: The park is on the shores of a small lobe of Lake Griffin. Camping and canoe rentals are available.

Fishing Index: Diane Henning says that this is a very good place to fish for largemouth bass.

Directions: From the intersection of FL 44 and US 27 in Leesburg, take US 27 north about 3.5 miles to the park entrance.

For more information: Call the park office at (352) 360-6760.

Lake (southern portion), Orange, Seminole and Volusia (southwestern portion) Counties

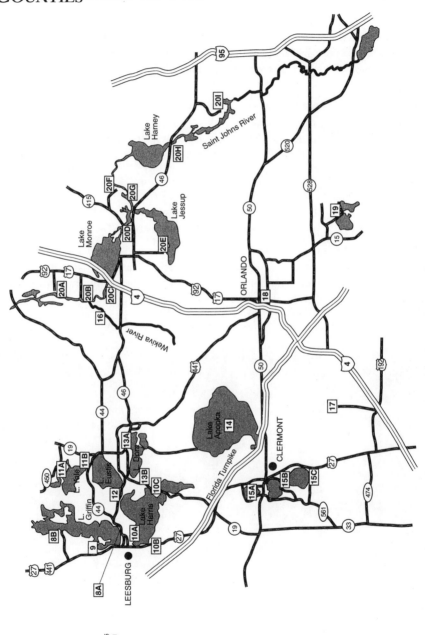

10. LAKE HARRIS AND LITTLE LAKE HARRIS ———————

Fresh; Boat and Bank; Ramp.

Description: The two lakes are linked where the FL 19 bridge crosses the lakes.

Fishing Index: Lake Harris has more deep water than other lakes in the chain according to guide Larry Fetter. To find them, you'll need one of the detailed topographic fishing maps that are widely available in the area and a good depth finder on your boat. In winter, crappie fishing is popular. The best crappie fishing, according to many anglers, is at night.

Access Points:

10A. VENETIAN GARDENS—*Pier and Boat; Ramp.*
Description: A City of Leesburg facility.
Directions: In Leesburg, from the intersection with US 27, US 441, and FL 44 (Dixie Avenue), take FL 44 about 1 mile east. The ramp is just off the highway.

10B. SINGLETARY PARK—*Pier and Boat; Ramp.*
Description: A GFC facility; docks are barrier-free.
Directions: In Leesburg. From the intersection with FL 44, drive about 2.5 miles south on US 27. The park is just off the highway.

10C. HICKORY POINT—*Pier and Boat; Ramp; $.*
Description: An outstanding facility for anglers. The site features a special boat ramp for deep-draft boats. Parking is ample. The combination dock and fishing pier is barrier-free and open to anglers at night.
Directions: From the intersection of FL 19 and US 441 in Tavares, take FL 19

At Hickory Point Park on Lake Harris, anglers fish around the emergent grasses for panfish. Cane pole fishing is a popular and inexpensive way to fish for these pint-sized fighters.

south 4.7 miles to the park entrance. It is just before the FL 19 bridge over the lakes.

For more information: Call the Lake County Water Authority at (352) 343-3357.

11. LAKE YALE

Fresh; Boat and Bank; Ramp.

Description: The lake connects to Lake Griffin through the Emerelda Marsh Wildlife Management Area.

Fishing Index: Some anglers report the number of trophy-sized fish being caught on this lake are really increasing.

Access Points:
11A. LAKE YALE BOAT RAMP—*Boat; Ramp.*
Directions: From the intersection with FL 44 in Eustis, take FL 19 north 5.5 miles to CR 450. Turn left on CR 450 and go 3.5 miles to Lake Yale Boat Ramp Road. Turn left and follow the road to the ramp.

11B. MARSH PARK—*Boat; Ramp.*
Directions: From the intersection with FL 19 in Eustis, take FL 44 west about 1.7 miles to CR 452. Take CR 452 0.6 mile to Yale Retreat Road. Turn right and follow the road to the ramp.

12. LAKE EUSTIS

Fresh; Boat and Bank; Ramp.

Description: Connects to Lake Griffin via Haines Creek and to Lake Harris via Dead River.

Fishing Index: The lake has a shoreline fringed in cypress and maidencane, a productive home for largemouth bass. Try fishing for them around the mouths of the canals connecting this lake to lakes Harris and Griffin, especially when the weather is cooler.

Directions: The ramp, in Tavares Park, is off US 441, about 0.9 mile west of the US 441-FL 19 intersection in Tavares. It's adjacent to the Dora Canal (also known as Dead River) connecting Lakes Eustis and Harris. A small fishing pier extends into the lake where US 441 crosses the canal. Park along the side of the road and walk to the pier. Parking is limited.

13. LAKE DORA

Fresh; Boat and Bank; Ramp.

Description: One of the mid-size lakes in the chain, it connects to Lake Eustis.

Fishing Index: A typical Harris chain lake that has good largemouth bass fishing in spring and fall and good summer bluegill fishing.

Access Points:
13A. GILBERT PARK—*Boat; Ramp.*
Directions: From the FL 19A - US 441 intersection near Mount Dora, turn right onto FL 19A and drive into Mount Dora. At the intersection with Tremain Street, turn right and travel 0.4 mile to the park.

13B. SUMMERALL PARK—*Boat; Ramp.*
Directions: From US 441 in Tavares, take FL 19 south about 0.9 mile to Wells Avenue. Turn left and go to the ramp.

14. LAKE APOPKA

Fresh; Boat and Bank; Ramp.

Description: This lake is too large and too well known to not mention. Unfortunately, it is not a highly recommended place to fish. Pollution has adversely affected the fish population here.

Fishing Index: Fish the southeast corner of the lake at Gourd Neck, also known as Apopka Springs. An active spring here ensures the best water quality in the lake and the greatest concentrations of crappie and sunshine bass. The lake is stocked with sunshine bass.

Directions: The closest ramp is in Monteverde. From Clermont drive 3.5 miles east on FL 50. Turn north on CR 455 and go 4 miles to Monteverde. Look for the ramp sign and turn right on the access road.

15. CLERMONT CHAIN

Fresh; Pier and Boat; Ramp.

Description: This chain of 13 small and mid-size scenic lakes surrounds Clermont. Some lakes are surrounded by cypress trees and are tannin stained. Those without cypress, notably Lake Minneola, are clear.

Fishing Index: Gordon Ball, one of the owners of Clermont Bait and Tackle, says, "January to April are the best months for catching largemouth bass. That's when the fish move into the shallow water and spawn. The lakes also have some big channel catfish in them, up to 40 pounds." The big catfish are taken with live baits, using a bobber to keep the bait a few feet off the bottom. Crappie fishing is popular in winter and where you find one you'll usually find more because the fish form tight schools when the water is cold.

Ball also points out that the fishing is "a little different in each lake. In Louisa the largemouth bass hang around the roots of the cypress trees. They are slightly smaller on the average but they're always there. In Minneola and Minnehaha the bass tend to school more and feed on shad. They can be in the deep holes or around the mouths of the canals connecting the lakes."

Access Points:
15A. LAKE MINNEOLA—*Pier and Boat; Ramp.*
Description: There is a free fishing pier adjacent to the ramp. A couple of fish

attractors are near the pier to help increase angler success.

Directions: From FL 50 in Clermont turn north onto 5th Street and go to Lake Minneola Drive. Turn right and look for the ramp and pier.

15B. LAKE LOUISA—*Boat; Ramp.*

Directions: From FL 50, turn south on 5th Street and go to Lake Shore Drive. Follow Lake Shore Drive about 3 miles to Hull Road (look for Lake Susan Lodge). Turn left onto Hull road and go 1.8 miles to the ramp.

For more information: Call Clermont Bait and Tackle at (352) 394-7000.

15C. LAKE LOUISA STATE PARK—*Bank and Canoe.*

Description: This park on the south shore features a swimming beach and picnic area. Canoes can be launched from shore.

Directions: Exit I-4 onto US 27 and drive about 9.5 miles north to CR 474. Turn left onto CR 474 and go 8.5 miles to the end of the road at FL 33. Turn north on FL 33 and go 2.3 miles to CR 561. Turn north and go 4.6 miles to Lake Nellie Road. Turn right and go 2.4 miles to the park entrance.

For more information: Call the park office at (352) 394-3969.

16. WEKIVA RIVER

Fresh; Boat.

Description: The river originates in Wekiva Springs State Park and flows north to the St. Johns River, joining it at DeBary. The narrow upper reaches are popular with canoeists.

A small boat is all you need to fish the Wekiva near Orlando. This scenic river is frequently used by canoeists and is rich in wildlife.

Fishing Index: Try fishing the river close to its junction with the St. Johns for largemouth bass. The upper part is not heavily fished.

Directions: The easiest access is from the ramps near Blue Spring State Park, Highbanks ramp, or Lake Monroe Park. Take the St. Johns River to the mouth of the Wekiva and head upriver.

17. DISNEY WORLD

Fresh; Boat.

Description: Yes, you can fish at Mickey's place and for real fish, too! The resort has two lakes, one natural and one man-made, for anglers to fish. Bring your own tackle or rent theirs. Disney allows only its own boats on the water and all fishing must be done with a member of the "cast," as they call their employees, on board.

Fishing Index: Anglers can fish Bay Lake and Seven Seas Lagoon for largemouth bass. Both produce lots of bass over 3 pounds.

Directions: Disney World is in Orlando. The main entrance is off of I-4 just south of Lake Buena Vista.

For more information: Call Walt Disney World at (407) 824-2222

18. LAKE IVANHOE

Fresh; Bank and Boat; Ramp.

Description: This is a designated urban fishery program site near downtown Orlando.

Fishing Index: The 125-acre lake is stocked with channel catfish. There are naturally occurring largemouth bass and several types of panfish. The lake is a good place to fish from the bank or in a small boat.

Directions: Exit I-4 at Orange Avenue. Park under the I-4 bridge for bank fishing or continue on Orange Avenue about 0.5 mile to the ramp.

19. MOSS PARK

Fresh; Boat and Bank; Ramp.

Description: This 1550-acre Orange County Park is located between lakes Hart and Mary Jane. It has a campground, swimming area, and abundant wildlife.

Fishing Index: Fish the lakes for largemouth bass, bluegills, and crappie.

Directions: Exit the Bee Line Expressway (FL 528) onto FL 15 and go south 2.6 miles to Moss Park Road. Turn left and go 4 miles to the park.

For more information: Call the park office at (407) 273-2327.

Largemouth bass are plentiful in Florida's freshwater. This one was caught in the lakes just outside of Walt Disney World's Magic Kingdom.

20. St. Johns River (FL 44 bridge to FL 520 bridge –

Fresh; Boat; Ramp.

Description: This part of the river includes lakes Monroe, Jessup, and Harney. The river splits below the FL 44 bridge, forming Hontoon Island. The island is a state park with camping, cabins, and an observation tower. Upriver from where Lake Jessup joins in is the Lemon Bluff area, one of the most scenic parts of the river. Above Lake Harney, the St. Johns has numerous sloughs branching off of the main course and the land around the river is totally undeveloped. The Econlockhatchee River, which originates southeast of Orlando, enters the river between Lake Harney and Puzzle Lake. The river from the FL 50 bridge to the FL 520 bridge is sometimes unnavigable due to low water.

Fishing Index: From roughly January to mid-April each year, American shad, a saltwater species that migrates from as far away as Canada, swims up the St. Johns to spawn. Most of the action is between Lake Monroe and Puzzle Lake. One of the best-known spots is Shad Alley, from the FL 46 bridge to Lemon Bluff. Fish for the 1- to 5-pound fish by trolling a locally available shad rig or gold or silver spoons. Fly fishers also target this species with lightweight rigs. Largemouth bass fishing is good along all parts of the river. In spring, good numbers of striped and sunshine (hybrid) bass are also taken. George Griffin, owner of Lindsay's Fish Camp on FL 46, says, "the area between Lake Harney and Puzzle Lake is under-fished. This part of the river is so far out of the way, people don't want to come out here. But this is where the old-timers come to fish. If you're not afraid to fish shallow water, you will do well. Plus you can't beat the scenery." Griffin also recommends fishing the Econlockhatchee River, a river he says is seldom fished but has lots of fish in it. It is accessible by boat up to the FL 419 bridge.

For more information: For information about the Lake Jessup to Lake Harney region, call J.J.'s Marina Isles Fish Camp at (407) 330-6155. For information about the area from Lake Harney to Puzzle Lake and the Econlockhatchee River, call Lindsay's Fish Camp at (407) 349-1110.

Access Points:

20A. Blue Spring State Park—*Bank and Pier; Ramp.*

Description: The park has a campground, cabins, swimming in the spring boil, and nature trails. Endangered West Indian Manatees winter over in the spring and are easily observed from shore. The ramp is not part of the park, though it is adjacent. It accesses the St. Johns River.

Directions: From US 17/92 in Orange City (4.6 miles south of Deland), turn west onto French Street and go 2.6 miles to the park. To reach the ramp, go past the park entrance and follow French Street until it ends at the ramp and the river.

For more information: Call the park office at (904) 775-3663.

20B. Highbanks Ramp—*Boat; Ramp.*

Directions: From US 17/92 in DeBary (4.3 miles south of Orange City), turn west onto Highbanks Road and go 2.9 miles to the ramp.

20C. LAKE MONROE PARK—*Pier and Boat; Ramp.*
Description: A Volusia County facility with camping and nature trails.
Directions: The park is on US 17/92 on the north side of the river where it widens to become Lake Monroe. Exit I-4 onto US 17/92 at Sanford and go north 0.8 mile to the park.

20D. CAMERON WRIGHT PARK—*Boat and Bank; Ramp.*
Description: A Seminole County Park with picnicking.
Directions: From the intersection with US 17/92 take FL 46 5.3 miles to the park. It is on the west side of the FL 46 bridge.

20E. LAKE JESSUP PARK—*Boat and Bank; Ramp.*
Description: A Seminole County Park with picnicking.
Directions: From the intersection with US 17/92 take Fl 46 0.5 mile to Sanford Avenue. Turn right and go south 4 miles to the park.

20F. LEMON BLUFF—*Boat; Ramp.*
Directions: From the intersection with US 17/92 in Sanford, Take FL 415 north about 6.6 miles to Lemon Bluff Road. Turn right and go 3.5 miles to the ramp at road's end.

20G. MULLET LAKE PARK—*Boat and Bank; Ramp.*
Description: This 151-acre Seminole County park has a campground. It is on the shores of Mullet Lake, part of the St. Johns River.
Directions: From the intersection with US 17/92 in Sanford, take FL 46 east 7.8 miles to Mullet Lake Road. Turn north and drive about 1 mile to the ramp.

20H. C.S. LEE PARK—*Boat; Ramp.*
Description: A Seminole County Park with picnicking.
Directions: From the intersection with US 17/92 in Sanford, take FL 46 east 15.8 miles to the bridge over the river. The park is on the west side. Or from I-95, exit onto FL 46 at Mims and drive west 11.2 miles to the park.

20I. HATBILL PARK—*Boat; Ramp.*
Description: This ramp may not be accessible when the water level is up on the river.
Directions: At Mims, exit I-95 onto FL 46 and go west 4.1 miles to Hatbill Park Road. Turn left and go about 4.9 miles to the ramp.

OSCEOLA, BREVARD (WESTERN PORTION), AND INDIAN RIVER (WESTERN PORTION) COUNTIES

21. WEST LAKE TOHOPEKALIGA ————————
Fresh; Boat; Ramp.

Description: The larger of the two "Toho" lakes. Veteran anglers of this lake agree that fishing here has declined. Too many nutrients and a rampant crop of hydrilla are to blame. With yearly hydrilla control, this lake still produces lots of bass, but this is only a temporary fix.

Fishing Index: "Learn how to fish the hydrilla—that's where the fish are," is the advice of Dwight Richardson, owner of Richardson's Fish Camp. That means finding the underwater edges or walls of the hydrilla, or looking for holes to pitch to. Inexperienced anglers will do best using live shiners and fishing when the water temperature is between 70 and 85 degrees. That means the best times are in fall and during the spring spawn. Crappie fishing is very good in winter.

Access Points:

21A. LAKE FRONT PARK—*Boat; Ramp.*
Description: A city park with plenty of parking.
Directions: From the intersection where US 17, 19, 92, 192, and 441 converge in Kissimmee, go south 0.6 mile on US 17/92 to FL 525 (Neptune Road) and turn left. Go 0.3 mile to Lake Shore Drive and turn right. The ramp is down Lake Shore Drive on the left.

21B. GRANADA RAMP—*Boat; Ramp.*
Directions: From the intersection where US 17, 19, 92, 192, and 441 converge in Kissimmee, go south about 3.8 miles on US 17/92 to Pleasant Hill Road (CR 531). Turn left and go about 4.5 miles to Granada Road. Turn left again and go to Ridgeway Road. Turn left and go to the ramp.

21C. SOUTH PORT RAMP—*Boat; Ramp.*
Directions: From the intersection where US 17, 92, 192, and 441 converge in Kissimmee, go south about 3.8 miles on US 17/92 to Pleasant Hill Road (CR 531). Turn left and go about 8 miles to Southport Road. Turn left again and go 5.5 miles to the ramp on the south end of the lake.

21D. WHALEY'S RAMP—*Boat; Ramp.*
Directions: From the intersection where US 17, 92, 192, and 441 converge in Kissimmee, go south about 6.9 miles on US 192/441 to CR 534. Turn right on CR 534 and go 0.4 mile to Kissimmee Park Road (CR 525). Turn left and go south 4 miles to Lake Toho Road (CR 525A). Turn left on Lake Toho Road and go 1.4 miles to the ramp.

For more information: Call Richardson's Fish Camp at (407) 846-6540 or Big Toho Marina at (407) 846-2124. Both are in Kissimmee.

22. EAST LAKE TOHOPEKALIGA
Fresh; Boat; Ramp.

Description: The smaller of the two "Toho" lakes, this nearly circular 12,000-acre lake also has a hydrilla problem. Public access is via the ramp at Chisholm Park, formerly East Lake Regional Park.

Fishing Index: A good lake for largemouth bass.

Directions: From the intersection of US 192/441 and Canoe Creek Road in St. Cloud, take US 192/441 south 2.9 miles to CR 15. Turn north and go about 3 miles to L Street. Turn left and go 0.5 mile to the park.

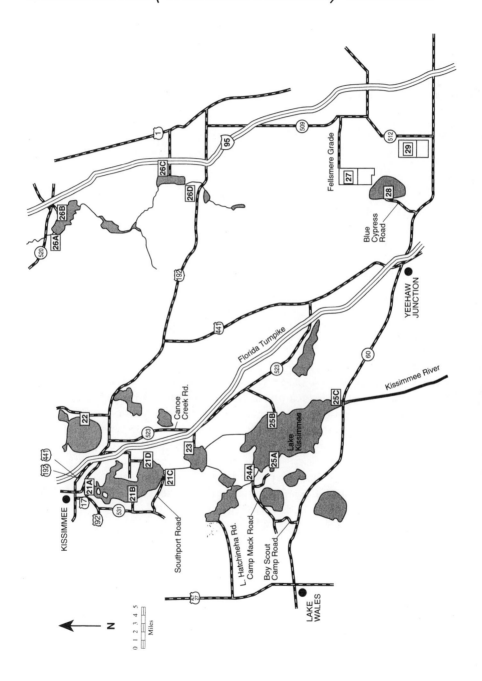

23. CYPRESS LAKE

Fresh; Boat; Ramp.

Description: Far from civilization, cypress trees surround much of the shoreline. In addition to the ramp, anglers access this lake via the canals from lakes Hatchineha and West Toho.

Fishing Index: Leo Cosce, owner of Camp Lester, says, "The lake is heavily fished during winter on bad weather days." Being smaller, the lake doesn't get as rough when it's windy. Crappie (specs) provide good action in winter and bluegills and shellcrackers are biting in spring and summer.

Directions: From the intersection of Canoe Creek Road (FL 523) and US 192/441 in St. Cloud, take Canoe Creek road south 11.2 miles to Lake Cypress Drive. Turn right and go 2.3 miles to the ramp.

24. LAKE HATCHINEHA

Fresh; Boat; Ramp.

Description: *The prettiest lake in the chain; cypress grows along much of the shoreline. There are no public boat ramps on this lake.*

Fishing Index: Another good largemouth bass lake in the Kissimmee chain. The waterway connecting this lake to Lake Kissimmee is also a good place to fish. Some current here helps hold down the hydrilla; fish the shoreline using traditional bass angling techniques.

Access Points:
24A. CAMPS LESTER AND MACK—*Fresh; Boat; Ramp.*
Description: These two fish camps have been in the area for years.
Directions: There is a ramp at Camp Lester on the waterway connecting Lakes Hatchineha and Kissimmee. From US 27 in Lake Wales, go east 9.2 miles on FL 60 to Boy Scout Camp Road. Turn left and go north about 3.2 miles to Camp Mack Road. Turn right and go about 6 miles to Camp Lester Road. Turn left to the camp. Camp Mack is adjacent to Camp Lester.
For more information: Call Camp Lester at (941) 696-1123 or Camp Mack at (941) 696-1108.

25. LAKE KISSIMMEE

Fresh; Boat; Ramp.

Description: The lake is scheduled for a drawdown in November, 1995. About 50 percent of the lake bottom will be exposed for six or seven months. Any surviving fish will concentrate in the remaining water and that should create some exciting conditions. There will also be special restrictions on the number and size of fish that you can keep. Catch-and-release will be emphasized. After the water level is brought back up, largemouth bass fishing should improve for several years as the bass population fills the acres of new prime habitat created by the drawdown.

Fishing Index: This lake has been a prime largemouth bass lake for many years. Despite dense mats of hydrilla, native Kissimmee grass flourishes in some areas. Fish the grassline. Leo Cosce, owner of Camp Lester, says, "If the weather is nice and the water temperature is above 70 degrees, you can catch bass in this lake on artificial lures. But when the water temperature is below 60 degrees, live bait is the only thing that works." The reason that so many bait shops and guides talk about using shiners, Cosce adds, is because, "the bait catches the fish. You just reel it in."

Access Points:
Besides the three public sites described here, try camps Lester and Mack (see site 24A) and the commercial facilities at the south end of the lake where it narrows to a river. These include River Oaks, Shady Oaks, and River Ranch Resort.

25A. LAKE KISSIMMEE STATE PARK—*Boat and Bank; Ramp; $.*
Description: The park has a campground and a living history demonstration of an 1876 cow camp. The park's ramp is at the end of a winding road. Some

Shorelines that have emergent vegetation growing in front of them create great habitat for largemouth bass. Anglers can use a trolling motor to work these areas.

people find it easier to use Camp Lester or Camp Mack, both just outside the entrance to the park.

Directions: From US 27 in Lake Wales, drive east 9.2 miles on FL 60 to Boy Scout Camp Road. Turn left and go north about 3.2 miles to Camp Mack Road. Turn right and go about 6 miles to the park entrance.

25B. OVERSTREET RAMP—*Boat; Ramp.*
Directions: From the intersection of Canoe Creek Road and US 192/441 in St. Cloud, take Canoe Creek road south 20.8 miles to Overstreet Road. Turn right and go 5.5 miles to the ramp at road's end.

25C. FL 60 RAMP—*Boat; Ramp.*
Directions: The ramp is just off FL 60 where it crosses the southernmost part of the lake. From the Florida Turnpike drive 19.8 miles west on FL 60. Or from US 27 in Lake Wales drive 26.5 miles east on FL 60. The ramp is adjacent to the locks that lead to the Kissimmee River.

26. ST. JOHNS RIVER (LAKE POINSETT TO LAKE HELEN BLAZES)

Fresh; Bank and Boat; Ramp.

Description: This part of the river also includes lakes Winder, Washington, and Sawgrass. The St. Johns River headwaters are in the marshes south of Lake Helen Blazes. The marshes around this part of the river help produce good fishing but also limit access. This is also a popular area for airboaters. According to Dave Cox, a biologist with the GFC who has 22 years of experience on the St. Johns River, "This part of the river is enjoyable and definitely wild. You're out in the wilderness once you leave the boat ramps." Cox warns boaters of a fixed crest weir at the north end of Lake Washington. Boaters can usually go over it when the river is at normal levels. Approach with caution and check the water depth.

Fishing Index: Lake Poinsett has the best largemouth bass fishing along this part of the river. The river between lakes Poinsett and Winder is also pretty good but Lake Winder has a severe hydrilla problem. Lake Washington is not heavily fished. Occasional fish kills here result in poor fishing conditions afterward. Cox says fish here when the water level begins to drop just after a period of high water. Upriver several miles are Sawgrass Lake and Lake Helen Blazes. Sawgrass is good for bluegills and shellcrackers. Helen Blazes has a hydrilla problem and can be difficult to fish. Anglers looking for a quality (not quantity) crappie fishing experience should try the river between Lake Washington and Sawgrass Lake.

Access Points:
26A. FL 520 RAMP—*Boat; Ramp.*
Directions: Exit I-95 onto FL 520 (at Cocoa). Drive about 4.5 miles west on FL 520 and look for the ramp on the south side of the river next to Lone Cabbage Fish Camp.

26B. LAKE POINSETT LODGE—*Bank and Boat; Ramp.*
Description: This fish camp allows bank fishing along its canals. Ask for an area map.
Directions: Exit I-95 onto FL 520 and go west 0.6 mile to Lake Poinsett Road. Turn left and follow the road 1 mile to the lake.
For more information: Call Lake Poinsett Lodge at (407) 636-0045.

26C. LAKE WASHINGTON RAMP—*Boat; Ramp.*
Description: This county-owned ramp was once a fish camp. Plans are to upgrade the ramp and increase access for boaters.
Directions: From US 1 near Eau Gallie, drive 5.8 miles west on Lake Washington Road to the ramp.

26D. CAMP HOLLY—*Boat; Ramp.*
Description: This commercial facility is a popular launch for airboats. The owners offer airboat rides to the public.
Directions: Exit I-95 onto US 192 and go west about 3 miles to the fish camp.

27. STICK MARSH AND FARM 13 (FELLSMERE RESERVOIR)
Fresh; Boat; Ramp.

Description: These are two adjacent waterbodies created in 1985 by flooding old farm fields. The area is strictly managed by the GFC as a trophy bass site. All largemouth bass caught must be immediately released unharmed. Plenty of guides along the central east coast fish this site. Check at a local bait and tackle shop or contact Stick Marsh Bait and Tackle.

Fishing Index: These two sites offer some of the best bass fishing in Florida. The biggest fish are caught in spring using live wild shiners. Other species, including crappie, bluegills, and catfish, can be harvested according to state regulations.

Directions: Exit I-95 at Fellsmere onto CR 512 and go west 4 miles to Fellsmere. Turn right on CR 507 and go north 4 miles to Fellsmere Grade. Turn left onto the Grade, which parallels the C-54 Canal on the south side. Follow the Grade 6 miles to the ramp.

For more information: Call Stick Marsh Bait and Tackle in Fellsmere at (407) 571-9855.

28. BLUE CYPRESS LAKE ─────────────
Fresh; Boat; Ramp.

Description: The lake is surrounded by marsh and cypress swamp. Kissimmee grass and lily pads provide cover for the fish.

Fishing Index: The lake is noted for crappie fishing and has a good largemouth bass fishery. Sunshine bass, near the southern limit of their range, are stocked here.

Directions: From US 441 in Yeehaw Junction, take FL 60 east about 6.6 miles to Blue Cypress Road. Turn left and go 4.3 miles to the ramp.

29. ANSIN-GARCIA RESERVOIR

Fresh; Boat; Ramp.

Description: This 10,750-acre reservoir is only a few miles south of Stick Marsh. CR 512 divides the site into east and west portions. The area is open to boaters without restriction except for the Ansin area, which is the southwest quadrant. It has a 10-horsepower limit on outboards.

Fishing Index: A very good place to fish for largemouth bass. The bass generally run slightly smaller than at Stick Marsh. Possession of bass is legal.

Directions: From the FL 60 exit off I-95, drive 7.5 miles west to FL 512. Go north on FL 512 for 1.5 miles to the ramp.

For more information: Call Stick Marsh Bait and Tackle in Fellsmere at (407) 571-9855.

VOLUSIA COUNTY (COASTAL AREA)

Volusia County has gone out of its way to provide public access for anglers. Dan O'Brien, executive director of the county's Port Authority, proudly states that they already have built more than 10,000 feet of fishing piers along the Halifax River and the upper part of Mosquito Lagoon. That is 4,100 feet more than the projected amount of pier footage needed for the population in 2010.

30. TOMOKA STATE PARK

Salt; Bank and Boat; Ramp.

Description: A scenic park with big oak trees on a peninsula between the Tomoka and Halifax rivers. There is a campground, picnic area, and cultural museum. The park is the site of an old Timucuan Indian Village.

Fishing Index: Park manager and avid angler Benny Woodham says anglers catch black drum and redfish in the Tomoka River and Basin in winter. "Most anglers use live bait when fishing in the river and basin, but you can use dead shrimp when fishing for black drum." In summer fish for spotted seatrout, flounder, and small snook and tarpon. Land-bound anglers can fish from the banks of the Tomoka River or off the North Beach Street bridge. Woodham adds that fly fishers who like to catch small tarpon, in the 15- to 20-pound range, should try the creeks around the park. The action can be very good.

Directions: From FL 40 in Ormond Beach, take Beach Street north 4.1 miles to the park entrance.

For more information: Call the park office at (904) 676-4050.

VOLUSIA AND BREVARD COUNTIES (COASTAL AREAS)

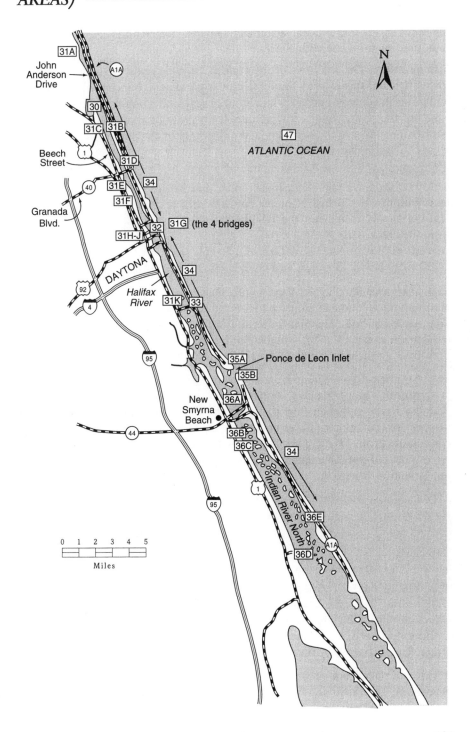

John Anderson Drive

31A

A1A

N

30

31C 31B

47

ATLANTIC OCEAN

Beech Street

1

31D

40

31E

34

31F

Granada Blvd.

31G (the 4 bridges)

32

31H-J

DAYTONA

34

92

Halifax River

31K

33

4

95

35A

Ponce de Leon Inlet

35B

New Smyrna Beach

36A

44

36B

36C

34

1

Indian River North

95

36E

A1A

36D

0 1 2 3 4 5
Miles

31. Halifax River
Salt; Boat, Bank, Bridge and Pier; Ramp.

Description: This coastal river begins near Tomoka marsh and is joined from the north by the Intracoastal Waterway. Daytona Beach and surrounding communities line much of both shores.

Fishing Index: The shallows of the Halifax provide good year-round angling for redfish and sheepshead. Snook fishing is good in all but the coldest months and peaks in summer and early fall. Spotted seatrout is best from April through June but the population is low, in part from years of commercial harvesting. Numerous piers and boat ramps make this part of the coast one of the most angler-friendly places in Florida.

Access Points:

31A. Highbridge Park—*Salt; Boat, Bank, and Bridge ; Ramp.*
Description: This Volusia County day-use park is along the scenic banks of Halifax Creek. Fish from the Highbridge Road over Halifax Creek or fish from the creek bank.
Directions: From FL 40 in Ormond Beach take A1A north 8.5 miles to Highbridge Road. Turn left and go 0.3 mile to the park.

31B. Seabridge Riverfront Park—*Salt; Pier.*
Description: A Volusia County park on the island side of the river across from Tomoka State Park. The pier is about 175 feet long.
Directions: From FL 40 (Granada Boulevard) in Ormond Beach turn north onto John Anderson Drive and go about 5.7 miles to the park.

31C. Sanchez Park—*Pier and Boat; Ramp.*
Description: The park ramp is on Strickland's Creek which empties into the Tomoka River and then into the Halifax River. Strickland's Creek and the majority of the Tomoka River and Basin are idle-speed zones.
Directions: From FL 40 (Granada Boulevard) in Ormond Beach, take Beach Street north about 2.5 miles to Sanchez Street. Turn left and follow the road until it ends at the park.

31D. Granada Riverfront Park—*Pier and Boat; Ramp.*
Description: The park is in Ormond Beach on the mainland side adjacent to the Granada Boulevard Bridge. The 1,500-foot pier, beneath the road bridge, is popular with anglers.
Directions: From US 1 in Ormond Beach, take FL 40 east 0.4 mile to the park.

31E. Sunrise Park—*Pier and Boat; Ramp.*
Description: The ramp is suitable only for small boats.
Directions: From the intersection of Beach Street and Granada Boulevard (FL40) in Ormond Beach, take Beach Street south approximately 2.75 miles to 11th Street. Turn left and continue one block to the park.

31F. Ross Point Park—*Pier.*
Directions: In Holly Hill. From FL 40 in Ormond Beach, take Beach Street south about 3.7 miles to the park.

31G. Seabreeze, Main Street, US 92, and Orange Avenue Bridges—*Bridge.*
Description: Within a 1.4-mile stretch, these four bridges cross the Halifax River in Daytona Beach.
Directions: Seabreeze Bridge is at the end of Mason Avenue (CR 430). Main Street Bridge is between Seabreeze and the US 92 bridge. And Orange Avenue Bridge is just south of the US 92 bridge. All are accessible from A1A and US 1.

31H. Daytona Beach City Island Park—*Pier.*
Directions: From the west end of the US 92 (Volusia Avenue) Bridge in Daytona Beach, turn south on Beach Street. The park is on the left.

31I. Halifax Harbor—*Pier and Boat; Ramp.*
Description: This is the municipal marina.
Directions: From the west end of the US 92 (Volusia Avenue) Bridge in Daytona Beach, turn south on Beach Street. The marina is 0.3 mile down Beach Street on the left.

31J. Bethune Point Park—*Pier and Boat; Ramp.*
Directions: From the west end of the US 92 (Volusia Avenue) Bridge in Daytona Beach, turn south on Beach Street. The park is 0.5 mile down Beach Street at the corner of Beach and Bellevue.

31K. Dunlawton Causeway—*Pier.*
Description: Fish the channel below from the west end of the causeway.
Directions: This is the A1A bridge over the Halifax River in Port Orange. From the intersection with US 92 in Daytona Beach, take US 1 south 4.9 miles to the A1A bridge. Turn left.

Other access points:
San Jose Fishing Dock—on the island side near Seabridge.

Riv-Ocean Drive Fishing Dock—on the island side near Seabridge.

Briggs Drive Fishing Dock—on the island side near Seabridge.

Roberta Drive Fishing Dock—on the island side near Seabridge.

Spruce Creek Park—near Dunlawton Causeway.

For more information: Call Volusia County Parks and Recreation at (904) 257-6000 (x5953) or the Port Authority at (904) 239-6425.

32. Main Street Pier

Salt; Pier; $.

Description: This 1,006-foot pier sits at the site of the original pier built in 1917. It has a bait and tackle shop and rod and reel rentals for pier patrons.

Fishing Index: Fish year-round for whiting and sheepshead. In summer add redfish, flounder, and black drum. Spanish mackerel and a few snook appear around the pier in fall. By the end of October, whiting become abundant and bluefish arrive. They are the staples on the pier through winter.

Directions: The pier is in Daytona Beach at the end of Main Street. From the intersection with US 1, take US 92 to the beach. Turn north on Atlantic Boulevard (A1A) and go 0.3 mile to the pier.

For more information: Call the pier office at (904) 253-1212.

33. SUNGLOW PIER
Salt; Pier; $.

Description: This pier is in Port Orange south of Daytona Beach. It extends 1,500 feet into the Atlantic. There is a restaurant at the beginning of the pier. Rod and reel rentals available.

Fishing Index: Whiting and bluefish are the main targets in winter. In spring Spanish mackerel arrive along with some big flounder, redfish, and pompano. In summer, the mackerel leave, the flounder get smaller, and some small sharks are caught. Spanish mackerel return in fall for a brief visit and bluefish return for winter.

Directions: From Daytona Beach, take A1A south 5.2 miles. A1A turns and goes back to the mainland via the Port Orange Causeway. Continue down the beach for three blocks to the pier.

For more information: Call the pier office at (904) 788-3364.

34. VOLUSIA COUNTY BEACHES
Salt; Surf.

Description: Almost every mile of the county's beaches is accessible to surf anglers. There are numerous beachfront parks and smaller pull-off areas where you can park and walk to the beach. In the Daytona Beach area, driving on the beach is permitted.

Fishing Index: Whiting is one of the year-round favorites of surf anglers. Pompano are around when the water is above 68 degrees. The best action comes in fall when baitfish begin their run. Starting around mid September big redfish, jacks, and bluefish show up to feed on the schools of small baitfish. Dave Rogers, manager of The Fishing Shack in Port Orange, says one of the better places for surf fishing is from Ponce de Leon Inlet north for about 3 miles. High tide is the better time to fish the surf and low tide is the time to go to the beach and look for the troughs and runouts—the places where the water moves back out to sea.

Directions: A1A runs from the Volusia-Flagler county line south to Ponce de Leon Inlet. It crosses over to the mainland in Port Orange and begins again south of the inlet in New Smyrna Beach. Anywhere you can legally park and get to the beach is worth trying.

For more information: Call The Fishing Shack in Port Orange at (904) 788-2120.

35. PONCE DE LEON INLET

Salt; Pier and Boat.

Description: Inlets are great places to fish and this one boasts excellent access. Water moving through Ponce de Leon Inlet enters the Halifax River and the northern end of Indian River. It is the only inlet for these two bodies of water. For boaters, the ramp beneath the North Causeway in New Smyrna Beach is the closest one to the inlet.

Fishing Index: Snook, redfish, seatrout, flounder, sheepshead, mangrove snapper, and black drum are the mainstays here. They don't all gather here at the same time, but every month has one or two "hot" species.

Access Points:

35A. LIGHTHOUSE POINT PARK—*Pier and Surf.*
Description: The barrier-free pier is a 1,000-foot paved portion of the inlet's north jetty. Some anglers, trying to get a better place to fish, climb onto the rocks. This is dangerous and anyone doing it must exercise extreme caution. Wearing shoes with good gripping soles is a must. Surf fishing is popular on the park's beach.

Directions: From US 92 in Daytona Beach, take A1A south about 10.3 miles to the intersection where A1A turns right and heads back to the mainland at Port Orange. Take the A1A spur that continues south and go about 5.2 miles to the park.

35B. SMYRNA DUNE PARK—*Bank and Surf.*
Description: Fish off of the south side jetty, but be careful on the rocks; it's a scramble.

Directions: From New Smyrna Beach, take the A1A Causeway toward the beach. Just across the bridge, turn left onto North Peninsula Drive and go to the park or cut over to the beach and drive on the beach to the park.

36. INDIAN RIVER NORTH

Salt; Pier and Boat; Ramp.

Description: The first 12 miles south of Ponce de Leon inlet are often referred to as part of the Mosquito Lagoon. But, according to veteran guide Captain Bill Mosseller, this part, which has hundreds of small islands, is the Indian River North. Mosquito Lagoon, he says, is the open-water segment of the Indian River south of the islands. Whatever you call it, it is an excellent place to fish. Fifteen tidal creeks, each 2 miles or longer, feed into this labyrinth of mangrove islands. Boaters in a hurry may not like this place: a year-round manatee speed zone is in effect. Observe the posted boat speed limits.

Fishing Index: This area, like Mosquito Lagoon, has a lot of big redfish. Captain Bill Mosseller (call Indian River Guides at (904) 428-6801) likes to fish this part of the river because the fish are more confined here than in the open waters of Mosquito Lagoon to the south. He seldom runs more than a few minutes from the boat ramp before he stops, switches on his trolling motor and starts to catch fish. One of the biggest problems he believes anglers have, is noise. "If you keep your trolling motor working at 50 percent of its pounds of thrust rating or less, you will catch fish if nothing else than by accident! It's a fact!"

Access Points:

36A. NORTH AND SOUTH CAUSEWAYS—*Salt; Pier and Boat; Ramp.*
Description: The twin bridges over the Indian River in New Smyrna Beach are a focal point for anglers. Beneath the high bridge of the South Causeway is a productive 500-foot fishing pier. A smaller pier is adjacent to the north bridge. The ramp at the north bridge provides the closest boating access to Ponce de Leon Inlet. Note that the water around the ramp is part of an idle-speed zone for manatee protection.
Directions: From US 1 in New Smyrna Beach, go west 0.3 mile on FL 44. A1A branches off to the right and is the South Causeway. FL 44 branches to the left and is the North Causeway.

36B. KENNEDY MEMORIAL PARK—*Boat; Ramp.*
Directions: On the mainland side. From US 1 in New Smyrna Beach go south 2.3 miles on US 1 to Edgewater. At the intersection with Park Avenue, turn left and go 0.2 mile to the ramp.

36C. VETERANS PARK—*Pier.*
Directions: On the mainland side. From the intersection of US 1 and FL 44 in New Smyrna Beach, take US 1 south about 3.1 miles to Edgewater. Turn left onto Riverside Drive and go 0.25 mile to the pier.

36D. RIVERBREEZE PARK— *Pier and Boat; Ramp.*
Description: On the mainland side. A new park in 1995, Riverbreeze has a campground and a long pier that should prove to be a good place to fish.
Directions: From the intersection of FL 44 and US 1 in New Smyrna Beach, take US 1 south about 11.5 miles to Oak Hill. If coming from Titusville it is about 19 miles from the US 1 and FL 406 intersection. In Oak Hill, turn east on Birch Avenue and follow it to the park.

36E. CANAVERAL NATIONAL SEASHORE NORTH RAMP—*Wade and Boat; Ramp.*
Description: The ramp provides access to Indian River North and Mosquito Lagoon from the island side of the river. Anglers can wade fish the flats around the ramp.
Directions: From the point where A1A begins to parallel the beach in New Smyrna Beach, take A1A south about 7 miles to the ramp. It is about 0.5 mile past the large national seashore entrance sign.

For more information: Call the Canaveral National Seashore north entrance station at (904) 428-3384.

37. MOSQUITO LAGOON

Salt; Pier, Wade, and Boat; Ramp.

Description: Mosquito Lagoon is within the boundaries of Merritt Island National Wildlife Refuge and Canaveral National Seashore. Most of the lagoon is 3 feet deep or less. Boaters leaving the Intracoastal Waterway must be able to operate in very shallow water. Weather is important to fishing success here. Captain Bill Mosseller (call Indian River Guides at (904) 428-6801) says the best times to fish are when the barometer is rising or steady. With about an 8-inch tide, winds are more of a factor than tides in the lagoon.

Fishing Index: This may be the best place for redfish in the entire state. Extensive seagrasses grow in the shallows—perfect cover for redfish. Many catches are well in excess of the current 27-inch maximum for redfish. Mosseller, who has guided here for 22 years, believes that "if you stand quietly in the boat and can cast into a 3-foot circle at 50 feet, you will catch all the fish you can handle." His preferred method is to sight cast for the fish. Spotted seatrout are also abundant in the lagoon. "Right now," Mosseller says, "you can catch 50 of them in half a day, but most of them will be small." This will soon change, now that the fish are no longer legal to harvest by nets. Anglers new to the area should try freelining a live shrimp. It's the tried and true way to catch a trout. With a noticeable lack of oyster bars and submerged branches to cut lines, this is an outstanding place to fish with 4- to 8-pound test line and ultralight rods and reels.

Access Points:

37A. HAULOVER CANAL—*Salt; Bank and Boat; Ramp.*
Description: The ramp is in Merritt Island National Wildlife Refuge. The canal connects Mosquito Lagoon and the upper part of Indian River; a good spot for bank fishing.
Directions: From US 1 in Titusville, drive 6.9 miles east on the Max Brewer Parkway to FL 3 (Kennedy Parkway). Turn north and go 4 miles to the ramp on the left.

37B. CANAVERAL NATIONAL SEASHORE EDDY CREEK—*Salt; Ramp. Boat; Ramp.*
Description: This dirt ramp allows access to the south end of the lagoon for boats less than 16 feet in length. The ramp and other facilities in the area are closed 72 hours before and 24 hours after a rocket launch. Call (407) 867-2805 for information on closures.
Directions: From US 1 in Titusville, take Max Brewer Parkway across the Indian River. Go to FL 402 (Beach Road). Turn right onto FL 402 and go 8.6 miles to Playalinda Beach. Turn north on the seashore road and go about 2 miles to the ramp.
For more information: Call the Canaveral National Seashore south entrance station at (407) 267-1110.

38. Upper Indian River (Volusia-Brevard County Line to Dragon Point)

Salt; Boat, Bridge, and Pier; Ramp.

Description: The amount of seagrass diminishes as you move south, but there is no shortage of places to fish along this stretch of river. Fishing is allowed from the relief bridges (smaller bridges on one or both sides of the main bridge), on several of the causeways connecting the mainland to Merritt Island, and the beaches. They are very popular with land-bound anglers, however parking is a problem; resist temptation and obey the posted no-parking signs. Fishing is not permitted on the NASA Causeway.

Fishing Index: Not as famous for fishing as nearby Mosquito Lagoon, but there are plenty of seagrass beds, especially along the river's eastern shore. This is a good place to fish for redfish and spotted seatrout.

Access Points:

38A. Marina Park—*Salt; Boat; Ramp.*
Description: A city facility adjacent to Veterans Memorial Park.
Directions: From the intersection with FL 406 in Titusville, take US 1 north about 0.3 mile to Marina Park Road. Turn right and go to the ramp.

38B. Veterans Memorial Park—*Salt; Pier.*
Description: This free 400-foot city pier extends into the Indian River. From September through the end of April, shrimping is popular. Shrimpers must sign up for the daily lottery for the numbered spots (assigned locations). Some spots are better than others and the drawing eliminates territorial disagreements. To catch shrimp you need a long handled net and a light to hang over the surface of the water. The concessionaire operating the bait and tackle shop rents equipment and manages the lottery.
Directions: The pier is on the mainland side of the Indian River in Titusville at the base of the Brewer Causeway (FL 402).
For more information: Call the pier bait house at (407) 383-2464.

38C. Parrish Park—*Salt; Boat and Pier; Ramp.*
Directions: The park is at the eastern end of the Brewer Causeway (FL 402) Bridge over the Indian River.

38D. Manatee Hammock Park—*Salt; Boat and Bank; Ramp.*
Description: A county park with a developed campground, swimming pool, and outdoor game area. Reservations accepted.
Directions: From the intersection with FL 50 south of Titusville, take US 1 south 2 miles and look for the campground on the left.

38E. Port St. John Ramp—*Salt; Boat; Ramp.*
Description: A highly popular, sometimes crowded ramp; heavily used by commercial clammers. Parking can be a problem.
Directions: From the intersection with FL 50 south of Titusville, take US 1 south 4.3 miles and look for the ramp on the left.

BREVARD COUNTY (NORTH PORTION, COASTAL AREA)

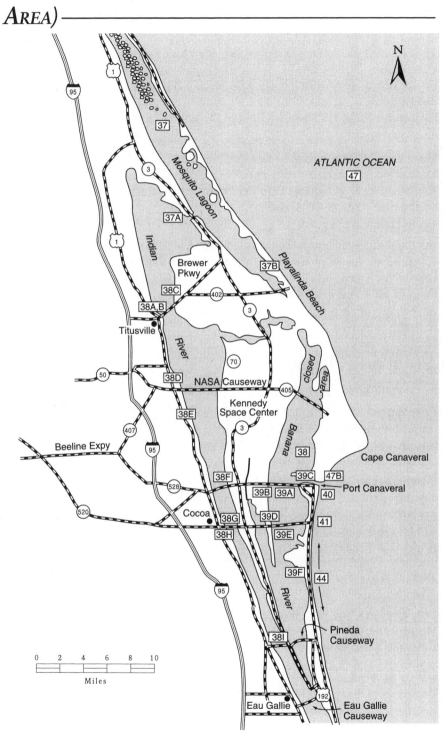

38F. FL 528 CAUSEWAY—*Salt; Boat and Bank; Ramp.*
Description: The facilities are on the east side of the Indian River.
Directions: From the junction with US 1 in Cocoa drive 2 miles east on the Bee Line Expressway (FL 528).

38G. HUBERT HUMPHREY BRIDGE—*Salt; Boat and Bridge; Ramp.*
Description: Part of the FL 520 (Merritt Island) Causeway from Cocoa to Cocoa Beach. Fish from the relief bridge. Facilities are on the east side of the Indian River.
Directions: From US 1 in Cocoa, take FL 520 east and cross the bridge.

38H. LEE WENNER PARK—*Salt; Boat and Pier; Ramp.*
Description: The old road bridge was converted into a fishing pier.
Directions: The park is at the base of the FL 520 Causeway on the mainland side of the river in Cocoa. Turn off FL 520 onto Riverside Drive. The park is on the south side of the causeway.

38I. PINEDA CAUSEWAY—*Salt; Bridge.*
Description: Fish from the causeway; parking is limited close to the areas where you can fish. A spit of land separates the Indian River from the Banana River.
Directions: From the intersection with FL 520 in Cocoa, take US 1 south 11 miles to FL 404 (Pineda Causeway). Turn left onto the causeway. Or from the intersection with FL 518 in Eau Gallie, take US 1 north 5.5 miles. Turn right onto the causeway.

39. BANANA RIVER

Salt; Boat, Bank Bridge and Wade; Ramp.

Description: This lagoon separates the east side of Merritt Island from the Canaveral Peninsula. The space shuttle launch pads are at the headwaters of this coastal waterway. Sykes Creek, a small creek that originates in Merritt Island, flows into the Banana River via Newfound Harbor.

Fishing Index: The area north of NASA Parkway (FL 405) is closed for security. From the FL 405 Parkway south to the FL 528 Causeway (FL 528) is a manatee refuge. No motor boats are allowed. This is an excellent place to fly fish for big redfish either from a canoe or by wading in the grass flats. South of the FL 528 Causeway to the end of the Banana River at Dragon Point is also excellent year-round for redfish. Boats are allowed here and the preferred method is to sight fish.

Access Points:
39A. FL 528 CAUSEWAY (BEE LINE EXPRESSWAY)—*Salt; Bridge and Wade.*
Description: This segment spans the Banana Riber from Merritt Island to Port Canaveral. Fish from the seawall around the bridge on the Merritt Island side and from the relief bridge over the Banana River. Wade the flats on the north side of the road.
Directions: From the FL 528 - FL 3 intersection on Merritt Island, take FL 528 east for 2.7 miles to the bridge. Pull off onto a dirt road on the north side of the road.

39B. KELLY PARK—*Salt; Boat and Bank; Ramp.*
Description: A Brevard County park. Good bank fishing on the Banana River.
Directions: From the FL 528 - FL 3 intersection on Merritt Island, take FL 528 east for 2.5 miles to the intersection with Banana River Road. Take Banana River Road south for 0.2 mile to the park. Bait and tackle are available at the convenience store across the street.

39C. PORT'S END PARK AND CENTRAL PARK—*Salt; Bank; Boat; Ramp.*
Description: These two small county parks have ramps along the south shore of the Port Canaveral Channel. Access is to the Atlantic Ocean and the Banana River. There is also good fishing from the seawall in Port's End Park.
Directions: From Cocoa, take the Bee Line Expressway (FL 528 Causeway) east towards the beach. Cross Merritt Island and the Banana River. To reach Port's End Park, turn left onto Dave Nisbet Drive (the first traffic light after crossing Banana River). Make an immediate left onto George King Boulevard, drive 0.1 mile and turn left onto Mullet Street. Continue 0.8 mile to Port's End Park. To reach Central Park, turn right onto George King Boulevard and then left onto Flounder Street (the first road after you turn onto George King Blvd.) Central Park is 0.1 mile down Flounder Street.
For more information: Call Sunrise Marina at (407) 783-9535 or Saltwater Concepts at (407) 784-9700.

39D. KIWANIS ISLAND PARK—*Salt; Boat; Ramp.*
Description: The park is on Sykes Creek on Merritt Island.
Directions: Take the Merritt Island Causeway (FL 520) from Cocoa toward Cocoa Beach. Cross the Indian River and go another 1.2 miles east on FL 520 from the intersection with FL 3 (Courtney Parkway). The park entrance is on the left.

39E. BANANA RIVER WAYSIDE PARK—*Salt; Bridge and Boat; Ramp.*
Directions: Take the Merritt Island Causeway (FL 520) from Cocoa toward Cocoa Beach. The park is on the causeway along the western side of the Banana River.

39F. RAMP ROAD PARK—*Salt; Boat, Bank and Pier; Ramp.*
Directions: Take the FL 520 Causeway to Cocoa Beach. Turn south at the A1A intersection and go about 3.2 miles to 4th Street. Look for the park signs and turn right.

40. JETTY PARK
Salt; Bank, Surf and Pier; $.

Description: This popular county park has a campground and offers a spectacular vantage point for watching the space shuttle blast off. Reservations are suggested during the winter tourist season. The Central Park boat ramp is nearby and charter boats operate out of the Port Canaveral area.

Fishing Index: Fish along a part of the seawall in the Port Canaveral Channel, from the jetty, or along the beach. Snook, flounder, bluefish, and mangrove snapper are common catches at any of these locations.

Directions: From Cocoa, take the Bee Line Expressway (FL 528 Causeway) east toward the beach. At the first traffic light after crossing the Banana River, turn left and then immediately right onto George King Boulevard. Go 0.9 mile on George King Blvd. until it ends at Jetty Drive. Turn left and continue 0.7 mile to the park.

For more information: Call Jetty Park at (407) 868-1108.

41. COCOA BEACH PIER
Salt; Pier; $.

Description: A restaurant and several gift shops at the base of the pier are the focal points here.

Fishing Index: Fish for mangrove snapper and sheepshead year-round.

Directions: From the A1A-FL 520 intersection in Cocoa Beach, drive 0.5 mile north on A1A to the pier.

For more information: Call the pier bait shop at (407) 783-7549.

BREVARD (SOUTH PORTION) AND INDIAN RIVER COUNTIES

42. NORTH-CENTRAL INDIAN RIVER (EAU GALLIE CAUSEWAY TO SEBASTIAN INLET)
Salt; Boat, Bank, Bridge, and Pier; Ramp.

Description: In this 18-mile reach, seagrasses are limited to a narrow fringe along the shoreline and around the shallow waters of most of the spoil islands.

Fishing index: In developed areas, fish around dock pilings for snook and sheepshead. Fish for trout and redfish wherever there is seagrass. Fishing tends to be better closer to Sebastian Inlet. Around the bridges and causeways anglers have good luck with mangrove snapper, sheepshead, redfish, and spotted seatrout. At night, try catching black drum.

Access Points:
42A. EAU GALLIE CAUSEWAY PARK BRIDGE—*Boat and Pier; Ramp.*
Description: Fish from the relief bridges or from the pier beneath the main span of the bridge.
Directions: From US 1 in Eau Gallie, take FL 518 east 0.6 mile to the start of the causeway. The park is on the causeway.

42B. BALLARD PARK—*Bank and Boat; Ramp.*
Directions: From the intersection with the Eau Gallie Causeway, take US 1 south about 1 mile to Thomas Harbor Drive. Turn left and go 0.5 mile to the park.

BREVARD (SOUTH PORTION) AND INDIAN RIVER COUNTIES

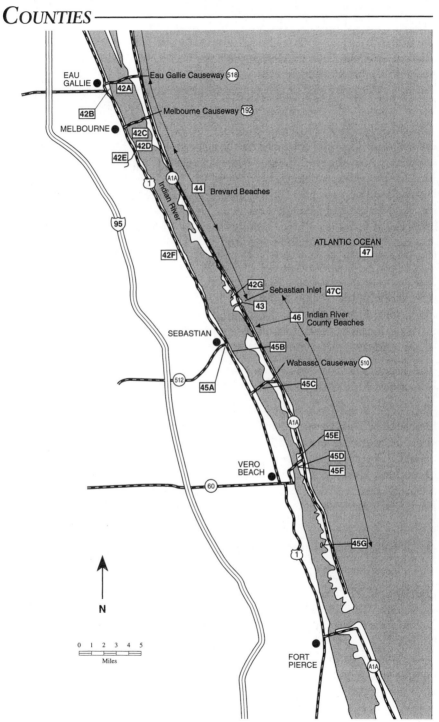

EAU GALLIE

Eau Gallie Causeway 518

42A

42B

Melbourne Causeway 192

MELBOURNE

42C

42D

42E

A1A

1

44 Brevard Beaches

95

ATLANTIC OCEAN
47

42F

42G

Sebastian Inlet 47C

43

46 Indian River
County Beaches

SEBASTIAN

45B

Wabasso Causeway 510

512

45A

45C

A1A

45E

45D

45F

VERO BEACH

60

45G

1

N

0 1 2 3 4 5
Miles

FORT PIERCE

A1A

42C. Melbourne Causeway—*Bank and Boat.*

Description: The causeway connects Melbourne to Indialantic and Melbourne Beach. There is no relief bridge but anglers can fish off the banks under the bridge. During the shrimp run, shrimpers work traps from the banks beneath the bridge.

Directions: From US 1 in Melbourne, take US 192 east to the causeway. Park at the east end of the causeway.

For more information: Call Richard's Gold Star Bait and Tackle at (407) 724-2566.

42D. Melbourne Beach Pier—*Pier.*

Description: This 636-foot pier on the eastern shore of the Indian River has a covered area at the end. Richard Smit, owner of Richard's Gold Star Bait and Tackle, says this is a great family place.

Fishing Index: In summer fish for spotted seatrout and redfish; in winter, whiting and sheepshead provide the action.

Directions: From US 192 in Indialantic, take A1A south 1.6 miles to Ocean Avenue. Turn right and go to the pier.

For more information: Call Richard's Gold Star Bait and Tackle at (407) 724-2566.

42E. Goode Park—*Boat; Ramp.*

Directions: From US 192 in Melbourne, take US 1 south 3.5 miles. Just after crossing Turkey Creek, turn right onto Port Malabar Boulevard. Go a few blocks and then turn right onto Bianca Road and follow it to the ramp.

42F. Jorgenson Landing—*Boat; Ramp.*

Directions: From Melbourne, drive 11 miles south on US 1 to the ramp.

42G. Long Point Park—*Bank and Boat; Ramp.*

Description: This Brevard County park has a campground with riverfront campsites, a swimming pond, and a many other amenities. Reservations are accepted and recommended.

Directions: From US 192 in Indialantic drive 15.2 miles south on A1A to the park. It's another 1.7 miles south to Sebastian Inlet.

For more information: Call the park office at (407) 952-4532.

43. Sebastian Inlet State Recreation Area ————

Salt; Boat, Bridge, Pier and Surf; Ramp.

Description: The inlet is one of the best known places to fish along Florida's east coast. The park has a ramp and campground on the south side of the inlet. The north side features swimming, surfing, and a bait and tackle shop. Landbound anglers can fish from the walkway on the north jetty or from the catwalk beneath the A1A bridge over the inlet.

Fishing Index: This is a great place for snook. Peter Kalata, owner of Whitey's Bait and Tackle, says, "It's like fishing for steelhead up north. Because of the current, the fish are holding in a spot and waiting for the food to come to

The fishing jetty at Sebastian Inlet State Recreation Area is one of the most popular and productive fishing piers along the east central Florida coast.

them." Live bait works best, he adds. "Make a quartering cast upstream and let the bait sink to the bottom and bounce along until it drifts by you."

Summer snook fishing is great but the season is closed so it's strictly catch and release. In fall, the bait run along the beach begins and the action in the inlet can be frantic. Anglers may catch some big snook, redfish, sharks, tarpon, and any other species that happens to be around. In winter, big flounder provide the top action. Fish for them on the bottom with a live shrimp or finger mullet. Kalata says the key to catching these doormats is to let the fish swim off with the bait before you try to set the hook. This may take a minute or more after you feel the first bite.

Directions: From US 192 in Indialantic, drive about 17.2 miles south on A1A to the park. Or from FL 60 in Vero Beach drive 15 miles north on A1A.

For more information: Call the park office at (407) 984-4852. For fishing information try Whitey's Bait and Tackle at (407) 724-1440.

44. Brevard County Beaches

Salt; Surf.

Description: Beginning at the county's northern boundary, surf anglers can enjoy the beautiful, undeveloped beaches of the Canaveral National Seashore. Beach access is restricted at the J.F.K. Space Center, but south of Port Canaveral Inlet the beach is open to the public all the way to Sebastian Inlet.

Fishing Index: Pompano and whiting are present year-round. Bluefish are the winter staple. Many seasoned surf anglers say that fall, when the baitfish make their run south, is the best time to surf fish. There's no telling what may bite. Snook, big redfish, tarpon, crevalle jack, and even a few king mackerel may take the bait. Big surf rods are essential to reach the fish, which are farther offshore from late fall to spring. Come summer, switch to light tackle and fish only a few feet from shore.

Directions: Wherever A1A runs along the beach, be on the lookout for a place to park and fish. When in Canaveral National Seashore, you must park in the designated parking lots and use the wooden walkways over the sand dunes to reach the beach. South of Port Canaveral, A1A is never more than a block or two from the ocean. Beginning with the beach at Jetty Park, numerous parks provide access to the beach. Anglers must be careful not to fish too close to swimmers and in the beach areas reserved exclusively for swimming.

Crevalle jack are tremendously strong fish. Even small ones, such as this one-pound fish, are exciting to catch.

45. SOUTH-CENTRAL INDIAN RIVER (SEBASTIAN INLET TO ROUND ISLAND)

Salt; Bridge, Bank, Pier and Boat; Ramp.

Description: A 21-mile reach of the Indian River within Indian River County. Vero Beach is the largest developed area.

Fishing Index: This is one of the favorite fishing grounds for veteran guide Captain Terry Parsons (call (407) 589-7782). He fishes the area for redfish and trout. Anglers can also catch some legal-size grouper along the edges of the Intracoastal Waterway according to Parsons. He believes that they come in through Sebastian Inlet, grow up on the grassflats, and then move into the deeper channels when they get bigger. Parsons also recommends the west side of the river south of Vero Beach for wade fishing.

For more information: Call Wabasso Tackle Shop at (407) 589-8518.

Access Points:
45A. SEBASTIAN RAMP—*Boat; Ramp.*
Directions: From the intersection with FL 60 in Vero Beach, take US 1 north 12 miles to Sebastian. Turn right on Main Street and follow it to the ramp.

45B. SEBASTIAN YACHT CLUB—*Boat; Ramp.*
Directions: From the intersection with FL 60 in Vero Beach, take US 1 north 11 miles to Sebastian. Turn right on Indian River Drive and follow it to the ramp.

45C. WABASSO CAUSEWAY BRIDGE—*Bank, and Boat; Ramp.*
Description: A popular spot for boaters and land-bound anglers alike. The next public ramp to the south is in Vero Beach.
Directions: From the intersection with FL 60 in Vero Beach, take US 1 north 8 miles to Wabasso. Turn right on FL 510 (Wabasso Causeway). The ramp is on the island side of the causeway.

45D. FL 60 BRIDGE—*Bridge.*
Description: The old FL 60 bridge, or Merrill Barber Bridge, was relocated and replaced. A catwalk for anglers runs beneath the new bridge.
Directions: From US 1 in Vero Beach, take FL 60 east about 1 mile to the bridge.

45E. MCWILLIAMS PARK—*Boat; Ramp.*
Directions: From US 1 in Vero Beach, take FL 60 east and cross the new Merrill Barber Bridge. Just over the bridge, turn left onto Indian River Drive and then make an immediate left onto the park road leading to the ramp.

45F. RIVERSIDE PARK—*Boat; Ramp.*
Directions: From US 1 in Vero Beach, take FL 60 east and cross the new Merrill Barber Bridge. Just over the bridge, turn right into the park.

45G. ROUND ISLAND—*Surf and Boat; Ramp.*
Description: This park on the island side of the river encompasses the land from the river to the Atlantic Ocean. Anglers can surf fish or launch a boat in

the Indian River. Just north of the Indian County-St. Lucie County line.
Directions: From FL 60 in Vero Beach drive about 7 miles south on A1A to the park. Fort Pierce Inlet is another 5 miles south.

46. Indian River County Beaches ——————————
Salt; Surf.

Description: Seven county beaches are open to swimmers and anglers. Parts of some beaches may be restricted for swimmers only, but there is plenty of room for surf anglers to find a place to fish.

Fishing Index: There are live "worm reefs" just offshore of the beaches in this county. Some of them are very close to shore and that creates good habitat for fish. Like all the surf zones along this part of Florida, late fall to early spring fishing for bluefish is very good. In spring and into early summer, pompano are a popular target. Surf fishing also yields snook, redfish, and occasionally tarpon and Spanish mackerel.

Directions: A1A parallels the beach. The county parks and other public parking areas are on this road.

47. Atlantic Ocean ——————————————
Salt; Boat.

Description: Offshore fishing along the East Central coast is varied. Captain Terry Parsons explains that this part of Florida has two populations of some species such as dolphin and Spanish and king mackerel. One population migrates up and down the Atlantic coast in spring and fall. The other moves up from south Florida and the Keys in summer. The result is longer seasons for some of the most popular offshore species.

Fishing Index: Close to shore, boaters seek Spanish and king mackerel during the spring and fall runs. Cobia, following the manta rays, also move close to shore most years in spring and fall. Farther out, dolphin fishing is very good spring through fall; sailfishing is best in fall and winter. Add to that the year-round presence of amberjack, wahoo, grouper, snapper, and cobia and anglers can always count on at least one or two species for good action.

Fleet Locations:
47A. Ponce Inlet.
Description: Most of this fleet is based in the community of Ponce Inlet on the north side of the inlet. A few boats also operate from New Smyrna Beach.
For more information: Call the "Critter Fleet" at (904) 767-7676.

47B. Port Canaveral.
Description: Anglers visiting the Orlando area are only 45 minutes from the fleet at Port Canaveral. It is a direct shot on the Bee Line Expressway to the port. Party and sportfishing boats are available.

For more information: Call the party boat Miss Cape Canaveral at (407) 783-5274. From Orlando the direct number is 648-2211. They book for several of the sportfishing boats plus two party boats.

47C. Sebastian Inlet.
Description: A few boats operate from small marinas near the inlet.
For more information: Call Wabasso Tackle Shop at (407) 589-7782.

Month by Month in East Central Florida

Note: *Offshore is defined as greater than 2 miles from the coast. Coastal waters include open waters inside of 2 miles including surf fishing, and all brackish water areas such as bays, the saltwater regions of rivers, and lagoons. Freshwater includes lakes, ponds, reservoirs, and rivers.*

January

Offshore: Sailfish and grouper are the best bets if the seas aren't too rough.

Coastal: An excellent time to surf fish for bluefish and whiting. Pompano may be plentiful when the water is above 68 degrees. Sand fleas are the top bait. Also the prime time for big flounder and spotted seatrout. Fish for them in the inlets and deeper spots of the Halifax, Banana, and Indian rivers. For flounder, anchor a big live shrimp or finger mullet on the bottom.

Freshwater: Striped and sunshine bass fishing is very good in the St. Johns River. Largemouth bass begin spawning in the lakes and rivers. Crappie action steadily improves this month. Shad anglers may see some fish toward mid-month.

February

Offshore: A repeat of the top sailfish and grouper action seen in January. Anglers will also find some wahoo, amberjack, blackfin tuna, and cobia out near the edge of the Gulf Stream. Bad weather dictates when it's most comfortable to go fishing.

Coastal: Bluefish, pompano, and whiting reward surf anglers this month. Use a 10- to 12-foot surf rod and expect to wade in to reach the trough that holds fish. Spotted seatrout action is very good with the bigger fish staying in deeper and warmer water near the flats. Try fishing for them later in the day. If the water on the flats is going to warm up and entice them to feed, this is when they'll show up, tides permitting.

Freshwater: This is one of the peak months for trophy largemouth bass. The best bait is live wild shiners. Normally, this is also one of the best American shad months on the upper St. Johns River. Add the excellent crappie fishing typical in February and this is one of the best months for freshwater fishing in the region.

MARCH

Offshore: Dolphin is on anglers' minds and this traditionally marks the beginning of the spring northward migration of the tasty fish. Closer to shore, Spanish and king mackerel also move north and the action is very good. If the waters warm up early, cobia will also make a strong showing.

Coastal: The big three—redfish, spotted seatrout, and snook—dominate the desires of anglers. Redfish and trout action is in its prime. Snook action is good but will improve in the next two months. If the net ban works like the biologists say it will, this could be a phenomenal month for fishing in the late 1990s and beyond. Surf fishing falls off as the bluefish leave, but a king mackerel or two may pick up the bait, especially if it's a live baitfish.

Freshwater: The peak time for shad will come and go in this month. Check the local conditions and don't procrastinate if you hear the fish are biting. Crappie action will begin to slow down for anglers who can't find the cooler waters in lakes and rivers. Largemouth bass are past peak spawning time but they are still around and hungry.

APRIL

Offshore: Dolphin are abundant. A wahoo, sailfish, or marlin may also liven up the day. Spanish and king mackerel continue to be very good. Small schools of cobia, following the manta rays, offer exciting sight fishing. An excellent way to find some blackfin tuna is to set out a chum slick behind the shrimp boats that anchor offshore during the day. Throw some chum in the water and if the tuna are present, you will see them. At that point, they are so worked up that they will hit just about any thing you toss their way.

Coastal: Around the inside of inlets and in lagoons, the redfish, snook, and seatrout action is excellent. Inlet specialists and surf anglers have a good chance of catching some cobia and Spanish mackerel. Drifting live bait, weighted down so there is just enough to keep the bait a few feet off the bottom, is a proven technique in the inlets. The shrimp run, if there is one, can be very good this month. Trouble is, the run is very unpredictable and success hinges on watching and waiting just about every night.

Freshwater: Largemouth bass move into the post-spawn feeding pattern and that makes for good fishing, but it is the last good month until late fall. Panfish lovers turn out in force as the bluegills begin to spawn.

MAY

Offshore: Spring has better-than-average fishing because of the migratory species moving past the east-central coast. May marks the tail end of the spring migration. Closer to shore, cobia are the best bet. Farther out, past the 100' contour, dolphin fishing is very good. The local peak season for blue marlin begins now.

Coastal: Snook fishing, especially around the inlets, is the best bet. Shark fishing also improves. The inlets and along the beaches are the most popular places to find them. Start your fishing early in the morning and late in the day or at night.

Freshwater: Bluegills and shellcrackers are on their beds and that translates into top action for both species. Largemouth bass and crappie action slows for summer unless you know how to fish the deeper spots in the lakes and rivers. Get the bait down to the fish and work it slowly. Heat makes the fish sluggish, even when eating.

JUNE

Offshore: Summer action is slower than in spring and fall but you can still catch fish. Expect average fishing for a variety of species including cobia, wahoo, king mackerel, amberjack, sailfish, and dolphin. Blue marlin fishing is in its prime and a trip to the Gulf Stream may be productive. Bottom fishing for grouper and snapper always brings in some fish. The question is how many will be legal size?

Coastal: Snook fishing is great but unless there is a change in the laws, you can't keep the fish this month. Snook spawn in summer and are catch-and-release only now. That's how we ensure there will be new fish for tomorrow's generation to catch. Shark anglers usually do well with the small coastal species such as blacktip. If you catch some pigfish (known by some as grunts), use them for bait for the big spotted seatrout that are around but reluctant to bite.

Freshwater: Early and late—those are the times of day for the best chance at catching some largemouth bass. There is very good year-round angling for catfish in virtually every freshwater body in the region. They are easy to catch and a catfish fry with some hushpuppies and cole slaw is hard to beat for great eating.

JULY

Offshore: Fishing for mangrove and lane snapper is popular for offshore anglers now. The best action is at night. Blue marlin action will still be better than average for the area. Other offshore fish are there, but summer is the slowest time of the year.

Coastal: Thanks to the excellent redfish habitat in the Indian River Lagoon, anglers can usually find some hungry redfish. Fish early in the morning or late in the day. At the end of the day watch for thunderstorms. Anyone can fish the surf this time of year. All you need is light tackle. The fish are in the first trough, which is always very close to shore. For pompano, use live sand fleas which you can dig on the beach. If none are found, go to the grocery store and buy some clams. They make an excellent bait for pompano and whiting.

Freshwater: The best bet are shellcrackers. If you are familiar with the places you fish, try a night trip for largemouth bass. The cooler evenings are likely times for bass to move into shallow waters to feed.

August

Offshore: A little of this and a little of that describes midsummer offshore fishing. The species swimming around include all the familiar names: cobia, dolphin, king mackerel, sailfish, wahoo, and others. Some days the fishing will be good and other times it will be tough. The best bets are night fishing for snapper and shark.

Coastal: Another month when experienced anglers can catch redfish in good numbers. If you lack experience but want to catch a lot of fish, try a trip with a guide. Snook and trout are caught in respectable numbers. In the surf, whiting and pompano are the most likely catches.

Freshwater: Limit your fishing to early in the morning or late in the day. The fish don't like the heat any more than you do. Actually it's harder on them because the warmer the water, the less life-sustaining oxygen it holds. If you know of a deep hole, work that area carefully. It should have fish in it.

September

Offshore: Anglers are ready for a change and September usually brings one. Baitfish, chased south by mackerel and cobia, run down the coast, signaling prime angling offshore all the way in to the beach. Water temperature apparently determines when the run begins.

Coastal: Surf and inlet anglers are also waiting for the bait to show up and stimulate the snook, tarpon, and seatrout action. Redfish provide the most reliable action until the feeding frenzy begins. Expect good fishing for mangrove snapper off bridges at night.

Freshwater: A slow month—still hot and humid—but better days are ahead. Not much change in activity or strategy since June.

October

Offshore: The action for cobia, both mackerel species, and tarpon swings into high gear. A trolled or cast silver spoon is usually irresistible for the mackerel once you've found them. This month and next are the best for offshore tarpon fishing. There may not be greater numbers of fish, but the action is noticeably better.

Coastal: Prime month to catch the big three: snook, redfish, and seatrout. Fish around the inlets, on the deeper flats, and within 0.5 mile of shore. Freeline a live bait and hold on. Tarpon also move close in now. A few are always caught from the surf.

Freshwater: The first signs of cooler weather bring largemouth bass anglers to the lakes and rivers and the bass back into the shallow water. Action is better but is not back to the peak experienced during spawning season. Sunshine and striped bass, if present, begin to bite again. So do crappie.

Offshore: Grouper action picks up as the fish move closer to the coast. King and Spanish mackerel and cobia are top choices this month. Sailfish activity begins to build toward the winter peak. Weather becomes a factor in making long offshore trips.

Coastal: Bluefish arrive and surf anglers dig out their big rods and reels. Snook, seatrout, tarpon, and redfish are in their fall prime. Flounder fishing begins to improve.

Freshwater: Cool water stimulates the appetites of the three bass species. Largemouths start to feed in anticipation of the spawn. Crappie action can be very good if the water cools off faster than normal.

DECEMBER

Offshore: This is one of the best times of year for grouper and sailfish. On warm days anglers can also find some amberjack, cobia, king mackerel, and blackfin tuna. Only the weather can spoil your plans.

Coastal: Bluefish from the surf and flounder in the inlets keep coastal anglers busy this month. Both are best bets. In the lagoons and saltwater rivers, sheepshead action is good around the numerous bridges and causeways that link the mainland to the beaches.

Freshwater: Prime crappie season begins this month. In the St. Johns, striped bass fishing enters its prime season.

EAST CENTRAL FLORIDA FISH AVAILABLITLITY CHART

NOTE: Refer to the month-by-month table for additional information. Information in this chart represents the seasonal patterns observed over the past three years. For saltwater species, the arrival of the migrant species and the peak times for each species are heavily dependent on water temperature. Unusually warm or cold periods will affect the patterns described above. Bream is the local name for bluegills and shellcrackers. Specs is a local name for crappie. Speckled trout is a local name for spotted seatrout.

■ signifies a reasonable chance of catching this species in that month.

❑ signifies the optimal months for catching the species.

SPECIES	JAN	FEB	MAR	APR	MAY	JUN	JUL	AUG	SEP	OCT	NOV	DEC
Redfish	■	■	❑	❑	❑	❑	❑	❑	❑	❑	❑	■
Snook	■	■	■	■	❑	❑	■	■	❑	❑	❑	■
Spotted Seatrout	❑	❑	❑	❑	❑	■	■	■	❑	❑	❑	■
Sheepshead	■	■	■	■	■	■	■	■	■	■	■	❑
Mangrove Snapper	■	■	■	■	■	■	■	■	■	■	■	■
Gag Grouper	❑	❑	■	■	■	■	■	■	■	❑	❑	❑
Bluefish	❑	❑	■	■	■	■	■	■	■	■	❑	❑
Flounder	❑	❑	■	■	■	■	■	■	■	■	■	❑

SPECIES	JAN	FEB	MAR	APR	MAY	JUN	JUL	AUG	SEP	OCT	NOV	DEC
Black Drum	■	■	■	■	■	■	■	■	■	■	■	■
Dolphin	■	■	□	□	□	□	■	■	■	■	■	■
Blackfin Tuna	■	■	■	■	■	■	■	■	■	■	■	■
Blue Marlin	■	■	■	□	□	□	□	■	■	■	■	■
Wahoo	■	■	■	■	■	■	□	□	■	■	■	■
Whiting	□	□	■	■	■	■	■	■	■	■	■	□
Amberjack	■	■	■	■	■	□	□	□	□	■	■	■
Sailfish	□	□	■	■	■	■	■	■	■	■	■	□
Cobia	■	■	■	□	□	■	■	■	■	□	□	■
Spanish Mackerel	■	■	□	□	□	■	■	■	■	□	□	■
King Mackerel	■	■	□	□	■	■	■	■	■	□	□	■
Crevalle Jack	■	■	■	■	■	■	■	■	■	■	■	■
Tarpon	■	■	■	■	■	■	■	■	□	□	□	■
Pompano	□	■	■	■	■	■	■	■	■	■	□	□
Shrimp	■	■	■	■	■							
Shark (all species)				■	■	□	□	□	■	■		
Largemouth Bass	□	□	□	□	■	■	■	■	■	■	■	■
Bluegills	■	■	■	□	□	□	■	■	■	■	■	■
Catfish	■	■	■	■	■	■	■	■	■	■	■	■
Shellcracker	■	■	■	■	□	□	□	■	■	■	■	■
Sunshine Bass	□	□	■	■						■	■	□
Striped Bass	□	□	■	■						■	■	□
Crappie	□	□	□	■	■						■	□
American Shad	■	□	□	■	■							

CHAPTER SEVEN
West Central Florida

COUNTIES: ▪ Levy (southern portion) ▪ Citrus ▪ Marion (western portion) ▪ Hernando ▪ Sumter ▪ Pasco ▪ Pinellas ▪ Hillsborough ▪ Polk ▪ Manatee ▪ Hardee ▪ Sarasota ▪ DeSoto ▪ Highlands

SALTWATER FISHING

No place along the West Central coast is far from good fishing. Most of the coastline along the upper part of this region, from Waccasassa Bay to Weeki Wachee, is still relatively undeveloped. Small tidal creeks and four larger rivers empty into the Gulf of Mexico, with salt marshes along most of the shoreline. The Gulf waters are shallow and seagrasses flourish—perfect conditions for spotted seatrout, redfish, tarpon, and flounder. In fact, most of the biggest tarpon landed in Florida come from Homosassa Bay in late spring and early summer when the fish move onto the flats to feed.

Farther south along the coast, development has mushroomed, spreading onto the barrier islands. The bays and sounds here, including Old Tampa, Hillsborough, Tampa, and Boca Ciega bays, Clearwater Harbor, and St. Joseph Sound, are recovering from years of pollution, and the fishing is improving. Anglers can fish from the area's many bridges, or launch a boat at local ramps. The passes—Hurricane, Clearwater, John's, and North Channel—are good places to look for big snook and predatory fish in summer. Fishing is good when the tide is going in or coming out.

South from Tampa Bay are the popular destinations of Bishop's Harbor, Terra Ceia Bay, and the flats around Snead Island. Anna Maria Island and the north half of Longboat Key have several access points for fishing the protected waters of Anna Maria Sound and Sarasota Bay. Public access points at Gulf Front Park, Sunset Beach, Manatee County Public Beach, and Beer Can Island allow surf anglers a convenient way to get on the beach.

Sarasota, Little Sarasota, and Blackburn bays offer excellent opportunities for snook, redfish, and spotted seatrout.

Charter boats operate from almost every coastal community, especially those near the passes connecting to the Gulf of Mexico. A few big party boats specialize in trips to the Florida Middle Grounds 100 miles offshore. These are one- or two-night trips where anglers bottom fish for grouper, snapper, amberjack, and other species. Call Hubbard's Marina for a schedule for near offshore and Middle Ground trips.

FRESHWATER FISHING

Hundreds of lakes dot this region and all contain fish. About half of the lakes are accessible from public or private ramps or via waterways that link some lakes.

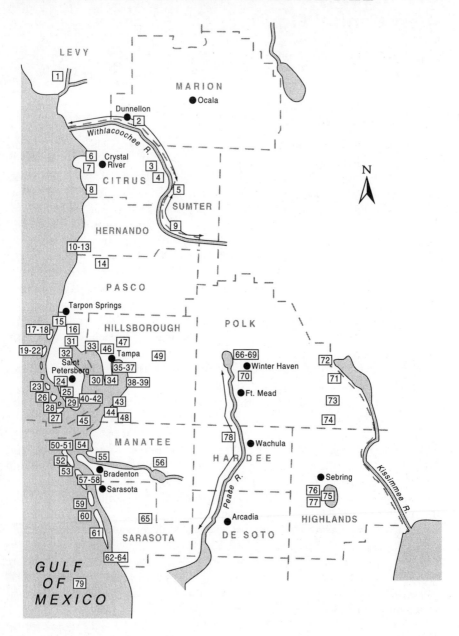

The bigger lakes attract most of the out-of-town anglers because outdoor magazines have popularized these over-sized fishing holes.

But fishing can be very good in the smaller, lesser known lakes too, including all those listed in this chapter. Stop at one of the local bait and tackle shops for tips on which lakes have the best action.

The region's rivers—particularly the Withlacoochee and Peace—are known for their scenic beauty and "old Florida" feel. The fishing is fine, but even devoted anglers may end up spending as much time watching wildlife as fishing.

Largemouth bass is the freshwater king in this region. The water is too warm for striped bass, and while the GFC stocks hybrid (sunshine) bass, the fish seldom reach the size they do in the cooler waters to the north. Crappie are another popular target, especially during the colder months.

LEVY (SOUTHERN PORTION), MARION (WESTERN PORTION), CITRUS, AND SUMTER COUNTIES

1. WACCASASSA RIVER

Salt; Boat; Ramp.

Description: There is a county boat ramp and a private ramp at Waccasassa Marina. Both are at the end of FL 326. Most anglers head downriver to fish the brackish waters of the river or the open waters of the Gulf of Mexico. It's about a 6-mile trip to the Gulf.

Fishing Index: Redfish and spotted seatrout are the most sought-after species. The area also produces some nice black drum. A hole at the mouth of the river is a frequent gathering spot for drum.

Directions: From US 19 in Gulf Hammock, drive 3.7 miles on FL 326 to the Levy County boat ramp.

For more information: Call the Waccasassa Marina at (352) 486-2339.

2. WITHLACOOCHEE RIVER (GULF OF MEXICO TO LAKE PANASOFFKEE)

Salt and Fresh; Boat and Bank; Ramp.

Description: This 90-mile river begins in the Green Swamp and flows northwest to the Gulf. The river is fresh except for the last 1.5 miles. This unusual situation is due to a hydroelectric dam, built on the river in the early 1900s. It also created Lake Rousseau stretching almost 10 miles upriver before the Withlacoochee returns to its narrow, meandering course.

Just south of the river mouth is the outlet of the Cross Florida Barge Canal. Originally the canal was to cut across the state from here to the Ocklawaha River and eventually connect to the St. Johns River. Because of numerous envi-

Pelicans, like this immature one, are always around fishing piers. Anglers must be very careful not to accidentally hook one of the birds. If you do, try to reel it in and remove the hook and all fishing line on the bird.

ronmental concerns, the project is defunct, but parts of the canal were constructed before the project officially died. Today the canal, from the lock to the Gulf, is used by anglers.

Just east of Dunnellon, the Blue Run joins the Withlacoochee, adding the clear water of Rainbow Springs to the river. The water in the run is a constant 70 to 72 degrees throughout the year. As you head upriver during low water, watch for rocks. Outlet River connects Lake Panasoffkee to the Withlacoochee River.

Fishing Index: Saltwater anglers will find some good redfish and seatrout spots along the lower reaches of the river and the canal. The shallow flats along the coast are also popular places to fish. Anglers also have a chance to hook up with some cobia around the channel markers seaward of the river mouth and a few legal size grouper where the old barge canal opens into the Gulf of Mexico.

Largemouth bass, crappie, and bluegills are the three top species in Lake Rousseau. February to May are the best months according to Brian Olear, manager of Buddy's Lakeside Park (at (352) 477-2513). "I like to fish deep in about 10 to 14 feet of water. The best place for this is in the channel. The rule of thumb I follow is that the big bass live on the bottom."

Captain Wayne Smith (at (352) 795-7302), who has fished the Withlacoochee and Lake Rousseau since 1969, has good luck catching big largemouth bass in the 3- to 4-foot-deep flats in spring and follows the fish to deeper water of the channel in summer on Lake Rousseau. He likes to use

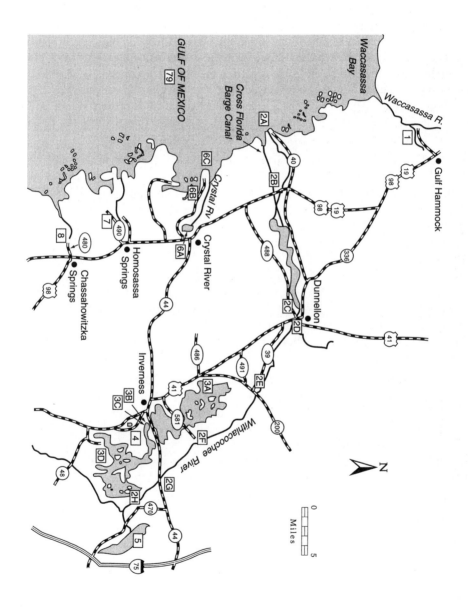

moccasin and blue-flake-colored artificial worms when fishing deep. In fall largemouth bass begin to move back into the shallow waters and stay there until the cold months of the winter. "Speckled perch, what other people call crappie, fishing is excellent from January through March. In April the shellcracker action picks up so there's always something to catch in the lake or the 'backwaters' which is what we call the upper part of the lake." The best chance of catching a trophy bass Smith says, "is to come in January or February and fish the open water flats with live native shiners. There are plenty of stumpfields in the shallow waters of the lake and that's the place to look for the big largemouths."

The lower part of Blue Run is a great place to fish for big bass in winter. The fish seek out the warmer water from the spring and congregate here, especially where the two rivers come together. From the Run upriver to the FL 200 bridge, Captain Wayne Smith says there are a series of old phosphate pits dating back to the late 1800s. These pits are connected to the river and offer anglers some good places to fish for largemouth bass. Upstream of the FL 200 bridge, the bottom is rocky and boaters need to exercise caution.

Directions: The river and lake form the boundary between Citrus and Levy and Marion and Sumter counties. Yankeetown is the last community before the river empties into the Gulf of Mexico and Dunnellon is the town at the eastern end of the lake. In addition to the sites described below, a number of fish camps and marinas are found along both the north and south shores of the lake.

Access Points:

2A. YANKEETOWN COUNTY PARK—*Salt; Boat and Bank; Ramp.*
Description: The Levy County park ramp provides access to the marsh-fringed shoreline along the Gulf of Mexico and the mouth of the Cross Florida Barge Canal segment that leads to Lake Rousseau.
Directions: From US 19 turn west onto FL 40 and go about 6 miles to the end of the road.

2B. CROSS FLORIDA GREENWAYS CANAL—*Salt; Bank and Boat; Ramp.*
Description: This facility is operated by the Florida Office of Greenways Management. The ramp provides access to the canal and the Gulf of Mexico. Access to Lake Rousseau is possible on the weekends from 8 a.m. to 4 p.m. when the lock is operating.
Directions: From US 19 on the south side of the canal, turn onto the access road and go about 0.2 mile to the ramp.

2C. GOLDENDALE RAMP—*Fresh; Boat; Ramp.*
Directions: From US 41 turn onto CR 488 just south of Dunnellon and the river. Drive 2.3 miles west on CR 488 to N. Goldendale Avenue. Turn right and go 0.3 mile to the ramp on Lake Rousseau.

2D. DUNNELLON—*Fresh; Boat; Ramp.*
Directions: The ramp is on US 41 on the north side of the river.

2E. EAST RIVERSIDE DRIVE RAMP—*Bank and Boat; Ramp.*
Directions: The Citrus County ramp is off of FL 200 along the south shore of the river. Turn onto CR 39 (Withlacoochee Trail) and go 1.3 miles to N. Oats Way and Riverside Drive. Turn right and go 0.1 mile to the ramp.

2F. TURNER CAMP—*Boat and Bank; Ramp.*
Directions: From US 41 in Inverness, drive 7.1 miles northwest on CR 581 to the end of the road and the ramp.

2G. RUTLAND BOAT—*Ramp; Boat; Ramp.*
Directions: The ramp is on the north side of the river on the west side of FL 44, 8 miles west of I-75.

2H. WYSONG PARK—*Boat and Bank; Ramp.*
Description: A small dock adjacent to the ramp is used by local anglers.
Directions: The facilities are on CR 300 off of FL 470. From Inverness drive about 10 miles east on FL 44. Turn right onto FL 470 and drive about 2 miles south to CR 300. Take CR 300 another 0.7 mile to the ramp. Or from I-75 at the town of Lake Panasoffkee, drive north about 4 miles on FL 470 to CR 307. Turn left and go 0.1 mile to CR 300. Turn right and go north 0.25 mile to the ramp.

For more information on the above sites: Call the GFC Central Region office at (352) 732-1225.

3. LAKE TSALA APOPKA ————————————————

Fresh; Boat, Bank, and Pier; Ramp.

Description: Lake Tsala Apopka is Florida's most unique lake. It is more like a collection of ponds surrounded by marsh. Sam McKinney of the GFC describes the lake as "a big marsh with some open holes." Those open holes are three pools that are now connected to each other by water control structures. The lake's connections to the Withlacoochee River are also via water control structures. The Floral City and Hernando pools are not as noted for fishing as the Inverness pool. The latter produces twice as many pounds of fish per acre, according to studies done by McKinney. Local anglers who know the area catch fish in all three areas but aren't real anxious to reveal all the best places. Who can blame them?

Fishing Index: The lake is a very good place to fish for largemouth bass and bream. Fluctuating lake levels affect fishing and navigation in the area.

Directions: There are four boat ramps and several private fish camps on the lake. The ramps are all accessible from US 41.

Access Points:
3A. HERNANDO BEACH—*Pier; Ramp.*
Description: A Citrus County facility with picnicking, a playground, and two ramps. Access to the Hernando pool.
Directions: From the intersection with CR 486 in Hernando, drive 0.2 mile north on US 41 to E. Orange Drive. Turn right and go 0.1 mile to the park.

Airboats offer anglers a chance to reach areas of Lake Tsala Apopka that anglers in boats can't reach. Dense mats of floating vegetation are characteristic of this lake.

3B. FL 44 Ramp—*Ramp.*
Directions: From US 41 in Inverness, drive 1 mile east on FL 44 to the ramp. Access to the Inverness pool.

3C. Eden Park—*Pier; Ramp.*
Description: A Citrus County park with a playground and picnic facilities.
Directions: From the intersection with FL 44 south of Inverness, go south on US 41 about 0.5 mile. Turn east on Eden Drive and go 0.5 mile to Park Lake Terrace. Turn left and go 0.1 mile to the park.

3D. Duval Island—*Ramp.*
Directions: From US 41 in Floral City, drive 0.75 mile southeast on FL 48 to Duval Island Road. Turn left and follow the road 0.1 mile to the ramp. Access to the Floral City pool.

4.   Fort Cooper State Park
Fresh; Bank and Canoe; $.

Description: The park features a horse trail, hiking trail, and campground. Only electric motors are allowed.

Fishing Index: Fish in the clear, spring-fed waters of Lake Holathlikaha for largemouth bass and bream.

Directions: From the intersection with FL 44 south of Inverness, drive 1 mile south on US 41. Turn left onto Old Floral City Road and go 1.1 miles to the park entrance.

For more information: Call the park office at (352) 726-0315.

5. LAKE PANASOFFKEE

Fresh; Boat; Ramp.

Description: Water levels in this spring-fed lake fluctuate in response to changes in the underlying aquifer. The developed part of the lake—including several fish camps—is along the lower western shore. Extensive marshes fringe the remainder of the lake. The lake and the Withlacoochee River are connected by the Outlet River.

Fishing Index: Panasoffkee has a reputation as a top shellcracker (redear sunfish) lake. This comes from the abundant supply of apple snails and freshwater clams that are the preferred food of this feisty panfish. Bass and speckled perch (crappie) fishing is also good in this shallow lake.

Directions: To reach the fish camps, exit I-75 and drive a couple of miles north on FL 470. The public ramp is on FL 470 where it crosses the Outlet River, about 4.9 miles north of I-75.

6. CRYSTAL RIVER

Salt and Fresh; Boat and Bank; Ramp.

Description: This is one of the best places in Florida to observe manatees. A series of springs here pumps millions of gallons of water into King's Bay. This nearly constant 72-degree water is a winter haven for manatees. The Crystal River National Wildlife Refuge was established in 1983 to specifically protect these endangered marine mammals. Special speed zones and boating closures within parts of the bay are enforced in winter, the prime time for manatees to be in the area. Please heed the posted regulations.

Fishing Index: Kings Bay has redfish and spotted seatrout during the coldest months of winter. The rest of the year these two species move onto the flats throughout the area. Fish for bass, panfish, and catfish in the river. In spring and summer some cobia move close to shore. Use a boat to fish for them around the rock jetties at the mouth of the Crystal River, or fish from shore at Fort Island Park.

Access Points:
6A. PETE'S LANDING—*Salt and Fresh; Boat; Ramp.*
Description: A county ramp accessed through Pete's Pier, a commercial business. There is no charge for the ramp but Pete's Pier charges for parking. The ramp provides direct access to Kings Bay.
Directions: From the intersection of US 19 and FL 44 in Crystal River, drive about 0.25 mile south on US 19. Turn west onto Kings Bay Drive. Go 0.6 mile to SW 1 Place. Turn right and go 0.2 mile to the marina.

6B. FORT ISLAND TRAIL PARK—*Salt; Boat and Bank; Ramp.*
Description: This county park is on the Crystal River and provides easy access to the Gulf of Mexico.
Directions: From the intersection of US 19 and FL 44 in Crystal River, drive

south 0.5 mile on US 19 to W. Fort Island Trail. Turn west and go about 5 miles to the park.

6C. FORT ISLAND GULF BEACH—*Salt; Boat and Bank; Ramp.*
Description: This beachfront county park is a popular place to picnic and swim. Anglers can fish from shore or around the nearby rock jetties.
Directions: From the intersection of US 19 and FL 44 in Crystal River, drive south 0.5 mile on US 19 to W. Fort Island Trail. Turn west and go about 9 miles to the park at road's end.

For more information on above sites: Call Citrus County Parks and Recreation Department at (352) 795-2202.

7. HOMOSASSA RIVER
Salt and Fresh; Boat; Ramp.

Description: This short river begins as a spring near busy US 19. A State Wildlife Park here is a great place to see manatees from the "underwater" walkway in the park. The river meanders toward the coast along miles of winding waterways and islands. Once away from the developed area, there are few signs of civilization. Several commercial marinas and motels are along the river close to the spring.

Fishing Index: This is one of the world's hotspots for tarpon. The big fish, in excess of 150 pounds, arrive in early May and leave by early June, according to Bill Korade, owner of Blue Water Bait and Tackle. "The school of big fish, in excess of 90 pounds, are around until early July." Anglers wanting to catch a world-record fish come here looking for the monster tarpon that will weigh 200 to 220 pounds. This time of year also draws the top tarpon guides from across the state. First-time anglers wanting to catch a big tarpon are advised to hire a guide because it takes local knowledge to find—and land—the fish.

The Homosassa is the only place where you can fish for big tarpon in shallow, crystal-clear water. Fly fishing is the predominant method of veteran tarpon anglers, although conventional plug fishing also works. Interestingly, Korade says live bait doesn't attract the really big fishes' attention. From July to October numerous tarpon move into the Homosassa River. Most are caught between the river mouth and three-fourths of the way up the river. A chunk of dead bait, such as a mullet head, can work well under these conditions. Around the spring there are some nice sized largemouth bass to be caught.

There is life after tarpon time in the Homosassa. Korade considers the Homosassa River and Bay system, "one of the greatest areas to fish anytime of the year because of the diversity of fish you can catch. We also have good fishing for redfish, spotted seatrout, cobia, Spanish and king mackerel, sharks, and grouper." Spanish mackerel make a strong run along the coast in the spring. The schools, feeding on shrimp and other bottom-dwelling organisms, create a highly noticeable patch of cloudy water called a "mud."

Directions: The only public access point is a county boat ramp at the end of

Fish Bowl Drive (CR 490). From US 19 turn onto Fish Bowl Drive and go about 2 miles to the ramp.

For more information: Blue Water Bait and Tackle at (352) 628-0414.

8. CHASSAHOWITZKA RIVER
Salt; Boat; Ramp.

Description: Most of the coastal waters south of the Homosassa River make up the Chassahowitzka (commonly pronounced Chass-o-whiskey) National Wildlife Refuge. A large part of the refuge is a manatee sanctuary and no boats are allowed in the area from October 15 to February 15.

Fishing Index: A great place to catch fish but dangerous for boating. Many local anglers refuse to fish the area because of the shallow water and rocky bottom characteristic of the Chassahowitzka. But some guides regularly fish the area and know how to keep from running aground. Some of them use a specially designed flat-bottomed, tunnel-drive boat so they can get to places few people fish and where they usually have good luck.

The area has very good to excellent angling for redfish and spotted seatrout. Sheepshead, flounder, and mangrove snapper are also common catches. Along the outer edges of marshes, cobia are taken from late spring through summer. Many tarpon anglers from Homosassa fish the flats along the outer edge of the refuge. Some very big fish are caught in this area.

Directions: The only public ramp is in a recreation area owned by Citrus County. There is a modern campground and small camp and bait store on-site. At the junction of US 19 and US 98, drive 1.8 miles west on W. Miss Maggie Road (CR 480) to the campground and ramp.

For more information: Call the campground office at (352) 382-2200.

HERNANDO AND PASCO COUNTIES

9. WITHLACOOCHEE RIVER (LAKE PANASOFFKEE TO GREEN SWAMP)
Fresh; Boat, Canoe and Bank; Ramp.

Description: Fishing success along the upper part of the river depends on water levels. Generally the river is narrow and difficult to fish when water levels are low.

Fishing Index: Redbreasts (Stumpknockers), bluegills, and warmouths are the most abundant species. Fishing success is variable.

Access Points:
9A. NOBLETON WAYSIDE PARK—*Bank and Boat; Ramp.*
Description: A Hernando County park with picnic facilities.

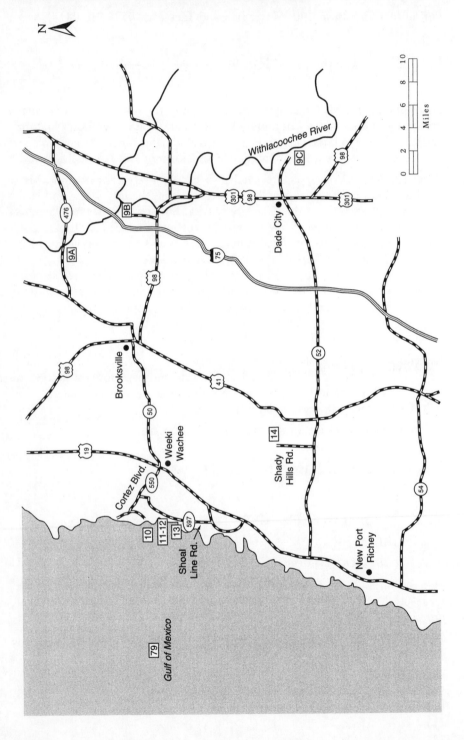

Directions: From the intersection with US 98 in Brooksville drive 6.3 miles north on US 41 to CR 476 (Lake Lindsey Road). Turn right and go about 4.7 miles to the ramp. Watch for signs.

9B. Silver Lake—*Bank and Boat; Ramp; $.*
Description: Part of the Withlacoochee State Forest. Camping.
Directions: From I-75, take the US 98 Brooksville exit and drive 1 mile east to Croom Rital Road. Turn left and go about 3.5 miles to the lake.

9C. Withlacoochee River Park—*Bank and Canoe.*
Description: A Pasco County Park with canoe dock, primitive camping, nature trails, and picnic area.
Directions: From Dade City turn off of US 301 onto River Road and go about 4 miles to the park.
For more information: Call the park office at (813) 567-0264.

10. Bayport Park.

Salt; Pier and Boat; Ramp.

Description: A Hernando County park with a lighted pier, picnicking, and ramp with direct access to the Gulf of Mexico.

Fishing Index: Fish for spotted seatrout and redfish along the coast or head farther offshore for cobia, grouper, snapper, and king mackerel.

Directions: From the intersection of US 19 and FL 550 (Cortez Boulevard) in Weeki Wachee, take FL 550 west about 5.8 miles to the park at road's end.

11. Rogers Park

Salt and Fresh; Bank and Boat; Ramp.

Description: A Hernando County park on the Weeki Wachee River, with picnicking and a ramp with access to the Gulf of Mexico.

Fishing Index: Fish for sheepshead, redfish, spotted seatrout, and offshore species. Boaters can also go upriver for largemouth bass.

Directions: From the intersection of US 19 and FL 550 (Cortez Boulevard) in Weeki Wachee, take FL 550 west about 3.2 miles to FL 597 (Shoal Line Road). Turn left and go about 1.5 miles to the park.

12. Jenkins Creek

Salt; Pier and Boat; Ramp.

Description: A Hernando County park. There are two lighted piers (one of which is barrier free), picnicking, and a ramp for boats 16 feet and under.

Fishing Index: Fish the tidal waters for redfish, sheepshead, spotted seatrout, and some snook.

Directions: From the intersection of US 19 and FL 550 (Cortez Boulevard) in Weeki Wachee, take FL 550 west about 3.2 miles to FL 597 (Shoal Line Road). Turn left and go about 2 miles to the park.

13. HERNANDO BEACH PARK

Salt; Boat; Ramp.

Description: A Hernando County park.

Fishing Index: The ramp provides direct access to the Gulf of Mexico. Fish for grouper, snapper, king and Spanish mackerel, and other offshore species. The coast offers numerous places to fish for redfish and spotted seatrout.

Directions: From the intersection of US 19 and FL 550 (Cortez Boulevard) in Weeki Wachee, take FL 550 west about 3.2 miles to FL 597 (Shoal Line Road). Turn left and go about 3.2 miles to Hernando Beach. Turn right onto Calienta Street. The ramp is on the left.

14. CREWS LAKE

Fresh; Pier and Bank; Ramp.

Description: A Pasco County park with nature and bike trails, picnicking, and tent camping. Boats are limited to motors of 10 horsepower or less.

Fishing Index: Fair fishing for largemouth bass and bluegills. Not a highly productive lake.

Directions: From US 41 in Gowers Corner drive 2.3 miles west on FL 52 to Shady Hills Road. Turn right and go north about 4 miles to Crews Lake Drive. Turn right and follow the road 1.4 miles to the park.

For more information: Call Pasco County Parks and Recreation Department at (813) 929-1260.

PINELLAS AND HILLSBOROUGH COUNTIES

These two counties boast well over 100 public launching ramps, bridges, waterfront parks, and beaches open to anglers. Listings of the most popular or convenient fishing spots or access points are supplemented here by brief notes on other sites worth trying.

15. TARPON SPRINGS (ANCLOTE RIVER)

Salt; Pier, Bank and Boat; Ramp.

Description: This Greek community near the Pinellas-Pasco County line is the center of the sponge-diving industry in Florida. The town is on the banks of the Anclote River. There are historical exhibits and a number of authentic Greek restaurants along the riverfront. Two Pasco County parks are the most popular places for anglers.

PINELLAS AND HILLSBOROUGH COUNTIES

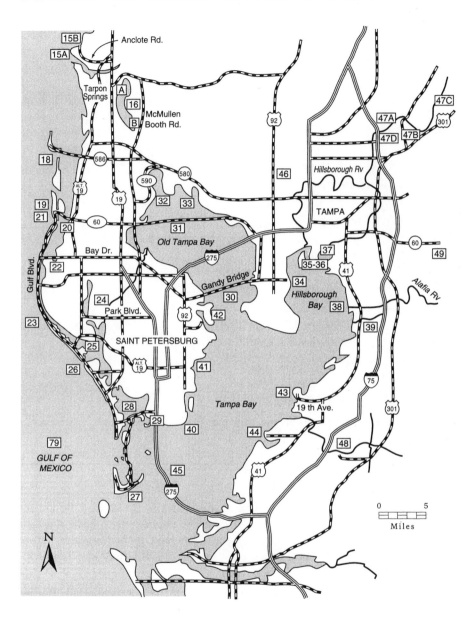

Anclote Rd.

15B
15A

Tarpon Springs

A
16
B

McMullen Booth Rd.

U.S. 92

47C
47A
301
47D 47B

18

586

Hillsborough Rv

46

TAMPA

590

580

19

ALT 19

32

33

19
21

60

31

20

Old Tampa Bay

60

49

Bay Dr.

Gulf Blvd.

I-275

22

37

35-36

41

Gandy Bridge

Hillsborough Bay

34

Alafia Rv

24

30

Park Blvd.

92

42

38

23

SAINT PETERSBURG

39

25

ALT 19

75

26

41

301

43

19 th Ave.

28

Tampa Bay

44

48

79

29

40

GULF OF MEXICO

45

27

275

N

0   5
Miles

Fishing Index: The river opens to the Gulf of Mexico at the Anclote Anchorage, a coastal area semiprotected by the Anclote Keys. Fish the mouth of the Anclote River and the seagrass flats just offshore for snook and spotted seatrout. The fishing pier at Anclote Gulf Park is adjacent to the outfall canal for a power plant. It is a great place to fish, especially in winter when most fish are looking for some warmer water. Anglers catch snook, spotted seatrout, redfish, tarpon, pompano, and sharks from the pier.

Ruben Hart, a life-long resident of the area and owner of Hart's 1 Stop, suggests freelining a live shrimp or greenback (a locally available baitfish) when fishing for redfish or spotted seatrout. "We don't have to go far, just to the mouth of the river or by the Anclote Keys, to have some good fishing."

Directions: Tarpon Springs is at the north end of Pinellas County. The major access road is US 19.

Access Points:
15A. ANCLOTE RIVER PARK—*Boat; Ramp.*
Description: The park's ramps provide direct access to the mouth of the Anclote River and the seagrass flats.
Directions: From Alternate US 19 in Tarpon Springs, turn west onto Anclote Road. Follow the road about 1.9 miles to the park.

15B. ANCLOTE GULF PARK—*Pier.*
Directions: From Alternate US 19 in Tarpon Springs, turn west onto Anclote Road. Follow the road about 2.8 miles to the park.

Other access points:
Howard Park—*surf fishing.*

Sunset Beach Park—*surf fishing.*

For more information: Call Hart's 1 Stop at (727) 938-5364.

16. LAKE TARPON
Fresh; Bank; Boat; Ramp.

Description: One of the few freshwater fishing sites in the county. Public access is via the A.L. Anderson or John Chesnut, Sr. county parks, both of which are in a heavily developed suburban area. Both have picnicking and nature trails but no camping. Several trailer park campgrounds with lake-front property are on US 19.

Fishing Index: Year-round fishing for largemouth bass and bluegill. Winter fishing for crappie. Considered a very good fishing lake.

Access Points:
16A. ANDERSON PARK—*Bank and Boat; Ramp.*
Directions: The entrance is on US 19 about 0.9 mile south of the intersection with Fl 582 (Tarpon Avenue) in Tarpon Springs.

16B. CHESNUT PARK—*Bank and Boat; Ramp.*
Directions: From US 19 take either CR 584 (Tampa Road) or CR 586 (Curlew

Road) east to McMullen Booth Road. Turn north on McMullen Booth Road and go about 2 miles from CR 584 or 2.2 miles from CR 586 to East Lake Road. Turn left on East Lake Road and follow it to the park.

For more information: Call the Anderson Park office at (727) 937-5410 or Chesnut Park office at (727) 784-4686.

17. DUNEDIN BEACH CAUSEWAY

Salt; Bank, Bridge and Boat; Ramp.

Description: The ramp is city operated. Like most ramps in Pinellas County, it is a very busy place on the weekends. Boaters have access to St. Joseph Sound and the Gulf of Mexico via Hurricane Pass.

Fishing Index: Fishing is allowed from the causeway, around the bridge embankments, and off of the main bridge. Fish for snook at night during the summer around the bridge pilings. Also try nighttime angling for tarpon and big reds in summer.

Directions: The ramps and bridges are along CR 586 (Curlew Road) about 3.5 miles from the intersection with US 19.

Other access points:
Edgewater Park and Marina—*ramp and bank fishing.*

18. HONEYMOON ISLAND AND CALADESI ISLAND STATE PARKS

Salt; Surf and Wade.

Description: These two parks are on undeveloped barrier islands near the city of Dunedin. Honeymoon Island has a bridge and road to it but Caladesi doesn't. It is accessible by private boat or scheduled ferry from Honeymoon Island and Clearwater Beach. Caladesi has a dock for overnight boaters.

Fishing Index: Surf fishing is popular on both islands. Anglers report good catches of spotted seatrout, snook, redfish, and Spanish mackerel. Try wade fishing the flats on the inside of the islands in summer for redfish, jacks, and small cobia.

Directions: Honeymoon Island State Park is at the western end of CR 586 in Dunedin. From US 19, turn west onto CR 586 (Curlew Road) and go about 4.9 miles to the park. To reach Caladesi Island State Park, take the ferry from Honeymoon's dock.

For more information: Call Honeymoon Island State Park office at (727) 469-5942 or Caladesi Island State Park office at (727) 469-5918.

19. BIG PIER 60

Salt; Pier.

Description: This 1,200-foot pier is operated by the City of Clearwater and was rebuilt in 1994.

Fishing Index: The pier regulars come here to fish for snook. The best action is at night. Some cobia, Spanish mackerel, redfish, and tarpon are taken seasonally. Winter fishing is for silver trout. Some flounder are caught throughout the year except during the coldest months.

Directions: The pier is on Clearwater Beach where FL 60 (Gulf to Bay Boulevard) ends and intersects with Gulf Boulevard.

For more information: Call the pier office at (727) 462-6466.

20. MEMORIAL CAUSEWAY

Salt; Bank and Bridge.

Description: Gulf to Bay Boulevard, where it crosses Clearwater Harbor, is called Memorial Causeway. Anglers can fish from the remains of the old bridge and off the seawall of the new causeway.

Fishing Index: Fish for spotted seatrout on the grassflats on the north side of the causeway and for snook, trout, and redfish off the south side. Summer flounder fishing can be very good.

Directions: The causeway is FL 60, the major road leading to Clearwater Beach. From the intersection with US 19 in Clearwater, take FL 60 (Gulf to Bay Boulevard) 5 miles west to the causeway.

21. SAND KEY PARK.

Salt; Surf and Bridge.

Description: This 90-acre county park is heavily used by beach goers. Anglers can park in one of the 674 metered parking places and walk to the beach to fish in the Gulf or along Clearwater Pass. Or fish from the walkway on the toll bridge near the park.

Fishing Index: The pass is a favorite hangout for snook and redfish. Use live baits for the big fish.

Directions: The park is just south of the Clearwater Pass Bridge on Gulf Boulevard.

For more information: Call the park office at (727) 595-7677.

22. Belleair Boat Ramp

Salt; Ramp.

Description: A Pinellas County facility with eight launching lanes. Gas and bait available.

Fishing Index: Access to Clearwater Harbor and the Gulf of Mexico via Clearwater Pass. The protected waters offer excellent fishing for snook, redfish, spotted seatrout, and flounder.

Directions: The ramps are on the mainland side of the Belleair Causeway, which is called West Bay Drive. From the intersection of East Bay Drive and US 19, head 5.7 miles west on East Bay Drive to the ramp. East Bay Drive changes to West Bay Drive at the intersection with Alternate US 19.

For more information: Call the ramp office at Belleair Causeway Bait and Tackle Shop at (727) 586-3474.

23. Long Pier

Salt; Pier.

Description: This 1,021-foot pier is also known as Redington Fishing Pier.

Fishing Index: Anglers catch a mixed bag including whiting, flounder, sheepshead, tarpon, cobia, Spanish mackerel, and redfish. Snook fishing, practiced at night by the local veteran anglers, is popular.

Directions: From the Tom Stuart Causeway (CR 666) drive about 2.3 miles north on Gulf Boulevard to the pier in Redington Shores.

Redington Long Pier, along the Gulf coast in Pinellas County is popular place for anglers.

For more information: Call the pier office at (727) 391-9398.

Other access points:
Park Boulevard boat ramp—*in Indian Shores along "The Narrows".*

24. LAKE SEMINOLE PARK

Fresh; Bank and Boat; Ramp.

Description: A 255-acre Pinellas County park with picnicking, a recreation trail, and play area. A good place to take the kids fishing. Visitors along the beach are only a few miles from this urban park and, if craving some freshwater fishing, can drive over and give it a try.

Fishing Index: Fair year-round fishing for bass, bream, and catfish.

Directions: From the intersection of US 19 and CR 694 (Park Boulevard), take Park Boulevard 5.6 miles west to the park entrance.

For more information: Call the park office at (727) 392-2972.

Other access points:
Ridgecrest Park—*county park in Largo with freshwater fishing.*

Walsingham Park—*county park in Largo with freshwater fishing.*

Taylor Park—*county park in Largo with freshwater fishing.*

25. WAR VETERANS' MEMORIAL PARK

Salt; Boat; Ramp.

Description: The ramps offer easy access to Boca Ciega Bay and the Gulf of Mexico via Johns Pass.

Fishing Index: Boca Ciega Bay has numerous grassflats that provide excellent spotted seatrout and redfish fishing for anglers in small boats.

Directions: From US 19, take Alternate US 19 (5th Avenue) north 6.9 miles to the ramp. Eventually it becomes Tyronne Boulevard and finally Bay Pines Boulevard. Follow signs to the Veteran's Hospital which is adjacent to the park.

For more information: Call the park office at (727) 293-9575.

26. JOHNS PASS

Salt; Bridge and Surf.

Description: One of the major inlets along this part of the coast. A large offshore fishing fleet is based here. Fish from the catwalk on the bridge, from the banks of the pass, and in the Gulf from the surf. There is a small beachfront park on the north side of the pass with plenty of metered parking.

Fishing Index: Fish the pass for snook day or night. Some big redfish and tarpon cruise the shoreline near the pass.

Directions: From Treasure Island Causeway go north on Gulf Boulevard 1.2 miles to the bridge and beach park.

Other access areas:
Treasure Island Causeway—*fish from the bank and bridge.*

Treasure Island Public—*Boat Ramp.*

Saint Petersburg Beach Causeway—*bridge fishing.*

27. FORT DESOTO PARK

Salt; Boat, Bank, Pier; Ramps.

Description: This county park is on five connected islands at the mouth of Tampa Bay. The park has a nice campground, miles of recreational trails, two fishing piers, more than 7 miles of beach, and historic Fort DeSoto. The boat ramps afford quick and easy access to the lower parts of Tampa and Boca Ciega bays and the Gulf of Mexico.

Fishing Index: The piers are good places to fish for Spanish mackerel during the spring and fall runs. At other times of the year, sheepshead and snook are the targets. Boaters can fish the flats of Mullet Key Bayou for spotted seatrout and redfish.

Directions: The Pinellas Bayway goes to the park. From the I-75 exit for the Bayway, at the north end of the Sunshine Skyway, follow the signs to the park.

At Fort DeSoto Park, anglers have two fishing piers from which to try their luck. Family Pier 1, on the Egmont Channel side, is a popular place to fish for Spanish mackerel.

For more information: Call the park office at (727) 866-2484; the baithouse concession stand at the Bay Pier at (727) 864-3345; or the Gulf Pier at (727) 864-9937.

28. Pinellas Bayway
Salt; Bridge.

Description: This causeway connects the southern tip of St. Petersburg to the beach. It crosses the lower part of Boca Ciega Bay. Fish from any of the three bridges along the causeway.

Fishing Index: Fish for sheepshead and snook around the pilings.

Directions: Exit I-75 at the first exit after crossing the Sunshine Causeway if heading north or the last exit before the bridge if going south. Follow the big overhead signs to St. Petersburg Beach. This is a toll road.

Other access areas:
Saint Petersburg Beach—*boat ramp.*

Saint Petersburg Beach access—*surf fishing.*

Merry Pier in Pass-a-Grille.

7th and 11th Avenue docks in St. Petersburg Beach.

29. Maximo Park
Salt; Boat; Ramp.

Description: A good place to launch your boat if you want to fish around the Sunshine Skyway bridge pilings or head into the lower part of Boca Ciega Bay.

Fishing Index: Fish the flats around the ramp for spotted seatrout.

Directions: Exit I-275 in St. Petersburg at Exit 3, Pinellas Point Drive. Follow the signs to 34th Street and go south to the park.

30. Gandy Bridge
Salt; Boat; Bridge and Bank; Ramp.

Description: The southernmost bridge over Old Tampa Bay. There are fishing catwalks on the east and west sides of the bridge. Land-bound anglers can also fish off the shoreline along the north side of the causeway on the Pinellas County side.

Fishing Index: The folks at Randy's Bait and Tackle say that the bridge is a good place to fish for snook at night, for cobia during summer, and for some top Spanish mackerel action in fall. Sheepshead hang around the pilings year-round.

Directions: From the Pinellas County side, exit I-275 at the Gandy Bridge exit. From the Tampa side exit I-275 onto Westshore Boulevard. Drive south about 3.7 miles to Gandy Boulevard. Turn right and you will be almost on the bridge. The eight-lane ramp is on the south side of Gandy Boulevard at the base of the bridge.

For more information: Call Randy's Bait and Tackle on the Pinellas County side at (727) 576-6465 or Gandy Bait and Tackle on the Tampa side at (813) 839-5551.

Other access points:
Picnic Island boat ramp at Port Tampa.

31. COURTNEY CAMPBELL CAUSEWAY
Salt; Bank, Wade and Boat; Ramp.

Description: The northernmost of the three bridges over Old Tampa Bay. Anglers can fish from shore, wade into the grassflats, or fish around the two bridges on the causeway. Watch for marked pull-off areas for vehicles.

Fishing Index: Spotted seatrout are on the flats near either end of the causeway. Snook and redfish are popular targets around the bridges.

Directions: From the Pinellas County side, turn onto FL 60 (Gulf to Bay Boulevard) and go east until you reach the causeway. From Tampa, exit I-275 at the airport exit and follow the signs to the causeway.

For more information: Call Buddie's Bait and Tackle on the causeway at (813) 287-1026.

32. PHILIPPE PARK
Salt; Boat; Ramp.

Description: A Pinellas County park. The day-use facility offers picnicking and a playground. The ramp provides access to Safety Harbor and upper Old Tampa Bay.

Fishing Index: Fish in Safety Harbor for seatrout, redfish, and snook.

Directions: From the intersection of FL 60 (Courtney Campbell Causeway) and CR 590, take CR 590 north about 3.3 miles to Philippe Parkway. Turn right and enter the park.

For more information: Call the park office at (727) 726-2700.

Other access points:
Safety Harbor Marina and Pier—*boat ramp and fishing pier.*

Safety Harbor Bridge (FL 590)—*bridge fishing.*

33. UPPER TAMPA BAY PARK

Salt; Bank, Wade, and Canoe; Canoe Launch.

Description: This county park and preserve is for anglers who like to fish in the small, quiet tidal creeks along this part of Old Tampa Bay. A great place to wade or fish from a canoe.

Fishing Index: Anglers catch redfish, spotted seatrout, snook, cobia, black drum, and sheepshead in Double Branch Creek.

Directions: FL 580 (Hillsborough Avenue on the Hillsborough County side) skirts the north end of Old Tampa Bay. From the intersection with Memorial Highway (FL 576), take Hillsborough Avenue about 3.5 miles northwest to Double Branch Road. Turn left onto Double Branch Road and go 2.3 miles to the park entrance.

For more information: Call the park office at (813) 855-1765.

34. BALLAST POINT PARK

Salt; Pier, Bank and Boat; Ramp.

Description: A city park with a small fishing pier and boat ramp on the west side of Hillsborough Bay.

Fishing Index: Anglers catch snook, redfish, sheepshead, and plenty of salt-water catfish.

Directions: From the intersection of Gandy Boulevard and Dale Mabry Highway (US 92) in Tampa, take Gandy Boulevard east 1.1 miles until it dead ends into Bayshore Boulevard. Turn right and go south on Bayshore Boulevard 0.6 mile to Interbay Boulevard. Turn left on Interbay Boulevard and go 0.3 mile to the park.

For more information: Call the bait house and restaurant at the pier at (813) 813-9585.

Other access points:
Bayshore Boulevard seawall—*bank fishing.*

35. MARJORIE PARK

Salt; Boat; Ramp.

Description: A city park on Davis Island. The ramp is in a congested area but does provide quick access to anglers wanting to fish around the downtown waterfront.

Fishing Index: Downtown Tampa, in the shadow of the tall buildings, is gaining a reputation as a good place to fish for snook, crevalle jack, redfish, sheepshead, and trout. Fish around the numerous pilings and use stout tackle to wrestle the fish from their hiding places.

Directions: From the Crosstown Expressway (FL 618) in downtown Tampa, take the Davis Island exit and follow the signs to Davis Island Boulevard. The park is on this road just after it crosses the bridge to the island.

Other access points:
Davis Island Boulevard seawall—*bank fishing in Seddon Channel south of Marjorie Park.*

36. DAVIS ISLAND
Salt; Boat and Bank; Ramp.

Description: Two ramps provide good access to Hillsborough Bay.

Fishing Index: Anglers fishing from the seawall catch snook, redfish, jacks, and, in summer, tarpon.

Directions: From the Crosstown Expressway (FL 618) in downtown Tampa take the Davis Island exit and follow the signs to Davis Island Boulevard. Follow the road around the island to the south end. Go past the airport and look for the ramp on the right.

37. 22ND STREET CAUSEWAY WAYSIDE PARK
Salt; Ramp.

Description: A convenient ramp for boaters wanting to fish in Hillsborough or McKay bays. Fishing is surprisingly good despite the heavily industrialized environs.

Fishing Index: Fish around the innumerable pilings for snook, crevalle jack, and redfish. In McKay Bay, look for snook and redfish.

Directions: The ramp is on the causeway (Business US 41). From the intersection of US 41 and Business 41, take Business 41 about 1.7 miles to the ramp.

38. WILLIAMS PARK
Salt; Pier and Boat; Ramp.

Description: A county park at the mouth of the Alafia River along the eastern shore of Hillsborough Bay. Boaters have easy access to the seagrass flats along the eastern shore of Hillsborough and Tampa bays. The pier extends into the Alafia River.

Fishing Index: The pier is a popular place for land-bound anglers to catch redfish, sheepshead, and snook. From the ramp, boaters can head south to the lower Hillsborough Bay hot spot known as "The Kitchen." The owner of Fisherman's One Stop had this tip for anglers wanting to catch a cobia: "Use a live pinfish, pigfish (grunt), or small blue crab. The bigger cobia are around the Big Bend power plant a few miles south of the mouth of the Alafia River.

Chumming with a block of frozen menhaden will increase your chances of catching a fish."

Directions: Exit I-4 onto US 41 and drive south about 7 miles to Riverview Drive. Turn right and follow the road to the park.

For more information: Call Fisherman's One Stop at (813) 677-5659.

39. BULLFROG CREEK

Salt; Bridge and Boat; Ramp.

Description: The US 41 bridge over Bullfrog Creek has a catwalk for anglers. It is a convenient place to fish from land. The ramp is county owned but maintained by 41 Bait and Tackle.

Fishing Index: A good place to fish for snook and to net blue crabs.

Directions: The bridge is 2 miles south of Gibsonton on US 41.

40. BAY VISTA PARK

Salt; Boat; Ramp.

Description: The ramp provides good access to the lower half of Tampa Bay.

Fishing Index: Boaters can head any direction between east and south and intersect the buoys that mark the main shipping channel. Fish around them for cobia. The fish could be there any month but May through September are best.

Directions: Exit I-275 at Pinellas Point Drive and drive east about 2.4 miles to road's end at 4th Street. The ramp is on the left.

For more information: Call the City of St. Petersburg Parks and Recreation Department at (727) 893-7171.

Other access points:
Grandview Park—*boat ramp.*

Bay Vista Park—*boat ramp, bridge, and bank fishing.*

Lewis Boulevard Bridge.

Lassing Park—*bank fishing.*

Poynter Park—*bank fishing.*

41. ST. PETERSBURG MUNICIPAL PIER

Salt; Pier.

Description: This pier is open to vehicular traffic and big enough at the end for a small shopping area and restaurant. At 0.7 mile long, it is the longest pier into Tampa Bay. It is a popular place for tourists to enjoy the sights.

Fishing Index: Although it may not look like a good place to fish, the pier has

3,000 pilings and that translates into plenty of habitat for sheepshead and snook. The best sheepshead fishing is from February through April according to Joe Piacenza, owner of the bait shop at the end of the pier. Whiting, mangrove snapper, and flounder are also taken from the pier. Piacenza has this advice for pier anglers: "Fish down or under the pier. The further under the pier, the bigger the fish."

Directions: In downtown St. Petersburg at the end of Second Avenue NE. Exit I-275 at "The Pier" exit and follow the signs.

For more information: Call The Pier Baithouse at (727) 821-3750.

42. WEEDON ISLAND PRESERVE
Salt; Bank, Wade, and Boat.

Description: This state-owned and county-operated preserve is a great place to come by boat or car and wade fish the quiet, seagrass-rich waters. Thirty-five percent of the waters in the preserve are closed to gasoline-powered motors. In

Anywhere in west central Florida where there are bridge or dock pilings, there's likely to be some sheepshead.

these areas, which are well marked, use a trolling motor or pushpole to get close to the fish. There is a small fishing pier just off the road that separates Riviera Bay from Bayou Grande.

Fishing Index: Wade fish for redfish, snook, and spotted seatrout. The outgoing tide is the preferred time to fish.

Directions: From US 92 (4th Street) in St. Petersburg, turn east on 83rd Avenue and drive about 3 miles to the preserve.

For more information: Call the preserve office at (813) 579-8360.

Other access points:
Crisp boat ramp—*Poplar Street and 35th Avenue NE.*

Demens boat ramp—*Bayshore Drive and 2nd Avenue S.*

43. E.G. SIMMONS PARK
Salt; Bank and Boat; Ramp.

Description: This county park along the eastern shore of Tampa Bay is a good place to take the family. There is a campground, picnic area, swimming beach, and several docks for land-bound anglers. Boaters have quick access to Tampa Bay.

Fishing Index: Fish from land or boat for redfish, spotted seatrout, flounder, and snook.

Directions: From US 41 about 1.5 miles north of Ruskin, turn onto 19th Avenue. Drive 2 miles west to the park.

For more information: Call the park office at (813) 761-7655.

44. COCKROACH BAY
Salt; Boat; Ramp.

Description: This mangrove-fringed bay along the southeast shore of Tampa Bay is one of the less developed stretches of the region. Adjacent to the boat ramp is a nature center operated by Hillsborough Community College.

Fishing Index: Seagrass flats along this part of the bay offer good fishing for spotted seatrout, flounder, and redfish. When the weather is cold, fish the deeper waters around the flats. That's where the fish wait for the water to warm up enough to move back on the flats and feed.

Directions: From Ruskin, drive 2.8 miles south on US 41 to Cockroach Bay Road. Turn right and go 3 miles to the ramp at road's end.

Other access points:
Ruskin Commongood Park—*boat, ramp—121st and 2nd streets in Ruskin.*

45. SUNSHINE SKYWAY BRIDGE

Salt; Bridge and Boat.

Description: Fish at the mouth of Tampa Bay from the remains of the old Sunshine Skyway bridge. Anglers fish off the old roadway on either side of the mouth of Tampa Bay. Fishing from this old bridge is a specialized sport. Use heavy duty tackle to keep the fish from getting under the bridge and cutting your line on the barnacle-encrusted pilings. A bridge net will be very handy when it comes time to bring a big fish out of the water.

Fishing Index: There is a wide diversity of fish to catch around the old bridges. At night, fish for snook and sharks. In the day, anglers can catch either of these species or cobia, sheepshead, Spanish mackerel, or mangrove snapper.

Directions: The access points are at the rest areas at either end of the main span of the Sunshine Skyway (I-275) bridge.

46. AL LOPEZ PARK

Fresh; Bank.

Description: One of the GFC urban fishing facilities. The park is a few blocks from Tampa Stadium, home of the Tampa Bay Buccaneers. For something different, try a morning fishing trip followed by a tailgate party and football game and maybe some more angling after the game while the traffic thins out.

Fishing Index: The 10-acre pond here is intensively managed to produce good fishing for catfish, bluegills, and largemouth bass. The bass fishing is strictly catch and release.

Directions: From Hillsborough Avenue (US 92) in Tampa, turn south onto Himes Avenue.

47. HILLSBOROUGH RIVER WILDERNESS PARK

Fresh; Bank and Boat; Ramp.

Description: A multisite county park that provides access to the Hillsborough River.

Fishing Index: The river has good cover for largemouth bass and bream.

Access Points:
47A. MORRIS BRIDGE PARK—*Fresh; Bank and Boat; Ramp.*
Description: The park has nature trails, picnicking, and a ramp for small boats.
Directions: Exit I-75 at Fletcher Avenue and Morris Bridge Road and take Morris Bridge Road (CR 579) north about 3.4 miles to the park.
For more information: Call the park office at (813) 987-6209.

47B. JOHN SARGEANT SR. MEMORIAL PARK—*Fresh; Bank and Boat; Ramp.*
Description: The park has a boardwalk, picnicking, and a ramp for small boats.

Directions: Exit I-75 onto Fowler Avenue and drive east 1.2 miles to US 301. Take US 301 north 3.4 miles to Stacy Road. Turn left and go to the park.
For more information: Call the park office at (813) 987-6208.

47C. DEAD RIVER PARK—*Fresh; Bank.*
Description: A park with a primitive trail, youth group camp, and picnicking.
Directions: Exit I-75 onto Fowler Avenue and drive east 1.2 miles to US 301. Take US 301 north 8.1 miles to Dead River Road. Turn left and go to about 2 miles to the park.
For more information: Call the park office at (813) 987-6210.

47D. TROUT CREEK PARK—*Fresh; Bank and Canoe; Canoe Launch.*
Description: On a small tributary of the Hillsborough River, this park has a boardwalk and picnicking.
Directions: From the Fletcher Avenue-Morris Bridge Road exit on I-75, follow Morris Bridge Road to the park entrance.
For more information: Call the park office at (813) 987-6200.

48. LITTLE MANATEE RIVER STATE RECREATION AREA——
Fresh; Bank and Canoe; $.

Description: 4.5 miles of this 40-mile river flow through this unit of the state park system. There is a campground, nature trails, and picnicking.

Fishing Index: Fish for largemouth bass and bream year-round. During winter cold spells some snook and redfish migrate upriver and mingle with the freshwater species. Snook, from the saltwaters of Tampa Bay, are year-round inhabitants of the lower freshwater regions of the river according to GFC fisheries biologist Tom Champeau.

Directions: From the intersection of FL 674 and US 301 in Sun City Center take US 301 south about 4.5 miles to Lightfoot Road. Turn right and follow the road to the park.

For more information: Call the park office at (813) 671-5005.

49. MEDARD PARK ——
Fresh; Boat, Bank and Pier; Ramp.

Description: The park has a 770-acre reservoir, a popular destination for anglers. There is also camping, several miles of bridal paths, a swimming beach, and picnicking. A 730-foot fishing pier/footbridge is barrier free. Boats can operate only at idle speed in the reservoir.

Fishing Index: The reservoir is a good place to fish for sunshine bass, stocked by the GFC. Anglers also have good luck catching crappie, bluegills, and catfish. Largemouth bass fishing is fair. The reservoir has a must-release policy for largemouths between 14 and 18 inches. The park staff suggest fishing at night during spring and summer. To do this, however, you must be a registered camper or buy an after-hours fishing permit.

Directions: Exit I-75 at FL 60 (Brandon Boulevard) and travel east 9.4 miles to South Turkey Creek Road. Turn south and drive about 1 mile to the park entrance.

For more information: Call the park office at (813) 757-3802.

Manatee and Sarasota Counties

50. Rod and Reel Pier and Anna Maria City Pier—
Salt; Pier.

Description: These two piers are only 0.5 mile apart at the northern tip of Anna Maria Island. Both have bait shops. Rod and Reel Pier, 250 feet long, is privately owned. The city pier, a 750-footer, has a restaurant and bait shop at its end.

Fishing Index: Fish either pier for sheepshead, black drum, redfish, snook, and seasonally for Spanish mackerel.

Directions: From US 41 in Bradenton, take FL 64 west to Anna Maria Island. The road dead ends at Gulf Boulevard (FL 789). Turn right and go north about 2.4 miles to Pine Street and turn right. The city pier is at the end of Pine Street. To reach Rod and Reel Pier, turn left at the end of Pier Street and go 0.5 mile.

For more information: Call the bait shop at Rod and Reel Pier at (941) 778-2816 or the bait shop at the city pier at (941) 778-0475.

The Rod and Reel Pier on Anna Maria Island is low to the water and easy to fish from. It may not be the longest pier along the west cost, but it is surprisingly productive.

MANATEE AND SARASOTA COUNTIES

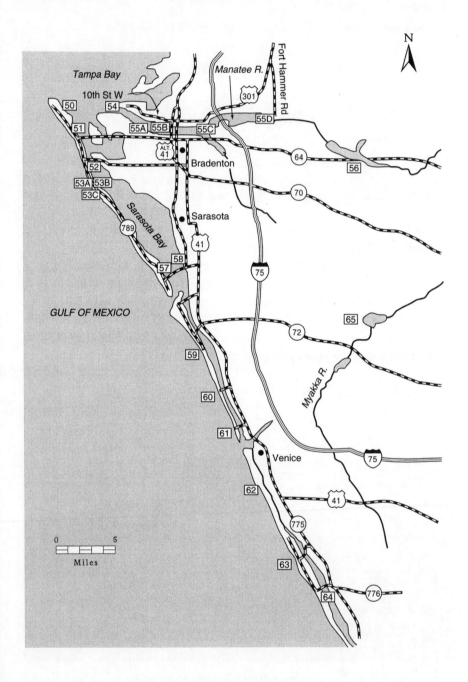

N

Tampa Bay

Manatee R.

Fort Hammer Rd.

10th St W

50

54

301

51

55A 55B 55C 55D

ALT. 41

64

Bradenton

56

52

53A 53B

70

53C

789

Sarasota

41

58

GULF OF MEXICO

57

75

72

65

59

60

61

Venice

75

62

41

775

0 ____ 5

Miles

63

64 776

51. KINGFISH BOAT RAMP

Salt; Bank and Boat; Ramp.

Description: Provides access to Tampa and Sarasota bays.

Fishing Index: Fish for redfish and snook from the banks around the ramp. From a boat, fish around the FL 64 bridge (Palma Sola Causeway) for snook and sheepshead.

Directions: The ramp is on the Anna Maria Island side of FL 64, about 8.3 miles east of the intersection of FL 64 and US 41 in Bradenton.

For more information: Call Manatee County Parks and Recreation Department at (941) 748-4501.

52. BRADENTON BEACH PIER

Salt; Pier.

Description: This city pier is part of the old bridge that connected Anna Maria Island to the mainland. A restaurant and bait shop are on the pier.

Fishing Index: Fish the flats around the bridge for snook, flounder, and spotted seatrout.

Directions: From the intersection of US 41 and FL 648 (Cortez Road), take FL 684 west, cross the Cortez Bridge, and go until the road dead ends at Gulf Drive. Turn south on Gulf Drive and go 0.3 mile to a roundabout. Exit the roundabout going east on Bridge Street. The pier is at the end of the road.

For more information: Call the pier bait shop at (941) 779-1706.

53. LONGBOAT PASS AND VICINITY

Salt; Bank, Bridge, Surf and Boat; Ramp.

Description: A locally famous fishing spot between Longboat and Anna Maria keys. The pass and the bay waters behind it are fertile ground for all of the region's most popular species.

Fishing Index: Snook, redfish, spotted seatrout, flounder, mangrove snapper, and tarpon move through the pass. Flounder and tarpon are seasonal and are most numerous in summer. The best fishing is when the tide is moving in or out.

For more information: Call Annie's Bait and Tackle at (941) 794-3580.

Access Points:
53A. LONGBOAT PASS BRIDGE—*Bridge and Bank.*
Description: Fish from the bridge or around the embankments beneath the bridge.

Mangrove shorelines provide the habitat that attracts big snook and other gamefish. The trick is to cast as close to the edge of the overhanging mangrove branches. Also always make a few casts around the points, such as the one at the far end of this small island.

Directions: The bridge is part of Gulf Drive. From the intersection of FL 64 (Manatee Avenue) and Gulf Drive on Anna Maria Key, take Gulf Drive south 1.7 miles to the bridge.

53B. COQUINA BEACH BAYSIDE—*Ramp.*
Description: A good ramp adjacent to Longboat Pass.
Directions: From the intersection of FL 64 (Manatee Avenue) and Gulf Drive on Anna Maria Key, take Gulf Drive south 1.5 miles to the ramp.

53C. BEER CAN ISLAND—*Bank and Surf.*
Description: At the northern tip of Longboat Key on the south side of Longboat Pass. It is a good place to fish the pass or in the surf.
Directions: The site is about 1.9 miles south of Gulf Drive's intersection with Manatee Avenue (FL 64) and 10.6 miles north of St. Armand's Key.

54. SNEAD ISLAND

Salt; Wade and Boat.

Description: The island guards the north shore of the mouth of the Manatee River. The island has many homes on it but the western tip is undeveloped and very pretty. It is a future county park site. Bait and tackle and a private fee ramp are at Tropic Isle Marina.

Fishing Index: The flats along the north side of the island are excellent wade fishing waters. Slightly farther out, boaters can fish the waters between Snead and Rattlesnake Key for snook and redfish.

Directions: Via land, take FL 43 (10th Street West) from its intersection with US 41 in Palmetto. Follow this road about 2.2 miles to the bridge to Snead Island. Just over the bridge turn right onto Tarpon Road. Go to the first road on the left; turn and drive 1.4 miles to road's end. The last half is unpaved.

For more information: Call Tropic Isles Marina near the Snead Island Bridge at (941) 729-8128.

55. MANATEE RIVER
Salt and Fresh; Bank, Pier, and Boat; Ramp.

Description: From its headwaters in northeastern Manatee County, the river flows west to the lower part of Tampa Bay with only one interruption along its 60-mile run. Half way down is a dam which impedes the river's flow and creates Lake Manatee, the freshwater supply for Manatee and Sarasota counties. The river is narrow and winding above the lake and also downstream until it reaches Fort Hammer where the river opens up and comes under tidal influence. The river is navigable by boat up to Fort Hammer. Beyond that, small boats may continue up to the Lake Manatee dam.

Fishing Index: Saltwater anglers will find plenty of places along the river to fish for redfish, snook, mangrove snapper, sheepshead, and spotted seatrout. When cold winter weather arrives, redfish and snook swim upriver, often moving into freshwater areas. Bass fishing is very good from Fort Hammer to Lake Manatee dam and in Lake Manatee.

Directions: The river begins in northeastern Manatee County and empties into the lower part of Tampa Bay.

Access Points:
55A. WARNER'S BAYOU RAMP (59TH STREET RAMP)—*Salt; Boat; Ramp.*
Description: A county-maintained facility that provides access to the lower Manatee River, the flats around Snead Island at the mouth of the river, and Terra Ceia Bay.
Directions: From Fl 64 (Manatee Avenue) in Bradenton, turn north on 59th Street and go 0.75 mile until the road ends at the river. Bear right on Riverview Boulevard. The ramp is on the left.

55B. GREEN BRIDGE PIER/RIVERSIDE PARK—*Salt; Bank, Boat, and Pier; Ramp.*
Description: The pier, which originates along the north shore, is part of the old US 41 bridge across the river. Bait and tackle available at Regatta Pointe Marina.
Directions: From US Business 41, turn westbound onto Riverside Drive on the north side of the Manatee River. The park and pier are just west of the US Business 41 bridge.
For more information: Call Regatta Pointe Marine at (941) 729-6021.

55C. BRADEN RIVER SHORES PARK—*Salt; Boat; Ramp.*
Description: This county ramp is on the Braden River, a tributary of the Manatee River.

Directions: The ramp is at the base of the FL 64 (E. Manatee Avenue) bridge over the Braden River in Bradenton.

55D. FORT HAMMER—*Salt and Fresh; Boat; Ramp.*
Description: This county ramp is a good access point for freshwater anglers to the Manatee River. It marks the official dividing line between fresh- and salt-water. Make sure you have the correct license when fishing in this area.
Directions: Exit I-75 onto US 310 and drive north about 5.6 miles to Fort Hammer Road. Turn right and go to the ramp at the end of the road, about 3 miles.

56. LAKE MANATEE STATE RECREATION AREA ————
Fresh; Bank and Boat; Ramp; $.

Description: The park extends along the south shore of Lake Manatee, a 2,500-acre impounded part of the Manatee River. There is a 20-horsepower limit on the lake.

Fishing Index: Tom Champeau of the GFC says the lake has good fishing for sunshine bass, bluegills, and redear sunfish.

Directions: Exit I-75 onto FL 64 and go about 8 miles east.

For more information: Call the park office at (941) 741-3028.

57. KEN THOMPSON PARK AT NEW PASS————————
Salt; Bank and Boat; Ramp.

Description: The park is on City Island just north of the upscale shopping district on St. Armand's Key. Mote Marine Laboratory, a private marine research and education facility, is adjacent to the park. The lab is open to the public and has an excellent marine center filled with large saltwater aquaria, a touch tank, and other exhibits.

Fishing Index: From the park, fish in New Pass for snook, mangrove snapper, and seasonally for tarpon and flounder. Land-bound anglers can also fish around the embankments of the bridge over New Pass. Boaters have access to the grassflats inside the pass and to several fish havens within a few miles of shore. These sites attract cobia, grouper, Spanish and king mackerel, and mangrove snapper.

Directions: From US 41 in Sarasota or by exiting at Fruitville off of I-75, go west on Fruitville Road. At Sarasota Bay, the road becomes the Ringling Causeway and signs lead to St. Armand's Key. From the roundabout on St. Armand's Key, exit onto FL 789. Go north about 1 mile to the park and Mote Marine Lab entrance on the right. The road is just before the New Pass bridge.

For more information: Call New Pass Bait Shop at (941) 388-3050. For more information about Mote Marine Laboratory call (941) 388-4441.

58. CAUSEWAY PARK AND TONY SAPRITO PIER ―――――

Salt; Pier and Boat; Ramp.

Description: The county park's ramp is suited only for boats less than 17 feet according to the staff at the on-site concession bait and tackle shop. A better ramp is located a few blocks away. The 10th Street ramp at the intersection of US 41 and 10th Street can accommodate larger boats and has more parking.

Fishing Index: Best fishing at the pier is at night for snook. Boaters can fish around the causeway bridges, on the grassflats, and around many other places in Sarasota Bay. New Pass is also nearby. Throughout the area, fishing is good year-round for snook and redfish, with flounder in summer.

Directions: From US 41 in Sarasota or by exiting at Fruitville off of I-75, go west on Fruitville Road. At Sarasota Bay, the road becomes the Ringling Causeway and signs lead to St. Armand's Key. Turn onto the service road just before the causeway.

For more information: Call Hart's Landing at (941) 995-0011.

Other access points:
Bird Key Park—*bank fishing, Ringling Causeway.*

Bay Island Park—*bank fishing, Siesta Drive Bridge.*

59. TURTLE BEACH ――――――――――――――――――

Salt; Surf, Bank, and Boat; Ramp.

Description: A county park just north of Midnight Pass, an inlet that is now completely filled with sand. The ramp provides boaters access to Little Sarasota Bay. The park has picnic shelters and a playground.

Fishing Index: Anglers can surf fish for snook, wade in the bay, or fish from boats for snook, redfish, mangrove snapper, and seatrout.

Directions: Exit I-75 onto Clark Road (FL 72) and drive west about 5.6 miles to Siesta Key. Turn south on CR 789 and go 2.8 miles to the park.

For more information: Call the Sarasota County Parks and Recreation Department at (941) 951-5572.

60. BLACKBURN POINT PARK AND VICINITY ―――――――

Salt; Bank, Boat, and Wade; Ramp.

Description: The park is good place to access the flats on the bay side of Casey Key. The ramp, also on Casey Key, is for small boats. The bridge from the mainland to the islands is the oldest operating swing bridge in Florida.

Fishing Index: Mangroves line Blackburn Bay and create very good cover for snook, redfish, spotted seatrout, and big sheepshead, according to Captain Mark Schindel.

Directions: From Venice, take US 41 north about 5.8 miles or from Sarasota take US 41 south about 10 miles to the intersection with Blackburn Point Road (CR 789). Take this road and cross the swing bridge. The park and ramp are on the island side.

61. NOKOMIS BEACH AND NORTH JETTY PARK————

Salt; Surf, Bank and Boat; Ramp.

Description: These two facilities are at the south end of Casey Key. The ramp is on the bayside area of Nokomis Beach. It provides access to Blackburn Bay and Venice Inlet. At North Jetty Park, anglers can fish in Venice Inlet.

Fishing Index: Fish for snook, redfish, and seatrout in the bay; snook in the surf; and snook, sharks, redfish, and tarpon in the inlet.

Directions: From US 41 in Venice, turn onto CR 789 (Albee Road). Go about 0.9 mile to the entrance road to the ramp. It's on a small island midway across the bay. Nokomis Beach is at the end of Albee Road where it intersects with Casey Key Road. North Jetty Park is 0.8 mile south of Nokomis Beach.

For more information: Call North Jetty Fish Camp at (941) 488-2408.

Fishing from the seawalls along Sarasota Bay is a popular pastime and a great place to take kids. This young angler gets a lesson on the fine point of how to cast.

62. Venice Pier

Salt; Pier.

Description: This 740-foot municipal pier is part of Brohard Park and is open 24 hours.

Fishing Index: Spanish mackerel migrate through the area in spring and good catches come off the pier. Snook and redfish are usually present except during the coldest months. Sheepshead action is good in fall and winter. In summer, mangrove snapper and cobia move in around the pier.

Directions: From US 41 in Venice take Venice Avenue west to Harbor Drive. Turn south on Harbor Drive and go about 1.7 miles to the park and pier.

For more information: Call the pier bait shop at (941) 488-9713.

Other access points:
Caspersen Beach—*surf fishing, south of Venice Pier.*

63. Manasota Beach

Salt; Surf, Bank and Boat; Ramp.

Description: The park is on Manasota Key south of Venice. It is recognized as a good shelling beach. The park has picnic shelters and year-round lifeguards.

Fishing Index: Surf fish for snook and redfish or fish from the shoreline of Lemon Bay near the boat ramp.

Directions: Drive south from Venice on US 41 to FL 775 (Englewood Road). Take FL 775 south 2.2 miles to Manasota Beach Road. Take this road about 1.5 miles to the park at road's end.

64. Lemon Bay Pier

Salt; Pier.

Description: This site, also known as Angler's Pier, is just across the line in Charlotte County. Across the road from the pier is Englewood Bait House, which offers boat rentals and charters. The pier is parallel to the road bridge to Englewood Beach.

Fishing Index: A good place to fish for snook day or night. There are plenty of submerged structures between the pier and the road bridge. Use a stout rod and reel if you're going after the big snook.

Directions: From US 41 in Murdock, go west 16.2 miles on FL 776 to Beach Road, just before Englewood. Turn left on Beach Road (toward Englewood Beach) and go 0.5 mile. The pier is on the left before crossing the bridge.

For more information: Call Charlotte County Parks Department at (941) 743-1313 or Englewood Bait House at (941) 475-4511.

65. MYAKKA RIVER STATE PARK —————————

Fresh; Bank, Canoe and Boat; Ramp.

Description: In addition to fishing in the upper Myakka River, this 30,000-acre park has miles of hiking and backpacking trails and is a great place for wildlife watching, especially birds. The river is also popular for canoeing. A campground, cabins, and interpretive exhibits round out the amenities here.

Fishing Index: The river has two wide spots known as Upper and Lower Myakka lakes. Both are good places to fish for largemouth bass, crappie, redear sunfish, and warmouth. The upper lake is in the developed part of the park and is easiest to access. On the river, anglers target largemouth bass and bluegills. Snook wander up into the freshwater regions of the river up to Lower Myakka Lake.

Directions: In Sarasota, exit I-75 onto FL 72 and drive east about 8 miles to the park entrance.

For more information: Call the park office at (941) 361-6511.

POLK, HARDEE, DeSOTO, AND HIGHLANDS COUNTIES

Lake fishing is a major activity in these four counties, especially Polk and Highlands, which have almost 550 and 100 lakes respectively. All lakes support at least a fair fishery, but some have a much better reputation than others. The ones listed in this section are considered the best lakes in the region as of the publication date of this book. Remember, Florida's lakes go through cycles and fishing conditions go through periods of ups and downs.

Most of the lakes can be fished only from a boat. Lakes with bank fishing sites include Arbuckle, Reedy, Rosalie, Weohyakapka, Parker, and the reservoirs at Saddle Creek Park.

The Central Florida Convention and Visitors bureau has several useful brochures about fishing in this part of the state. To request information give them a call at 1 800 828-7655.

66. TENOROC FISH MANAGEMENT AREA —————————

Fresh; Boat; Ramp.

Description: This 6,000-acre site has 1,000 acres of fish-filled phosphate pits that remain from the active mining days of the 1960s and '70s. The site is tightly regulated and all anglers must check in and out of the sites. Fishing is allowed only Thursday through Sunday. Anglers surrender their fishing licenses when entering the site and are given a daily fishing permit and a creel information sheet which they must fill out. Special rules apply at Tenoroc and anglers will be informed of the specific regulations in effect. Most of the fishing is catch and release.

If all the special rules sound harsh, consider this: Tenoroc lakes consistently produce trophy-size bass. Each lake is managed for this purpose. Be-

POLK, HARDEE, DESOTO, AND HIGHLANDS COUNTIES

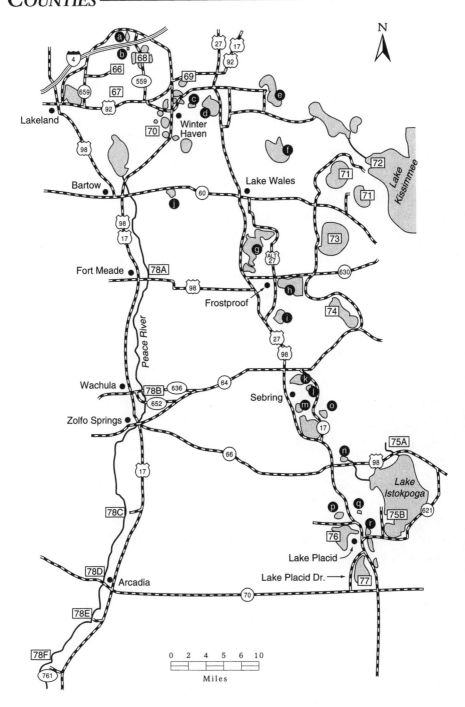

cause of tightly controlled fishing pressure, and rules adapted to enhance the fishery, those who fish here have an excellent chance for a high-quality experience.

Fishing Index: Trophy-sized largemouth bass are the main attraction at Tenoroc. Fishing is good year-round for this species. The lakes also have good populations of crappie, bluegill, redear sunfish, and catfish.

Directions: From US 98 in Lakeland, take US 92 east 3 miles to Combee Road (FL 659). Turn north and go 3.5 miles to Tenoroc Mine Road. Turn right and follow the road to the Headquarters and Check-in.

For more information: Call the Tenoroc office at (941) 499-2422. Anglers can make a reservation for a fishing permit by calling this number. This is recommended for weekends.

67. SADDLE CREEK PARK

Fresh; Boat and Bank; Ramp.

Description: The park features an old 326-acre phosphate-pit lake. There are several boat ramps, numerous sites for bank fishing, a place to swim, a campground, and other recreational facilities. This is a good family place.

Fishing Index: Heavily fished but still a better than average place for big bass.

Directions: From US 98 in Lakeland, take US 92 east 3.7 miles to the park entrance.

For more information: Call the park office at (941) 665-0966.

68. LAKES JULIANA AND MATTIE

Fresh; Boat; Ramp.

Description: Lake Mattie is reached via a waterway connecting it to Lake Juliana. The ramp is at Fish Haven Camp.

Fishing Index: Lake Mattie is an excellent crappie lake. The best time to fish is during the colder months.

Directions: From US 92 in Auburndale, turn north on CR 559 and go 4.5 miles. Turn onto Fish Haven Road and follow it to the camp.

For more information: Call Fish Haven Camp at (941) 984-1183.

69. NORTH WINTER HAVEN CHAIN

Fresh; Boat; Ramp.

Description: The north chain consists of lakes Haines, Rochelle, Conine, and Smart.

Fishing Index: The chain has good bass and bluegill fishing.

Directions: There is a ramp on Lake Rochelle. It is just past the junction of US 92 and US 17 near the town of Lake Alfred. From this ramp, you can access the other lakes via canals.

70. SOUTH WINTER HAVEN CHAIN
Fresh; Boat and Bank; Ramp.

Description: The south chain consists of nine lakes within the city of Winter Haven and to the south of town.

Fishing Index: The chain has good bass and bluegill fishing. It is heavily fished and there is considerable boat and jet ski traffic. Try fishing during the week.

Directions: There is a ramp at Lake Cannon Park. From US 17 take FL 544 (Havendale Boulevard) west about 1 mile. Turn left onto Lake Cannon Drive and follow it to the park. Another ramp is on Lake Shipp. From the intersection of US 17 and FL 540 in Winter Haven, drive about 0.5 mile south. Turn west onto Avenue X and follow it a short distance to the ramp.

Additional access points:
Lake Howard ramp.

Lake Hartridge ramp.

Lake Summit ramp *(on the same lake as Cypress Gradens).*

71. LAKES ROSALIE AND TIGER
Fresh; Boat and Bank; Ramp.

Description: Water flows from Lake Rosalie to Tiger Lake and then to Lake Kissimmee. Both are shallow, sandy-bottomed lakes.

Fishing Index: The lakes are good for largemouth bass. Tiger Lake also has a reputation for producing nice stringers of crappie.

Directions: From US 27 in Lake Wales, drive east about 13 miles on FL 60 to Tiger Lake Road. Turn left and go 2 miles to Lake Rosalie Road. Turn left and follow the road 1.1 miles to a county park and boat ramp. Access to Tiger Lake is from either Bud's Ramp and Camp off Tiger Lake Road or Camp Rosalie off Sam Keene Road 1.7 miles east of FL 60.

For more information: Call Buds Ramp and Camp at (941) 696-2274 or Camp Rosalie at (941) 696-2662.

72. KISSIMMEE RIVER STATE PARK
Fresh; Boat and Bank; Ramp.

Description: The park's boat ramp provides access to Lake Kissimmee. A more detailed listing is provided in the East Central Florida chapter under the Lake Kissimmee site.

73. LAKE WEOHYAKAPKA

Fresh; Boat and Bank; Ramp.

Description: With a name as hard to pronounce as this, no wonder it's usually called Lake Walk-in-the-Water. This is the largest lake in Polk County at 7,000 acres. Limited bank fishing.

Fishing Index: A bass and crappie lake.

Directions: From Alternate US 27 in Frostproof, go east 9.3 miles to Lake Walk-in-the-Water Road. Turn right and go 4.5 miles to the county park and boat ramp.

For more information: Call Harvey's Minit Mart at (941) 635-5234.

74. LAKE ARBUCKLE

Fresh; Boat and Bank; Ramp.

Description: The most pristine lake in Polk County, according to the GFC *Central Florida Fishing Guide.* Access is via the ramp at Lake Arbuckle Park.

Fishing Index: The lake has excellent crappie fishing during the colder times of the year. It also has a good year-round largemouth bass fishery.

Directions: From Alternate US 27 in Frostproof, drive 0.6 mile east on CR 630. Here the road jogs to the left and Lake Reedy Boulevard goes straight ahead. Take Lake Reedy Drive around the lake about 4.5 miles to Lake Arbuckle Road. Turn left and go 3.2 miles to the ramp.

For more information: Call Harvey's Minit Mart at (941) 635-5234.

75. LAKE ISTOKPOGA

Fresh; Boat; Ramp.

Description: One of the best-known lakes in central Florida. Some anglers prefer to fish this lake over Lake Okeechobee. There are several fish camps around the lake.

Fishing Index: An excellent reputation for largemouth bass and bluegills. The amount of hydrilla has been increasing and that is changing the fishing strategy on this lake. When the aquatic weeds are dense, fish the edges of the weedlines or the holes in the weeds. When the weed level is reduced, return to the tradition of fishing along the shoreline.

Dan Clark, a full-time guide on the lake, realizes that the mats of exotic hydrilla are a benefit to the good bass fishing in Lake Istokpoga. "Hydrilla is one of the best bass covers there is," he says, and fisheries biologists won't argue with him on that point. Clark recommends using live wild shiners if you want to catch the big trophy fish.

Access Points:

75A. ARBUCKLE CREEK—*Boat; Ramp.*
Directions: From US 27 south of Sebring, take US 98 east along the north shore of the Lake. The ramp is about 7.4 miles to the east, just off the highway.

75B. HIGHLANDS LAKE DRIVE—*Boat; Ramp.*
Directions: The ramp is at the south end of the lake. From US 27 in Lake Placid turn onto FL 621 and go west 2.6 miles to Highlands Lake Drive. Turn left and go to Windy Point, the first paved road on the right. Turn right and follow the road to the ramp.

For more information: Call Dan Clark of Fishy Fingers Guide Service at (941) 465-8139 or J.W. Bait and Tackle in Lake Placid at (941) 699-0650.

76. LAKE JUNE IN WINTER
Fresh; Boat and Bank; Ramp.

Description: Everyone refers to this water body as Lake June although the official name includes the "in Winter." At H.L. Bishop Park there is a fishing pier and boat ramp.

Fishing Index: A good lake for largemouth bass. The lake has numerous deep holes, good places to fish for largemouth in summer when the surface water is hot. Anglers should fish these locations throughout the year except for the spawning period in early spring when the fish move into the shallows. Also, try crappie fishing at night in summer.

Directions: You can see the fishing pier and park from US 27 in Lake Placid. Turn west onto CR 621 (Lake June Road) at the north end of the lake.

For more information: Call J.W. Bait and Tackle in Lake Placid at (941) 699-0650.

77. LAKE PLACID
Fresh; Boat; Ramp.

Description: This is a clear-water lake just south of Lake June. Jim Turner of J.T. Bait and Tackle says that in addition to the big three lakes near the city of Lake Placid (June, Istokpoga, and Placid), there are 26 other lakes in the area with "sufficient fish in them."

Fishing Index: Turner suggests fishing the deep, 48- to 52-foot hole in the southwest corner of the lake for largemouth bass. "Use a deep diving crank bait or live shiners." This lake is also very productive for crappie (specs) in late winter and early spring and an excellent place to fish for bluegills in summer.

Directions: From the intersection with FL 621, drive 1.4 miles south on US 27. Turn onto Placid View Road. The ramp is about 2 miles down the road.

For more information: Call J.W. Bait and Tackle in Lake Placid at (941) 699-0650.

More Lakes to Try

All the following have ramps and or are accessed by a nearby lake with a ramp. While they are not considered top producers, each lake can have periods of good to above-average fishing. Local knowledge, usually available from bait and tackle shops throughout the region, is very helpful in finding a sleeper lake waiting for you to discover its secrets. On the map on page 245 these lakes are identified by a circle with an upper case letter within.

Lake Name	Nearby City	Ramp Location
A Lake Agnes	Polk City	Lake Agnes Drive
B Lake Tennessee	Polk City	Old Berkely Road
C Lake Fannie	Winter Haven	Lucerne Park Road
D Lake Hamilton	Winter Haven	US 27
E Lake Marion	Haines City	Jim Edwards Road
F Lake Pierce	Dundee	Timberline Road
G Crooked Lake	Frostproof	FL 630
H Reedy Lake	Frostproof	Lake Reedy Drive
I Lake Livingston	Frostproof	Lake Livingston Road
J Lake Garfield	Bartow-Lake Whales	CR 655 A
K Lake Lelia	Avon Park	off US 98 and US 27
L Lake Letta	Avon Park	FL 17
M Lake Sebring	Sebring	FL 17A
N Red Beach Lake	Sebring	FL 17
O Dinner Lake	Sebring	FL 17A
P Lake Francis	Lake Placid	4-H Road off US 27
Q Lake Apthorpe	Lake Placid	off US 27
R Lake Clay	Lake Placid	Lake Clay Drive

78. Peace River

Fresh; Boat and Bank; Ramp.

Description: This river originates from the waters of Lake Hancock, one of the more polluted lakes in the region. From the lake, the river flows a little more than 100 miles until it empties into Charlotte Harbor near Punta Gorda. Tannins from trees along the riverbanks give the water a brownish tea-colored look. Despite it's start from a polluted lake and the fact that it flows through areas of active phosphate mining, the Peace River is fairly clean and healthy south of Bartow. It is a very scenic river and popular with canoeists.

Fishing Index: The upper part of the river is an excellent place to fish from a canoe or small boat for largemouth bass and catfish. From Bartow southward, freshwater anglers will find saltwater snook swimming in the river. The further south you go, the more snook there are. Flip a lure under some brush along the river bank to entice a bass or snook to take the bait.

For more information: Call the South Region office of the GFC at (941) 648-3203.

Access Points:

78A. FORT MEADE—*Boat and Bank; Ramp.*
Directions: From US 17 in Fort Meade drive 1.1 miles east on US 98. Turn onto NE 9th Street and drive to the ramp.

78B. CR 652 NEAR WACHULA—*Boat and Bank; Ramp.*
Directions: From US 17 in Wachula turn onto Main Street (CR 636) and go east 0.6 mile to CR 652. Turn south and go 1 mile to the bridge over the river and the ramp.

78C. GARDNER—*Boat and Bank; Ramp.*
Directions: From US 17 in Gardner, turn onto River Road and go west 1.5 miles to the end of the road and the ramp.

78D. ARCADIA—*Boat and Bank; Ramp.*
Directions: The ramp is on FL 70 1.3 miles west of the intersection of US 17 and FL 70.

78E. NOCATEE—*Boat and Bank; Ramp.*
Directions: The ramp is on CR 760 1.1 miles west of US 17 in Nocatee.

78F. FORT OGDEN—*Boat and Bank; Ramp.*
Directions: From US 17 in Fort Ogden, turn onto CR 761 and drive 1.4 miles to Lettuce Lake Road. Turn left and go to Reese Street. Turn onto Reese Street and follow it to the ramp.
For more information: Call Lettuce Lake Campground at (941) 494-6057.

79. GULF OF MEXICO
Salt; Surf and Boat.

Description: The beaches of the barrier islands in this region are popular for sunbathers and swimmers. The beaches offer excellent fishing in early morning or whenever there aren't a lot of people in the water.

Fishing Index: Surf fishing is very good along most of the beaches north and south of Tampa Bay. Try for snook, redfish, and whiting in the trough that lies just a few feet off the beach. In addition, smoker king mackerel and tarpon appear in spring and fall. For offshore species, try one of the party boats or sportfishing boats (which hold six passengers or less). Popular targets are grouper, snapper, Spanish and king mackerel, amberjack, and cobia for the boats that fish inside the 100-foot line. Beyond that, the charters may go after these same species or look for dolphin and sailfish. Several party boats make overnight trips to the middle grounds where big catches are usually the rule.

Captain Mark Schindel (call (941) 924-6490) says tarpon are one of the species he targets. "The fish range from right off the beach to 2 miles offshore and the best time to find them there is from the end of April to the end of June. We sight fish for them and use large live blue crabs for bait until the fish spawn. After that I switch to live baitfish. One of the best areas to find the tarpon is from Point O'Rocks to Siesta Key Beach."

Anglers with boats capable of going offshore and who are not familiar with the region can visit any of the numerous artificial reefs, well-known wrecks, and natural hard-bottom areas. Local marinas often have inexpensive charts or lists of LORAN numbers for the better-known sites. As long as you have a LORAN or GPS and a good fathometer, finding these sites is relatively easy. And although the sites are widely known, new fish are always moving in to replace ones that anglers harvest.

Directions: Anglers can reach the beach at numerous public access sites or by staying at a beachfront hotel and walking out the door. A list of local fishing guides offering offshore or backcountry trips is in every phone directory. If you talk to a bait and tackle shop, the owners will usually recommend several guides that would be the best for the type of fishing you want to do. The offshore boats tend to congregate at the marinas around the passes. Look for their brochures in hotels and other tourist spots.

MONTH BY MONTH IN WEST CENTRAL FLORIDA

Note: Offshore is defined as greater than 2 miles from the coast. Coastal waters include open waters inside of 2 miles including surf fishing, and all brackish water areas such as bays, the saltwater regions of rivers, and lagoons. Freshwater includes lakes, ponds, reservoirs, and rivers.

JANUARY

Offshore: This is a tough month for offshore anglers because of the high number of bad-weather days. When the fronts aren't blowing through and stirring up the seas, grouper grabbers will find keeper-sized fish within 10 miles of shore.

Coastal: This is one of the months when anglers head up the region's tidal creeks and rivers. That's where the snook, spotted seatrout, and redfish go to escape the cold, windswept waters of the bays and coastline. Another good bet is to fish around one of the power plant discharge canals. The warm water attracts a wide variety of fish. Bridge anglers will find a good supply of sheepshead this month and next.

Freshwater: Largemouth bass start to spawn in the shallow waters of the region's many freshwater lakes. Live wild shiners are the bait of choice for trophy-sized fish. This is also a top month for crappie.

FEBRUARY

Offshore: The rough winter will peak this month, so anglers must resign themselves to heading out between the northwesters. When the weather is good so is the fishing. Grouper are always biting but finding out where they are takes some work. Try trolling until you get a hit then stop and fish that area for a while.

Coastal: Look for the warm water this month. Anything above 70 degrees is where you want to be. Snook, redfish, and seatrout lurk in these warm spots. Late in the day, after the sun has warmed the water on the flats, look for some fish to move in and feed. Best bet is around the power plant outfalls.

Freshwater: This is peak time for the big bass. The fish are spawning in the shallows around the lakes and the females are on their nests. Live wild shiners are as sure-fire a bait as you'll ever find this time of year. If you have to use artificials, try something that looks like a shiner or shad. Also expect great crappie action.

March

Offshore: The Gulf water begins to warm up in March and by the end of the month offshore action will be in high gear. Spanish and king mackerel follow the schools of baitfish moving up from the south.

Coastal: This is the time when fishing along the coast gets really exciting. Baitfish move into the area and are the apple of every fish's eye and mouth. Hoping to avoid becoming a meal, the baitfish will seek what cover they can get. The huge number of bridge and dock pilings in the region attract the bait and bring along mackerel, snook, redfish, and tarpon. Best places to go for this action are the Gulf fishing piers and the Sunshine Skyway.

Freshwater: The last month for the females to spawn and for good big bass fishing. Live shiners are the preferred bait. Crappie action will begin to slow as the water warms up, but this is still usually a good month.

April

Offshore: King and Spanish mackerel are at their peak. Sometimes you must set several lines out at different depths to find where in the water column the fish are congregating. Lines set closer to the bottom will also find grouper, cobia, and snapper. Those closer to the surface might be hit by blackfin tuna or a sailfish. Use what locals call whitebait, an encompassing name for several species of white-sided baitfish.

Coastal: The snook, redfish, and seatrout that were up the creeks over the winter are moving closer to the coast and the open water of Tampa Bay. Tarpon are more numerous than last month. You can always count on sheepshead and mangrove snapper around the bridges and piers this time of year.

Freshwater: Largemouth bass are entering the postspawn period and some veteran anglers say that while there are plenty of fish around, getting them to bite takes more work than the previous three months. Look for bluegill and redear sunfish action to pick up as their spawning time approaches.

May

Offshore: Depending on how warm the Gulf water is there may be some king mackerel around but chances are most are farther north by now. Anglers can return to the reliable grouper and snapper fishing or look in the water column for summer's pelagic fish: blackfin tuna, sailfish, and maybe a marlin.

Coastal: Anglers are looking for big tarpon to appear. The site of a 150-pound fish leaping out of the water is something that die-hard anglers and novices will remember for a long time. Look for the big fish along the coast, within a few miles of shore. Toward the north end of the region, the fish will move onto the flats around Homosassa and anglers will be waiting for them with fly rods in hand. This is also a great time for snook and redfish. Seatrout are on the flats and there are plenty of cobia in Tampa Bay. A good time to be in west-central Florida.

Freshwater: Bluegills and shellcrackers (redear sunfish) are spawning and it's easy to catch your limit of these fish. Largemouth bass seek deeper water during the day and move into shallower water to feed during the early and late hours of the day.

JUNE

Offshore: Offshore anglers have to start moving farther offshore for good grouper action. Gag grouper tend to move to deeper water in summer. Forty miles out and farther will get you into the best dolphin, wahoo, sailfish, blackfin tuna, and marlin fishing there is along the west-central coast. It's not as convenient as fishing in the Atlantic, but the experienced charter boat operator knows how to bring these fish to the boat.

Coastal: Tarpon, tarpon, tarpon. Now is the time for the monsters. The biggest fish, in excess of 200 pounds, are on the flats around Homosassa. That's also where you will find some of the best guides in the state taking their clients in search of record fish. If tarpon aren't your bag, this is a prime month for snook. The fish will be in the passes and along the beach, making them accessible to surf anglers. Spanish mackerel are plentiful close to shore and at the mouth of Tampa Bay.

Freshwater: Worm fishing for largemouths early in the morning or late in the day is a standard tactic this month. In midday, the bass are down deep and anglers willing to use deep-diving crank baits or live shiners down deep will catch fish.

JULY

Offshore: The bluewater fish—dolphin, wahoo, sailfish, and blackfin tuna—are the target of anglers with open-water boats that can make the trip more than 40 miles out. This is the peak month for these species. Grouper are in at least 70 feet of water. For a change of pace, try night fishing for snapper. Mangroves, yellowtails, and a few reds are active feeders after dark.

Coastal: Along the shore, usually within 0.5 mile, 50- to 125-pound tarpon cruise the channels paralleling shore. They're looking for a whitebait breakfast so use some fresh cast-netted fish. Toss your bait ahead in the direction they're heading and hold on. Cobia are plentiful in Tampa Bay both around the shipping lane markers and in the open sandy holes in the grassflats.

Freshwater: If you want largemouth bass either fish the shallow waters of the lakes very early in the morning or just as the sun sets. The rest of the time go to the deepest spots in the lake and fish deep. You will also find some crappie there.

AUGUST

Offshore: Those bluewater fish, in 100 feet of water and deeper, continue to provide good summer action. Grouper are in at least 70 feet of water. Chumming them out of their holes may help increase your chances of getting one to the boat. If you fish the bottom, it's essential to turn their heads up as quickly as possible. If you don't, the fish will duck into a hole and you will never muscle it out. At this point just leave the rod alone for a half hour and then try again. Maybe the fish will move back into open water.

Coastal: Shark anglers like to fish in the passes at night during summer. Sharks are abundant in west central Florida. The traditional flats fish—snook, redfish, and seatrout—move to the deep side of the flats now that it's hot. Fish early and late in the day, especially when the tide is moving.

Freshwater: Look for lakes with deeper water and fish for bass and crappie there. Local anglers don't take advantage of this enough and may tell you not to bother fishing in the middle of the day. But if you can stand the heat, give it a try. Otherwise consider night fishing for bass and crappie. It works.

SEPTEMBER

Offshore: This will be the last good month for the bluewater species. Dolphin like to travel with anything that's floating in the water. Grass or algae lines are ideal places to look but so is any piece of debris. Grouper will start to move slightly closer to shore if the water starts to cool a bit. Trolling a big lure 5 to 10 feet above the bottom will attract the fish. It's possible some king mackerel will show up, but if you really want one wait until next month.

Coastal: Redfish are the top inside fish this month but snook aren't far behind. Sight fishing reds on the flats is a popular way to catch these fish. You will need a shallow draft boat to reach them or be prepared to get wet and wade. Trout fishing, which everyone predicts will dramatically improve now that there is a net ban in coastal waters, may be terrific on the flats. Ask locally about the status.

Freshwater: After the long hot summer, largemouth bass might start to be easier to find in shallow water. Now it's time to work the plastic worm along the lake's shoreline vegetation.

OCTOBER

Offshore: King mackerel traditionally make their return performance this month, coming down from their summer home along the north Gulf coast. They move in schools, so not every day will be great, but you'll have more action than you can handle if you find the fish. Grouper are getting closer to shore and that makes them more accessible to smaller open-water boats.

Coastal: This is a great month for coastal and backwater anglers because there is top action for redfish, snook, cobia, flounder, and Spanish mackerel. The snook and reds start to move out of the passes and coastal areas and head toward the rivers where they eventually move whenever the weather turns cold.

Freshwater: Activity starts to pick up as there are more bass spending more time in the shallow waters that anglers like to fish. Crappie fishing will still be better in the deeper waters.

NOVEMBER

Offshore: Grouper have anglers excited this month. The Gulf populations of gag grouper are as close to shore as they will get and that means the fish are in 20 to 40 feet of water. The fastest way to find the fish, unless you have a book full of LORAN numbers of secret grouper holes, is to troll a lure along the bottom. Try this along stone crab trap lines because crabbers set their traps along edges where the bottom drops onto a hard bottom area. The king mackerel run continues through this month before most of the fish disappear until next spring.

Coastal: The creeks and rivers are still bringing warm water to the Gulf and Tampa Bay and that's why snook, redfish, and seatrout are attracted to these areas. Fish the sea grass beds around any of these places; the action will be hot. This is also a great month for flounder. Fish for them on open sandy patches in the sea grass beds or around the edges of oyster bars.

Freshwater: Crappie action should turn on toward the end of the month. The quicker it gets colder the better the fishing will be. Live Missouri minnows are a favorite, reliable bait. Bass anglers will find fish around the edges of aquatic weeds and shorelines and the number of bigger fish being caught will increase. The females are preparing for the spawn which can begin in December in mild weather years.

DECEMBER

Offshore: This is one of the best months for gag grouper. The only problem is the weather. Fronts sweep down from the northwest, kicking up the seas and making it impossible to get offshore. On calm days there's very good fishing within 10 miles of the coast. Live bait works best, but you may want to refrain from using it until you slow-troll up a good location.

Coastal: The fish are up the creeks and around the power plant outfalls now. You can fish inside even on windy days. There's always a lee side of an island or the mainland where the water will be calm and you can fish in relative comfort. Cobia, pompano, and permit join redfish, snook, and spotted seatrout around the power plants. Freelining a shrimp is a good tactic to use in winter.

Freshwater: Crappie are spawning and the fish bite readily. All you need to catch these fish is a cane pole and that's what many anglers use. Simple still works when it comes to fishing. The first largemouth bass of the season will begin to spawn in the shallower, warmer lakes. They won't be the biggest females but it does make this a better-than-average month.

West Central Florida Fish Availability Chart

NOTE: The information contained in this chart represents the seasonal patterns observed over the past two or three years. For salt water species, the arrival of the migrant species and the peak times for each species is heavily dependent on water temperature. Unusually warm or cold periods will effect the patterns described above. Bream is the local name for bluegills and shellcrackers. Specked Perch or Specs are crappie. Speckled trout is another name for spotted seatrout.

■ signifies a reasonable chance of catching this species in that month.

□ signifies the optimal months for catching the species.

Species	Jan	Feb	Mar	Apr	May	Jun	Jul	Aug	Sep	Oct	Nov	Dec
Snook	■	■	■	□	□	□	■	■	■	□	□	■
Redfish	■	■	■	■	■	■	□	□	□	□	■	■
Spotted trout	■	■	■	□	□	□	■	□	□	■	■	■
Sheepshead	□	□	□	■	■	■	■	■	■	■	□	□
Mangrove Snapper	■	■	□	□	■	■	□	□	□	■	■	■
Gag Grouper	■	■	□	□	■	■	■	■	■	■	□	□
Amberjack	■	■	■	■	■	■	■	■	■	■	■	■
Flounder	■	■	■	□	■	■	■	■	■	■	□	■
Black Drum	■	■	■	■	■	■	■	■	■	■	■	■
Crevalle Jack	■	■	■	■	■	■	■	■	■	■	■	■
Shark (all species)	■	■	■	■	■	■	□	□	■	■	■	■
Black Sea Bass	■	■	■	■	■	■	■	■	■	■	■	■
Spanish Mackerel	■	■	■	□	□	□	■	■	■	□	□	
Whiting	□	□	■	■						■	■	□
Blackfin Tuna		■	■	■	■	■	■	■	■			
King Mackerel	■	■	■	□	□	□	■	■	■	□	□	
Tarpon			■	■	■	□	□	■	■			
Cobia				■	□	□	■	■	■	□	■	■
Tripletail				■	■	■	■	■	■			
Sailfish					■	■	■	■	■	■		
Wahoo						■	■	■	■	■		
Largemouth Bass	□	□	□	■	■	■	■	■	■	■	■	■
Catfish	■	■	■	■	■	■	■	■	■	■	■	■
Shellcracker	■	■	■	□	□	□	■	■	■	■	■	■
Sunshine Bass	■	■	■	■	■	■	■	■	■	■	■	■
Crappie	□	□	■	■	■	■	■	■	■	■	■	□
Bluegills	■	■	■	□	□	□	■	■	■	■	■	■

Southwest Florida Regional Map

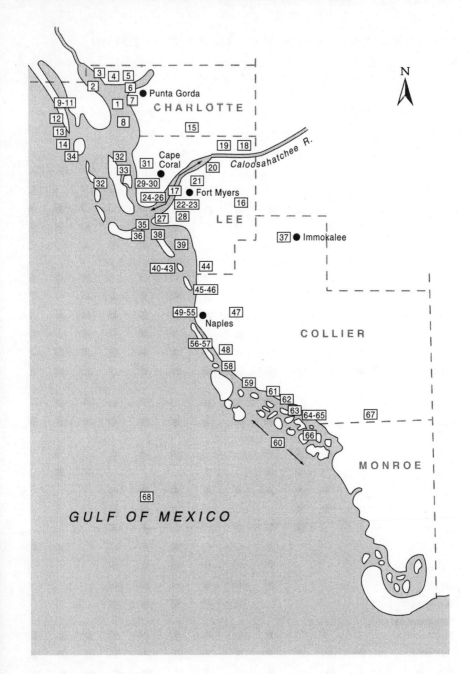

N

3 4 5
2
6
● Punta Gorda
9-11   7
1
CHARLOTTE
12   8
13
14
34   15
32   19 18
Cape   Caloosahatchee R.
31 Coral
33   20
32   29-30   21
24-26 17 ● Fort Myers
22-23
16
LEE
35   28
27
36   38   37 ● Immokalee
39
40-43   44
45-46
49-55   47
● Naples   COLLIER
56-57   48
58
59
61
62
63
64-65   67
66
60
MONROE
68
GULF OF MEXICO

CHAPTER EIGHT
Southwest Florida

COUNTIES: ▪ Charlotte ▪ Lee ▪ Collier

The southwest region extends from Charlotte Harbor in the north to the famous Ten Thousand Islands in the south. This part of the state has the dual distinction of being one of the fastest growing communities in the country and having some of last tracts of wilderness east of the Mississippi River. With that comes a legacy of good fishing.

SALTWATER FISHING

Southwest Florida has some of the best backwater fishing (in the extensive network of bays, mangrove islands, and tidal creeks) in the state. Thousands of miles of shoreline, countless oyster bars, and acres of seagrass beds attract an abundance of saltwater fish. Roaming these waters are four of the state's most sought after gamefish: snook, redfish, spotted seatrout, and tarpon. While there are peak months to catch each species (see the species availability chart and month-by-month table), all four are year-round residents of this region. Thousands of anglers come to southwest Florida each year for the chance at a grand slam, catching one fish of each species in one day.

The region's excellent fishing is due in large part to the vast tracks of unspoiled fresh- and saltwater wetlands. The Charlotte Harbor/Pine Island Sound area, one of the state's largest estuaries, has relatively clean water that supports extensive grass beds and stands of mangroves. Several large sections of this estuarine complex are designated as state aquatic preserves and strict regulations protect the water quality and marine life in the system. Rookery Bay, between Naples and Marco Island, and the waters from Marco Island into the upper part of the Ten Thousand Islands, are also aquatic preserves. The upper part of the Ten Thousand Islands is slated to become a National Wildlife Refuge by 1996, while the lower portion has been a part of Everglades National Park for many years.

Twenty saltwater fish species are permanent residents in southwest Florida. Of course there are peak periods for each species (see fish availability chart), but virtually anywhere a line is wetted anglers have a chance of catching one or more of these species at any time. These year-round residents are supplemented with seasonal appearances of king mackerel, permit, tripletail, silver trout, and dolphin—enough action to keep even ardent anglers busy.

FRESHWATER FISHING

Southwest Florida, at first glance, may not look like a freshwater angler's paradise. The region has only a handful of natural lakes and only one, Lake Trafford in the farming community of Immokalee, is accessible to the public. Many other lakes dot the region, but they are all man-made rock pits or water retention areas for the numerous housing and golf course developments. Most of them are stocked and offer some excellent bass, catfish, and panfish fishing. But, because they are located on private property, fishing is usually restricted to residents and their guests. If in doubt, assume the lake is private and ask permission before wetting your line.

Don't construe the shortage of natural lakes and the restricted-use man-made lakes as a lack of places to freshwater fish. Hundreds of miles of drainage canals here contain tons of fish. Three major canal systems serve the region: Lehigh Acres, Cape Coral, and Golden Gate. Certain parts of each system are locally famous for bass and panfish. Each system has a few boat ramps, some bridges to fish from, and plenty of bank fishing spots.

Drainage canals also line many of the major roads. Don't overlook these as possible fishing spots. If there is a safe place to pull off the road, stop and give it a try. Canal fishing is common here and its proponents usually catch fish.

This part of the state has year-round largemouth bass and panfish fishing. Most of the bigger bass are caught during the cooler months when the fish are more actively feeding and at their peak bedding time. Panfish, including bluegills and shellcrackers, will almost always bite a worm, cricket, or small minnow. Black crappie, preferring colder waters, aren't as prevalent in this part of the state. Lake Trafford has the best crappie fishing in the region with the winter months being best. Oscars, exotic fish that are working their way into southwest Florida from the Miami area, can be very abundant in the freshwater canals, particularly along the US 41 canal in eastern Collier County. Catfish, mudfish, and several species of gar are also common freshwater residents.

CHARLOTTE AND LEE (NORTHERN PORTION) COUNTIES

Boaters who are not familiar with Charlotte Harbor waters should exercise caution: many areas outside marked channels are exceedingly shallow.

Besides being a great place to fish, Charlotte Harbor is home to a significant manatee population. Always be on the lookout for these large but harmless marine mammals. The Boaters Guide to Charlotte Harbor is a free publication that is very useful. To obtain a copy, write to Florida Sea Grant College Program, P.O. Box 110409, University of Florida, Gainesville, FL 32611, or call (904) 392-2801.

1.   CHARLOTTE HARBOR AND VICINITY ———————————
Salt; Boat, Bridge, and Pier; Ramp.

Description: Charlotte Harbor, Gasparilla Sound, and the brackish-water portions of the Peace and Myakka rivers form one of the most famous fishing areas in Florida. Anglers will find a multitude of places to fish and species to catch. Allen Ogle, owner of Bill's Tackle Shop in Punta Gorda, sums up the fishing in Charlotte Harbor by saying, "The diversity of fish is unsurpassed for both shore and boat anglers."

CHARLOTTE AND LEE (NORTHERN PORTION) COUNTIES

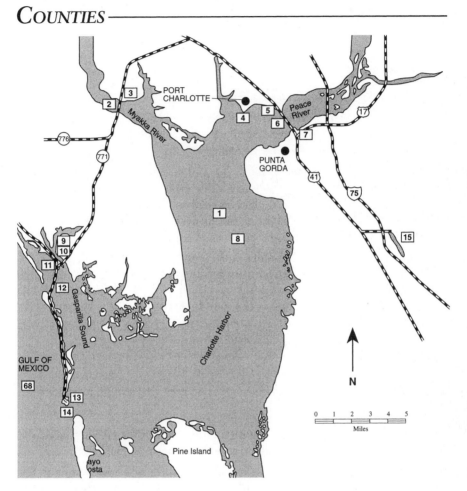

PORT CHARLOTTE

Peace River

Myakka River

PUNTA GORDA

Gasparilla Sound

Charlotte Harbor

GULF OF MEXICO

N

0 1 2 3 4 5
Miles

Pine Island

ayo
osta

Fishing Index: Numerous bridges across these bodies of water offer land-bound anglers a chance to fish for snook, tarpon, cobia, black drum, and sheepshead. The pilings attract and hold fish especially when baitfish are plentiful. Snook fishing from the bridges or in a boat around the pilings is popular at night during summer. Anglers dangle Coleman lanterns and bright lights over the water to attract baitfish and hungry snook. Redfish are caught throughout the region all year, although the best time seems to be in late summer and early fall. Extensive seagrass flats along much of the mangrove fringed shoreline are frequented by snook, redfish, seatrout, and other species. A popular artificial reef, home to species normally seen offshore, is in the middle of Charlotte Harbor (see separate listing in this chapter). Boca Grande Pass, at the mouth of Charlotte Harbor, is world renowned for the mammoth tarpon that move through the area in late spring and early summer.

Directions: See the piers, ramps, and special areas of interest described in this section.

2.   MYAKKA RIVER NORTH AND SOUTH PIERS

Salt; Pier and Boat.

Description: This pier is a section of an abandoned railroad trestle that ran to Port Boca Grande. It crosses the Myakka River about 3 miles upriver from where the river empties into Charlotte Harbor.

Fishing Index: Fish for snook, sheepshead, and mangrove snapper around the pilings. Redfish swim by from July to October and a few tarpon show up in late spring and early summer. Anglers on the pier and in boats like to fish for snook around the pilings at night in summer. Use a bright light close to the water's surface to attract the fish.

Directions: From US 41 in Murdock, turn west on FL 776 and go 6 miles to the bridge over the Myakka River. Just before crossing the bridge, turn right onto Sturkie Road and follow it to the parking lot for the Myakka North Pier or cross the bridge and park along the road by the sign to fish the South Pier.

For more information: Call Charlotte County Parks Department at (941) 743-1313.

3.   EL JOBEAN PARK

Salt; Boat; Ramp.

Description: A small county park with a single ramp that provides access to the lower part of the Myakka River and upper Charlotte Harbor.

Fishing Index: The ramp is the closest access point for boaters wanting to fish around the FL 776 bridge over the Myakka River and the grassflats along the western edge of upper Charlotte Harbor.

Directions: The ramp is in El Jobean on FL 776 just before the Myakka River Piers. Next to the ramp is Gulf Coast Marine Center, which has another ramp and sells bait, tackle, and licenses.

For more information: Call Gulf Coast Marine Center at (941) 629-9666.

4.   PORT CHARLOTTE BEACH PIER

Salt; Boat and Pier; Ramp.

Description: The pier is on Alligator Bay, a small bay along the north shore of Charlotte Harbor. This is a great place to bring the family. The pier is part of a county park. There is a boat ramp, snack bar, pool, playground, beach, tennis courts, and bocci court at the park.

Fishing Index: Like any of the piers along Charlotte Harbor, be on the lookout for snook at any time of the day or night. Silver trout action can be very good in winter. Try for seatrout and Spanish mackerel in January and February on live shrimp. To find out what's biting ask at the snack bar.

Directions: From US 41 in Port Charlotte, take Harbor Boulevard south 1.6 miles to the pier. Or turn west from US 41 onto Edgewater Road and go 0.8 mile to Harbor Boulevard. Turn left and go 0.7 mile to the park.

For more information: Call Charlotte County Parks Department at (941) 743-1313.

5. BAYSHORE PARK PIER (CHARLOTTE HARBOR PIER) ——
Salt; Pier.

Description: A narrow wooden pier with no facilities on-site.

Fishing Index: The pier regulars are there to fish for snook. Most of the activity on this lightly used pier is at night in summer. Spanish mackerel fishing can be good January to March.

Directions: From US 41, turn westbound on Bayshore Road, which is on the north side of the Peace River. Take Bayshore Road about 0.8 mile. The pier is on the left.

For more information: Call Charlotte County Parks Department at (941) 743-1313.

6. US 41 PEACE RIVER BRIDGE ——————
Salt; Bridge and Boat.

Description: Fish off the catwalks from either side of the bridge. They are separate from the road traffic. Boaters can fish around the bridge pilings.

Fishing Index: Snook are year-round residents around the pilings. Some tarpon pass through the area from spring through fall. Spanish mackerel are caught from January to March. Allen Ogle, owner of Bill's Tackle Shop in Punta Gorda and current all-tackle world record holder for hammerhead shark, says there are lots of places around Punta Gorda and Port Charlotte to fish for snook. Just find some pilings from a bridge or pier and give it a try.

Directions: US 41 is the major highway along the southwest coast. There are fishing areas on the north- and southbound spans

For more information: Call Bill's Tackle Shop in Punta Gorda. They have information on upper Charlotte Harbor. (941) 639-1305.

7.   PUNTA GORDA PIER

Salt; Boat; Pier and Bank; Ramp.

Description: Operated by the City of Punta Gorda. Fish from the pier or along the seawalled area of the park. A free boat ramp is next to the pier. Boaters don't have far to go to reach the US 41 and I-75 bridges over the Peace River and the seagrass beds along the upper east side of Charlotte Harbor.

Fishing Index: Fish for snook around the pier pilings especially at night. Mangrove snapper and sheepshead also gather around the pier and seawall throughout the year. In winter, some seatrout and Spanish mackerel are found. Fish for them with live shrimp.

Directions: On the south side of the Peace River just off US 41 in Punta Gorda look for the entrance to Laishley Park on the east side of the highway. The pier and ramp are in the park.

For more information: Call the City of Punta Gorda at (941) 639-6255.

8.   CHARLOTTE HARBOR REEF

Salt; Boat.

Description: A concrete culvert and rubble reef located in mid Charlotte Harbor.

Fishing Index: Here anglers can catch all of the backwater species and several offshore fish including cobia, sharks, Spanish mackerel, and tripletail.

Directions: LORAN coordinates 14162.8, 44020.57 (Lat. 26 50.50', Long 82 05.32').

9-10. CORAL CREEK AND GASPARILLA NORTH PIERS

Salt; Pier.

Description: These piers are part of the old railroad trestle that went to Port Boca Grande.

Fishing Index: Fish for sheepshead and mangrove snapper around the pilings. Redfish move through the area from July to October. A few tarpon show up in late spring and early summer. Anglers on the pier and in boats like to fish for snook around the pilings at night in summer.

Directions: Off FL 771 near Placida. Drive from Placida on FL 771 toward Port Charlotte. Just before the road makes a sharp bend left, look for signs directing you to these piers. Access to the Coral Creek Pier (9) is on the left and the Gasparilla Pier (10), part of the old train trestle, is on the right.

For more information: Call the Charlotte County Parks Department at (941) 743-1313.

11. PLACIDA BOAT RAMP

Salt; Boat; Ramp.

Description: A public ramp provides access to upper Charlotte Harbor via Gasparilla Sound, lower Lemon Bay, and the Gulf of Mexico via Gasparilla Pass.

Fishing Index: For boaters planning a trip offshore, this is a convenient place to launch and be close to Gasparilla and Boca Grande passes. Numerous bridges and grassflats offer good fishing.

Directions: Look for the signs to Boca Grande on FL 775 in Placida. Turn onto Gasparilla Road, the only road to Boca Grande. Go about 0.75 mile to the ramp on the left. Adjacent to it is Eldred's Marina which also has a boat ramp and sells bait and tackle.

For more information: Call Eldred's Marina at (941) 697-1431.

12. GASPARILLA SOUTH PIER

Salt; Pier.

Description: This pier is part of the old railroad trestle that ran to Port Boca Grande.

Fishing Index: Like the other sections of this old railroad trestle, this is a good place to fish for snook at night.

Directions: Take Gasparilla Road 2.5 miles from the intersection with FL 775. Look for the signs and access road on the left as you head toward Boca Grande.

For more information: Call Charlotte County Parks Department at (941) 743-1313.

13. PORT BOCA GRANDE

Salt; Surf.

Description: A good place to surf fish is at the southern tip of Gasparilla Island around the Florida Power and Light Company bulk fueling dock. Access to the site is via Gasparilla Island State Park and Boca Grande Pass Marina. Bait and tackle are available at the marina. The state recreation area also offers swimming, shelling, and picnicking. For those who enjoy lighthouses, the Boca Grande Light is located here.

Fishing Index: Snook, grouper, and redfish are routinely caught around the pilings. Bring along a small cast net to catch your own live bait. Free line a live bait during the incoming or outgoing tide, fish the bottom with live shrimp, or cast surface plugs around the pilings.

Directions: Take Gasparilla Road to Boca Grande. At the intersection with 5th Street, turn right and follow Gulf Boulevard 2.5 miles to its end. Park at the

Boca Grande Pass Marina or Gasparilla Island State Recreation Area (there is a user fee) and walk to the beach.

For more information: Call Gasparilla Island State Recreation Area at (941) 964-0375 or Boca Grande Pass Marina at (941) 964-0607.

14. Boca Grande Pass

Salt; Boat.

Description: The pass is the mouth of Charlotte Harbor. It is renowned as one of the best tarpon spots in the world. At one time, bulk phosphate ore was loaded from docks in the pass. The remains of these docks, along the north shore, are also a popular place to fish when the tarpon aren't biting.

Fishing Index: If you are looking to catch a tarpon, this is one of the best places to hook up with one of the big silver kings. Tarpon fishing, particularly in late spring and early summer, draws large numbers of anglers. Small live crabs, known locally as pass or moon crabs, are one of the preferred baits. During tarpon season the pass becomes very crowded. Experience is necessary to stay out of the way of other anglers and avoid colliding with other vessels. The Boca Grande Fishing Guides Association developed a protocol for tarpon fishing in the pass. To receive a copy, send a self-addressed stamped envelope to the Boca Grande Fishing Guides Association. (see address below). Your best chance of success, if you are unfamiliar with the area and with the operation of a boat, is to hire a guide. To obtain a list of guides, their specialties, and phone

Flatboats are very popular for getting anglers into the shallow waters around mangroves.

numbers write to the association. The old phosphate dock along the north shore of the pass just inside of the bulk fuel docks is highly regarded as a hot snook spot in summer, especially at night.

Directions: The closest access point to the pass is from the marinas in Boca Grande. Only Whidden's Marina—(941) 964-2878—has a boat ramp. The closest public ramp is the Placida ramp (see site 5).

For more information: Write the Boca Grande Fishing Guides Association, P.O. Box 676, Boca Grande, FL 33921 or call Whidden's or Boca Grande Pass Marinas.

15. WEBB LAKE

Fresh; Boat and Bank; Ramp.

Description: This is one of the GFC's fish management areas. It is one of the old quarries that provided fill dirt for part of the I-75 road bed. Fishing this lake is not for the average angler. In addition to complying with the freshwater fishing license requirements, anglers must also have a valid special Wildlife Management Area Stamp ($25 in 1995), available at any Tax Collectors office. Stamps are not sold on site.

Fishing Index: In an effort to provide long-term, quality sportfishing, Webb Lake is a catch-and-release lake for largemouth bass. In addition no gasoline engines can be used on the lake. If you like to fly fish, this is a good lake to try fly fishing for bass.

Directions: The lake is in the Cecil Webb Wildlife Management Area. From Punta Gorda, drive 7 miles south on I-75 (or 20 miles north from Fort Myers) to Exit 27 for Tuckers Grade Road (FL 762). Drive 0.1 mile east to the entrance and office. Follow Tuckers Grade Road past the office and look for Webb Lake Road on the right. Three boat ramps are along the access road.

LEE COUNTY (CENTRAL PORTION)

The heart of Lee County is a hotbed of activity for saltwater enthusiasts. The Caloosahatchee River flows through downtown Fort Myers and connects to the lower parts of Pine Island Sound and Matlacha Pass at the coast. Redfish, snook, and tarpon are top targets for saltwater anglers throughout these waters. Boaters can motor up the Caloosahatcheee, cross through Lake Okeechobee, and connect with a canal that leads to the state's east coast. And, you can fish along the entire route!

16. LEHIGH ACRES CANALS

Fresh; Bank and Boat.

Description: The second of three large developments that have extensive drainage canals associated with them. The Lehigh Acres canal system is fished primarily by local residents.

Fishing Index: Bass and panfish angling is fair to good year-round.

Directions: From the FL 82 exit of I-95 in Fort Myers, drive southeast 10.6 miles on FL 82 (toward Immokalee) to Alabama Road. Turn left and go 2.5 miles to the beginning of Lehigh Acres.

17. CALOOSAHATCHEE RIVER

Salt and Fresh; Boat, Bridge and Bank.

Description: The Caloosahatchee River runs from Lake Okeechobee through downtown Fort Myers and empties into San Carlos Bay and the Gulf of Mexico. An excellent fishery.

Fishing Index: From December through April, anglers congregate around the power plant effluent that enters the Caloosahatchee via the Orange River. The warm water attracts lots of big snook and tarpon. In summer, snook preparing to spawn gather near the river's mouth and draw crowds of anglers.

Directions: The next nine sites described below are access points to the Caloosahatchee River.

18. CALOOSAHATCHEE RIVER, ALVA ACCESS AREA

Fresh; Boat and Bank; Ramp.

Description: Less developed than the Franklin Lock and Dam (site 19). There is a boat ramp but no campground. Bank fishing is limited.

Fishing Index: Anglers on the Caloosahatchee usually fish in the remnants of the old oxbows from the river's original course. What is called the river now is a dredged channel. Bass and panfish thrive in the quiet oxbows.

Directions: Access is on the north side. In Alva, take Josephine Street 0.5 mile east to the ramp.

19. CALOOSAHATCHEE RIVER, FRANKLIN LOCK AND DAM

Salt and Fresh; Boat and Bank; Ramp.

Description: This facility is operated by the U.S. Army Corps of Engineers. The dam and lock serve as the dividing line between fresh- and saltwater fishing. A campground and boat ramp are found on both banks of the river; the south bank gives access to the saltwater side of the lock and the north bank accesses the freshwater side. Recreational boats can pass through the locks. Note: you cannot drive across the river at this point, there is no bridge. Limited bank fishing opportunities are available.

Fishing Index: Fish for tarpon and snook around the locks and downriver during the colder months of the year.

LEE COUNTY (CENTRAL PORTION)

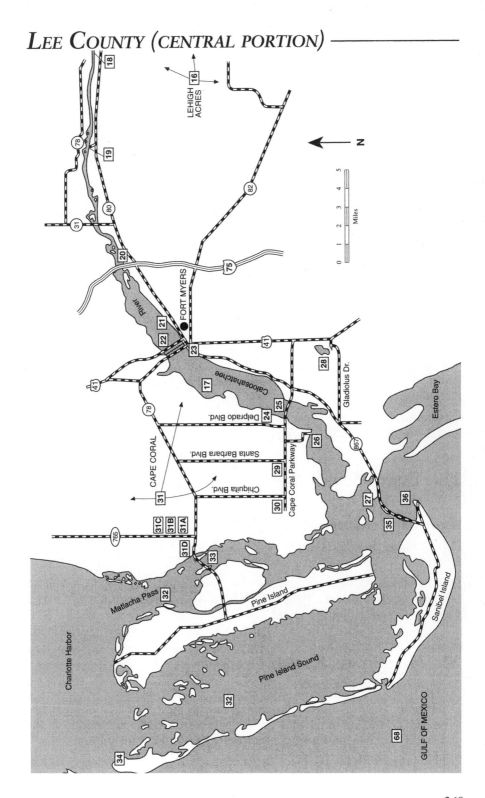

Directions: To reach the south bank facilities, take Exit 25 on I-75 and drive east about 6.4 miles on FL 80. Look for the informational road sign, and turn left. To reach the north bank facilities from Exit 25, drive about 4 miles east on FL 80 and then 2.5 miles north on FL 31. Turn right onto FL 78 East and drive about 4.3 miles to the sign for the lock and boat ramp on the right. Facilities are 0.25 mile down the access road.

20. ORANGE RIVER

Salt; Boat.

Description: There is an electric power generating plant along the shore of the Caloosahatchee that uses river water to cool its generators. The effluent empties into the Orange River, which then flows into the Caloosahatchee. This plume of warm water, especially in winter, is a popular place to fish. Manatees also congregate in this area to take advantage of the warm water. To protect the manatees boaters must use extreme caution and travel slowly when fishing this area in winter.

Fishing Index: The warm water is a natural attractant for snook and tarpon in winter. Tarpon seem to like live bait but you won't find any to cast net around the power plant. If you have a fast boat or can take the time, go to the mouth of the river and cast net some live baitfish around Sanibel. Get what you need and then make the 23-mile trip upriver. It's a lot of effort but is usually very rewarding.

Directions: The Orange River enters the Caloosahatchee just upstream from the I-75 bridge. Look for the twin smoke stacks of the power plant.

21. TARPON STREET PIER

Salt; Pier.

Description: A small, city-maintained fishing pier on the Caloosahatchee River.

Fishing Index: Snook are around the pier all year, but summer nights are the best time.

Directions: From US 41 in downtown Fort Myers, go about 2 miles northeast on Palm Beach Boulevard. Turn left at Tarpon Street (watch for Terry Park). The pier is at the end of the street.

22. NEW EDISON BRIDGE

Salt; Bridge and Boat.

Description: This is the US 41 Business Route bridge over the Caloosahatchee River that is inbound to downtown Fort Myers from the north. Fish from the pedestrian walkway on the bridge or from a boat around the pilings.

Fishing Index: Fish for big black drum around the pilings with heavy tackle.

Spanish mackerel and seatrout can be caught in January and February on live shrimp.

Directions: From US 41 on either side of the river, follow the signs to Business 41.

23. CENTENNIAL PARK PIER

Salt; Boat and Pier; Ramp.

Description: A 200-foot pier with a T at the end on the shores of the Caloosahatchee River in downtown Fort Myers. This is a good place to bring the family. At the east end of the park there is a free boat ramp.

Fishing Index: Spanish mackerel and seatrout can be caught in January and February on live shrimp. Snook are around the pier all year.

Directions: The pier is in Fort Myers. Park beneath the US 41 bridge over the Caloosahatchee on the south side of the river. The pier is about 150 feet east of the bridge.

24. JAYCEES PARK

Salt; Bank.

Description: Fish on the banks of the Caloosahatchee River estuary. This small park has picnic tables and places for the kids to run and play.

Fishing Index: Sheepshead, black drum, and mangrove snapper are caught around the oyster bars and rock rubble along the river bank.

Directions: From Cape Coral Parkway, go north 0.8 mile on Del Prado Boulevard. Turn east onto Beach Parkway and go 0.7 mile to the park at the end of the road.

25. CAPE CORAL BRIDGE

Salt; Bank and Boat.

Description: This is the main access road to Cape Coral from Fort Myers. It spans the lower part of the Caloosahatchee River. Fishing is not allowed from the toll bridge, but land-bound anglers can wet a line from the sea wall beneath the bridge. Boaters can anchor and fish around any of the bridge pilings.

Fishing Index: A good place to fish for snook and tarpon as they move up and down the Caloosahatchee River. Also, because this is close to the Gulf, look for cobia and Spanish mackerel.

Directions: From Cape Coral, take Cape Coral Parkway to the bridge. From the Fort Myers side, take College Parkway past the University of South Florida and Edison Community College campuses to the bridge.

26. Cape Coral Community Pier

Salt; Boat, Pier and Bank; Ramp.

Description: A good place to take the family. This pier on the lower Caloosahatchee River is a favorite hangout for some local anglers. The water around the pier is shallow except for a slightly deeper hole on the right side of the T at the end of the pier. There is a boat ramp, fuel dock, beach, pool, and other amenities on-site.

Fishing Index: Sheepshead like to hang around the pier pilings during winter.

Directions: The pier is in southern Cape Coral. From Cape Coral Parkway, turn south onto Coronado Parkway and go 1.7 miles to the pier. Follow the signs to the Yacht Club. The pier is across the street.

27. Punta Rassa

Salt; Boat; Ramp; $.

Description: This popular ramp allows anglers quick access to the Gulf of Mexico, San Carlos Bay, Pine Island Sound, Matlacha Pass, and the Caloosahatcheee River.

Fishing Index: From here it is a short run to the grassflats around Sanibel Island, the Edison Reef offshore from Sanibel, and some good snook, tarpon, and redfish angling in the Caloosahatchee River.

Directions: The ramp is at the base of the Sanibel Causeway bridge on FL 867. Just before the toll booth, turn onto Punta Rassa Road. Look for the ramp just after the turnoff.

28. Lakes Park

Fresh; Bank and Boat; $.

Description: Operated by Lee County. A day-use park featuring bank fishing areas, swimming, picnicking, and a playground. A great place to introduce kids to fishing. Boats are available for rent.

Directions: Just east of US 41 on Gladiolus Drive. From Fort Myers, go south on US 41 about 4.5 miles past Page Field Airport and turn right onto Gladiolus Drive.

For more information: Call Lakes Park office at (941) 432-2000.

29-30. Cape Coral Parkway

Salt; Bridge.

Description: Cape Coral Parkway is the major east-west road in the southern part of Cape Coral. The two short bridges over the canals might not look impressive, but these are locally favorite places to fish. Be careful about parking on private property.

Fishing Index: Tides Bait and Tackle store owner Pete Pavletich says these are two of the better snook fishing spots in Cape Coral. Summer nights are the best time to fish here.

Directions: The toll bridge from Fort Myers to Cape Coral is on the parkway. The first site, 29, is 2.5 miles west from the toll bridge on Cape Coral Parkway where the road crosses a canal just east of the intersection with Santa Barbara Boulevard. The second site, 30, is 6.3 miles from the toll bridge where the Parkway crosses another canal just east of the intersection with Chiquita Boulevard.

31. Cape Coral Canals

Fresh; Boat and Bank; Ramp.

Description: An extensive maze of canals threads through this large, partially developed community. Most of them are freshwater but some, particularly those close to saltwater, are brackish. Although this looks like an urban setting on the maps, many parts of Cape Coral are sparsely developed. Most of the property along the canals is privately owned; please respect the rights of property owners. However, with the number of roads and bridges in the area, there are plenty of places to fish. Three easy-to-find sites and a boat ramp along Burnt Store Marina Road in northwest Cape Coral are shown on the map as sites 31A, B, C, and D.

Directions: Cape Coral is west of Fort Myers. Sites 31 A, B, and C are in northwest Cape Coral. Located north on Burnt Store Marina Road (CR 765) from Pine Island Road are three canals that cross Burnt Store Road where you can fish from the banks. Site 31A is 2 miles north of Pine Island Road, just past the intersection with Tropicana Parkway. Site 31B is 2.7 miles north of Pine Island Road at the intersection with Diplomat Parkway, and site 31C is almost 4 miles north of Pine Island Road. In addition to these sites, a small park and boat ramp (site 3D) provide access to a part of the freshwater canal system 0.6 mile north of Pine Island Road.

32. Pine Island Sound and Matlacha Pass

Salt; Boat and Bridge.

Description: This area extends south from Charlotte Harbor. Extensive, shallow seagrass flats cover large parts of the sound and pass.

Fishing index: The grassflats along much of the shoreline are very popular places to sight fish for redfish especially in spring and fall. Paul Hobby (at (941) 768-1466), a guide who specializes in fishing in Pine Island Sound, says that seatrout hang out year-round. "Look for them on the deeper grassflats, the ones that are 6 to 8 feet deep. If you're looking for snook and redfish use live bait and try along the mangrove shoreline during the higher part of the tide. The fish will be here all year." Captain Mike Rehr (at (941) 472-3308), a dedicated fly fisher whose favorite target is redfish in the sound, suggests getting out of the boat and wading. "In September, the redfish begin to school and the majority of them can be found along the edges of the grassflats in about 4 to 6 feet of water. In October, the redfish move onto the flats following and feeding around the spawning southern common rays. This is by far my favorite month for wade fishing." According to Rehr, "Getting out of the boat is the best way to lower your profile and noise level." That, he says, will "reduce the chances of a fish seeing and hearing you."

Directions: Refer to the site descriptions for the public boat ramp at Punta Rassa, Sanibel Causeway, Matlacha Pass bridge, and Cayo Costa State Park. Numerous private ramps are at the marinas throughout the area.

33. MATLACHA PASS BRIDGE
Salt; Bridge.

Description: Two short bridges span the pass. Between and around them is the fishing community of Matlacha. If you don't catch fish here, try one of the numerous seafood restaurants for some fresh local seafood.

Fishing Index: A good snook spot, especially at night.

Directions: The bridges are on FL 78 (Pine Island Road). From the intersection of US 41 and FL 78 in north Fort Myers, drive about 10.9 miles west on FL 78 to Matlacha.

34. CAYO COSTA STATE PARK
Salt; Surf.

Description: The park is on Cayo Costa Island and can be reached only by boat. From the park, surf fish along the beach or wade fish small grassflats on the Pine Island Sound side. The park has a primitive campground, cabins, and also one of the best shelling beaches in southwest Florida.

Fishing index: On the Gulf side, fish for redfish, snook, pompano, and maybe a tarpon any time of year. Look for seatrout and redfish on the grassflats.

Directions: This barrier island park is south of Boca Grande. If you don't have a boat, there are scheduled ferry services from Boca Grande Pass Marina (call (941) 964-0607) and Bokeelia on Pine Island (Tropic Star Ferry at (941) 283-0015).

For more information: Call the park office at (941) 964-0375.

Although it's not very long, the Sanibel Pier's location is one that attracts fish and anglers.

35. SANIBEL CAUSEWAY
Salt; Bank and Wade.

Description: The causeway is part of the only road to Sanibel and Captiva islands. Anglers can fish along the causeway and then try the Sanibel Pier (site 36). Nonanglers can enjoy the beach and shopping at the many gift shops and boutiques on the islands. Top off the day with dinner at one of the many fine restaurants.

Fishing Index: A popular way to fish this area is to wade fish the flats around the causeway. When the water is warm, look for redfish, trout, and snook on the flats. When it's cooler try the "potholes" and oyster bars. Flounder and pompano are also caught on the flats. Try fishing from the seawalls around the bridges. Boaters can fish around bridge pilings for snook, cobia, Spanish mackerel, tarpon, redfish, trout, and more.

Directions: From Fort Myers follow FL 867 to Sanibel. Pay the toll and cross over the draw bridge. There is ample parking along the causeway.

36. SANIBEL FISHING PIER
Salt; Pier and Surf.

Description: Fish off the pier or along the shore. Non-anglers can go shelling along the beach, visit Sanibel Lighthouse, swim, and enjoy the sun.

Fishing Index: Although this is a short pier, its location makes it a good place to catch Spanish mackerel, snook, redfish, pompano, flounder, and sheepshead.

Directions: Take the Sanibel Causeway onto the island. Turn left at Periwinkle Drive and go about 1.4 miles. Take the left fork in the road to the parking lot.

For more information: Call the city of Sanibel at (941) 472-3373.

Lee (southern portion) and Collier (northern portion) Counties

This part of southwest Florida is one of the fastest growing areas in the country. Growth moving south from Fort Myers and north from Naples is converging on Estero Bay and vicinity. Right now the fishing is very good but a number of large developments threaten the region's water quality and wetlands. The next few years will tell whether the fishing remains good or deteriorates.

37. Lake Trafford

Fresh; Boat; Ramp.

Description: This 1,500-acre lake is one of two natural lakes in Collier County. For south Florida, it is reputedly a very good place to fish for largemouth bass. The abundance of aquatic weeds creates plenty of places to fish. This lake is best fished by boat. Lake Trafford Marina, the only one on the lake, has boats and motors to rent, a complete line of tackle, and a campground.

Fishing Index: Lake Trafford Marina owner Ski Olesky says the best time for bass is from mid-February until the first of May. He encourages anglers to use artificial lures, particularly plastic worms, when fishing for bass. A lake this size, he contends, has a limited supply of big bass. Since the biggest fish are usually females caught during the bedding season, he also likes to see most of the fish released. Apparently most of the local bass anglers agree and the lake continues to be a good place to fish. If you're looking for crappie try the lake during the colder months. They're caught year-round, but most of the activity is in winter with Missouri minnows the preferred bait. Bluegills provide good action in spring and summer.

Directions: From the intersection of FL 29 and Lake Trafford Road in Immokalee, turn west and follow the lake road until it ends at the lake. Lake Trafford Marina is next to the free ramp.

For more information: Call the Lake Trafford Marina at (941) 675-2401.

38. Fort Myers Beach Pier

Salt; Pier.

Description: The pier is in a commercial resort area and is popular with tourists who want to fish and sightsee. Bait and tackle are available at the pier.

Fishing Index: Schools of redfish and Spanish mackerel move by the pier and

LEE (SOUTHERN PORTION) AND COLLIER (NORTHERN PORTION) COUNTIES

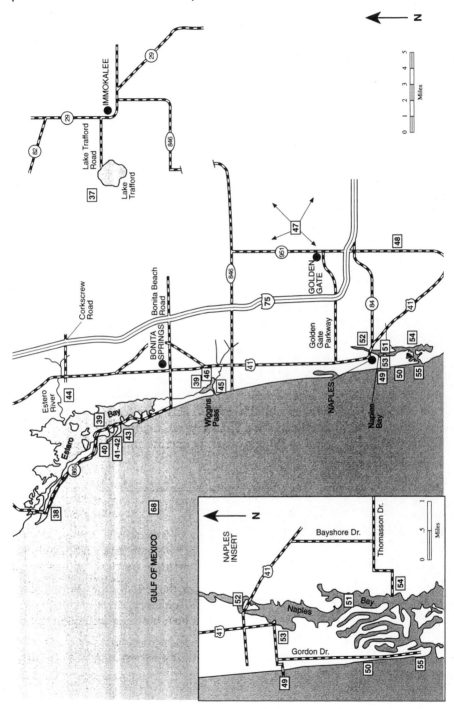

turn periods of calm into wild action in a matter of minutes. While this doesn't happen every day, there are snook, black drum, whiting, and sheepshead to keep anglers coming to the pier.

Directions: In Fort Myers Beach at the north end of Estero Island. From the north, drive south on FL 865 and cross the bridge to the island. The pier is on the beach just over the bridge. From the south, take FL 865 to just before the road makes a right turn to the bridge. The pier is on the left.

For more information: Call the pier office at (941) 335-2438.

39. ESTERO BAY AND WIGGINS PASS

Salt; Boat and Bridge.

Description: Estero Bay, Wiggins Pass, and the surrounding wetlands are much smaller estuarine systems than Charlotte Harbor. They are good places to fish but they are often overlooked by anglers unfamiliar with southwest Florida.

Fishing Index: Estero Bay has several seagrass flats, making it an excellent place to sight fish for redfish with light tackle and fly rods. Fishing the flats requires a small shallow draft boat. Many anglers will wade these flats to avoid spooking the fish.

The bridges between the barrier islands provide land-bound anglers with some excellent snook and sheepshead fishing sites. With a small boat anglers can fish Estero Bay's four passes for some big tarpon, sharks, and the ever present snook and redfish. Wiggins Pass, just south of Estero Bay but not connected by a navigable waterway, has some good mangrove shoreline for snook fishing. A county boat ramp provides easy access.

Directions: Refer to the site descriptions for the Big Carlos Pass bridge, New Pass bridge, and Carl Johnson and Koreshan parks for access points to Estero Bay. Wiggins Pass State Recreation Area and the boat ramp at Cocohatchee County Park offer access to Wiggins Pass. Numerous marinas are in the area.

40. BIG CARLOS PASS BRIDGE

Salt; Boat, Bank, and Bridge.

Description: Fish off the protected walkway or around the bridge embankment. Look for dolphins mating in the pass. The female has a reddish underside while in heat and will have a number of males in pursuit.

Fishing Index: A variety of fish move through the pass on the incoming and outgoing tide. Snook, redfish, tarpon, sharks, and sheepshead are commonly caught when fishing from the bridge and in a boat between the bridge and the pass opening to the Gulf.

Directions: This is the FL 865 bridge connecting Estero Island (Fort Myers Beach) to Black Island.

41. LOVERS KEY STATE RECREATION AREA

Salt; Bridge; $.

Description: On Black Island, a barrier island that is part of the Estero Bay complex. From the parking lot, follow the walkway to the bridge and fish there.

Fishing Index: Fish for snook, mangrove snapper, and sheepshead off the bridge spanning the island's brackish-water lagoon.

Directions: From Fort Myers Beach, drive south on FL 865. The entrance is well marked.

For more information: Call the park office at (941) 463-4588.

42. CARL JOHNSON PARK

Salt; Boat, Bridge and Surf; Ramp.

Description: A nice coastal park. To reach the beach where you can surf fish, take the tram or enjoy the walk through the mangroves and tidal flats. Several small bridges along the way also offer fishing access. Across the road on the bay side a free boat ramp provides access to the backwater and the Gulf via New Pass or Big Carlos Pass.

Fishing Index: Surf fish for snook in summer and tarpon in spring and summer. From the boat ramp, it is only a few minutes' boat ride to the seagrass flats fishing and some great fall sight fishing for redfish in Estero Bay.

Sheepshead activity peaks during the winter in southwest Florida. Great bait stealers, they put up a good fight once hooked.

Directions: On Black Island immediately south of the entrance to Lovers Key. The parking lot is visible from FL 865.

43. NEW PASS BRIDGE
Salt; Bank and Boat.

Description: Another of the bridges over the passes to Estero Bay. Fish from the embankments beneath the bridge or in a boat.

Fishing Index: Passes are always good places to fish. Snook, redfish, tarpon, and sharks follow their food sources in and out of the backwaters as the tide moves in and out. Look for sheepshead around the pilings throughout the year.

Directions: This is the FL 865 bridge that connects Black Island to Bonita Beach.

44. KORESHAN STATE HISTORIC SITE
Salt; Boat and Bank; Ramp; $.

Description: Bank fishing is permitted in the park on the scenic Estero River. The park has a campground and boat ramp that provides access to Estero Bay. This is a also a very good river to canoe; rentals are available in the park and at the canoe outpost across the highway.

Fishing Index: Fish for snook in the river and the residential canals downstream from the park during the colder months. Launch your boat here for easy access to the upper part of Estero Bay.

Directions: The park entrance is at the intersection of US 41 and Corkscrew Road in Estero. This is about 20 miles north of Naples and 14 miles from Fort Myers.

For more information: Call the park office at (941) 992-0311.

45. DELNOR WIGGINS PASS STATE RECREATION AREA
Salt; Boat and Surf; Ramp; $.

Description: A very popular and sometimes crowded beachfront park. The boat ramp provides access to backwater fishing and the Gulf via Wiggins Pass. Navigation of the pass is often difficult due to shoaling. A boat that draws more than 3 feet may not be able to go through the pass. From the park, landbound anglers can fish from the beach in the swift moving water of Wiggins Pass. Drive to the north end, park in the last parking lot, and walk to the pass.

Fishing Index: Some big tarpon, snook, and redfish move through the pass when the tide is running. To catch them, make sure you have the tackle to do the job.

Directions: From the US 41 and Immokalee Road intersection, drive 1.1 miles west on 111th Avenue to the park.

For more information: Call the park office at (941) 597-6196.

46. COCOHATCHEE RIVER PARK

Salt; Boat and Bank; Ramp.

Description: A boat ramp here provides access to Wiggins Pass and vicinity. Or fish from the docks adjacent to the playground.

Fishing Index: Some snook, sheepshead, and mangrove snappers hang around the docks.

Directions: On Vanderbilt Drive 0.75 mile north from 111th Avenue.

47. GOLDEN GATE CANALS

Fresh; Bank and Boat.

Description: The southernmost of the three residential areas with an elaborate canal system. There are canals in the city as well as in the extensive estates area. Fish around any of the bridges at the ends of some of the roads. There are several primitive ramps to launch a small boat. Local information, as in Cape Coral and Lehigh Acres, is very helpful.

Fishing Index: Bass, panfish, catfish, and a couple of oscar hot spots provide steady year-round fishing. The biggest bass are usually taken when the water is coldest, in January and February.

Directions: Golden Gate is east of Naples. To access the canals in the "city," take Golden Gate Parkway east from Naples. From the intersection of the Parkway and US 41 in Naples (at the north end of Coastland Mall), drive approximately 5.5 miles east. To fish the canals in the estate section, take Golden Gate Parkway east until it ends at CR 951, approximately 7 miles from US 41 in Naples. Turn left and drive north for about 2.9 miles to the intersection with Golden Gate Boulevard. Turn right; fish any of the canals in this large rural area.

For more information: Call Jess Mootispaw at Golden Gate Bait and Tackle Box at (941) 348-8771 to find out where the fish are biting.

48. FLORIDA 951 CANAL

Fresh; Bank.

Description: Motorists are likely to see anglers anywhere along this stretch of road. The adjacent canal is a frequent stop for people who work all day but want to get in a few minutes of freshwater fishing on their way home. Pull well off the busy road onto the wide shoulder.

Fishing Index: The bank is unvegetated and there is easy access to the canal and its abundance of 1- to 3-pound bass. The open banks are good for fly fishing for bass and panfish. This is also a good place to watch wildlife. Alligators, turtles, anhingas, and several species of herons and egrets frequent the canal.

Directions: This drainage canal parallels FL 951 from its intersection with Davis Boulevard (FL 84) south for 5.5 miles.

49. NAPLES PIER

Salt; Pier.

Description: This landmark structure, only a few blocks from the swanky shops of Third Street South, has a reputation for excellent fishing. Midway out on the pier is a concession stand with snacks, drinks, a limited supply of tackle, and plenty of bait. If you ask, the staff will be happy to tell you what's biting.

Fishing Index: Depending on the time of year, redfish, Spanish mackerel, whiting, and snook action can be outstanding. See the fishing index for Fort Myers Beach Pier. It's also a great place to take a kid fishing.

Directions: From the intersection of US 41 and Fifth Avenue South, go south on 9th Street to Broad Avenue. Turn right on Broad Avenue and go to the end of the road and Gulf Shore Boulevard. Turn left and go south one block. The pier is on the right.

For more information: Call the pier concession stand at (941) 434-4696.

50. NAPLES BEACH

Salt; Surf.

Description: About 1 mile south of the Naples pier, the beach offers a popular place to surf fish. Just off the beach is a trough. Anglers wade through this low area and walk on the shallow sand bar seaward of the trough. In summer the water is very clear (especially in the morning), and it is possible to sight fish in the trough. This is a good place to fly fish.

Fishing Index: This is a particularly good spot for pompano, redfish, and, during summer, some big snook. The best time to fish here is early morning. Dig for sand fleas and use them to tempt a few pompano to swim in the direction of your hook.

Directions: From the intersection with Broad Avenue, take Gulf Shore Drive south about 1.6 miles. Look for the public beach access on 32nd and 33rd Avenues South.

51. NAPLES BAY

Salt; Boat; Ramp.

Description: The waterfront along the bay long ago changed from a mangrove fringed, fish-rich water body to a highly developed and sea-walled area. The bay is in the center of this upscale community, now replete with big, expensive waterfront homes and many well-appointed yachts.

Fishing Index: Although Naples Bay is highly developed and doesn't enjoy the best reputation for water quality, enough fish live here to make fishing a worthwhile activity. The lower part of the bay has the cleanest water and the best fishing. Snook addicts are often seen fishing off and around the docks of residential canals, especially at night. In the day, some anglers have good luck fishing the oyster bars just south of where Haldeman Creek enters the bay.

Directions: Refer to the following site descriptions for the Gordon River bridges, city of Naples boat ramp, and Bayview Park. Numerous marinas are in the area.

52. GORDON RIVER BRIDGES

Salt; Bridge.

Description: Two short bridges span the Gordon River in downtown Naples.

Fishing Index: Many locals fish these bridges at night for snook. Watch out for boats passing under the bridge.

Directions: On US 41 in Naples about 0.5 mile from the downtown shopping district.

53. CITY OF NAPLES BOAT RAMP

Salt; Ramp.

Description: Use of the ramp is free, but there is only metered parking. The ramp is fairly steep. It accesses Naples Bay.

Fishing Index: Head down the bay from here and fish for snook along the residential canals.

Directions: From US 41, go six blocks south on 9th Street to the ramp.

54. BAYVIEW PARK

Salt; Bank; Ramp.

Description: A popular ramp for boaters heading into the Gulf or toward Rookery Bay. Anglers can also fish the lower part of Naples Bay from the bank. This is the closest ramp to Gordon Pass.

Fishing Index: From the ramp, you are only minutes from some good snook and redfish angling along the mangrove-fringed shoreline of the inland waterway that heads south to Marco Island.

Directions: From Naples on US 41 East, turn right on Bayshore Drive and go 1.5 miles to Thomasson Drive. Turn right and go 0.5 mile to Fern Street. Turn left and go about 0.3 mile to Danford Street. Turn right and drive about 0.4 mile to the park at the end of the road.

55. GORDON PASS
Salt; Boat.

Description: This is the major pass that connects Naples Bay to the Gulf of Mexico. It is very popular with local anglers.

Fishing Index: When the tide is moving in or out, boaters fish the rock jetty on the south side of the pass for snook and redfish. Be careful where you anchor. The best fishing is near the rocks, but there may be many boats coming and going, making the waters very choppy. Have a good anchor and use it.

Directions: Accessible to fishing only by boat. Follow the channel markers south through Naples Bay to the pass.

COLLIER (SOUTHERN PORTION) AND MONROE (NORTHERN PORTION) COUNTIES

56. ROOKERY AND JOHNSON BAYS AND VICINITY
Salt; Boat.

Description: To reach these bays take the inland waterway south from Naples or north from Marco Island. The boat ride is pleasant and many osprey nest on channel markers along the way. Manatees also frequent the area.

Fishing Index: Rookery Bay, about halfway between Naples and Marco Island, is a popular fishing destination for many anglers. Fish either the north or south entrances to the bay, the flats at the north end, or along the mangrove shoreline toward the south end of the bay. Immediately south of Rookery Bay is Johnson Bay. It has some good grassflats for redfish. Both bays are the preferred hangout for snook, redfish, seatrout, and small tarpon. Don't overlook the mangrove shoreline along the inland waterway between the city of Naples and the resort community of Marco Island. As at the shoreline of the bays, there is some excellent and easily accessible backwater fishing. With a small boat you can fish the waterway and the small bays adjacent to it. Any of the numerous points created by the erratic shoreline are good places to look for snook. Captain Todd Geroy at (941) 793-7141, a well-respected and highly knowledgeable backwater guide, fishes this area on a regular basis. "I like to fish with the moving water by starting outside along the coast if the tide is

Redfish, like this one, are making a strong comeback in the state's coastal waters now that the fish is no longer commercially harvested.

going in and work my may into the backwaters as the tide rises. When the tide is moving out, I reverse my approach." Geroy believes that August to October are some of the best months to fish this area. "Sometimes we catch redfish, snook, and small tarpon in the same location within minutes at this time of year."

Directions: Anglers reach these bays via boat from Marco Island and Naples. Shell Point, described next, is a good place for land-bound anglers.

57. SHELL POINT

Salt; Boat and Bank; Ramp.

Description: One of the most scenic places to fish in Collier County is Shell Point in the Rookery Bay National Estuarine Research Reserve. Take few minutes to stop at the Briggs Nature Center (about 1 mile off FL 951 on Shell Island Road) and learn more about the reserve. The primitive ramp is designed for boats less than 17 feet and drawing no more than 1 foot. It provides access to Rookery and Johnson bays. A small, secluded fishing spot is on the bank at the mouth of Henderson Creek.

Fishing Index: The most productive fishing is when the tide is running in or out. This is a good place to use live shrimp or baitfish and wait for a big snook to show interest. Take some insect repellent, especially in the early morning and at dusk.

Directions: To reach the bank fishing site from US 41, drive 2 miles south on FL 951 toward Marco Island. Turn right on Shell Island Road and drive about 3 miles to road's end. Park and follow the path to the left of the natural boat ramp.

58. FLORIDA HIGHWAY 951 BRIDGE

Salt; Boat; Bridge and Bank; Ramp.

Description: This is the main bridge to Marco Island. It is one of the best places to fish in the area if you don't have a boat. You can fish along the seawall or shoreline around the bridge embankments, but the best place to fish is from the walkway beneath the bridge.

Fishing Index: The bridge is a locally-known hotspot for snook, especially at night. The two most popular techniques to connect with old linesides are to hook a live shrimp and let it float with the current or jig a small Bett's spec rig. According to Dan Gewant, owner of Angler's Answer Bait and Tackle, you must look in the water to decide which bait to use. If glass minnows are in the waters beneath the walkway, use the spec rig. If you see shrimp, then liveline a big, lively shrimp and hold on.

Directions: From US 41, drive about 8 miles south on FL 951. Park on either

COLLIER (SOUTHERN PORTION) AND MONROE (NORTHERN PORTION) COUNTIES

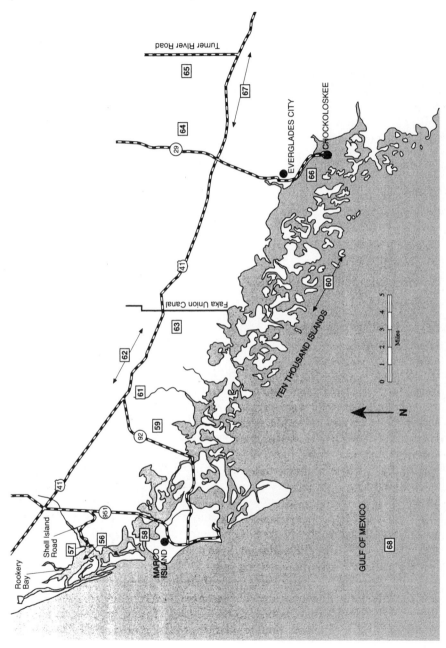

side of the bridge. About 0.25 mile north of the mainland side of the bridge is a county-maintained boat ramp.

For More Information: Call Angler's Answer at (941) 775-7336.

59. FLORIDA HIGHWAY 92 —————————————
Salt; Bank.

Description: This is the southern access route to Marco Island. The road has a wide shoulder for the most part and there are numerous places to pull off the highway and fish in the tannin-colored, mangrove-fringed waters. You can pull your car right up to where you will fish, and have everything that you need only a few steps away.

Fishing Index: Snook, redfish, mangrove snapper, sheepshead, and maybe some small tarpon swim in these waters. A good place for a lazy day of low stress fishing.

Directions: This highway runs from US 41 to the south side of Marco Island. A canal parallels the road from the Goodland Bridge east for about 3 miles. Coming from Miami, turn left onto FL 92 about 0.25 mile past Collier Seminole State Park.

For more information: Call Angler's Answer at (941) 775-7336.

60. TEN THOUSAND ISLANDS —————————————
Salt; Boat.

Description: If you've never fished the Ten Thousand Islands, you owe it to yourself to visit at least once. You'll want to come back again and again. Winding through the labyrinth of water created by the mangrove islands and tidal creeks, boaters can experience Florida as the early Spanish explorers saw it. The Ten Thousand Islands has at least that many islands if not more. Becoming "temporarily" lost among the maze of islands and waterways is easy to do. My grandfather always taught me to look over my shoulder when heading into the wilderness because I'd have to recognize the way back at the end of the day. Looking back is very important when heading into this area, especially if it's your first trip. To the inexperienced eye, most of the area looks the same and it's easy to get confused. Always have a compass and navigational chart of the area with you. A Global Positioning System (GPS) unit will also be helpful if you are really worried about getting lost.

If the beauty of the area overcomes you and you temporarily forget where you are, follow the flowing water. The stronger flows usually are or lead to the major tidal channels that connect to the Gulf. By following these routes in a southwesterly direction you should find the open water of the Gulf. Once you're outside, look for a well-defined landmark to regain your bearings.

Except for US 41 and FL 29 (which runs to the small fishing villages of Everglades City and Chokoloskee), there are no roads in the Ten Thousand

Islands. This makes fishing from a boat the preferred method. Only a few land access points offer very good fishing.

With a small boat not only can you reach more fishing spots, but you'll have the opportunity to enjoy the beauty of the mangrove swamp and the wildlife of the area. Ospreys are a common site and bald eagles also frequent the area. In the water you can see bottle-nosed dolphins and, during all but the coldest months, manatees.

Fishing Index: The islands are famous for snook and redfish. Snook love the shady habitat provided by a mangrove tree overhanging the water. When the tide is up, try casting a lure or live bait under an overhanging branch. Snook like to wait here for an easy meal. If the fish doesn't have to move very far to get a meal, it's more likely to strike. The numerous small bays throughout the area are sometimes loaded with redfish. Look for seagrass flats. The region also has a number of tidal channels that connect the Gulf of Mexico to the interior bays. These are excellent places to fish for snook, redfish, shark, and tarpon. Just offshore of the Ten Thousand Islands the water is very shallow and there are extensive seagrass beds. Commercial netting in recent years has decimated the trout population in this area, but this is still a good area to look for the spotted seatrout.

Anglers who want to increase their odds of catching more fish can travel a little farther south and fish in the Everglades National Park portion of the Ten Thousand Islands. The park's waters have been closed to commercial fishing for many years and many anglers and some guides swear that the fishing is better. Captain Joe McNichols at (813) 262-4132 specializes in fishing this area. "My favorite species to fish for are the tarpon, especially when they are "laid up" in the shallow bays. Generally this happens in March, April, and May. We pole around the bays until we find the fish. Then comes the hard part—trying to tell which is the head end and which is the tail end of the dark shadow you see in the water. If you cast to the tail end, the fish usually swims away and you've lost your chance. If you cast to the head end, hold on. Catching fish this way on flies or plugs is a lot of fun."

Many of the tidal channels penetrate deep into the mangrove wilderness. If you are familiar with the region, try fishing some of the deep holes along these waterways. Several species of grouper, normally caught offshore, inhabit these remote locations.

This is one part of Florida where fishing with a guide is highly recommended. The captains who fish these waters know their way around, and have the local knowledge necessary to find the fish.

Directions: Refer to the following site descriptions for Collier Seminole State Park, Port of the Islands Resort, and Chokoloskee Causeway. The shortest boat rides to this area are from Everglades City. Many boaters also make the trip by water from Marco Island. Backwater guides operate throughout the area. Consult the Naples telephone directory for listings. Captain Mark Ward's store, Everglades Angler, specializes in fly fishing this area. For more information call (941) 262-8228.

61. COLLIER SEMINOLE STATE PARK

Salt; Boat and Bank; Ramp; $.

Description: In the park, you can fish from a wooden walkway around the boat basin. The ramp allows boaters access to the upper part of the Ten Thousand Islands via the Blackwater River. The park has canoes for rent, a campground, a nature trail through a tropical hardwood hammock, and a 6.5-mile hiking trail. It can be very buggy in summer.

Fishing Index: Anglers have varied luck catching snook, mangrove snapper, sheepshead, and small tarpon around the dock.

Directions: The entrance to the park is on US 41, 0.25 mile south of the highway's intersection with FL 92.

For more information: Call the park office at (941) 394-3397.

62. US 41, SEGMENT 1

Fresh; Bank.

Description: US 41, the Tamiami Trail, is a busy, two-lane highway. The canal along the side of the road can be fished along the entire length. However, it is not safe to stop and leave your car unless you can pull well off the highway. The easiest places to stop are around the small bridges that allow water to move from the north side of the road to the south side.

Fishing Index: Anglers have good luck catching small bass and panfish throughout the year. In addition to the freshwater species, you may also catch some small snook and tarpon. Bring all necessities with you, including insect repellent, because there are no facilities once past the park except for Port of the Islands Resort.

Directions: From the intersection with FL 92, drive east on US 41 toward Miami. Around the bend past Collier Seminole State Park, a canal appears on the north side of the road. This canal is fishable until just before the intersection with FL 29.

63. PORT OF THE ISLANDS

Fresh and Salt; Boat; Bridge and Bank; Ramp.

Description: You can fish in saltwater from the US 41 bridge or along the bank between the bridge and the weir. Caution is advised when fishing off the bridge. US 41 is a very busy road. Port of the Islands is a well-known landmark in Florida. There is a campground, and guests can fish freshwater on the banks north of the weir on the Faka Union Canal. A primitive boat ramp at the campground on the north side of the highway is open to the public. From the marina you can launch a boat, rent one, or fish with a guide in the famous Ten Thousand Islands. There is a skeet and trap facility adjacent to the campground.

Fishing Index: On the freshwater side, most anglers use the boat ramp to access an area called the "Big T." Head north up the Faka Union Canal for several miles to where the canal dead-ends into an east-west canal. That's the "Big T" and it is a very popular bass hole. Don't be surprised if you also see tarpon rolling and snook feeding on the surface. Both saltwater species can tolerate freshwater and routinely make their way to this area from their saltwater haunts. Saltwater anglers leaving from the resort's marina are heading for the Ten Thousand Islands to fish for snook, redfish, and seatrout. The waters around the marina and in the Faka Union Canal are a state-designated manatee sanctuary; all boats must travel at slow speed until they reach the end of the canal about 3.5 miles from the marina. The leisurely trip is worth it because the fishing and the scenery in this part of the world are always interesting and productive.

Directions: Head toward Miami on US 41; the resort is 6 miles from Collier Seminole State Park.

For more information: For saltwater fishing information, call the marina at (941) 394-3101. The campground and freshwater boat ramp are operated by a different company. Its number is (941) 642-5343.

64-65. FLORIDA 29 AND TURNER RIVER ROAD ————

Fresh; Bank.

Description: These are north-south roads that cut through the Big Cypress Swamp. FL 29 goes from Everglades City to Immokalee. Fish the canals that parallel the roads. Freshwater fishing is north of US 41. It is easier to fish along Turner River Road because there is less traffic. This limerock road goes to the Bear Island campground of the Big Cypress National Preserve. The canal is fishable from US 41 north to the intersection with I-75. The canal by Turner River Road is fishable to the I-75 overpass.

Fishing Index: If you want to do some wildlife watching with your fishing try either of these locations. There is good year-round bass and panfish fishing in the canals alongside these roads. This is a remote area and it is possible to see a variety of birds, numerous alligators, some deer, and perhaps a black bear.

Directions: FL 29 intersects with US 41 and I-75. Turner River Road can be reached only off US 41. The intersection is about 6.3 miles east of FL 29.

66. CHOKOLOSKEE CAUSEWAY ————

Salt; Boat and Bank; Ramp.

Description: About the only place to fish from land in the Ten Thousand Islands is along the causeway to Chokoloskee Island. On your way, stop at the Everglades National Park Visitor Center and Ranger Station to learn about the region and go on a guided boat tour. After fishing along the causeway, head down to Chokoloskee and visit the Smallwood Store. The beautifully restored facility was one of the first Indian trading posts in this part of the world. The public ramp is next to the Outdoor Resorts Campground at the south end of the causeway.

Fishing Index: Fish from land for mangrove snapper, sheepshead, redfish, and snook.

Directions: From US 41, drive south 4 miles on FL 29 to Everglades City. Go through town and follow the signs to Chokoloskee. There are several places to pull off the road along the causeway and fish. The ramp is about 7.4 miles south of US 41 on FL 29.

67. US 41, SEGMENT 2
Fresh; Bank.

Description: A continuation of the "borrow canal" that provided the fill for US 41. To stop and fish along this road, make sure that you can park well off the road. Out here civilization is miles away. A great place to watch for and see lots of alligators and birds.

Fishing Index: A top spot for Oscars. The fish can be so prevalent that you will get tired of catching them long before the supply runs out.

Directions: Heading toward Miami on US 41, you can fish in the Tamiami Canal on the north side of the highway from the intersection with FL 29 to the Dade County line.

68. GULF OF MEXICO
Salt; Boat.

Description: The charter boats operating out of ports from Fort Myers Beach to Everglades City stay busy much of the year. Most of the captains fish from 5 to 50 miles offshore. There are some artificial reefs close to shore, but these are heavily fished by private boats. The charter boats tend to fish rocky bottoms and submerged wrecks 12 miles or more offshore. Like any open water angling, LORAN numbers are essential for success.

Some of the boats operate out of numerous small marinas throughout the area. One of my personal favorite captains is Dennis Smith at (941) 394-4907. He docks his boat, the Kay-Dee II, at a small marina and restaurant called Pelican Bend. It's on the Isle of Capri, which is just north of Marco Island. After a day of fishing, you can have the cooks at the restaurant prepare your catch for a very reasonable cost. If you decide to save your catch for another day, try the restaurant's sauteed grouper. It is the best fish I've ever had.

Fishing Index: Most of the fish caught in the Gulf are taken where there is some relief on the bottom. Snapper, grouper, cobia, king mackerel, tarpon, amberjack, and all the other Gulf species prefer to hang around any type of bottom relief. That's why a good depth finder is also essential. If you detect something other than a smooth bottom, it is worth investigating.

Bottom fishing for grouper and snapper is the most common type of off-shore fishing. If you have only half a day to fish, this is what most captains will fish for. Full-day charters, which make for a better trip, can venture further offshore and that increases your chances of catching cobia, amberjack, and permit. In the spring and fall, if you request it, the captains will fish for Spanish and king mackerel.

For those who have a boat that can handle offshore waters, the numerous artificial reefs placed by the state and local governments are the best bet. A LORAN or GPS and a good depth finder are necessary to find these spots. The numbers for the major sites are listed in Appendix B in the back of this guide.

There are acres of hard bottom off the southwest Florida coast. Depending on who you ask, some marinas and bait and tackle stores may part with a few numbers for some of the more popular spots. Although these areas are heavily fished at certain times of the year, the local wanderings of resident species and the seasonal movement patterns of migratory fish ensure that a constant supply of fish will be found around these submerged structures and natural areas.

Fleet Locations: Charter boats are for hire throughout the region. Some of the larger fleets are in Fort Myers Beach, Bonita Beach, Naples, and Marco Island. Consult the local phone directories for listings. Hotels usually have several boats they work with on a regular basis. If you're visiting the area, ask your hotel concierge or at the front desk.

Permit are a common summertime catch off the southwest Florida coast. Look for them in the water above submerged wrecks and other structures.

Month By Month in Southwest Florida

Note: Offshore is defined as greater than 1 mile from the coast. Backwaters include all waters inside of the passes and landward of the barrier islands and all other brackish water area such as bays and the saltwater regions of rivers. Freshwater includes, lakes, ponds, reservoirs, rivers and phosphate pits.

January

Offshore: Spanish mackerel, gag grouper and mangrove snapper are in close to shore. It's always worthwhile to cruise a line of stonecrab trap floats to look for tripletail. Wear polarized glasses so you can see the fish. When you find one, freeline a shrimp under its nose and the fish will bite.

Backwaters: Snook escape the cold this time of year by moving way up the tidal creeks and residential canals. These are great places to fish on cold and windy days. This is also a good time for spotted seatrout if you can find them. Try the grass flats in the Ten Thousand Islands and Estero Bay. There will be plenty of big sheepshead around bridge and pier pilings. Although it's a small fish and not much of a fighter, this is best time for silver trout.

Fresh: The cool waters inspire large bass to prepare for the bedding season and that means the action will pick up as the fish fatten up. Crappie action will be at its peak and the best place to try is Lake Trafford in Immokalee.

February

Offshore: Another good month for catching legal-sized gag grouper, big mangrove snapper and jumbo sheepshead on nearshore artificial reefs. This can be a tough month for offshore enthusiasts if a lot of northwesters blow through.

Backwaters: The snook are still way up the creeks and if you want to catch one, that's where you need to go. Spotted seatrout will be on the grass flats on warm days and in the slightly deeper water near the flats when it is cooler. The hot sheepshead action continues around the bridges.

Fresh: Largemouth bass beginning to bed and now is the time to look for the trophy fish. Live shiners are the preferred bait.

March

Offshore: The water is warming and the cobia, permit and amberjack will reappear around the wrecks, reefs, and other structures. Lucky anglers may find some hungry big tarpon on offshore reefs. Sometime this month the king mackerel will appear, moving up from the south.

Backwaters: This is the transition month for snook. They will be moving out of the deep backwaters and into the bays. Towards the south end of this region, anglers will find a few big tarpon. With the net ban in place as of 1995, look for spotted seatrout action to become top-notch within five years.

Fresh: This should be another very good month for big bass unless it gets real hot. Panfish activity will begin to pick up as spawning season approaches.

APRIL

Offshore: Gag grouper will begin to move offshore and red grouper will start to move closer in. Look for northward-migrating king and Spanish mackerel in the nearshore waters. Trolling is the way to find them. Some big tarpon will be found on the reefs. Permit, cobia, and amberjack fishing will continue to improve.

Backwaters: The big tarpon will be in the passes in the south of the region. Snook fishing will be very good throughout the area. Try for redfish in the passes. This has the potential to be another great month for spotted seatrout.

Fresh: This is traditionally a top month for panfish. By now most of the largemouth bass are finished bedding and the fish are beginning to disperse.

MAY

Offshore: This is the last good month to catch the migrating kind mackerel and amberjack. Shark anglers will find the action really picks up this month. The barracuda will become noticeably thick around any submerged structure and they will take half of many of the fish you pull off the bottom. Look for the permit fishing to be very good, especially if you have some small live crabs for bait.

Backwaters: This is a good month to fish for sharks in passes and the backwaters. Small blacktip sharks are common and are good eating. This is a top month for tarpon and snook. Fish for tarpon in the passes and close to shore. The snook will be around the mangroves and in the passes.

Fresh: The last good month for top panfish activity. Anglers can expect only average bass fishing from now through the end of the summer.

JUNE

Offshore: The best gamefish for this month is the permit. A live crab is the bait of choice. Plentiful supplies of cobia and red grouper will be around the most popular offshore fishing holes. If you want to catch a dolphin, this is one of the months to try. They seem to be easier to find towards the north end of this region. Good catches of yellowtail snapper reward anglers lucky enough to find a hotspot.

Backwaters: Although the season is closed, this is one of the best months for snook. Bend down the barbs and remember to release every snook you catch. This is big tarpon time in Boca Grande Pass and the waters are often congested. This is the time too for boaters to be extra courteous and cautious. Shark anglers love the summer and do well in the backwaters and in the passes especially when fishing at night.

Fresh: Now, and for the rest of the hot summer months, fish early in the morning or late in the day. In the heat of the day the fish won't bite but you're sure to swelter.

Yellowtail snapper move onto the offshore reefs and wrecks in the summer off the state's lower west coast. Averaging 1-2 pounds, they aren't the biggest of the snappers but they are one of the tastiest.

JULY

Offshore: Around the wrecks and artificial reefs, look for abundant supplies of permit and a steady stream of cobia. The permit won't be at every site all the time, but if you're patient and wait in one spot for a while, a school or two will pass through. This is one of the best times to find red grouper close to the shore. Some mangrove snapper will be around, too. Get the fish up quickly, otherwise the 'cudas will take their share. Barracuda are so abundant that they can be a nuisance unless you like catching them. This is also the time of year to watch out for thunderstorms. Leave the water if one approaches.

Backwaters: This marks the beginning of the better months to angle for redfish. Look for them feeding on the flats. Snook action is very good although not as many anglers go for this fish during the closed season. The big tarpon are gone, but there will be plenty of smaller ones to be caught. For any of these species it is best to fish early in the day or later in the afternoon, tides permitting, to beat the heat.

Fresh: For largemouth bass try topwater plugs in the early morning and run worms deep in the day if you can take the heat.

AUGUST

Offshore: Consider a nighttime outing. Snapper are nocturnal feeders and if you can chum up a few fish, more are bound to show up. The standard summer selection—permit, cobia, grouper, snapper, and barracuda—will be around just about every structure. You may also encounter some lunker snook on the artificial reefs. It's not unheard of for a few schools of Spanish mackerel to show up, too.

Backwaters: Redfish action is usually top-notch on the flats. This is a good time to sight fish for them. It is one of the most exciting types of backwater fishing. Snook fishing is good at night around docks with lights on. It is the perfect thing for insomniac anglers.

Fresh: Panfish action is your best bet. Persistent anglers will catch some bass during the cooler times of the day. For something different, try a nighttime trip; the fish will bite.

SEPTEMBER

Offshore: Cobia, moving south from the upper Gulf, begin to join the resident fish, creating a very good month for this member of the ling family. The red grouper will begin to move offshore and the gag will start to move a little closer. More schools of Spanish mackerel will show up by the end of the month. This is peak hurricane month, so keep your eyes and ears tuned to the forecast.

Backwaters: Redfish action is hard to beat, but a lot of anglers will turn their attention to snook now that the summer closed season is over. If you're a fly rodder, try fishing for reds on the flats.

Fresh: No surprises this moth, just follow the summer pattern.

OCTOBER

Offshore: If the pattern holds, the king mackerel will show up some time this month. More cobia will also arrive, making this one of the best months for these strong-fighting fish. Live bait seems to be especially effective. Gag grouper fishing will begin to improve as the fish move closer to shore.

Backwaters: This is a great time of the year to fish for snook and redfish. Schools of reds will be throughout the area and there seems to be a snook beneath every overhanging mangrove branch. The spotted seatrout fishing will also take a positive turn this month. It could be very, very good in some spots.

Fresh: Look for the largemouth bass fishing to improve slightly but that's only if the weather begins to cool off. There are always panfish to be caught but not in numbers to brag about.

NOVEMBER

Offshore: Get the mackerel while they move through the area. Look for terns and pelicans feeding on schools of baitfish—chances are very good that some of either species of mackerel will be nearby. Some cobia will be around but not in the numbers of the summer. Now is the time to look for tripletail around crab floats and floating debris.

Backwaters: Usually a solid snook and redfish month unless the weather is unusually cold. Give spotted seatrout a try, too. Troll until you find one, mark the spot and fish the area with jigs. Trout don't swim alone.

Sheepshead, the favorite of many wintertime residents, will be plentiful and as clever as ever in stealing your bait.

Fresh: The bass action begins to pick up as water cools. The fish become more aggressive and will be caught throughout the day.

December

Offshore: This is usually one of the best months for king mackerel. Anglers are looking for the big "smokers" to be in the area. It's also possible to find some jumbo redfish hanging around the nearshore wrecks and reefs. Don't overlook tripletail around the crab trap buoys.

Backwaters: The snook will be thinking about heading to warmer waters up the tidal creeks at the first sign of cold weather. Traditionally, this is one of the best seatrout months. Anglers will have luck trolling the grass flats throughout the region. Sheepshead action will be on the increase and so will the number of anglers looking for them.

Fresh: Bass fishing gets better, especially if the weather cools off. It may not be too early to try for crappie on Lake Trafford.

Southwest Florida Fish Availability Chart

NOTE: Refer to the month by month table for additional information. Information in this chart represents the seasonal patterns observed over the past three years. For salt water species, the arrival of the migrant species and the peak times for each species is heavily dependent on water temperature. Unusually warm or cold periods will effect the patterns described above.

■ signifies a reasonable chance of catching this species in that month.

□ signifies the optimal months for catching the species.

Species	Jan	Feb	Mar	Apr	May	Jun	Jul	Aug	Sep	Oct	Nov	Dec
Snook	■	■	■	■	□	□	■	■	■	□	□	■
Redfish	■	■	■	■	■	■	□	□	□	□	□	■
Spotted Seatrout	□	□	□	□	■	■	■	■	■	■	■	□
Sheepshead	□	□	□	■	■	■	■	■	■	■	■	■
Mangrove Snapper	■	■	■	■	■	■	■	■	■	■	■	■
Crevalle Jack	■	■	■	■	■	■	■	■	■	■	■	■
Tarpon	■	■	□	□	□	□	■	■	■	■	■	■
Pompano	■	■	■	■	■	■	■	■	■	■	■	■
Flounder	■	■	■	■	■	■	■	■	■	■	■	■
Spanish Mackerel	■	■	■	□	□	■	■	■	□	□	■	■

Species	Jan	Feb	Mar	Apr	May	Jun	Jul	Aug	Sep	Oct	Nov	Dec
Cobia	■	■	■	■	■	■	■	■	■	□	□	■
Red Grouper	■	■	■	■	■	■	□	□	■	■	■	■
Gag Grouper	□	□	■	■	■	■	■	■	■	■	■	□
Yellowtail Snapper	■	■	■	■	■	■	□	□	■	■	■	■
Lane Snapper	■	■	■	■	■	■	■	■	■	■	■	■
Black Drum	■	■	■	■	■	■	■	■	■	■	■	■
Barracuda	■	■	■	■	■	□	□	□	□	■	■	■
Shark (all species)	■	■	■	■	□	□	□	□	□	■	■	■
King Mackerel	■	■	□	□	□	■				■	□	□
Amberjack	■	■	□	□	■	■					■	■
Tripletail	■	■	■	■	■					■	■	■
Bluefish	■	□	■									
Whiting	■	■	■								■	■
Silver Trout	□	□	■								■	■
Permit			■	■	■	□	□	□	■	■	■	
Dolphin						■	■	■	■			
Largemouth Bass	□	□	□	□	■	■	■	■	■	■	■	■
Panfish	■	■	■	□	□	■	■	■	■	■	■	■
Crappie	■	■	■	■	■	■	■	■	■	■	■	■
Catfish	■	■	■	■	■	■	■	■	■	■	■	■
Oscar	■	■	■	■	■	■	■	■	■	■	■	■

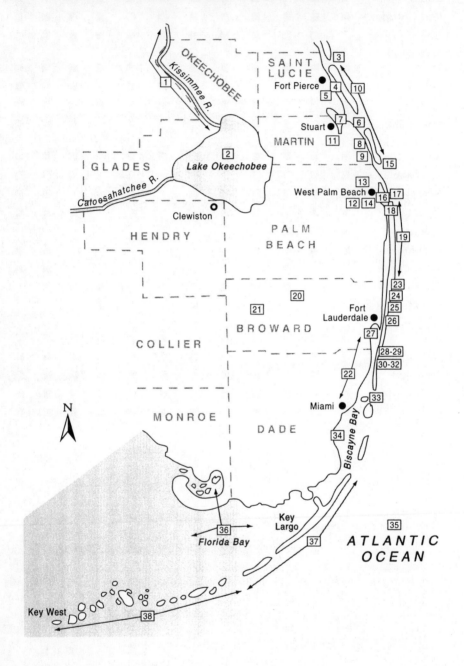

CHAPTER NINE

Southeast Florida

COUNTIES: ▪ Saint Lucie ▪ Martin ▪ Okeechobee ▪ Glades ▪ Hendry ▪ Palm ▪ Beach ▪ Broward ▪ Dade ▪ Monroe (Florida Bay and the Keys)

SALTWATER FISHING

Bluewater fishing for sailfish, marlin, wahoo, and dolphin reaches its zenith in the Gulf Stream waters of southeast Florida. Less than 10 miles from the mainland, the Gulf Stream is easy to reach from any port along the coast. Closer to shore are coral reefs which begin as small patches around West Palm Beach and blossom into ornate reefs in the Florida Keys. There are also several ocean fishing piers from Fort Pierce to Miami that provide land-bound anglers the chance to hook some ocean species.

For inside angling, the lower part of Indian River and Lake Worth are good for snook, redfish, and spotted seatrout. The Loxahatchee River, which empties into the Atlantic Ocean at Jupiter Inlet, is also a snook mecca. Farther south, sea grasses flourish in the lower part of Biscayne Bay, a good spot for bonefish.

At Florida's tip, the shallow waters of Florida Bay are also highly regarded fishing grounds. Anglers leaving from Flamingo in Everglades National Park fish the out-front area, as they call Florida Bay, for snook, redfish, spotted seatrout, and tarpon. The bay is also easy to reach from the upper Florida Keys. Here anglers call the bay the backcountry and they fish the flats for bonefish and tarpon.

The Florida Keys are the most unique and diverse place to fish in Florida. With bonefish, permit, and tarpon on the flats; snapper and grouper on the reefs and wrecks; dolphin, king mackerel, sailfish, marlin, tuna, wahoo, and many others in the blue water; and sharks and barracuda everywhere, the hardest decision to make is what to fish for first.

FRESHWATER FISHING

Southeast Florida is one of the most developed parts of the state. While growth continues in the region, plenty of angling adventures remain. The freshwater canals of Dade and Broward counties harbor a thriving population of the exotic butterfly peacock bass, deliberately stocked by the GFC to control the forage fish population and for the pleasure of anglers. Hundreds of miles of canals in the Everglades offer excellent fishing for largemouth bass, panfish, and Oscars, an exotic escapee from the freshwater aquarium world. The Osborne chain of lakes in eastern Palm Beach County has surprisingly good largemouth bass fishing for an urban area. Finally, the Big O, Lake Okeechobee, is world-famous for bass and crappie. Miles of drainage canals around the lake are also good places to fish.

OKEECHOBEE, GLADES, HENDRY, MARTIN (WESTERN PORTION) AND PALM BEACH (WESTERN PORTION) COUNTIES

1. KISSIMMEE RIVER

Fresh; Boat and Bank; Ramp.

Description: The Kissimmee River, currently undergoing massive restoration after it was forced into man-made channels by the US Army Corps of Engineers, promises to return to the days when it held a productive fishery. Give it another ten years before the river is truly a good place to fish.

Fishing Index: Fishing in the channelized parts of the river is limited to a small section of the river's original course that again holds water. There is some largemouth bass fishing in the restored part of the river.

Access Points:
1A. FL 60 RAMP—*Boat; Ramp.*
Directions: The ramp is just off FL 60 where it crosses the southern-most part of Lake Kissimmee, about 26.5 miles west of US 27 in Lake Wales. It is adjacent to the locks that lead to the Kissimmee River.

1B. S-65B LOCK—*Boat; Ramp.*
Description: This is the closest access area to the partially restored section of the river. Access is from the Highlands County (west) side of the river.
Directions: From the intersection with US 27 south of Sebring, take US 98 about 11 miles east to Bluff Hammock Road. Turn left and go north 4 miles to the lock and ramp.
For more information: Call the South Florida Water Management District at (561) 686-8800 or (800) 432-2045.

2. LAKE OKEECHOBEE

Fresh; Bank and Boat; Ramp.

Description: At 450,000 acres or 730 square miles, the Big O is the largest freshwater lake in Florida and one of the largest in the United States. Its fishing reputation matches its size. Despite recent pollution problems, Lake Okeechobee provides outstanding bass and world-class spec (crappie) fishing.

The GFC's Everglades Region Fishing Guide states that fishing success for largemouth bass in 1991-92 was 0.69 fish per hour and that there was an average of 142 bass per vegetated acre. For crappie, the GFC reports a catch rate of 2.17 fish per hour in 1991-92, down from a peak of 3.11 fish per hour in 1989-90. In 1990-91, an estimated 2 million specs were taken!

Lake Okeechobee's future as a famous fishing hole is threatened by rampant hydrilla and pollution. Decades of runoff from dairy ranches and back-pumped water from sugarcane fields have poured excess nutrients into the lake. This led to algae blooms that killed parts of the lake. Today, plans call for cleaning up the problems to save the fisheries.

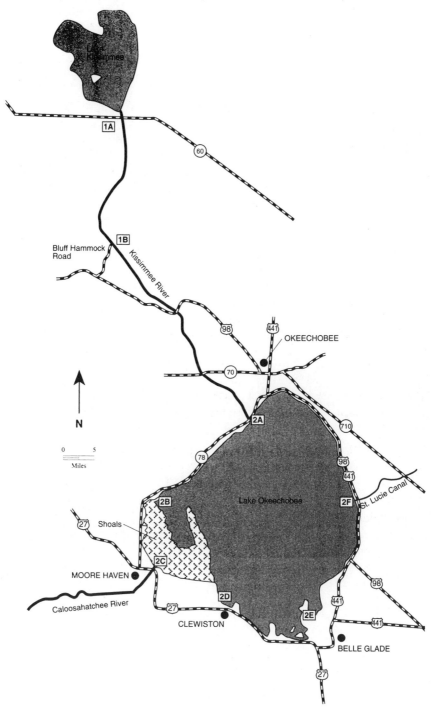

Fishing Index: First-time visitors to Okeechobee should hire a guide. Or expect to spend days trying to find a hot spot and getting un-lost. Guides are also familiar with the lake's weather. Intense thunderstorms boil up in a hurry during summer and winter's northwest winds bring cold fronts. Sam Griffin, creator of the Jerkin' Sam lure, was born in a houseboat on the lake and has lived nearby all his life. Sam says, "Respect the lake's vastness. You can get into trouble in a hurry." The best fishing (and more than half of the action) takes place along the lake's western shore. This area is more secluded and sheltered than the more open, windy eastern side.

The peak fishing seasons follow a pretty consistent pattern. Bass are taken year-round, Griffin says, with the largest fish caught from December to March (the spawning season), and the most fish caught from March to June and September to November. Where fish congregate depends on the lake's water level, which is regulated by the local water management district. Always check with a local bait and tackle store or marina about lake conditions before going fishing.

For bass, if you aren't experienced using artificial lures, use live bait such as shiners. Griffin suggests trolling for bass to find where they are. Once one takes the bait, stop, break out the lures, and fish the area. Where there is one bass, more are sure to be around.

Spec (crappie) fishing is best in winter. Although you can catch them all year, cooler temperatures stimulate the fish to feed with a vengeance. November to May is when most crappie are taken. During summer when bass and crappie fishing is the slowest, bluegills and shellcrackers are spawning and the action is top notch.

Anglers who don't know the lake but want to try it on their own should fish the rim canal, which runs along the southern half of the lake. It is protected from the open waters by a series of vegetated islands. The fishing is very good here; frequent openings along the route create some excellent points for anglers to cast to.

For more information: Several fishing maps and books on Lake Okeechobee are available; ask at marinas and fish camps. For a guide, try the marinas listed below or call the Lake Okeechobee Guides Association at 1 800 284 BIG-O or (941) 763-2248.

Access Points:

Nearly two dozen public ramps and at least that many commercial marinas and fish camps are on the lake. Listed below are the six most popular public launches. Several marinas or fish camps near these ramps sell bait and tackle and offer information on fishing conditions.

2A. OKEE-TAINTIE RECREATION AREA—*Boat and Bank; Ramp.*
Description: The Kissimmee River empties into Lake Okeechobee here. Bait and tackle, boat rentals, guide services, a campground, and picnic area are on site. From this ramp, anglers can fish the north end of the lake or the Kissimmee River.

Directions: From the town of Okeechobee drive 3 miles south on US 441/98. Where US 441/98 bears left, turn right onto FL 78 and drive 3.7 miles south to the site.

For more information: Call the recreation area office at (941) 763-2622, Nix's Fishing Headquarters at 1 800 284-2246 or (941) 763-2248, or Garrard Tackle Shop at (941) 763-3416.

2B. HARNEY POND CANAL ACCESS AREA—*Boat and Bank; Ramp.*

Directions: From the town of Okeechobee, drive 3 miles south on US 441/98. Where US 441/98 bears left, turn right onto FL 78 and drive about 19.8 miles south to the access area. Or from US 27 in Moore Haven, drive about 13 miles north on FL 78 to the site.

For more information: Call Becks Food Store at (941) 946-1622.

2C. MOORE HAVEN RECREATION AREA-WEST—*Boat and Bank; Ramp.*

Description: A campground, picnic area, boat rentals, bait and tackle, and guide service are on-site.

Directions: From US 27 in Moore Haven, take Daniels Road north 0.5 mile to Canal Avenue. Turn right to enter the site.

2D. CLEWISTON RECREATION AREA—*Boat and Bank; Ramp.*

Description: A picnic area is on-site; bait and tackle and guide services are nearby.

Directions: From US 27 in Clewiston, turn north on Francisco Street and go 3 blocks to the recreation area.

For more information: Call Angler's Marina at (941) 983-2128 or Roland Martin's Clewiston Marina at 1 800 473-6766 or (941) 983-3151.

2E. BELLE GLADE RECREATION AREA—*Boat and Bank; Ramp.*

Description: A campground and picnic area are on site with bait and tackle and guide services nearby.

Directions: The recreation area is on Torry Island. In Belle Glade, turn west off of North Main Street onto CR 717 and go 3.2 miles to the recreation area.

For more information: Call Slim's Fish Camp at (561) 996-3844.

2F. PORT MAYACA RECREATION AREA—*Boat and Bank; Ramp.*

Description: This site along the eastern side of the lake is a good point of departure for anglers wanting to fish for specs (crappie). The ramp is located where the Saint Lucie Canal begins. There are no additional facilities nearby.

Directions: From Belle Glade drive about 27 miles north on US 441/98 to Port Mayaca and the site.

Other access points:

Lock 7 Recreation Area—*Near intersection of US 441/98 and FL 78.*

Indian Prairie Canal Access Area—*8 miles south of Okee-Taintie on FL 78.*

Bear Beach Access Area—*1 mile north of Harney Pond Area on FL 78.*

Fisheating Creek Access—*4.5 miles south of Harney Pond Area on FL 78.*

Sportsman's Village Access Area—*6 miles north of Moore Haven on FL 78.*

South Bay Access Area—*About 13 miles east of Clewiston on US 27.*

Canal Point Lions Club Park—*At the junction of US 441 and US 98 north of Belle Glade.*

SAINT LUCIE AND MARTIN (COASTAL AREAS) COUNTIES

The Saint Lucie River and the southern part of the Indian River provide anglers with miles of sheltered, fishable waters. Wade anglers can access the rivers from bridges, causeways, and roadside pulloffs. Surf fishing access is excellent and outstanding angling for pompano and bluefish in winter make a trip to the beach worthwhile. The Savannahs add a touch of freshwater angling that's only a few miles from the beaches. Offshore fishing fleets out of Fort Pierce and Stuart target sailfish, king mackerel, snapper, and grouper.

3. FORT PIERCE INLET ─────────────────────

Salt; Boat.

Description: The inlet is stabilized with jetties on both sides. There is land access for anglers from the north and south; several boat ramps provide easy access to the inlet. Be careful of the strong currents in the inlet.

Fishing Index: Snook is the fish on the minds of most inlet anglers. Fall and spring are the best times although the fish are in the area all year. In summer, anglers will find the big spawners in the inlet, but since snook season is closed in June, July, and August, the fish must be released immediately when caught. Mangrove snapper action is very good from mid June to the end of August. Try fishing for them at night. Tarpon are a popular catch-and-release fishery from summer through October. In winter, bluefish and flounder are the best bets. The fishing varies weekly, but locals know what's biting; just ask.

For more information: Call Al's Bait and Tackle at (561) 461-8338 or Whites Tackle Shop at (561) 461-6909.

Access Points:
3A. NORTH BEACH CAUSEWAY—*Bridge and Boat; Ramp.*
Description: There is a park on the small island between the two bridges that cross this part of the Indian River. Anglers can fish off either bridge. The ramp is in the park.
Directions: From the intersection of US 1 and North Beach Causeway (A1A North), take the causeway 0.6 mile toward the beach.

3B. FORT PIERCE INLET STATE RECREATION AREA—*Surf, Pier; $.*
Description: Fish from the surf or off the rock jetty. Jetty anglers must use extreme caution. This jetty does not have a cap on it like the south inlet jetty. The rocks are slippery and if the seas are rough, waves routinely break over the top.
Directions: From the intersection of US 1 and North Beach Causeway (A1A North), take the causeway about 2.2 miles to the beach. The park entrance is on the right.

Saint Lucie and Martin (coastal areas) Counties

A1A
3A
3B
3
Ft. Pierce Inlet
N
Fort Pierce
3D
3C
ATLANTIC OCEAN
35
4B
A1A
5
Power Plant
Indian River
4
4B
10
Port St. Lucie
4A
1
4C
Saint Lucie River
707
4D
7
7C
7B
Stuart
6A
Florida Turnpike
6
Saint Lucie Inlet
7D
7A
6B
A1A
76
95
Cove Rd.
11
1
8
76
1
9

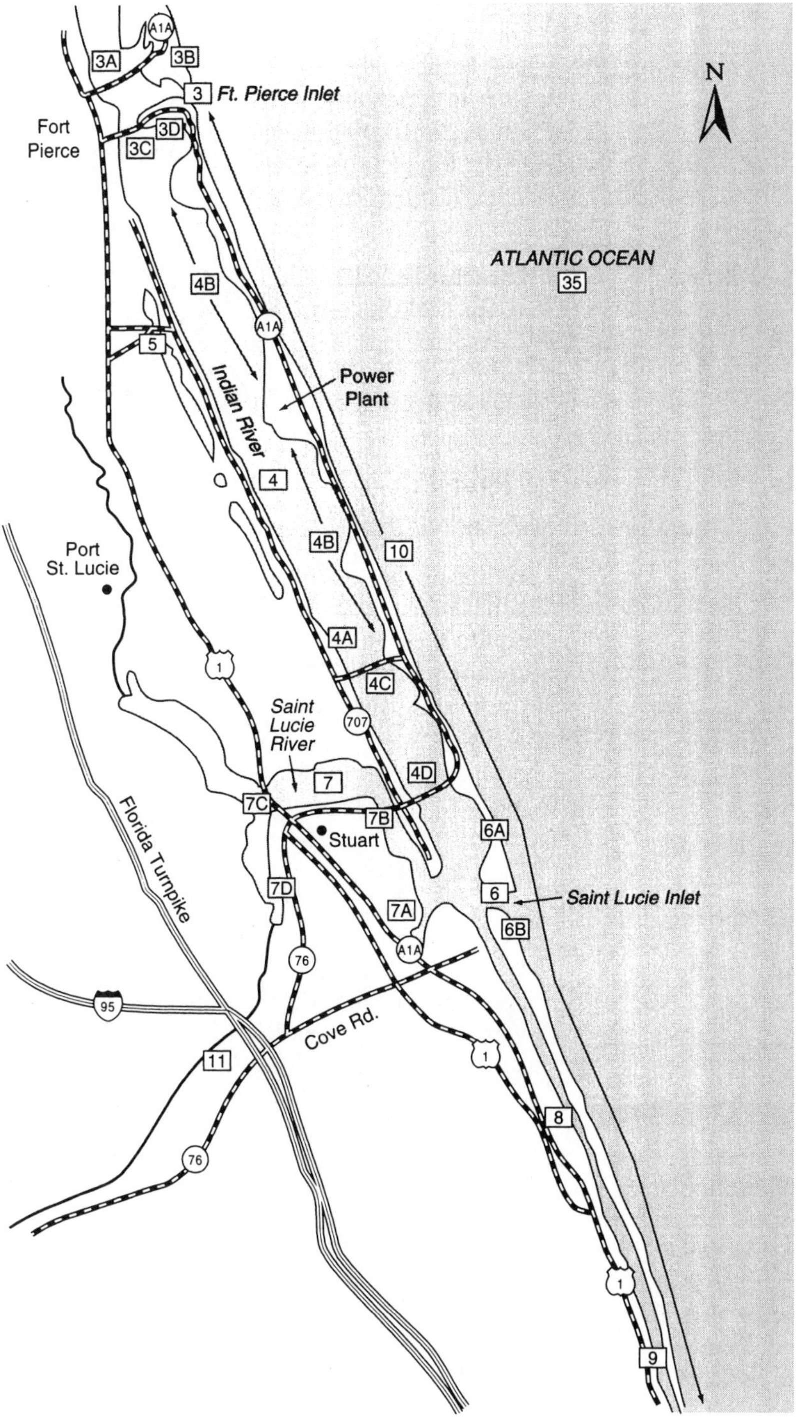

For more information: Call the park office at (561) 468-3985.

3C. SEAWAY DRIVE—*Boat and Bridge; Ramp.*
Description: Locals also call this the Peter Cobb Bridge. Fish off the bridge from a catwalk beneath the span. The ramp midway across the causeway is suitable only for john boats. Most boaters prefer the ramp at the base of the bridge on the mainland side. It is only 100 yards or so by boat to a locally popular fishing hole known as the Turning Basin.
Directions: From US 1 in Fort Pierce take Seaway Drive toward Hutchinson Island. The ramp is on the left just before the bridge.

3D. SOUTH JETTY PARK—*Pier, Surf.*
Description: This county beachfront park allows access to the inlet's south jetty. The jetty has a paved cap, making it easily accessible and much safer for anglers than the northside jetty.
Directions: From US 1 in Fort Pierce, take Seaway Drive 2.2 miles to Hutchinson Island. The park is on the left where A1A bends right and goes south.

4. SOUTH INDIAN RIVER

Salt; Wade, Bridge, Pier and Boat; Ramp.

Description: The south section of the Indian River, from just north of Fort Pierce Inlet to Jupiter Inlet, has the highest average salinity of anywhere in the lagoon system except Mosquito Lagoon. With an inlet at each end, flushing is better and sea grass flats are abundant. Midway between the two inlets on the island side of the river is the Saint Lucie Nuclear Power Plant.

Fishing Index: Spotted seatrout, redfish, and snook are the big three targets in this section of the river. There is also some very good summer tarpon fishing around Big Mud Creek, which is adjacent to the power plant.

Access Points:
4A. INDIAN RIVER DRIVE (FL 707)—*Wade.*
Description: This road parallels the river on the mainland side. There are a few places to pull off the road and wade fish the sea grass flats along the shoreline. Most of the property is private and access is limited.
Directions: Indian River Drive splits from US 1 at the intersection with Seaway Drive in Fort Pierce. Driving south from Stuart, you can reach this road by taking the Stuart Causeway toward the beach. After crossing the first bridge (over Saint Lucie Inlet), turn north on Indian River Drive in Sewall's Point.

4B. HIGHWAY A1A—*Wade.*
Description: This road parallels the river on the Hutchinson Island side. Extensive sea grass beds begin just north of the power plant and extend toward Fort Pierce for about 2 miles. Walk through the mangrove fringe from the road to the open waters. Access to the grassflats south of the power plant, an area known as Herman's Bay, is easier for anglers who like to wade but don't like walking through soft muddy areas. Access to the river is better here than from Indian River Drive.

Directions: From Fort Pierce, take A1A south. Or head north on A1A from Stuart. Look for places where other cars have pulled off the road to access the flats.

4C. JENSEN BEACH CAUSEWAY PARK—*Bridge, Pier and Boat; Ramp.*
Description: The causeway is a popular and productive spot for snook. Anglers can fish from catwalks beneath the main channel bridge and from Mosquito Bridge at the eastern end. A fishing pier is next to the boat ramp on the north side of the causeway. The site provides good access to the southern half of the Indian River and is crowded on weekends.
Directions: From US 1 in Stuart, take A1A toward the beach. After crossing the Saint Lucie River, turn left on Indian River Drive, which is just before the causeway crossing the Indian River. Take Indian River Drive 3.7 miles north to FL 732, the Jensen Beach Causeway.

4D. STUART CAUSEWAY PARK—*Wade and Bridge.*
Description: Wade fish the grassflats around the spoil islands or fish off the main bridge. Fish off the bridge for pompano from winter to spring.
Directions: From US 1 in Stuart, take A1A toward the beach. The Indian River portion of the causeway begins 3.2 miles from this intersection.

5.   THE SAVANNAS
Fresh; Bank and Boat; Ramp.

Description: This 550-acre Saint Lucie County park preserves a series of shallow coastal lakes. Anglers are limited to motors of 7.5 horsepower or less.

Fishing Index: The lakes are locally recognized for their largemouth bass fishing.

Directions: From the intersection with Orange Avenue (FL 68) in Fort Pierce, take US 1 about 4.9 miles south to Midway Road. Turn left and go 1.2 miles to the park. Or from Stuart, take US 1 about 12 miles north to Midway Road and turn right.

For more information: Call the park office at (561) 464-7855.

6.   SAINT LUCIE INLET
Salt; Boat, Surf, and Wade.

Description: The only practical access is by boat. The closest vehicle access point leaves almost a mile of hiking to the inlet, pretty far to carry your gear. Despite the hike, some anglers do make the trek.

Fishing Index: A tremendous diversity of fish feed here on everything from shrimp and crabs to schools of baitfish swept in and out by the strong tide. In winter, flounder, bluefish, pompano, mangrove snapper, and snook are common catches. Summer brings tons of tarpon and some great snook fishing.

For more information: Call Mitchell's Bait and Tackle at (561) 287-0486.

Access Points:
6A. BATHTUB BEACH—*Surf and Wade.*
Description: This is the closest land-based access point to the inlet—about a 1-mile hike down the beach. To break up the walk, try a little surf fishing along the way.
Directions: From US 1 in Stuart, take Ocean Boulevard (A1A) about 4.7 miles east across the Stuart Causeway to the beach. Here A1A turns north. Instead turn south (right) on MacArthur Boulevard. Go 2.3 miles to the end of the public road and the parking. Walk to the beach and continue south to the inlet.

6B. SAINT LUCIE INLET STATE PRESERVE—*Surf.*
Description: There are no roads to the preserve and access is only possible by boat. Anchor along the beach and surf fish.
Directions: The site occupies the north end of Jupiter Island up to the south side of the inlet.
For more information: Call the park office at (561) 744-7603.

7. SAINT LUCIE RIVER

Salt; Bank, Bridge, Pier, and Boat; Ramp.

Description: The river is deep compared to the Indian River, making it a good place to fish in winter. The North Fork goes to Port Saint Lucie, and the South Fork connects to the Saint Lucie Canal.

Fishing Index: When the weather is cold, redfish and snook hole up in the deeper spots in the two forks waiting for the waters to warm again. Flounder fishing is also good in winter.

For more information: Call Mitchell's Bait and Tackle at (561) 287-0486.

Access Points:
7A. SANDSPRIT PARK—*Pier and Boat; Ramp.*
Description: This Martin County park provides the quickest access to Saint Lucie Inlet for boaters.
Directions: From Ocean Boulevard (A1A) in Stuart, take US 1 south 2.5 miles to Saint Lucie Boulevard in Port Salerno. Turn left onto Saint Lucie Boulevard and drive 1 mile to the park.

7B. SAINT LUCIE RIVER Bridge
Description: A popular spot for winter pompano fishing.
Directions: This is the A1A bridge over the Saint Lucie River. From US 1 in Stuart, take Ocean Boulevard (A1A) 2.4 miles east to the beginning of the bridge.

7C. ROOSEVELT BRIDGE—*Bridge and Boat.*
Description: By the end of 1996 the existing bridge will be replaced. When the new vehicular bridge is completed, the old bridge will become the fishing pier.
Directions: This is the US 1 bridge over the Saint Lucie River in Stuart.

7D. LEIGHTON PARK—*Bridge and Boat; Ramp.*
Description: The park is on the shores of the South Fork of the Saint Lucie River. From this ramp, boaters can head up the Okeechobee Waterway to the Saint Lucie Locks, which are the dividing line between fresh- and saltwater. Around the bridge, anglers do well on sheepshead and mangrove snapper.
Directions: From the intersection of US 1 and A1A in Stuart, turn onto Palm City Avenue and go south 1.4 miles to Monterey Road. Turn right onto the Leighton Bridge. The park is on the west side of the river. Or from the US 1-A1A intersection, take US 1 south 2 miles to Monterey Road.

8. MARTIN COUNTY PARK

Salt; Boat; Ramp.

Description: This new and unnamed (at press time) facility will be open in 1996. It provides boaters with access to the Intracoastal Waterway between Saint Lucie Inlet and Hobe Sound.

Fishing Index: Fish in Peck Lake, the site of the old Saint Lucie Inlet, for redfish, spotted seatrout, and snook.

Directions: From Stuart, take US 1 south about 10.5 miles to Osprey Road. Turn left and go 0.6 mile to Gomez Avenue. Turn right and go south about 0.3 mile to the park.

9. JONATHAN DICKINSON STATE PARK

Salt and Fresh; Bank and Boat; Ramp; $.

Description: At 11,300 acres, this is one of the largest state parks in Florida. The Loxahatchee River is the park's focal point for anglers and canoeists. Several freshwater lakes offer fishing from canoes or banks (no motors allowed). The park has camping, river tours, hiking and horseback trails, and cabins.

Fishing Index: Fish the small freshwater lakes for largemouth bass and bream.Saltwater anglers can fish the Loxahatchee River for snook and tarpon from spring through fall. Sand perch and mangrove snapper provide year-round action that is also tasty table fare.
Directions: From Stuart, take US 1 south about 15 miles. From West Palm Beach take US 1 north approximately 22 miles. The park entrance is off US 1.
For more information: Call the park office at (407) 546-2771.

10. SAINT LUCIE AND MARTIN COUNTY BEACHES

Salt; Surf.

Description: Take your pick from nearly three dozen public access areas along the beaches in these two counties. Every spot is worth a try. Three of the more popular spots are Bob Graham, Bathtub, and Hobe Sound beaches.

Fishing Index: Winter fishing is primarily for bluefish and pompano; action peaks from November to May. Spring brings snook, which remain through summer. The fall bait run attracts a variety of fish to the surf. Anglers may find snook, tarpon, or Spanish mackerel. Whiting are present all year with the best action in spring.

The beach in the Hobe Sound area is a top surf fishing spot. The area is unusually good because of a reef about 100 yards offshore with a trough between the beach and the reef. Anglers catch tarpon, kings, snook, sennet, cobia, permit, pompano, and whiting in the trough.

Directions: All of the surf access points are off of A1A on Hutchinson Island, except several areas on FL 707 where it runs south from Hobe Sound along the beach. Heading south from Fort Pierce on A1A, the larger beach areas are: Pepper Park and Fort Pierce State Recreation Area (both north of Fort Pierce Inlet); South Jetty Park, South Beach, Surfside, Green Turtle, Frederick Douglas, Walton Rocks, Jensen Beach, Bob Graham, Stuart, House of Refuge, and Bathtub. From here follow A1A west to Stuart and then drive south on FL 707.

11. PHIPPS PARK AND SAINT LUCIE LOCK ———————

Fresh and Salt; Bank, Pier and Boat; Ramp.

Description: This county park and its ramp are on the saltwater side of the lock. The US Army Corps of Engineers operates a campground and ramp on the freshwater side.

Fishing Index: The pool below the lock is a great place for snook in winter. Sheepshead are another common catch. Fish around the dam and along the shoreline of the waterway for largemouth bass.

Directions: From US 1 in Stuart, take Kanner Highway (FL 76) south 6.9 miles. Turn right onto Lock Road and go 1.25 miles. The lock is on the left and Phipps Park is on the right.

PALM BEACH COUNTY (EASTERN PORTION)

12. LOXAHATCHEE NATIONAL WILDLIFE REFUGE ———

Fresh, Bank and Boat; Ramp.

Description: The refuge encompasses the South Florida Water Management District's Water Conservation Area 1.

Fishing Index: The bulk of the conservation area is marsh and is not easily accessible. However, a perimeter canal is popular with bass and panfish anglers. Dense patches of aquatic weeds make boating difficult. The fishing is best when water levels are low. This concentrates fish in the canals.

PALM BEACH COUNTY (EASTERN PORTION)

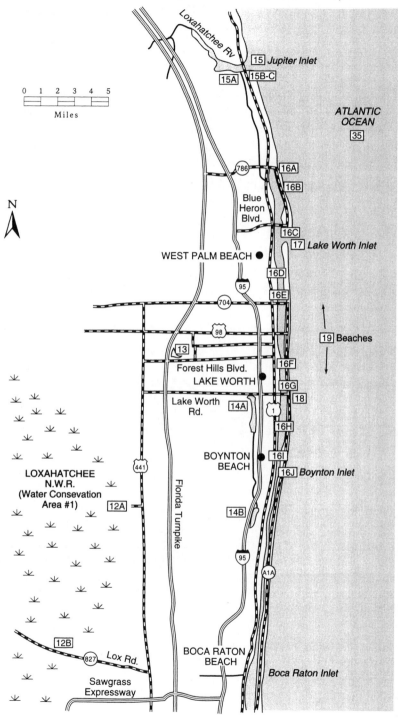

Loxahatchee Rv

15 Jupiter Inlet
15A
15B-C

0 1 2 3 4 5
Miles

ATLANTIC
OCEAN
35

N

786   16A
      16B

Blue
Heron
Blvd.

16C
17 Lake Worth Inlet

WEST PALM BEACH ●

16D
95
704   16E

98

19 Beaches

13

Forest Hills Blvd.
LAKE WORTH ●   16F
                16G

Lake Worth
Rd.   14A   18

16H

BOYNTON
BEACH ●   16I

16J Boynton Inlet

441

Florida Turnpike

14B

LOXAHATCHEE
N.W.R.
(Water Consevation
Area #1)

12A

95

A1A

12B
827   Lox Rd.

BOCA RATON
BEACH

Boca Raton Inlet

Sawgrass
Expressway

Access Points:

12A. HEADQUARTERS BOAT RAMP—*Bank and Boat; Ramp.*
Description: This ramp is adjacent to the refuge headquarters. Bank fish around the ramp.

Directions: From the intersection of US 441 and US 98, take US 441 about 12.7 miles south to Lee Road. Turn west, go 0.6 mile to refuge headquarters.

12B. LOXAHATCHEE RECREATION AREA—*Bank and Boat; Ramp.*
Description: This site provides access to the Loxahatchee National Wildlife Refuge (Water Conservation Area 1) and Water Conservation Area 2.

Directions: West of Boca Raton, exit the Sawgrass Expressway onto US 441 and drive north 1.7 miles. Turn left on FL 827 and go 6 miles to the ramp.

For more information: Call the refuge office at (561) 732-3684.

13. OKEEHEELEE PARK

Fresh; Bank and Boat; Ramp.

Description: A 157-acre lake here is part of the GFC's Urban Fishing Program. The lake has a fish feeder, attractor, and an aerator to help improve angling success.

Fishing Index: Largemouth bass are catch-and-release only. The lake is regularly stocked with channel catfish.

Directions: Exit I-95 onto Forest Hills Boulevard and drive 5.7 miles west to the park entrance.

14. LAKES OSBORNE AND IDA

Fresh; Bank and Boat; Ramps.

Description: The two lakes, 5.5 miles apart, are connected by a navigable canal. Miles of additional canals also join this system and offer a vast freshwater source for fishing. There are ramps at the Palm Beach County parks on each lake.

Fishing Index: The lakes are best fished early or late in the day. At other times anglers will be sharing the waters with pleasure boaters and water skiers. In summer, fish the lakes at night. Both lakes plus the canals have largemouth bass, bluegill, and catfish. In addition, the lakes are stocked with sunshine (hybrid) bass, which bite better during colder months.

Access Points:

14A. JOHN PRINCE PARK—*Bank and Boat; Ramp.*
Description: The park has a large campground and is only minutes from shopping districts and a few miles from the beach.
Directions: Exit I-95 onto 6th Avenue North and drive 1 mile west to the park entrance.

For more information: Call the park office at (561) 582-7992.

14B. LAKE IDA WEST PARK—*Bank and Boat; Ramp.*
Directions: Exit I-95 at Atlantic Boulevard (the Delray Beach exit). Go one block west on Atlantic, turn north on Congress Avenue, and go about 0.9 mile to Lake Ida Road. Turn right, go under the I-95 overpass, and look for the park on the left.

15. JUPITER INLET AND THE LOXAHATCHEE RIVER ———
Salt; Bank, Bridge and Boat; Ramp.

Description: The inlet is the mouth of the Loxahatchee River, a short, primarily tidal river that flows northeast to Jonathan Dickinson State Park. Officially this is not a maintained inlet. It does have shoals, but boaters use it on a daily basis. Use caution.

Fishing Index: Snook and tarpon are the major targets here. Both species are here year-round, but snook fishing is best from spring to fall and the largest tarpon show up in October and November.

For more information: Call Inlet Bait and Tackle at (561) 743-2248.

Access Points:
15A. BURT REYNOLDS PARK—*Bank and Boat; Ramp.*
Description: This is the closest ramp to Jupiter Inlet. Anglers can fish the Intracoastal Waterway from the banks. Sand perch and mangrove snapper are common catches.
Directions: The park is off of US 1 about 0.3 mile south of the US 1 bridge over the Loxahatchee River.

15B. DUBOIS PARK—*Bank.*
Description: The park is on the south shore of the Loxahatchee River. Anglers can fish the shoreline close to the inlet.
Directions: The park is just to the east of where A1A and US 1 split, south of the US 1 bridge over the Loxahatchee River.

15C. JUPITER BEACH PARK—*Pier; Surf.*
Description: This beachfront park provides access to the south jetty at Jupiter Inlet. A diversity of fish are found here thanks to the close proximity of the Gulf Stream. Look for snook, tarpon, bluefish, mutton snapper, whiting, pompano, and sand perch. In 1996, a paved cap over the rocks will make it easier and safer for anglers to fish from the jetty.
Directions: From the US 1 bridge over the Loxahatchee River, drive south and take A1A south 0.6 mile to the park.

16. LAKE WORTH

Salt, Bank, Pier, and Boat; Ramp.

Description: This 22-mile lagoon is recovering nicely from a long history of development and pollution. The sea grass beds have come back and so have the fish. A power plant in Riviera Beach discharges warm water into Lake Worth and is a local landmark for anglers.

Fishing Index: With a mix of sea grass flats, dock pilings, deep holes, mangroves, seawalls, channel markers, bridges, and the power plant "boil" there is no shortage of fishing spots. Deeper areas hold bluefish and snapper in winter. Go to the flats for snook. A crevalle jack can show up just about anywhere, and the warm water of the power plant boil attracts fish in winter, especially snook and tarpon.

The folks at Perks Bait and Tackle say the snook fishing is good at the south end from March to September. In fall, bluefish, pompano, and permit move in.

For more information: For the north part of Lake Worth, call Lott Brothers Tackle Shop at (561) 844-0244. For the central part, call 25th Street Bait and Tackle at (561) 655-3887. For the south end, call Perks Bait and Tackle at (561) 582-3133.

Access points:

16A. JOHN D. MAC ARTHUR BEACH STATE PARK—*Surf and Wade; $.*
Description: The park has a swimming beach, nature center, and an excellent example of a coastal hammock. Anglers can surf fish or wade the flats.
Directions: From US 1 in North Palm Beach, take A1A south 2.3 miles to the park.
For more information: Call the park office at (561) 624-6950.

16B. BURNT BRIDGE—*Bridge and Wade.*
Description: A locals' hangout. From the bridge, bottom fish for sand perch, sheepshead, and mangrove snapper. Or wade the flats around the bridge and fish for snook and redfish.
Directions: This is the A1A bridge at the north end of Lake Worth. From US 1 in North Palm Beach, take A1A south 2.3 miles to the bridge. The bridge is just outside the entrance to John D. Mac Arthur Beach State Park (Site 16A).

16C. PHIL FOSTER PARK—*Pier and Boat; Ramp.*
Description: This is the only public ramp close to Lake Worth Inlet. The pier is the remains of the old bridge across Lake Worth.
Directions: From US 1 in Riviera Beach, take Blue Heron Boulevard east 0.75 mile to the park. It is on Singer Island, a small patch of land midway between the bridges connecting the mainland to Palm Beach Shores.

16D. CURRY PARK—*Salt; Boat, Bank and Pier; Ramp.*
Description: This city park offers excellent access for land-bound anglers and boaters. There are three piers, a long seawall, and a 6-lane boat ramp.

Directions: Exit I-95 onto Palm Beach Lakes Boulevard and drive east to road's end at Flagler Drive. Turn left and go about 0.6 mile north to the park.

16E. FLAGLER BRIDGE—*Bridge, Bank and Boat.*

Description: Ed Weiner of 25th Street Bait and Tackle says this bridge is one of the best places locally to catch snook. Prime time is early fall. The bridge is also good for sheepshead, sand perch, pompano, black drum, and mangrove snapper.

Directions: Exit I-95 onto Palm Beach Lakes Boulevard and drive east to road's end at Flagler Drive. Turn right and go about 0.5 mile south to the bridge.

16F. LAKE WORTH SPILLWAY PARK—*Salt; Pier.*

Description: The spillway regulates freshwater discharge from the West Palm Beach Canal, which originates in Lake Okeechobee. This is a good snook hole when the spillway is open and during the colder months.

Directions: From the intersection with US 98 in Lake Worth, take US 1 (Olive Street) south 2.3 miles to Maryland Drive. Turn right and go 0.2 mile to the park.

16G. BRYANT PARK—*Salt; Boat, Bank and Bridge; Ramp.*

Description: The pier is part of an old bridge over Lake Worth.

Directions: From US 1 in Lake Worth, take FL 802 (Lake Worth Road) east 0.4 mile to the bridge. The ramp and pier are on the north side on the mainland.

16H. BICENTENNIAL SPORTSMAN'S PARK—*Bank, Bridge, and Boat.*

Description: The park is on the mainland side of the Lantana Bridge across Lake Worth; a good place for sheepshead, sand perch, mangrove snapper, and snook.

Directions: From US 1 in Lantana or A1A in Lantana Beach, turn onto Ocean Avenue and go 0.2 mile to the park from either direction.

16I. BOYNTON INLET PARK—*Boat; Ramp.*

Description: This is the closest ramp to Boynton Beach Inlet. From here you can also go south in Lake Worth about 0.5 mile to fish the Boynton Spillway on the mainland side. It is a good place for snook.

Directions: The ramp is on US 1 about 1.7 miles south of the US 1-Hypoluxo Road intersection or 1 mile north of the US 1-FL 804 intersection.

16J. BOYNTON BEACH INLET (OCEAN INLET)—*Bank and Surf.*

Description: Fish from the seawall along this narrow man-made inlet or from the surf by the southside jetty. There is a marina but no ramp inside the inlet. The water moves through this pass at an incredible rate when the tide is going in or out. Use caution, especially in winter. A sand bar outside the inlet sometimes snags boaters on rough-water days.

Directions: From the Lake Worth Pier, drive 4.6 miles south on A1A and look for the parking area on the south side of the inlet.

17. LAKE WORTH INLET

Salt; Boat.

Description: This urban inlet at Riviera Beach is completely surrounded by some of the most expensive real estate in Florida. The inlet serves a variety of recreational and commercial vessels including several cruise ships. The channel, blasted from the limestone rock bottom, reaches 40 feet in some places. Two boulder jetties protect and stabilize the inlet. The north jetty drops off sharply to the bottom while the south side has a slope to it before it reaches the channel drop off.

Fishing Index: The inlet produces some spectacular fishing. The Gulf Stream is very close offshore, bringing bluewater and pelagic fish close enough for a visit. Catching a sailfish or king mackerel is not unusual. Caught with more regularity are snook, tarpon, mangrove snapper, and crevalle jack. Snook action peaks in summer; redfish, African pompano, gag grouper, bluefish, and permit show up in winter. Anglers unfamiliar with the inlet's idiosyncrasies have the best luck drifting through the inlet using live baits or bouncing jigs off the bottom.

Directions: The inlet is near Riviera Beach. Access is from Phil Foster Park (16C) and Curry Park (16D).

18. LAKE WORTH PIER

Salt; Pier; $.

Description: This 960-foot pier has a reputation as one of the best fishing piers on Florida's Atlantic coast. Bait and tackle are available and there is a restaurant on the pier.

Fishing Index: Schools of live bait always seem to be around the pier and that's what brings in big fish. In summer, mangrove snapper and permit provide good action. It is not unusual for permit greater than 20 pounds to be taken here using sand crabs as bait. During the fall baitfish run, bluefish, pompano, and Spanish mackerel produce flurries of activity. By winter, cobia (in the 40- to 60-pound range) move in and are joined by a return of pompano in spring. Ted Rougas, the pier master, recommends fishing on the south side of the pier. "There are rocks from halfway out to the end and that's where you catch most of the snapper and snook. During snook season, in spring and fall the best time to fish for snook is from 7 to 9 a.m. and 4 to 7 p.m."

Directions: From US 1 in Lake Worth, take FL 802 (Lake Worth Road) east 0.9 mile to the junction with A1A. The pier is at this intersection.

For more information: Call the pier bait shop at (561) 582-9002.

19. PALM BEACH COUNTY BEACHES

Salt; Surf.

Description: Beach access is good in this county. Do not fish within the designated swimming areas where lifeguards are present. Those unfamiliar with the area can ask a lifeguard for directions or ask at a local tackle shop.

Fishing Index: Surf fishing is very good for a wide range of fish because the Gulf Stream runs close by. Spanish and cero mackerel, whiting, snook, tarpon, pompano, permit, and several species of snapper are caught from the beaches.

Directions: From north to south, the beach areas are Coral Cove, Jupiter Beach, Carlin, Juno Beach, Ocean Reef, Kreusler, Ocean Inlet, Caloosa, Gulf Stream, and South Inlet. All are accessible from A1A.

BROWARD AND DADE COUNTIES

20. WATER CONSERVATION AREA 2

Fresh; Boat and Bank; Ramp.

Description: The majority of this 210-square-mile marsh is not accessible to boaters. Instead, fish the perimeter canal if it's not choked with weeds. Check with a local bait and tackle store before you go.

Fishing Index: The canal is a popular place to fish for largemouth bass, bream, and Oscars. Land-bound anglers can pull off US 27 or FL 827 wherever it is safe and fish from the canal banks. This is a good place to cane pole fish for bluegills and Oscars.

Access Points:
20A. SAWGRASS RECREATION AREA—*Bank and Boat; Ramp.*
Description: Campground, boat rentals, and bait and tackle are on-site.
Directions: Exit I-75 onto US 27 and drive 2 miles north. The site is on the right.

20B. LOXAHATCHEE RECREATION AREA—*Bank and Boat; Ramp.*
Description: This site provides access to the Loxahatchee National Wildlife Refuge (Water Conservation Area 1) and Water Conservation Area 2.

Directions: West of Boca Raton, exit the Sawgrass Expressway onto US 441 and drive north 1.7 miles. Turn left on FL 827 and go 6 miles to the ramp.

For more information: Call Sawgrass Recreation Area at (561) 389-0202.

21. WATER CONSERVATION AREA 3

Fresh; Bank and Boat; Ramp.

Description: This section of the Everglades covers 730 square miles in western Dade and Broward counties. Fishing is limited to the perimeter canals. Miles of banks can be fished along the few local roads. Boat access is more limited but several ramps do the job.

Fishing Index: Largemouth bass are the top attraction for boaters. You can also bank fish for bass but the majority of land-based anglers go for bream, Oscars, and catfish. The GFC advises that largemouth bass, mudfish (bowfin), and gar caught in Water Conservation Areas 2a and 3 should not be eaten due to high mercury levels. Oscars are an aquarium escapee that has adapted to canal life and is proliferating. Oscars will bite almost any type of dead bait. They are not regulated by the GFC; anglers can keep as many as they want. The slightly pinkish and firm meat from the average 1-pound oscar is tasty.

Access Points:
21A. Everglades Holiday Park—*Boat and Bank; Ramp.*
Description: The park has a campground, bait and tackle, johnboat rentals, fishing guides, and airboat rides.
Directions: Exit I-75 onto US 27 (just east of the I-75 toll both), and drive south 5.75 miles to Griffin Road. Turn right and go about 0.5 mile to the park.
For more information: Call the park office at (954) 434-8111.

21B. Interstate 75 Recreation Areas—*Fresh; Bank and Boat; Ramp.*
Description: I-75 replaced the old two-lane toll road known as Alligator Alley that connected Fort Lauderdale to Naples. But it cut off what had been unlimited access along the old road and replaced it with five recreation areas. Each area has a ramp and bank fishing. The problem is access to the sites. Two sites are accessible only to westbound traffic, and the other three can be reached only by eastbound traffic. There are no turning lanes that allow you to cross the median. You will have to go to the Seminole Indian Reservation exit or to the east-end toll booth on I-75 in order to reverse direction.
Directions: From the toll booth at the east end of I-75 (near the junction with US 27), drive 6.5 miles to the first site on the westbound side. The next site westbound site is 13.5 miles from the toll booth. To reach the eastbound sites, take the exit for the Seminole Indian Reservation and return east on I-75. The eastbound sites are 7.9, 13.1, and 16.9 miles east from the Seminole Reservation exit.

21C. US 41 Boat Ramps—*Fresh; Bank and Boat; Ramp.*
Description: US 41 (the Tamiami Trail) connects Miami to the west coast of Florida beginning in Naples. Fish from miles of canal banks or launch at one of three boat ramps.
Directions: From Krome Avenue and US 41 (Dade Corners), take US 41 west. For the next 22 miles a canal runs along the north side of US 41. Pull off only where you can get completely off the road; this two-lane road is heavily traveled. Three dirt ramps accommodate boats up to 17 feet under ideal conditions. They are located about 12.5, 13.2, and 16.1 miles from the US 41-Krome intersection.

BROWARD AND DADE COUNTIES

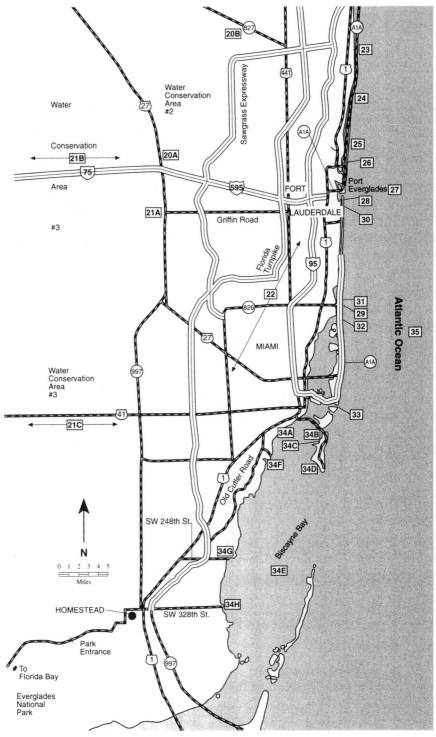

22. DADE AND BROWARD COUNTY URBAN CANALS ———

Fresh; Bank and Boat; Ramp.

Description: Several major and many minor canals around greater Miami and Fort Lauderdale are popular for peacock bass. Because this is a totally urban area, local knowledge is essential to finding the access points and the fish. Your best bet, if unfamiliar with the area is to hire a guide.

Fishing Index: Anglers fish these canals for butterfly peacock bass. Introduced by the GFC in 1984 to help control other exotic fish, butterflies flourished. They feed only during the day and prefer live bait. Some anglers use artificial baits that resemble small fish. Most fish caught weigh between 1.5 and 2 pounds. The South American peacock bass also lives in the canals. It is a much larger fish but is not caught as often. Anglers can keep two butterfly bass under current regulations, but all South American bass must be released unharmed as soon as they are caught.

Directions: Consult the bait and tackle shops in Dade and Broward counties. Most of them can direct you to areas where it is safe to fish and launch a boat. They also can recommend a guide who specializes in butterfly peacock bass fishing.

For more information: Call Neil Cobo at The Fishing Line (the epicenter for peacock bass enthusiasts) at (305) 598-2444.

23. DEERFIELD PIER ———

Salt; Pier; $.

Description: This beach pier was rebuilt in 1993. The pier bait shop is never closed.

Fishing Index: This 920-foot pier places anglers within easy casting distance of cobia and king mackerel. Look for them migrating north in spring and south in fall. Spanish mackerel are year-round residents. Snook are common and bluefish make an appearance in fall. Live bait is the choice of experienced anglers.

Directions: From US 1 in Deerfield Beach, drive 0.9 mile east on Hillsboro Boulevard. Turn left onto A1A and go 0.3 mile to the pier.

For more information: Call the pier bait shop at (954) 480-4423.

24. FISHERMAN'S WHARF PIER ———

Salt; Pier; $.

Description: The 1,080-foot pier has a restaurant, bar, and bait and tackle shop. Nearby is a playground on the beach.

Fishing Index: Snook, tarpon, and mangrove and yellowtail snapper are plentiful in summer. Spanish mackerel are caught year-round along with jacks and barracuda. In fall, bluefish and pompano arrive in good numbers and are joined by some cobia. These fish remain through winter in lower numbers but then increase in spring.

Directions: From the intersection of US 1 and Atlantic Boulevard (FL 814), take Atlantic Boulevard east 0.7 mile to A1A. Turn left and go two blocks to Second Street. Turn right and go 1 block to Pompano Beach Boulevard and the pier.

For more information: Call the pier office at (954) 943-1488.

25. ANGLIN'S FISHING PIER
Salt; Pier; $.

Description: This 875-foot pier in Lauderdale-by-the-Sea has been a favorite for anglers for years.

Fishing Index: Fish year-round for snook, crevalle jack, barracuda, and Spanish mackerel. In summer, the best action comes from blue runners, jacks, and barracuda in the day and mangrove snapper and tarpon at night. Pompano make a good showing in spring and fall along with large numbers of Spanish mackerel. Snook are popular in fall mainly because it's legal then to keep up to two fish.

Directions: From the intersection of Commercial Boulevard and US 1, take Commercial Boulevard east 1.1 miles to the intersection with A1A. Continue east two blocks on Commercial to the pier.

For more information: Call the pier bait shop at (305) 491-9403.

26. HUGH TAYLOR BIRCH STATE RECREATION AREA
Salt; Bank; $.

Description: A beachfront park with a group campground, canoe trail, and exercise course.

Fishing Index: Fish the Intracoastal Waterway off the seawall for mangrove snapper.

Directions: The park is at the intersection of East Sunrise Boulevard and A1A in Fort Lauderdale.

For more information: Call the park office at (954) 564-4521.

27. PORT EVERGLADES
Salt; Boat.

Description: A major shipping and cruise ship port that offers good boat fishing. During the coldest months fishing is very good in the canals around the port. The warm outflow canal of the power plant draws many fish then.

Fishing Index: Mangrove snapper and small tarpon are caught around the rock jetties of the port entrance year-round. Snook are there much of the year but are a best in summer. A good pompano run in fall is followed by the season peak of bluefish and Spanish mackerel in winter. Sheepshead are caught all year but the best fishing is during winter around the jetties and around the docks. The best time for big tarpon is in winter around the power plant canals.

Directions: The port is in Fort Lauderdale. Closest boat access is John U. Lloyd Beach State Recreation Area (see Site 28).

For more information: Call T and R Tackle at (954) 776-1055.

28. JOHN U. LLOYD STATE RECREATION AREA
Salt; Pier, Surf and Boat; Ramp; $.

Description: The park occupies a small peninsula on the south side of Port Everglades. Anglers can fish from the jetty on the south side of the port entrance. It is capped and is easily accessed.

Fishing Index: The waters of the inlet are good for Spanish mackerel in spring and fall, pompano in fall and early winter, and grouper and snapper year-round. Boaters who fish the port entrance can follow the big tarpon that show up in October and gradually move into nearby warm-water canals.

Directions: From Fort Lauderdale, drive south on US 1 to Dania Beach Boulevard (A1A) in Dania. Drive about 2.1 miles east on A1A to the park.

For more information: Call the park office at (954) 923-2833.

29. NEWPORT FISHING PIER
Salt; Pier

Description: This 918-foot pier is open 24 hours and has bait and tackle.

Fishing Index: Spanish mackerel fishing is best during fall and spring. A few king mackerel are also caught during their yearly run south. In summer fish for mangrove snapper, jacks, and barracuda. In winter, whiting, sharks, and some cobia make up the bulk of the action.

Directions: The pier is located where Sunny Isles Boulevard dead ends into A1A in North Miami Beach.

For more information: Call the pier bait shop at (305) 949-1300

30. DANIA PIER
Salt; Pier; $.

Description: This 922-foot pier was completely rebuilt in 1994. It has a reputation for consistently good fishing. Bait, tackle, and rentals are available.

A long-handled gaff comes in handy when bringing a small shark on board.

Fishing Index: Seasonally, snook, pompano, and Spanish mackerel are caught along with a near constant supply of yellowtail and mutton snapper.

Directions: From US 1 in Dania, drive about 2 miles east on Dania Beach Boulevard (A1A) to the pier.

For more information: Call the pier bait shop at (954) 927-0640.

31. OLETA RIVER STATE RECREATION AREA ——————
Salt; Pier and Bank.

Description: This large urban park is on Biscayne Bay in North Miami.

Fishing Index: Fish from the park's pier for sheepshead, mangrove snapper, and small tarpon.

Directions: From US 1 in North Miami, take Sunny Isles Boulevard (FL 826) east 1 mile to the park entrance on the right.

For more information: Call the park office at (305) 919-1846.

32. HAULOVER INLET ——————
Salt; Bank and Boat.

Description: A small county park affords landbound anglers access.

Fishing Index: Fish the rock-lined banks for mangrove and mutton snapper. The inlet is a favorite hangout for snook and tarpon.

Directions: From the intersection of Collins Avenue and the Sunny Isles Causeway (FL 826), take Collins Avenue south 2 miles to the park.

For more information: Call Haulover Inlet Park at (305) 947-3525.

33. GOVERNMENT CUT ——————
Salt; Boat.

Description: This is the main shipping channel to the port of Miami. It is also popular with anglers.

Fishing Index: Bottom fish for grouper and snapper around ocean jetties; also a very good place for tarpon. Winter brings the best fishing, biggest fish.

Directions: The cut passes through the upper part of Biscayne Bay. The closest public ramp is at Crandon Marina on Key Biscayne. From US 1 in Miami, take the Rickenbacker Causeway to Key Biscayne where it becomes Crandon Boulevard. Take this road 5.8 miles to the marina (see site 34C).

34. BISCAYNE BAY

Salt; Boat; Ramp.

Description: Biscayne Bay's clear, shallow water is rich with sea grass. A series of islands shelters the bay from the Atlantic Ocean. The southern two-thirds of the bay are part of Biscayne National Park.

Fishing Index: Bonefish have made Biscayne Bay famous. The best fishing is south of Cape Florida in or near Biscayne National Park. Stiltsville is one of the best known spots. Anglers fish the flats on either side of the finger channels here. Bonefish move onto the flats to feed when the water is between 74 and 86 degrees.

Live shrimp is the preferred natural bait but a jig tipped with a piece of fresh shrimp also works well. Fly fishing is also popular.

Permit also feed on the flats and are a popular target for sight-casters. Small crabs are the preferred bait. Snook, Spanish mackerel, bluefish, mangrove and mutton snapper, barracuda, and small sharks are also caught in the bay.

To avoid the crowds, fish here during the week.

Access Points:

34A. DINNER KEY MARINA—*Boat; Ramp.*
Description: A Dade County park.
Directions: From US 1 in Miami, take SW 27th Avenue about 0.8 mile south to road's end at the park.
For more information: Call the marina office at (305) 579-6980.

34B. BEAR CUT BRIDGE—*Bridge.*
Description: Fish in the cut between Biscayne Bay and the Atlantic Ocean from the bridge catwalk.
Directions: From US 1 in Miami, take the Rickenbacker Causeway to Key Biscayne, where it becomes Crandon Boulevard. Continue 5.6 miles to the bridge.

34C. CRANDON PARK MARINA—*Boat; Ramp.*
Description: The marina is home to several charter boats that fish the Atlantic Ocean and Biscayne Bay.
Directions: From US 1 in Miami, take the Rickenbacker Causeway to Key Biscayne, where it becomes Crandon Boulevard. Continue 5.8 miles to the marina. It is just across the Bear Cut Bridge on Key Biscayne.
For more information: Call the marina office at (305) 361-1281. For fishing charter information try L and H Charters at (305) 361-9318.

34D. CAPE FLORIDA STATE RECREATION AREA—*Bank; $.*
Description: This day-use park was severely damaged by Hurricane Andrew but has been rebuilt. Fish for snook, crevalle jack, and snappers (from the seawall.)
Directions: From US 1 in Miami, take the Rickenbacker Causeway to Key

Biscayne, where it becomes Crandon Boulevard. Follow this road about 6.6 miles until it ends at the park entrance.

For more information: Call the park office at (305) 361-5811.

34E. BISCAYNE NATIONAL PARK—*Boat.*

Description: The waters of Biscayne Bay make up the majority of this 181,500 acre park. The only land areas are the mainland shoreline and several islands. The park does not maintain any public boat ramps. Access is from three Dade County parks. All state fishing regulations apply in the park except those for lobstering (Florida crayfish). The park is a lobster sanctuary and is closed to harvesting.

Directions: The park headquarters and visitor center are located at Convoy Point. From US 1 in Homestead, take SW 328 Street (North Canal Road) east about 8.1 miles to the visitor center.

34F. MATHESON HAMMOCK PARK—*Boat; Ramp.*

Description: A Dade County park.

Directions: From US 1 in South Miami, take Kendall Drive (FL 94) east 2.3 miles to where it deadends at Old Cutler Road. Turn right and go about 0.5 mile to the park entrance.

34G. BLACK POINT PARK—*Boat; Ramp.*

Description: A Dade County park.

Directions: Exit the Florida Turnpike onto Allapattah Road and go north 0.2

There are plenty of charter boats for hire in Florida. Don't be afraid to ask questions and tell the captain what you are interested in catching. They want you to be happy so you'll recommend them to your friends.

mile to SW 248 Street (Coconut Palm Drive). Turn right and go east 2.6 miles to the park entrance.

34H. HOMESTEAD BAYFRONT PARK—*Boat; Ramp.*
Description: A Dade County park. The national park headquarters is next door.
Directions: From US 1 in Homestead, take SW 328 Street (North Canal Road) east about 8.1 miles to the park.
For more information: Call the park headquarters at (305) 230-7275.

35. ATLANTIC OCEAN (FORT PIERCE TO MIAMI) ———
Salt; Boat.

Description: Offshore fishing is a major activity along the southeast coast and in the Keys. The Gulf Stream swings toward shore around Palm Beach and brings blue water and ocean sport fish within reach of anglers with smaller offshore boats.

Fishing Index: Wahoo action is best off Fort Pierce in spring and fall but fish are present all year. Sailfish are caught all year. Winter is traditionally best, but a fair number of fish can be caught in summer by changing tactics and fishing in deeper water. KDW is how local offshore anglers refer to the top three species they catch. King mackerel are caught year-round but peak in spring and fall. Dolphin (mahi-mahi on the menu of local restaurants) are in their prime in summer but remain well offshore. Wahoo are caught every month of the year.

Grouper and snapper are popular bottom fish. In summer, fish for snapper after dark.

Directions: Stop in any community between Fort Pierce and Miami. More than 100 charter boats operate in this area. Most of the ocean-going charters are based near Fort Pierce, Saint Lucie, Jupiter, and Lake Worth inlets. Indian River and Lake Worth guides often use the ramps closest to their customers or where the best fishing happens to be. From Fort Lauderdale to Miami, charter boats operate from local marinas.

For more information: Look in the phone book under fishing charters.

MONROE COUNTY (FLORIDA BAY AND THE KEYS)

The only major road in the Keys, US 1, runs 110 miles from Key Largo to mile marker 0 at Key West. Everybody refers to the mile markers along the route when giving directions ("Joe's Bait Shop is at mile 63"), and the terms "bay side" and "ocean side" are used to distinguish one side of the road from the other. Many of the old highway bridges, bypassed by newer spans, are open for anglers to use.

36. FLORIDA (UPPER PART) AND WHITEWATER BAYS————

Salt; Boat; Ramp.

Description: Florida Bay spreads between the Keys and the mainland's southern tip. Whitewater Bay is an inland brackish-water bay surrounded by mangrove forests. Both bays are within the boundaries of Everglades National Park and are linked by the man-made Buttonwood Canal near the park's Flamingo Visitor Center. There are two ramps here. One provides easy access to Florida Bay and the other is the quickest way to Whitewater Bay.

Fishing Index: Anglers come here to fish for snook, redfish, spotted seatrout, and tarpon, and to enjoy the spectacular scenery. Captain Ned Lentz, one of five guides operating out of Flamingo Lodge, says there is more to fishing this area than catching a fish every few casts. "Here, you can see an alligator and a crocodile in the same glance, then turn your head and watch a flock of a hundred birds. When fishing in this area, look beyond your cast; the scenery is magnificent."

Snook fishing is very good year-round. Snook are everywhere when the water is warm. When it cools off, they head up the tidal creeks in search of deep holes, frequently moving into the freshwater currents. Redfish and spotted seatrout prefer sea grass beds in the bays. During all but the hottest and coldest days of the year, you can easily sight cast to the fish if the water is clear enough. Trout action is traditionally best during winter. Tarpon anglers looking for the biggest fish should come between mid-May and early July.

Fishing "out front" in Florida Bay is centered within a 5-mile radius of Flamingo. The bottom here is too muddy to wade fish (walking clouds the water), so plan on using a flat-bottomed boat. Florida Bay is also usually too murky to fish during much of the winter and spring. Whitewater Bay is known as the "backwater," a popular winter angling spot.

Hire a guide if you're new to the area. If you use your own boat, take a good chart and refer to it often. The bay is shallow and it is easy to stray off course, run aground, or cut across a sea grass bed. You will be fined for mowing through sea grass or running into coral. Prop scars take years to grow back and hasten the decline of sea grasses. Also carry a copy of the state and national park fishing rules and an accurate measuring device. Law enforcement rangers will check your catch.

Directions: From US 1 in Florida City, take SW 344th Street west and follow the signs 8.3 miles to the park entrance. From the main visitor center follow the park road 38 miles to Flamingo.

For more information: For general information about fishing in the area, call the Flamingo Lodge (305) 253-2241 and ask for the marina. To make a reservation at the lodge or book a guide, call 1 800 600-3813. For general information about Everglades National Park, call (305) 247-6211.

MONROE COUNTY (FLORIDA BAY AND THE KEYS)

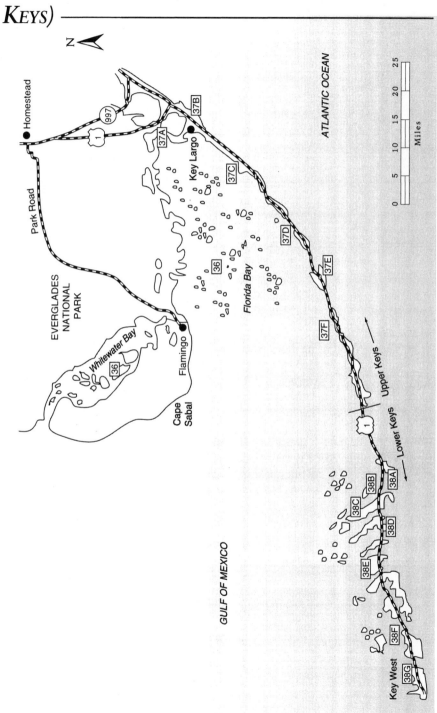

37. Upper Keys

Salt; Boat, Bridge, and Wade; Ramp.

Description: From Key Largo to Marathon on Upper Matecumbe Key, anglers can access the backcountry waters of Florida Bay, the ocean-side and bay-side flats, most of the bridges connecting the individual Keys, the reefs and wrecks in the Atlantic Ocean, and the blue waters of the Gulf Stream.

Fishing Index: Fishing is always good in the Keys because most species are present year-round. But peak times vary for specific species. Refer to the following list when planning a trip to the upper Keys.

Species	Location	Peak Time
Bonefish	Ocean and bayside flats	March-May; Sept-Nov
Snook	Backcountry (Florida Bay)	December-February
Redfish	Backcountry (Florida Bay)	October-November
Tarpon	Backcountry, Channels	mid April-June
King mackerel	Bluewater, Channels	June-August
Reef Fish	Reefs, Channels	June-August
Permit	Reefs (calm weather days)	July-August
Dolphin	Blue Water	June-August
Sailfish	Blue Water	November-January
Blue marlin	Blue Water	June-August

Access Points:
There are numerous marinas in the Keys. Most have ramps or hoists. The fees for using a private facility range from $10 to $20. While this is expensive compared to every place else in Florida, this is the normal fee for the Keys. The number of free ramps is very limited so your best bet is to go to your destination and use the marina most convenient to where you want to fish.

37A. Little Blackwater Sound—*Boat; Ramp.*
Description: The ramp is maintained by Everglades National Park. There is no charge to use the ramp but parking is limited. From this site, anglers can access the backcountry of eastern Florida Bay. The water is very shallow; use extreme caution.
Directions: The ramp is on the bay side near mile marker 111 on US 1.

37B. John Pennekamp State Park—*Boat; Ramp; $.*
Description: 70 nautical square miles of coral reefs, mangroves, and sea grass beds form the first underwater state park in the United States. The heavily used park offers a campground, picnic area, canoe trails, glass-bottom boat tours, snorkeling, and SCUBA diving. The park ramp provides easy access to the reefs in the park and beyond.
Directions: The park is on the ocean side at mile marker 102.5.
For more information: Call the park office at (305) 451-1202.

37C. Harry Harris Park—*Boat; Ramp.*
Description: A Monroe County park on the bay side.
Directions: In Tavernier at mile marker 92.5, turn onto Burton Drive. The

park is at the end of the road. Look for the signs.

37D. INDIAN KEY—*Boat; Ramp.*
Description: A limerock ramp maintained by the Florida Department of Transportation. Adequate parking.
Directions: Bay side at mile marker 78.

37E. LONG KEY STATE RECREATION AREA—*Salt; Wade; $.*
Description: The park has a campground and swimming beach. Anglers can wade fish the flats for bonefish, permit, and tarpon.
Directions: The park is ocean side at mile marker 67.5.
For more information: Call the park office at (305) 664-4815.

37F. COUNTY BOAT RAMP—*Boat; Ramp.*
Description: A Monroe County facility on the bay side.
Directions: The ramp is at the north end of Marathon at mile marker 54.

Additional sources of information in the upper Keys:
Papa Joe's Marina - 1 800-539-8326; mile marker 79.7. Good source of information about backcountry fishing; eleven guides that fish the backcountry.

Bonefish Bob's - (305) 664-9420; in Islamorada. Owner Bob Berger is a good source of information.

Rod-bending action is easy to come by in the Keys.

Bud and Mary's Marina - (305) 664-2461; at mile marker 80. Owner Richard Stanczyk and his employees in the bait and tackle shop have a wealth of information about offshore fishing. A large charter boat fleet operates from the marina.

Whale Harbor Marina - (305) 664-4511; at mile marker 84. Another good place to get information or charter a boat for offshore fishing.

38. LOWER KEYS

Salt; Boat, Bridge, and Wade; Ramp.

Description: From Seven Mile Bridge to Key West there are many angling opportunities in the ocean- and bayside flats, channels, Gulf of Mexico and Atlantic Ocean wrecks, coral reefs, and the blue water.

Fishing Index: Again, fishing is good year-round (except for redfish), but peak times vary for specific species. Refer to the following list, courtesy of Captain Jim Sharpe of Sea Boots Charters. The backcountry here consists of islands on the Gulf side that extend from Big Pine Key to Key West.

Species	Location	Peak Time
Bonefish	Ocean and bayside Flats	August-October
Snook	Bridges and Backcountry	September-December
Tarpon	Flats and Channels	January-August
King mackerel	Bluewater, Channels	Jan-April; Nov-Dec
Reef Fish	Reefs, Channels	June-October
Permit	Flats, Channels, Wrecks	October
Dolphin	Blue Water	March-October
Sailfish	Blue Water	Jan-May; Aug-Dec
Blue Marlin	Blue Water	April-November
White Marlin	Blue Water	Feb-March; May-July
Wahoo	Blue Water	Jan-April; Aug-Dec

Access Points:
38A. BAHIA HONDA STATE RECREATION AREA—*Wade and Boat; Ramp; $.*
Description: This popular park has ocean- and bay-side facilities. During peak season there may be a waiting line to enter the park. The park has a campground, swimming beach, bayside cabins, and commercial dive trips to Looe Key. The park's two boat ramps offer convenient access to the Atlantic Ocean or the lower Keys backcountry.
Directions: The park entrance is on the ocean side at mile marker 36.5.
For more information: Call the park office at (305) 872-2353.

38B. SPANISH HARBOR WAYSIDE PARK—*Boat; Ramp.*
Description: The ramp is free and there is good parking.
Directions: On West Summerland Key, at mile marker 34.

38C. KOEHN AVENUE RAMP—*Boat; Ramp.*
Description: A small county ramp that is suitable for shallow draft boats. Water

near the ramp is about 2 feet at low tide. It is a good access point to the lower Keys backcountry.

Directions: At the north end of Big Pine Key. From US 1 in Big Pine Key, turn north on Key Deer Boulevard. Go about 3.4 miles to Big Pine Street. Turn right and go 0.6 mile to Koehn Avenue. Turn left and go to the ramp at road's end.

38D. LITTLE TORCH KEY RAMP—*Boat; Ramp.*
Description: A free Monroe County ramp on Newfound Harbor Channel. A good paved ramp with adequate parking.
Directions: On Little Torch Key, at about mile marker 28, turn south on Old State Road 4A. The ramp is just off of US 1.

38E. CUDJOE KEY RAMP—*Boat; Ramp.*
Description: This free ramp accesses the backcountry via Kemp Channel. Suitable only for shallow draft boats.
Directions: On Cudjoe Key, at about mile marker 23, turn north on Blimp Road. The ramp is about 2.5 miles north of US 1.

38F. SHARK KEY RAMP—*Boat; Ramp.*
Description: An ocean-side Monroe County ramp. Beware of the tight turns for trailers.
Directions: The ramp is at mile marker 11.5.

38G. STOCK ISLAND RAMP—*Boat; Ramp.*
Description: An ocean-side Monroe County ramp.
Directions: The ramp, at mile marker 5, is the closest public ramp to Key West.

Boats in the Keys often congregate in the same area once they locate a school of yellowtail snapper.

The Florida Keys

No place in Florida hosts as many species of saltwater gamefish as the Keys. Choosing from the 70 or so species is surpassed in difficulty only by selecting from the hundreds of places to fish for them. The easiest way to get a handle on fishing the Keys is to think in terms of six fishing grounds: flats, coral reefs, bridges, channels, wrecks, and blue water. These areas are described below:

Flats

Flats are shallows with anywhere from a few inches to a few feet of water, depending on the tide. Typically the bottom is covered with dense sea grass beds with scattered open, sandy areas. Extensive flats are found on the Florida Bay and Gulf of Mexico side of the Keys. A comparatively narrow but highly productive ribbon of flats is also found along the nearshore ocean-side waters.

Bonefish—year-round residents—are one of the most sought-after species on the flats. Captain Paul Tejera (call (305) 852-7888), a fly fishing specialist, fishes the upper Keys for bonefish. "I like to fish the ocean-side flats on a low rising tide." In the lower Keys, Captain Jim Sharpe, owner of Sea Boots Charters (call 1 800-238-1746), says the best time for bonefish is in September and October.

Also expect barracuda and small sharks throughout the Keys and permit in the lower Keys. All are fun to catch on light spinning tackle or by fly fishing. While the majority of the flats are accessible only by boat, there are several areas where anglers can park their car and wade. In the upper Keys try the ocean-side flats near Newport, just south of John Pennekamp Coral Reef State Park. In the lower Keys, walk from shore onto the ocean-side flats from Bahia Honda State Recreation Area.

Coral Reefs

Anglers flock to the reefs in search of snapper, grouper, barracuda, and other species. Boaters should refer frequently to good charts here to find the best spots and to avoid running aground. Some of the reefs are heavily used by divers and a few areas are closed to anglers. Before you go, check with a local tackle or dive shop to make sure you have the latest information.

Reef fishing is good throughout the Keys but is considered better in the lower Keys. The lower Keys see less boat traffic and fishing pressure. Fish for yellowtail snapper by using a chum line to get the fish biting. It takes some skill to do this and if you haven't done it before, consider a day trip on a party boat. Captain David Jensen operates the party boat Caloosa out of Whale Harbor Marina at mile marker 83.5; call (305) 852-3200 for more information. Jensen specializes in yellowtail snapper fishing. "One of the keys to a successful trip," he says, "is to fish at the level where the yellowtails are."

While that sounds simple, only experience can tell you how much lead is needed to get your bait to the right depth.

Sometimes sailfish temporarily leave the deep water to raid schools of baitfish on the ocean-side of a reef. Because the transition from reef to deep water is so well defined, this is a good area to look for that errant sailfish.

The reefs are also prime locations for spiny lobster "fishing." This crawfish lacks the claws found on New England lobsters, but the meat from the tail is sweet and tender. There is a two-day sport fisherman's season on the last consecutive Wednesday and Thursday in July. The regular season, open to recreational divers and commercial trappers, begins in early August. Strict rules govern the taking of crayfish.

BRIDGES

The many bridges that link the Keys are fish magnets. Anglers with boats can fish around any bridge pilings they can safely reach. Anglers without boats can fish from many bridges, and also around the embankments of any bridges they can access.

Snook, tarpon, shark, snapper, grouper, and occasionally some open water fish such as king mackerel are caught around the bridges here. Boaters have the advantage over land-based anglers because they can reach more bridges, have the ability to drift with a big fish they are fighting, and don't have to haul their catch from the water to the bridge's road surface, a distance frequently over 25 feet. Nonetheless, with a stout rod and reel, some heavy line, and a good bridge gaff (a weighted grappling hook tied to a rope), bridge anglers routinely catch big tarpon, shark, grouper, and snapper.

Sight casting to fish on the flats is easy in the clear waters of the Florida Keys. The thrill of seeing a big tarpon like this one is more than enough to get an angler's attention.

CHANNELS

In addition to the channels between islands, there are numerous channels between the flats in Florida Bay. Navigating the channels on the shallow bay side of Key Largo requires considerable local knowledge.

The channels in the lower Keys are a completely different story. There is good fishing for a variety of fish. Anglers are likely to encounter snapper, bonefish, barracuda, shark, and tarpon just about any time. Fish the channels during the hottest parts of the summer days.

WRECKS

Hundreds of wrecks off the lower Keys offer reliable fishing. Many are well-known sites and their LORAN coordinates are common knowledge.

Grouper, snapper, permit, barracuda, shark, amberjack, cobia and king, cero, and Spanish mackerel are regular inhabitants of wrecks. Like the other fishing grounds in the Keys, wrecks are great places to fish all year. Standard baits include cut bait, live shrimp, and jigs tipped with shrimp and crabs. If there is any complaint about wreck fishing it's the barracuda. The voracious predators are abundant around most wrecks and frequently share half of your fish with you. Usually they take the rear half of what you've hooked and so seldom hook themselves.

BLUEWATER

Dolphin, sailfish, wahoo, tuna, king mackerel, blue and white marlin, and big, big sharks inhabit the 200- to 2,000-foot deep waters of the Atlantic Ocean. Water depths in excess of 200 feet begin a few miles off shore in some areas.

Islamorada and Key West are the focal points for offshore charter boats. Sailfish and dolphin are the popular targets here. Both species are caught year-round; the best sailfish action is from November through January and the best dolphin fishing is during summer in the upper Keys. In the lower Keys, sailfish season peaks from December through April and prime time for dolphin is from April through September.

Boats fishing for marlin in the upper Keys often head to an area in the Atlantic called The Humps. Here mounds rise from the ocean floor and come to within a few hundred feet of the surface.

About 20 miles south of Key West, The Wall is one of the most famous locations for marlin, big sharks, tuna, and wahoo. Here the bottom plummets 2,000 feet below the surface. Anglers who want the best shot at catching these fish should plan a trip to the lower Keys in April or May, according to Captain Jim Sharpe. Go on a charter boat—the best offshore captains will often interview prospective clients to find out what they really want to catch.

This good-sized yellowtail snapper was caught with a piece of cut bait in a chum slick. Chumming is a traditional method used by anglers in the Keys for catching these tasty fish.

Month by Month in Southeast Florida*

Note: Offshore is defined as farther than 2 miles from the coast. Inshore/Bays are open waters within 5 miles including surf fishing areas, and all brackish waters such as bays, the saltwater regions of rivers, and lagoons. Freshwater includes lakes, ponds, reservoirs, and rivers.

*This chart does not reflect the monthly activity in the Florida Keys. Generally, all the fish species in the Keys are year round residents. The peak season for the major species is provided in the Fishing index section for the upper and lower Keys listings.

January

Offshore: Sailfish is the best bet if the seas aren't too rough.

Inshore/Bays: An excellent time to surf fish for bluefish and whiting. Snook and spotted seatrout action is very good in Florida Bay. Excellent sheepshead fishing in Port Everglades.

Freshwater: First of the best months for largemouth bass. Crappie action rapidly escalates this month.

February

Offshore: A repeat of the top sailfish action seen in January; also some wahoo and blackfin tuna in the Gulf Stream. Weather dictates when to go fishing. Several shark species in their prime this month and next.

Inshore/Bays: Bluefish and whiting reward surf anglers this month. Use a 10- to 12-foot surf rod; may need to wade to reach the fish in the trough. Spotted seatrout action is very good in Florida Bay. Another top month for snook. Fish for them up the tidal creeks of Whitewater Bay. Some big tarpon hide in the canals around Port Everglades.

Freshwater: One of the peak months for trophy largemouth bass. The best bait are live wild shiners. Also prime crappie fishing season. Fish Lake Okeechobee with Missouri minnows.

March

Offshore: A top month for king mackerel as they begin migrating north. Dolphin also become more numerous. Spanish mackerel also migrate north; fish for them from piers. A prime month for offshore shark fishing.

Inshore/Bays: Traditionally an above-average month for the backwater big three: redfish, spotted seatrout, and snook. Redfish and trout action is prime. Snook action is good, but improves during next two months. Surf fishing slows as bluefish head north. In Palm Beach County, anglers using live bait may find a king mackerel. Bonefish prowl the flats in good numbers.

Freshwater: The peak bass spawn is ending; fishing is still good but may have some slow periods. Crappie action also slows unless you can find cooler water in Lake Okeechobee and the canals.

APRIL

Offshore: King mackerel are abundant; dolphin and wahoo are consistent. A sailfish or marlin may also be caught. Spanish mackerel continue to be very good. Small schools of cobia add to the mix.

Inshore/Bays: Another above-average month for redfish, snook, and spotted seatrout, especially around the inside of the inlets and in the lagoons. A top month for bonefish on the flats. There may be a few permit around too.

Freshwater: Largemouth bass have moved off their beds. Anglers should work weedlines and pepper grass patches in Lake Okeechobee. Bluegill start to bed by the end of the month—good fishing for the next three months.

MAY

Offshore: Peak dolphin season begins this month. Wahoo, sailfish, marlin, and king mackerel may also take the bait. Traditionally a very good month for bluewater anglers. Pier anglers will see Spanish mackerel.

Inshore/Bays: Snook fishing around inlets is a best bet. If it doesn't get too hot early in the year, there will still be good fishing for redfish and spotted seatrout in Florida Bay. A great month for bonefish. Because of the midday heat, start fishing early or late in the day or at night.

Freshwater: Bluegills are on their beds and that translates into top action. Largemouth bass and crappie action slow for summer. Crappie still bite but only if you fish the deeper spots. Bass anglers should avoid fishing in midday for the next few months.

JUNE

Offshore: Dolphin lead the way for top action in summer. Over the wrecks, anglers will find good snapper and grouper action. This is the beginning of the best months for big mangrove snapper.

Inshore/Bays: Snook fishing is always very good in Florida Bay, but mosquitoes emerge in hordes. Snook season is closed so it's strictly catch-and-release for this species. The flats and deeper channels between them are good places to look for tarpon now.

Freshwater: Fish early or late in the day for a chance at catching largemouth bass. Catfish are easy to catch year-round in Lake Okeechobee but not too many anglers fish for them. A catfish fry is a great activity for the weekend.

JULY

Offshore: Mangrove and yellowtail snapper are a popular summer quarry. The best action is at night. Dolphin still run the blue waters.

Inshore/Bays: Bonefish and permit, fished early or late in the day, are the best bet. Check the tide table to make sure the water is either coming onto or going off the flats. Big tarpon are found in Florida Bay now. They move around a lot, so try to get some information from a local source. Surf fish with light tackle and live sand fleas or clams for pompano.

Freshwater: A slow month. Try night fishing for largemouth bass. For fun, try Oscar fishing in the US 41 canal in the Everglades. The fish bite readily and give a good fight on ultralight tackle.

August

Offshore: Tops on the list are dolphin for bluewater anglers and grouper and snapper for bottom anglers. Some days will be better than others. The best bet for guaranteed fish is a night snapper trip to the reefs or a wreck.

Inshore/Bays: Fish for snook at night in the tidal rivers and canals. In Biscayne Bay, permit are on the flats longer during the day than bonefish because they can tolerate slightly higher water temperatures.

Freshwater: If you really want to catch fish, find a good guide. The fish are out there, but knowing where and when to fish, especially in Lake Okeechobee, is important. Remember, the fish don't like the heat any more than you do.

September

Offshore: Usually, this is the last of the hot, thunderstorm-infested months. Fishing is a mixed bag. No bluewater fish is at its peak but all the typical species are out there. Night fishing for snapper may be the best bet.

Inshore/Bays: Night is the best time to fish for snook and snook are one of the best bets this month. With a boat, try fishing the saltwater canals in Fort Lauderdale. Snook hang out around the docks.

Freshwater: A slow month; not much change in activity or strategy since June.

October

Offshore: The migrants are returning and that signals the start of the fall king mackerel run. Cobia accompany the mackerel. Grouper, amberjack, and snapper are still caught in good numbers over wrecks and reefs.

Inshore/Bays: Redfish and spotted seatrout activity begins to pick up in Florida Bay. Bonefish and permit are on the flats but will head for the deeper waters of the adjacent channels if it gets too cool. Snook anglers will be out in force once the season opens. Surf anglers start to see more pompano.

Freshwater: The first sign of cooler weather perks up largemouth bass action in Lake Okeechobee and surrounding canals.

November

Offshore: King and Spanish mackerel and cobia are top choices this month. Sailfish activity begins to build toward the winter peak.

Inshore/Bays: Bluefish arrive and surf anglers dig out their big rods and reels. Snook, seatrout, and redfish are in their fall prime.

Freshwater: The cool water stimulates the appetites of largemouth bass. You may not catch many big fish, but you can catch a lot of fish this month. Crappie action can be very good if the water temperature cools off faster than normal.

DECEMBER

Offshore: Above-average month for Spanish and king mackerel. These fish will be around for a month or so before the kings head south to the Keys for winter. Spanish mackerel stay in the area through winter. Dolphin activity slows but the peak for sailfish begins this month or next.

Inshore/Bays: Bluefish and pompano action from the surf are best bets. In the lagoons and saltwater rivers, sheepshead are in top form around the bridges and causeways. Snook, redfish, and trout angling is best in upper Florida Bay.

Freshwater: Prime crappie season begins this month. Some largemouth bass spawning may start toward month's end.

SOUTH EAST FLORIDA FISH AVAIALABILITY CHART*

NOTE: Refer to the month-by-month table for additional information. Information in this chart represents the seasonal patterns observed over the past three years. For saltwater species, the arrival of the migrant species and the peak times for each species is heavily dependent on water temperature. Unusually warm or cold periods will affect the patterns described above. Bream is the local name for bluegills and shellcrackers. Specs is a local name for crappie. Speckled trout is a local name for spotted seatrout.

*This chart does not reflect the fish availability in the Florida Keys. Generally, all the fish species in the Keys are year-round residents. The peak season for the major species are provided in the Fishing indices for the upper and lower Keys listings.

■ signifies a reasonable chance of catching this species in that month.

□ signifies the optimal months for catching the species.

Species	Jan	Feb	Mar	Apr	May	Jun	Jul	Aug	Sep	Oct	Nov	Dec
Redfish	■	■	□	□	□	■	■	■	■	□	□	■
Snook	□	□	□	□	□	□	□	□	□	□	□	□
Spotted Seatrout	□	□	□	■	■	■	■	■	■	□	□	□
Bonefish	■	■	■	□	□	□	□	□	□	■	■	■
Sheepshead	□	□	□	■	■	■	■	■	■	■	■	□
Snapper species	■	■	■	■	■	□	□	□	□	■	■	■
Gag Grouper	■	■	■	■	■	■	■	■	■	■	■	■
Bluefish	□	□	■	■	■	■	■	■	■	■	■	□
Flounder	■	■	■	■	■	■	■	■	■	■	■	■
Permit	■	■	■	■	■	□	□	□	□	■	■	■
Dolphin	■	■	■	■	□	□	□	□	■	■	■	■
Blackfin Tuna	■	■	■	■	■	■	■	■	■	■	■	■

Species	Jan	Feb	Mar	Apr	May	Jun	Jul	Aug	Sep	Oct	Nov	Dec
Blue Marlin	■	■	■	■	■	■	■	■	■	■	■	■
Wahoo	■	■	■	■	■	■	■	■	■	■	■	■
Whiting	□	□	■	■	■	■	■	■	■	■	■	□
Amberjack	■	■	■	■	■	□	□	□	■	■	■	■
Sailfish	□	□	■	■	■	■	■	■	■	■	□	□
Cobia	■	■	■	■	■	■	■	■	■	■	■	■
Spanish Mackerel	■	■	□	□	□	■	■	■	■	■	□	□
King Mackerel	■	■	□	□	□	■	■	■	■	■	□	□
Crevalle Jack	■	■	■	■	■	■	■	■	■	■	■	■
Tarpon	□	□	■	■	■	■	□	□	■	■	□	□
Pompano	■	■	■	■	■	■	■	■	■	□	□	□
White Marlin	■	■	■	■	■	■	■	■	■	■	■	■
Shark (all species)	■	□	□	■	■	□	□	□	■	■	■	■
Largemouth Bass	□	□	□	■	■	■	■	■	■	■	■	■
Bluegills	■	■	■	□	□	□	■	■	■	■	■	■
Catfish	■	■	■	■	■	■	■	■	■	■	■	■
Oscar	■	■	■	■	■	■	■	■	■	■	■	■
Butterfly Peacock	■	■	■	■	■	■	■	■	■	■	■	■
Sunshine Bass	■	■	■	■						■	■	■
Crappie	□	□	□	■							■	□

Mangrove snapper, also referred to as gray snapper, is the most commonly caught of the snappers in Florida.

Appendix I
Government Agencies

Florida Game and Fresh Water Fish Commission (GFC)

The GFC publishes regional freshwater fishing guides, brochures about the fish management areas and urban fishing sites, special reports about freshwater fish and fishing in Florida, and an annually updated sportfishing guide and regulations summary.

Headquarters
620 South Meridian Street
Farris Bryant Building
Tallahassee, FL 32399-1600
(850) 488-4676
(850) 488-9542 (TDD)

Regional Offices

Northwest Region
3911 Highway 2321
Panama City, FL 32409-1658
(850) 265-3670

Everglades Region
551 North Military Trail
West Palm Beach, FL 33415-1396
(407) 640-6100

South Region
3900 Drane Field Road
Lakeland, FL 33811-1299
(941) 648-3203

Central Region
1239 S.W. 10th Street
Ocala, FL 34474-2797
(352) 732-1225

Northeast Region
RFD 7, Box 440
Lake City, FL 32055-8713
(904) 758-0525

The Commission operates a Wildlife Alert program to report violations. You can remain anonymous and you will not have to testify in court. When calling in a violation, try to provide information about the vehicles or boats, descriptions of persons involved, exact location and time of day, and any other information that may be helpful.

To report a violation call the regional hotline for your area.

Northwest Region:	1-800-342-1676
Northeast Region:	1-800-342-8105
Central Region:	1-800-342-9620
South Region:	1-800-282-8002
Everglades Region:	1-800-432-2046

The Commission also maintains the Florida Sport Fishing Information Line, a toll-free number that anglers can call to hear recorded messages about fresh- and saltwater fishing. By following the instructions, anglers can obtain regional fishing reports, information about licenses, locations of ramps, and answers to commonly asked questions. The number to call is: 1 800 ASK FISH (275-3474).

Department of Environmental Protection

This agency, formerly the Departments of Natural Resources and Environmental Protection, is responsible for managing Florida's marine resources. This includes marine research, the marine patrol, land management activities, and environmental permitting. The state park system is also managed by this agency.

Saltwater fishing is regulated by the Department of Environmental Protection. Unfortunately, it does not have regional offices or field staff assigned to assist the public with recreational saltwater fishing issues. The department does have an excellent publication summarizing the saltwater fishing regulations in Florida. Ask for a copy of *Fishing Lines*. It is available at most bait and tackle shops, marinas, and tax collector offices.

Boaters will also want a copy of the Florida Boater's Guide available from the Florida Marine Patrol.

Florida has an excellent state park system. There are more than 110 park areas throughout the state and many of them provide access points for salt- or freshwater anglers. The Florida State Parks Guide is available for persons wanting more information about the resources and recreational opportunities at each site.

Copies of *Fishing Lines*, *Florida Boater's Guide*, and the *Florida State Parks Guide* are available from:

Department of Environmental Protection
3900 Commonwealth Boulevard
Tallahassee, FL 32399-3000
(904) 488-7326

The Florida Marine Patrol is the primary enforcement agency for saltwater related issues. You are encouraged to report any suspicious activities or violations to the Patrol's hotline: 1-800-DIAL-FMP (1-800-342-5367).

Florida Marine Fisheries Commission

This seven-member, governor-appointed commission has the job of managing the state's marine resources. It does this by recommending, reviewing, and revising the laws related to commercial and recreational fishing.

Florida Marine Fisheries Commission
2540 Executive Center Circle West, Suite 106
Tallahassee, FL 32301
(850) 487-0554

National Marine Fisheries Service/Fisheries Management Councils

The National Marine Fisheries Service is a federal agency that manages commercial and recreational marine fisheries in the federal waters of the Atlantic Ocean and Gulf of Mexico. These waters begin 9 nautical miles offshore in the Gulf of Mexico and 3 nautical miles offshore in the Atlantic and extend to 200 miles offshore.

Two Fisheries Management councils, the Gulf of Mexico and South Atlantic, manage the fish stocks for their respective regions. Generally the size and bag limits for the popular sport fish are the same in state and federal waters. Anglers are advised to periodically check for changes to the federal regulations. Copies of the recreational rules are available form the Fisheries Management Councils.

National Marine
Fisheries Service
9450 Koger Blvd.
St. Petersburg, FL 33702
(727) 570-5301

Gulf of Mexico Fisheries
Management Council
Lincoln Center, Suite 331
5401 West Kennedy Blvd.
Tampa, FL 33609
(813) 228-2815

South Atlantic Fisheries
Management Council
One Southpark Circle
Suite 306
Charleston, SC 29407
(803) 571-4366

Florida Marine Extension Agents

The Florida Sea Grant Program is a part of the University of Florida. Marine Extension Agents work with individuals, schools, local government agencies, and businesses on marine related issues and education programs.

For a list of agents contact: **Florida Sea Grant College Program**
P.O. Box 110409
University of Florida
Gainesville, FL 3264-0409

Water Management Districts

The state has five water management districts. Their mission is to manage the state's ground and surface waters. Although the districts are not directly involved in maintaining recreational facilities, they do own land from which anglers can access places to fish. To find out more about the various programs each district offers, contact the addresses below.

Northwest Florida Water
Management District
Route 1, Box 3100
Havana, FL 32333-9700
(850) 539-5999

Suwannee River Water
Management District
Route 3, Box 64
Live Oak, FL 32060-9573
(904) 362-1001

St. Johns River Water
Management District
P.O. Box 1429
Palatka, FL 32178-1429
(904) 329-4500

Southwest Florida Water
Management District
2379 Broad Street
Brooksville, FL 34609-6899
(352) 796-7211 or 1 800 423-1476

South Florida Water Management District
P.O. Box 24680
West Palm Beach, FL 33416-4680
(407) 686-8800 or 1 800 432-2045

APPENDIX II
Additional Publications of Interest to Anglers

Florida Sportsman Magazine - The premier magazine for anglers interested in fishing in Florida. Subscriptions are $18.95 (1995 price) plus 6 percent tax for Florida residents. Send orders to: **Florida Sportsman**
Subscription Service Department
P.O. Box 59200
Boulder, CO 80323-9200

Gulf Coast Angler -   A new publication that focuses on west coast fishing. Subscriptions are $13.86. Send order to: **Gulf Coast Angler**
Circulation Dept.
406 Sarasota Quay
Sarasota, FL 34236

Florida Wildlife - The Game and Fresh Water Fish Commission's excellent bimonthly magazine. Subscriptions are $10/year. Send orders to:

Florida Wildlife
620 S. Meridian
Tallahassee, FL 32399-1600

Florida Sea Grant - Has two publications of interest to anglers. One is "Common Saltwater Fishes of Southwest Florida" (SGEB-25). Printed on waterproof paper, this useful booklet has information and drawings of 86 species of fish from southwest Florida. Copies are $4.00.

"Atlas of Artificial Reefs in Florida" (SGEB-20) is a detailed listing of offshore artificial reefs that includes the latitude and longitude, LORAN coordinates, and composition of each site. Copies are $6.00. To order either publication send a check to: **Florida Sea Grant College Program**
P.O. Box 110409
University of Florida
Gainesville, FL 32611-0409

World Record Game Fishes - The official directory of record fish maintained by the International Game Fish Association. Anglers and businesses who want to support the organizations goals of wisely maintaining and perpetuating game fish and the sport of game fishing can join the IGFA. Memberships for individuals are $25.00/ year (1995) which includes a copy of the annual book. To join, send a check to: **International Game Fish Association**
1301 East Atlantic Boulevard
Pompano Beach, FL 33060

APPENDIX *III*
Artificial Reefs in Florida

The following sites represent some of the many artificial reef sites in Florida. The state, in conjunction with local governments, has an active artificial reef program. New sites are continuously being added around the state. The sites listed below are current as of 1995.

The sites chosen are well-known ones that come recommended by local marinas and tackle store owners. They are all sufficiently large that anglers with a LORAN or GPS unit should be able to find them with little difficulty.

The closest port or inlet to each group of sites is listed in the table. Off shore anglers are encouraged to stop at local bait and tackle stores to inquire about new sites and other existing sites not listed here. Many areas have local charts with coordinates for the best-known sites printed on the chart.

SELECTED NORTHWEST FLORIDA ARTIFICIAL REEF LOCATIONS

Name	Lat./Long	LORAN C	Depth (feet)	Distance (N. miles)	Composition
FROM SAINT MARKS					
St. Marks Reef	30/00/00 84/09/15	14478.1 46426.1	20	5.00	Concrete culverts
Ochlockonee Reef	29/54/42 84/13/07	14449.4 46421.0	30	9.00	DC-3 fuselage
FROM APALACHICOLA					
V Tower	29/24/32 84/21/32	14310.4 46202.9	70	15.00	Barge, concrete rubble
K Tower	29/30/28 84/22/03	14368.0 46346.6	60	13.00	Barge, concrete rubble
S Tower	29/17/03 84/36/28	14227.8 46245.3	105	35.00	Barge, concrete rubble
O Tower	29/32/07 84/37/03	14288.4 46376.2	70	13.00	Barge, concrete rubble
Franklin Co. Reef	29/32/31 84/45/46	14256.0 46431.3	75	10.00	Bridge material

Name	Lat./Long	LORAN C	Depth (feet)	Distance (N. miles)	Composition
Apalachicola Reef	29/30/30 84/50/30	14217.0 46414.0	75	10.00	Bridge material
C Tower	29/24/14 84/51/28	14198.2 46393.7	85		Barge, concrete rubble

FROM MEXICO BEACH

Name	Lat./Long	LORAN C	Depth (feet)	Distance (N. miles)	Composition
J.C. Reef	29/50/20 85/29/30	14115.7 46804.1	45	0.50	Concrete, rubble auto frames
Lumber Ship	29/53/44 85/27/52	14142.9 46830.5	25	1.50	Metal ship, framework
Mexico Beach Site	29/54/04 85/32/00	14116.5 46845.6	55	3.00	Boxcars

FROM PANAMA CITY

Name	Lat./Long	LORAN C	Depth (feet)	Distance (N. miles)	Composition
Liberty Ship	30/00/00 85/40/30	14065.1 46918.6	72	8.00	Ship
Stage I West	30/00/00 85/48/00	13949.8 46950.0	115	9.00	Concrete bridge trusses
Stage I East	30/00/00 85/48/00	13995.2 46923.3	105	9.00	Concrete bridge trusses
Chippewa	30/00/00 85/48/00	14012.3 46921.2	96	9.00	Tugboat
Warsaw Site	30/04/00 85/48/07	14037.2 46977.4	75	4.50	Concrete bridge trusses
BJ Putnam		13991.6 46909.1	100	10.00	Freighter
Fountainblieu Site	30/09/00 85/53/00	14020.1 47022.8	73	9.00	Concrete bridge trusses
Grey Ghost	30/02/49 86/05/32	13891.1 46991.7	105	21.00	Steel tug, tires

From Destin

Name	Lat./Long	LORAN C	Depth (feet)	Distance (N. miles)	Composition
Liberty Ship Reef	30/12/47 86/48/21	13515.2 47083.9	85	10.75	Ship
Bridge Rubble Reef	30/22/00 86/30/00	13720.4 47131.0	73	1.90	Concrete rubble
Brown Barge	30/21/00 86/35/00	13660.7 47134.1	80	3.00	Barge, rubble
Liberty Ship Reef Site 4	30/19/36 86/36/06	13648.1 47115.7	87	13.00	Ship

From Pensacola Beach

Name	Lat./Long	LORAN C	Depth (feet)	Distance (N. miles)	Composition
Tenneco Reef	30/00/00 87/04/00	13324.5 47012.7	156	22.00	Oil platform
Russian Freighter	30/11/20 87/10/38	13263.8 47077.1	84 ship	9.00	Navy target
Miss Jenny	29/57/11 87/12/24	13248.8 47006.5	115	19.30	Steel supply ship
Three Barges	30/16/57 87/12/50	13270.6 47107.6	54	6.90	Barges, rubble
Tug Philip	30/08/09 87/13/09	13256.2 47059.4	95	8.50	Tugboat
Born Again	30/08/09 87/13/09	13247.6 47060.8	95	8.50	Tugboat, pipes
Tugboat Heron	30/08/09 87/13/09	13253.0 47060.6	91	15.00	Tugboat
Monsanto Boxes	30/11/07 87/14/05	13247.7 47079.7	69	8.33	Steel modules
Avocet		13248.2 47007.2	115	20.00	Dredge
Pete Tide II		13250.7 47063.4	100	12.00	Crewboat
Deliverance	30/11/07 87/14/05	13247.7 47074.7	79	8.33	Steel tugboat

SELECTED BIG BEND FLORIDA ARTIFICIAL REEF LOCATIONS

FROM CEDAR KEY					
Name	Lat./Long	LORAN C	Depth (feet)	Distance (N. miles)	Composition
Cedar Key #2	28/58/57 83/11/53	14375.4 45466.4	26	11.00	Conrete culverts, boulders, slabs
Cedar Key #3	29/06/50 83/25/37	14375.0 45640.0	36	13.00	Concrete culverts
Cedar Key #1	29/07/00 83/12/30	14398.5 45549.3	23	9.00	Concrete culverts

FROM STEINHATCHEE					
Name	Lat./Long	LORAN C	Depth (feet)	Distance (N. miles)	Composition
Steinhatchee Reef	29/39/48 83/37/38	14459.7 46011.3	21	11.00	Boat molds & concrete rubble
White City Bridge		14359.5 45770.5			Bridge rubble

SELECTED NORTHEAST FLORIDA ARTIFICIAL REEF LOCATIONS

FROM FERNANDINA BEACH					
Name	Lat./Long	LORAN C	Depth (feet)	Distance (N. miles)	Composition
FA Site		45318.5 61912.9			
FB Site	30/40/07 81/09/34	45307.7 61874.4	60	12.00	
Whittakers Hole	30/38/13 81/13/22	45326.8 61915.2	60	13.00	Steel tug
FC Site		45290.0 61897.0			
HH Site	30/34/03 81/08/26	45253.8 61888.8	80		
Amberjack Hole	30/32/49 81/03/10	45210.2 61852.6	80	18.50	Barge

From Bayport

Name	Lat./Long	LORAN C	Depth (feet)	Distance (N. miles)	Composition
Montgomery Reef	30/26/47 81/13/12	45237.3 61958.6	65	8.40	120' Steel Barge
Nine Mile Reef	30/23/32 81/10/11	45193.2 61944.5	63	10.40	Tug
Huggins	30/22/20 80/53/52	45077.3 61814.0	90	24.50	Freighter
Pablo Grounds	30/20/18 81/11/41	45179.2 61969.6	73	9.90	Barge
Jacksonville Beach Wreck	30/16/19 81/13/34	45168.7 62001.7	60	10.50	Culverts

From Saint Augustine

Name	Lat./Long	LORAN C	Depth (feet)	Distance (N. miles)	Composition
Dumpsters	29/55/14 81/05/20	44952.6 62025.0	56	8.90	Dumpsters
Concrete Culverts	29/55/14 81/05/20	44959.4 62025.3	56	8.90	Concrete Culverts
Desco Boat	29/53/16 81/00/31	44903.1 61975.5	70	12.80	Desco Shrimp Boat
Inner Plane Wreck	29/51/12 80/58/14	44873.4 61969.8	70	15.10	Airplane Pieces
Outer Plane Wreck	29/50/04 80/57/39	44858.3 61963.4	72	16.40	Airplane Pieces
Ponte Vedra Wreck		45105.0 61982.0			
Hospital Grounds		45050.0 61900.5			

Selected East Central Florida
Artificial Reef Locations

From Ponce de Leon Inlet

Name	Lat./Long	LORAN C	Depth (feet)	Distance (N. miles)	Composition
Port Authority Reef Site #1	29/07/15 80/41/39	44396.3 61972.8	80	11.00	Culverts
Port Authority Reef Site #2	29/09/36 80/40/33	44407.4 61959.5	80	16.00	Culverts
Port Authority Reef Site #3	29/11/58 80/44/45	44453.8 61982.3	85	14.00	Culverts
Port Authority Reef Site #4		44521.6 61960.2			
Port Authority Reef Site #5	29/07/18 80/48/00	44437.8 62020.0	55	6.00	Culverts
Port Authority Reef Site #6	29/03/06 80/43/00	44370.2 61995.6	60	9.70	Culverts
Port Authority Reef Site #7	29/01/18 80/41/00	44341.3 61986.6	62	27.00	Culverts
Port Authority Reef Site #8	28/55/30 80/42/24	44296.5 62011.1	55	13.50	Culverts

From Port Canaveral

Name	Lat./Long	LORAN C	Depth (feet)	Distance (N. miles)	Composition
Damocles	28/25/30 80/17/30	43866.0 61920.0	85	17.00	Vessel & Culverts
Humminbird Reef	28/25/06 80/14/05	43866.2 61898.8	110	18.00	Launchpad Rubble
Tiger Red	28/24/13 80/17/50	43842.0 61926.0	85	12.00	Tug boat
Brevard Artificial Reef	28/18/25 80/27/17	43866.2 62000.0	60	9.10	Dumpsters, Drums

Selected West Central Florida
Artificial Reef Locations

From Big Sarasota or New Pass

Name	Lat./Long	LORAN C	Depth (feet)	Distance (N. miles)	Composition
M10 Reef	27/02/00 82/42/33	14114.8 44391.5	67	15.50	Barge, boat, molds
M6 Reef	27/11/08 82/43/40	14135.1 44451.5	55	11.00	Boats, culverts, drums
M8 Reef	27/12/28 82/48/16	14128.2 44495.4	65	12.20	Landing craft, boxcars
M7 Reef	27/16/04 82/48/10	14137.8 44516.9	50	11.60	Boxcars
I2 (Alan E. Fisher) Reef	27/17/55 82/37/06	14166.1 44437.4	30	2.00	Bridge rubble, Piles
I3 (Donald Roehr) Reef	27/18/04 82/35/36	14169.5 44425.8	22	2.00	Bridge rubble & pilings
M2 Reef	27/18/38 82/43/03	14155.1 44490.4	42	7.00	Concrete culvert, pipes, drums
M3 Reef	27/18/38 82/43/17	14149.5 44480.5	42	7.00	Concrete catchbasins & boxes, culvert
M1 Reef	27/19/06 82/43/20	14155.8 44494.8	42	7.10	Barge & boats

From Pinellas County ports

Name	Lat./Long	LORAN C	Depth (feet)	Distance (N. miles)	Composition
Blackthorn	27/52/30 83/11/24	14181.7 44942.7	80	12.80	Ship
Madeira Beach Reef	27/46/18 82/54/54	14201.0 44768.0	33	5.70	Cement culverts, rubble
Clearwater Reef	28/00/57 82/53/42	14243.0 44861.5	27-29	3.30	Concrete pilings, steel barges

FROM TARPON SPRINGS					
Name	Lat./Long	LORAN C	Depth (feet)	Distance (N. miles)	Composition
Pasco Reef No. 1	28/15/04 82/57/28	14275.8 45000.0	25	11.00	Steel vessels, cylinders, concrete culverts
Pasco Reef No. 2	28/17/27 83/01/14	14274.8 45048.2	40	13.20	Barge, concrete culverts & poles
A.H. Richardson Reef	28/30/00 82/55/00	14325.3 45111.1	22	18.00	Tires, concrete rubble
Jim Champion Reef	28/36/01 82/57/01	14337.0 45160.0		17.00	Concrete culverts
Don Bendickson	28/31/07 82/58/07	14319.8 45140.0	25		US Army Tanks

FROM CRYSTAL RIVER					
Name	Lat./Long	LORAN C	Depth (feet)	Distance (N. miles)	Composition
Crystal River Artificial Reef	28/47/24 83/03/30	14356.2 45305.5	30	19.20	Concrete & iron culverts, boat molds, bridge rubble

SELECTED SOUTHWEST FLORIDA ARTIFICIAL REEF LOCATIONS

FROM NAPLES OR MARCO ISLAND					
Name	Lat./Long	LORAN C	Depth (feet)	Distance (N. miles)	Composition
Marco Island 5 Mi. Reef	25/52/42 81/47/48	14074.0 81/47/48 53714.0	35	4.4	Drege pipe and pontoon material
Gordon Pass 5 Mi. Reef	26/05/13 81/53/26	14089.8 43777.3	28	5.00	Airplane fueselage
Doctors Pass 5 Mi.Reef	26/10/13 81/54/18	14098.9 43818.0	28	5.00	Concrete culvert
Wiggins Pass 14 Mi. Reef	26/14/52 82/05/50	14085.0 43900.0	48	14.50	Concrete culverts

Name	Lat./Long	LORAN C	Depth (feet)	Distance (N. miles)	Composition
Wiggins Pass 5 Mi. Reef	26/17/09 81/55/29	14110.6 43828.3	30	5.00	Busses, Coke trucks
Wiggins Pass 4.6 Mi. Reef	26/17/18 81/54/51	14111.9 43823.5	30	4.80	Barge & Crane

FROM SANIBEL

Name	Lat./Long	LORAN C	Depth (feet)	Distance (N. miles)	Composition
Jaycees Reef	26/24/07 82/05/05	14100.0 43913.0	33	8.50	Barge with rubble & tires
Sanibel Reef	26/24/35 82/02/50	14113.1 43900.9	20	2.90	Concrete rubble, tires
Edison Reef	26/28/30 82/13/32	14078.1 43970.2	40		Bridge rubble
CSX Boxcar Reef	26/42/00 82/36/00	14082.6 44239.6	70	18.00	Boxcars, barges, culverts
Charlotte Harbor Reef	26/50/30 82/05/19	14162.8 44024.7	8-11	1.50	Bridge rubble, beams

SELECTED SOUTHEAST FLORIDA
ARTIFICIAL REEF LOCATIONS

FROM FORT PIERCE INLET

Name	Lat./Long	LORAN C	Depth (feet)	Distance (N. miles)	Composition
Fishing Club Reef	27/26/48 80/10/24	43262.0 62005.0	55	65.50	Concrete Rubble
Tug No. 1	27/23/48 80/02/00	43204.5 61954.2	190	13.00	Tug boat
Tug No. 2	27/23/48 80/02/00	43200.0 61960.7	150	16.00	Tug boat
Tug No. 3		43210.0 61963.0	127		Tug boat
USS Mulliphen	27/23/48 80/02/00	43207.4 61958.4	168	16.50	Cargo Vessel

From Saint Lucie Inlet

Name	Lat./Long	LORAN C	Depth (feet)	Distance (N. miles)	Composition
Toilet Bowl Reef	27/12/37 80/06/32	43107.3 62013.8	57	3.50	Porcelain Toilets, Tanks, etc.
Mercedes II Reef	27/12/18 80/02/18	43091.1 61993.0	100	7.50	Freighter
Stern USS Rankin	27/12/18 80/02/18	43079.7 61986.8	100	7.50	USS Rankin Stern
David T Reef	27/12/18 80/02/18	43090.8 61993.1	100	7.5	Repair Ship David T.
Bow USS Rankin	27/12/18 80/02/18	43079.0 61986.8	100	7.5	USS Rankin Bow
Dr. Edgar Ernst Reef	27/09/18 80/03/18	43063.7 62000.4	60	5.00	School Buses

From Jupiter Inlet

Name	Lat./Long	LORAN C	Depth (feet)	Distance (N. miles)	Composition
Esso Bonaire	26/58/54 80/01/04	14351.3 62006.5	90	3.40	Tanker

From Lake Worth Inlet

Name	Lat./Long	LORAN C	Depth (feet)	Distance (N. miles)	Composition
Classic Barges	26/47/40 79/59/34	14334.7 62019.1	235	2.50	Hopper Barge
Palm Beach Reef Site #1	26/47/40 79/59/34	14335.7 62021.5	250	2.10	Frames. culverts, rubble, tanks
Amaryllis	26/45/37 80/01/00	14331.4 62030.0	95	1.00	Freighter
Blue Heron	26/45/35 80/01/08	14330.7 62033.0	40-75	0.70	Rock Pile of Statue Remnants
Bud Bar	26/28/48 80/02/15	14301.2 62066.0	90	1.00	Freighter, culverts
Boyton Kiwanis —Miller Lite		14301.5 62051.2	200	2.00	Freighter

Name	Lat./Long	LORAN C	Depth (feet)	Distance (N. miles)	Composition
Corey & Chris	26/13/45 80/03/23	14274.2 62093.4	244	1.60	Dredge
Chevron Tanks	26/13/45 80/03/23	14271.3 62097.1	170	1.50	Fuel Tanks
Jim Atria	26/08/51 80/05/00	14266.5 62103.5	110	1.30	Freighter
Grouper Grotto	26/08/51 80/05/00	14263.6 62104.5	150	1.40	Fuel tanks, culverts, pipes
Mercedes	26/08/51 80/05/00	14265.2 62105.2	97	1.00	Freighter
Tenneco	25/58/50 80/04/55	14247.3 62121.0	190	2.10	Oil Platform legs
Tenneco II	25/58/50 80/04/55	14246.9 62122.7	105	1.60	Oil platform decks

FROM GOVERNMENT CUT AND BISCAYNE BAY

Name	Lat./Long	LORAN C	Depth (feet)	Distance (N. miles)	Composition
Haulover Reef	25/54/08 80/04/43	14237.7 62129.4	120	2.10	Concrete Pipe
Narwal	25/54/08 80/04/43	14239.7 62127.8	115	2.10	Freighter
Andro	25/54/08 80/04/43	14237.7 62129.4	103	2.00	Freighter
Deep Freeze	25/49/34 80/04/54	14230.7 62133.0	135	1.75	Transport vessel
Anchorage Reef	25/48/42 80/05/40	14229.3 62137.5	45	1.60	Concrete girders
Leon's Barge	25/48/42 80/05/40	14229.3 62136.9	50	1.60	Barge
Belzona One	25/42/04 80/05/21	14217.8 62144.9	68	3.70	Steel tug
Key Biscayne Reef	25/42/04 80/05/21	14218.6 62143.8	135	1.6	Bridge girders
Proteus	25/42/04 80/05/21	14218.7 62144.3	72	3.75	Freighter

Name	Lat./Long	LORAN C	Depth (feet)	Distance (N. miles)	Composition
Lakeland	25/42/04 80/05/21	14218.6 62143.8	140	4.25	Steel ship
Ultra Freeze	25/37/24 80/04/54	14211.1 62150.0	120	5.00	Freighter
Tarpoon	25/37/24 80/04/54	14210.2 62151.4	71	4.50	Ship
Blue Fire	25/33/42 80/05/02	14204.6 62155.5	110	6.50	Freighter
Doc De Milly	25/22/03 80/07/37	14181.7 62180.4	140	5.00	Freighter
Berry Patch	25/22/03 80/07/37	14181.8 62180.4	150	5.00	Freighter

FROM THE UPPER KEYS

Name	Lat./Long	LORAN C	Depth (feet)	Distance (N. miles)	Composition
CG Cutter Bibb	24/59/50 80/22/46	14123.0 62270.0	130	5.87	Ship
CG Cutter Duane	24/59/50 80/22/46	14122.2 62270.9	122	5.87	Ship
Islamorada Artificial Reef	24/51/41 80/34/05	14094.0 43291.1	115	4.50	Bridge rubble
Long Key Artificial Reef	24/43/36 80/49/42	14054.4 3365.5	26	4.25	Bridge rubble
Thunderbolt	24/39/34 80/57/58	14034.0 43403.4	115	4.00	Freighter

FROM THE LOWER KEYS

Name	Lat./Long	LORAN C	Depth (feet)	Distance (N. miles)	Composition
Seven Mile Bridge Reef	24/36/20 81/10/00	14006.8 43460.4	115	2.00	Bridge rubble
KW Fish. Tourn. Reef	24/27/15 81/46/15	13922.2 43639.7	180	7.00	Navy Cable Vessel
Key West Gulfside Reef	24/41/08 81/52/44	13933.4 43679.1	32	9.75	Concrete & Steel
Gunbor Artificial Reef	24/57/00 81/46/00	13972.3 43651.5	52	19.55	Superstructure from "Cayman Salvage Master"

INDEX OF FISHING SITES

ABOUT THE AUTHOR

Kris Thoemke has lived in Florida most of his life. He began fishing and enjoying the outdoors in the late 1950s. He has a Ph.D. from the University of South Florida in marine biology. Prior to pursuing a career as a full-time outdoor and environmental communicator five years ago, Kris was the manager of the Rookery Bay National Estuarine Research Reserve near Marco Island.

Wanting to share his knowledge about Florida's natural resources with a broad audience, Kris embarked on a mission to inform people about Florida's outdoors. It began as the host of *Florida Outdoors* on WNOG radio. The talk radio show, now in its ninth year, is a popular program in the Naples area.

In 1990 he became the host and, a year later, the co-producer of *Exploring Florida*, a popular television series on PBS. He has also worked as the environmental and outdoor editor for the Fort Myers-Naples ABC television affiliate.

AS a writer, Kris credits in several newspapers including his regular outdoor features in the *Naples Daily News*. His magazine articles and photographs have appeared in *Florida Sportsman*, *Gulf Coast Angler*, *Florida Wildlife* and other publications.

A popular speaker, he is in demand at conventions and as a naturalist guide in south Florida. He is an active member of the Outdoor Writers Association and has won numerous awards, including the Outdoor Communicator of the Year from the Florida Wildlife Federation.

FALCON GUIDES® Leading the Way™

FIELD GUIDES

Bitterroot: Montana State Flower
Canyon Country Wildflowers
Central Rocky Mountains
 Wildflowers
Chihuahuan Desert Wildflowers
Great Lakes Berry Book
New England Berry Book
Ozark Wildflowers
Pacific Northwest Berry Book
Plants of Arizona
Rare Plants of Colorado
Rocky Mountain Berry Book
Scats & Tracks of the Pacific
 Coast States
Scats & Tracks of the
 Rocky Mountains
Sierra Nevada Wildflowers
Southern Rocky Mountain
 Wildflowers
Tallgrass Prairie Wildflowers
Western Trees
Wildflowers of Southwestern
 Utah

FISHING GUIDES

Fishing Alaska
Fishing the Beartooths
Fishing Florida
Fishing Georgia
Fishing Glacier National Park
Fishing Maine
Fishing Montana
Fishing Wyoming
Fishing Yellowstone
 National Park
Trout Unlimited's Guide to
 America's 100 Best Trout
 Streams
America's Best Bass Fishing

BIRDING GUIDES

Birding Georgia
Birding Illinois
Birding Minnesota
Birding Montana
Birding Northern California
Birding Texas
Birding Utah

MORE GUIDEBOOKS

Backcountry Horseman's
 Guide to Washington
Camping Arizona
Camping California's
 National Forests
Camping Colorado
Camping Oregon
Exploring Canyonlands &
 Arches National Parks
Exploring Hawaii's Parklands
Exploring Mount Helena
Exploring Southern California
 Beaches
Family Fun in Montana
Family Fun in Yellowstone
Hiking Hot Springs of the Pacific
 Northwest
Recreation Guide to WA
 National Forests
Touring Arizona Hot Springs
Touring California & Nevada
 Hot Springs
Touring Colorado Hot Springs
Touring Montana & Wyoming
 Hot Springs
Trail Riding Western Montana
Wilderness Directory
Wild Montana
Wild Utah
Wild Virginia

ROCKHOUNDING GUIDES

Rockhounding Arizona
Rockhounding California
Rockhounding Colorado
Rockhounding Montana
Rockhounding Nevada
Rockhound's Guide to New
 Mexico
Rockhounding Texas
Rockhounding Utah
Rockhounding Wyoming

HOW-TO GUIDES

Avalanche Aware
Backpacking Tips
Bear Aware
Desert Hiking Tips
Hiking with Dogs
Hiking with Kids
Leave No Trace
Mountain Lion Alert
Reading Weather
Route Finding
Using GPS
Wild Country Companion
Wilderness First Aid
Wilderness Survival

WALKING

Walking Colorado Springs
Walking Denver
Walking Portland
Walking Seattle
Walking St. Louis
Walking San Francisco
Walking Virginia Beach

■*To order any of these books, check with your local bookseller*
or call FALCON ® at **1-800-582-2665**.
Visit us on the world wide web at:
www.falcon.com

FALCON

FALCON GUIDES ®Leading the Way™

HIKING GUIDES

Best Hikes Along the Continental Divide
Hiking Alaska
Hiking Arizona
Hiking Arizona's Cactus Country
Hiking the Beartooths
Hiking Big Bend National Park
Hiking the Bob Marshall Country
Hiking California
Hiking California's Desert Parks
Hiking Carlsbad Caverns
   and Guadalupe Mtns. National Parks
Hiking Colorado
Hiking Colorado, Vol. II
Hiking Colorado's Summits
Hiking Colorado's Weminuche Wilderness
Hiking the Columbia River Gorge
Hiking Florida
Hiking Georgia
Hiking Glacier & Waterton Lakes National Parks
Hiking Grand Canyon National Park
Hiking Grand Staircase-Escalante/Glen Canyon
Hiking Grand Teton National Park
Hiking Great Basin National Park
Hiking Hot Springs in the Pacific Northwest
Hiking Idaho
Hiking Indiana
Hiking Maine
Hiking Maryland and Delaware
Hiking Michigan
Hiking Minnesota
Hiking Montana
Hiking Mount Rainier National Park
Hiking Mount St. Helens
Hiking Nevada
Hiking New Hampshire
Hiking New Mexico
Hiking New Mexico's Gila Wilderness

Hiking New York
Hiking North Carolina
Hiking the North Cascades
Hiking Northern Arizona
Hiking Northern California
Hiking Olympic National Park
Hiking Oregon
Hiking Oregon's Eagle Cap Wilderness
Hiking Oregon's Mount Hood/Badger Creek
Hiking Oregon's Central Cascades
Hiking Pennsylvania
Hiking Ruins Seldom Seen
Hiking Shenandoah
Hiking the Sierra Nevada
Hiking South Carolina
Hiking South Dakota's Black Hills Country
Hiking Southern New England
Hiking Tennessee
Hiking Texas
Hiking Utah
Hiking Utah's Summits
Hiking Vermont
Hiking Virginia
Hiking Washington
Hiking Wisconsin
Hiking Wyoming
Hiking Wyoming's Cloud Peak Wilderness
Hiking Wyoming's Teton
   and Washakie Wilderness
Hiking Wyoming's Wind River Range
Hiking Yellowstone National Park
Hiking Yosemite National Park
Hiking Zion & Bryce Canyon National Parks
Wild Country Companion
Wild Montana
Wild Utah
Wild Virginia

■ *To order any of these books, check with your local bookseller*
or call FALCON ® *at* **1-800-582-2665**.
Visit us on the world wide web at:
www.Falcon.com

FALCON®

FALCONGUIDES ®Leading the Way™

FALCONGUIDES are available for where-to-go hiking, mountain biking, rock climbing, walking, scenic driving, fishing, rockhounding, paddling, birding, wildlife viewing, and camping. We also have FalconGuides® on essential outdoor skills and subjects and field identification. The following titles are currently available, but this list grows every year. For a free catalog with a complete list of titles, call FALCON® toll-free at 1-800-582-2665.

SCENIC DRIVING GUIDES

Scenic Driving Alaska and the Yukon
Scenic Driving Arizona
Scenic Driving the Beartooth Highway
Scenic Driving California
Scenic Driving Colorado
Scenic Driving Florida
Scenic Driving Georgia
Scenic Driving Hawaii
Scenic Driving Idaho
Scenic Driving Indiana
Scenic Driving Kentucky
Scenic Driving Michigan
Scenic Driving Minnesota
Scenic Driving Montana
Scenic Driving New England
Scenic Driving New Mexico
Scenic Driving North Carolina
Scenic Driving Oregon
Scenic Driving the Ozarks
Scenic Driving Pennsylvania
Scenic Driving Texas
Scenic Driving Utah
Scenic Driving Virginia
Scenic Driving Washington
Scenic Driving Wisconsin
Scenic Driving Wyoming
Scenic Driving Yellowstone and
  the Grand Teton National Parks
Scenic Byways East & South
Scenic Byways Far West
Scenic Byways Rocky Mountains
Back Country Byways

HISTORIC TRAIL GUIDES

Traveling California's Gold Rush Country
Traveling the Lewis & Clark Trail
Traveling the Oregon Trail
Traveler's Guide to the Pony Express Trail

WILDLIFE VIEWING GUIDES

Alaska Wildlife Viewing Guide
Arizona Wildlife Viewing Guide
California Wildlife Viewing Guide
Colorado Wildlife Viewing Guide
Florida Wildlife Viewing Guide
Indiana Wildlife Viewing Guide
Iowa Wildlife Viewing Guide
Kentucky Wildlife Viewing Guide
Massachusetts Wildlife Viewing Guide
Montana Wildlife Viewing Guide
Nebraska Wildlife Viewing Guide
Nevada Wildlife Viewing Guide
New Hampshire Wildlife Viewing Guide
New Jersey Wildlife Viewing Guide
New Mexico Wildlife Viewing Guide
New York Wildlife Viewing Guide
North Carolina Wildlife Viewing Guide
North Dakota Wildlife Viewing Guide
Ohio Wildlife Viewing Guide
Oregon Wildlife Viewing Guide
Puerto Rico & the Virgin Islands
  Wildlife Viewing Guide
Tennessee Wildlife Viewing Guide
Texas Wildlife Viewing Guide
Utah Wildlife Viewing Guide
Vermont Wildlife Viewing Guide
Virginia Wildlife Viewing Guide
Washington Wildlife Viewing Guide
West Virginia Wildlife Viewing Guide
Wisconsin Wildlife Viewing Guide

*To order any of these books, check with your local bookseller
or call FALCON ® at **1-800-582-2665**.
Visit us on the world wide web at:
www.falcon.com*

FALCON

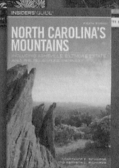